*To d[...]
Best Wishes!
G. Thomson
Fraser*

In the Claw of the Tiger

Courtesy LaCoste/Thurber family

In the Claw of the Tiger

BASED ON THE TRUE STORY OF
WORLD WAR II POW AND SURVIVOR OF THE
BATAAN DEATH MARCH
FRANKLIN "PORKY" LACOSTE

G. Thomson Fraser

Copyright © 2007 by G. Thomson Fraser.

Library of Congress Control Number: 2007903567
ISBN: Hardcover   978-1-4257-7492-9
               Softcover   978-1-4257-7483-7

All rights reserved. No part of this book may be reproduced or transmitted in any form or by any means, electronic or mechanical, including photocopying, recording, or by any information storage and retrieval system, without permission in writing from the copyright owner.

In the Claw of the Tiger is a World War II novel based on a true story which falls within the genre of literature referred to as narrative or creative nonfiction. It contains accurate and well-researched information that has been "fictionalized" in places to tell a story.

This book was printed in the United States of America.

To order additional copies of this book, contact:
Xlibris Corporation
1-888-795-4274
www.Xlibris.com
Orders@Xlibris.com
31327

Dedication

To my parents, Louise and Donald Fraser, my brothers and sisters, daughter and grandchild, and all the other members of my beloved family who have offered love and encouragement through the years. My deepest gratitude.

Preface

In the early 1990s I worked as an aide for Massachusetts State Senator Robert D. Wetmore (D-Barre), who was a veteran of the Korean Conflict. The senator was particularly conscious of veterans' issues, so I often found myself out in the district meeting with veterans on his behalf. In my travels I met a key player in the DAV (Disabled American Veterans), retired air force major Alan Bowers who had suffered a spinal cord injury while ejecting from a disabled OV-10 aircraft over Vietnam in 1972. Alan was compiling tape-recorded stories of area veterans who served in armed conflicts and transcribing them for publication. I asked him if one of the stories might be sufficiently compelling to be adapted into a screenplay or novel. He said he knew just the man for me to meet—"Porky" LaCoste—a survivor of the Bataan Death March and POW camps in the Philippines and Japan. The transcriptions were later published by Haley's in several volumes titled *On Duty: Interviews with Military Veterans from North of Quabbin*. In 2003, Alan Bowers was elected national commander of the DAV.

I periodically met with Porky at his home, his daughter Caryl's home, or at the local McDonald's during each spring, summer, and fall. We worked on getting every detail he could recall down on paper and creating workable dialogue. During the winter, Porky golfed and relaxed in the Florida sunshine with his beloved wife, Helen, while I reworked the material. By 1999 I had transformed the first portion of the story into a screenplay format titled *In the Claw of the Tiger* but had come to realize that only a novel would allow the complete story to be told.

The draft screenplay was read before a live audience on August 14, 1999, at the Drama Circle at Mount Wachusett Community College in Gardner, Massachusetts, and was filmed by AOTV-Channel13, a local access television station serving Athol and Orange. The reading met with success, at least locally, where the tape was rebroadcast over and over again, and Porky became a local celebrity. Cast members included Paul Martin, who performed the role of Porky; State Representative David Bunker as Pint Lawson; Jeremy Thurber (Porky's grandson), who played Herman Hausmann; Kevin LaCoste (Porky's grandson) as Billy Freeman; Seth Leary as Bobby Doolan; Chris King as Franny Robichaud; and David Agans as Pinky Dower. Additional cast members included Arthur Koykka, David Henshaw, Joan LaBonte, Kim Osbourne, Richard Cunningham, Glenn McDonald, Matthew Richardson, Katherine North-Erickson, and Porky's granddaughters Becky Jillson and Lori LaCoste. The pianist was Marilyn Hyson.

Pinky and Porky reunion at 1999 reading
Courtesy LaCoste/Thurber Family

With the support and encouragement of Porky's daughter, Caryl Thurber, I eventually returned to the story, bit the bullet, and did the research (thanks to Google) necessary to complete a creative nonfiction work that spans time and place to tell a survivor's tale from a world at war. *In the Claw of the Tiger* is not a war story in the traditional sense of macho exploits—though there are moments of blood, guts, and gore—but the story of young men caught up in circumstances of the single deadliest conflict the world has seen, involving tens of millions of deaths. Despite the odds, Porky survived with a little help from his friends and, on occasions, with help from individuals on the other side of the conflict, the enemy.

Acknowledgments

The author photo was taken in 2005 by my granddaughter, MacKenzie Coffman, who was eight years old. I thank her for her loving patience during the dozens of attempts to indulge my vanity.

Along with Caryl Thurber and her family, I wish to thank Russell Kennedy, of the Athol Historical Society, and Paulie Perkins, who lives in Porky's old neighborhood and shared her school-day memories one bright fall afternoon.

Special thanks to Richard Chaisson, a retired reporter and local historian who shared dozens of local photographs gifted to him by the Hames Photo Shop, the Athol Daily News, and others; Federico Baldassarre, researcher/archivist for the Battling Bastards of Bataan, who was a great help with Philippine historical and geographical details; Kathy Vinson with the Department of Defense Media Services; Wes Injerd, who helped identify maps and photos of POW camps; the FDR Library and Museum; Helen Wykle, reference librarian at the D.H. Ramsey Library Special Collections, University of North Carolina at Asheville; Jim Opolony—Faculty Advisor for Proviso School Bataan Project (192nd Tank Battalion); the National Archives and Library of Congress; Dana Armstrong, a digital imaging specialist, for help with the photographs; Richard J. Chase, Jr., publisher of the Athol Daily News; Carol Courville, executive director of AOTV-Channel13; the staff at the Athol Public Library; Athol Veterans agent Toni Phillips; Mike Hoctor, the nephew of Francis Hoctor, whose story commands an entire chapter in part 2; Kevin Lecy, owner of the Royale Pub in downtown Athol; James Baird, who shared his war story; members of Billy Freeman's family: Patricia Gerard, Sarah Sonn, and Bill Greene, as well as Margaret Robinson, who helped me locate Billy's sister Pat; and Philip "Pinky" Dower, who was the first of Porky's friends to sign up for military service.

Billy Freeman enjoyed taking photos, as did several of his friends, including Roland Stickney (also mentioned in the story). In going through old photo albums, the LaCoste and Thurber families found dozens of photos. The photos are marked by topic, numbers, or letters, and most bear Porky's stamp from the 27th Material Division. None of the photographs identify the photographer. Many of the photos are being published for the first time as part of this book. We extend our gratitude to Billy and other unnamed photographers who contributed to this remarkable archive.

I am also deeply grateful to my niece, Susanni Douville Hull, who edited parts of the first draft and later returned to the project to serve as the copy editor for the final draft of the manuscript; my sister, Lillian Douville, whose valuable conversations led to many edits; my daughter, Rebekah, who also lent a hand editing; Janice Lanou, who made many helpful comments; my first English professor, Philip Nicoloff, who offered valuable insight into Japanese culture; Robert and Masako Stiver, who helped me transliterate Japanese dialogue; and Lisa and John DeWitt, whose friendship and encouragement helped more than they will ever know.

Roxanne Rooney Kennedy typed reams and reams of my indecipherable notes, retired air force major Chet Lubelczyk offered comments on military and other aspects of the narrative, and Senator Wetmore provided detailed background information on local history.

The final draft was copyedited by Xlibris' Richard Le Blanco and reviewed by Christine Gerra. The book cover was designed by Sherwin Soy.

I also thank the webmasters who posted World War II websites. I suspect I have visited them all and am deeply grateful for the insight offered. However, there are three Web sites in particular that were extremely helpful: Louis Morton's *US Army in World War II: The War in the Pacific, the Fall in the Philippines*, at *http://www.ibiblio.org/hyperwar/USA/USA-P-PI/index.html*; the Center for Research, Allied POWs under the Japanese at *http://www.*

mansell.com/pow-index.html; and Old Tokyo: Vintage Images from Japan at *http://www.oldtokyo.com/index.html*.

Many of the World War II prisoner-of-war photographs available on websites are from the Ira Kaye Collection, ARC ID #559254, Photographic Prints of Allied Prisoners of War in Japan, 1944-1945, at the National Archives.

There is a traditional Native American saying, "Only the Creator is perfect." When we make mistakes, it is an acknowledgement of our humanity and a tribute to the Creator's perfection. I have tried my best to avoid mistakes. Those that exist within this narrative are my humble tribute to the Creator.

Genevieve
May 7, 2007
Orange, Massachusetts

Part 1

Emperor Hirohito
Courtesy Library of Congress

Chapter 1

Luzon, Philippine Islands
Summer 1942

Raw, red, and vibrant, the sun birthed through the navy rim of the Pacific, radiated up the Sierra Madre, across the bombed-out airbase at Clark Field to prisoner of war camps O'Donnell and Cabanatuan. As light broke over the water, flags emblazoned with the radiant sun were raised at Imperial Command posts throughout the island. Japanese soldiers emerged in formation from semidarkness, faced north and lowered their heads perpendicular to their waists, in a solemn bow to the heavenly sovereign, the emperor, a direct descendant of the sun goddess, Amaterasu.

As the stark light spread over the terror-stricken countryside—now occupied by Imperial Forces—it lit pathways through the war-torn jungle of the Bataan Peninsula and the abandoned American island fortress at Corregidor, in the mouth of Manila Bay, now blockaded by Japanese vessels. Beyond the island, dark pulsating waters of the South China Sea transformed into dazzling blue-green, animated and electric, while beneath the waves, an aquatic graveyard lay awash with sunken hopes of the battle dead.

POW Camp Cabanatuan

In a field along a river plateau, a boyish figure slept clad in coveralls, head on a towel, like Tom Sawyer with a pail and pole by his side. Layers of tall grass that he had pulled down over himself served as a blanket, crisscrossing his chest, pinned down by thin arms. Hot from a bout of malaria, his scarred forehead beaded with sweat as insect chirps and birdsong reached a crescendo and droplets of dew formed on the grass.

The man, whose twenty-fifth birthday had come and gone unnoticed, slipped into an ice-cold dream of years past—of walking by a frozen pond that lay ten thousand miles due east-northeast from this place.

Arms pulled back, he gripped a rope tightly in his fists. A red wood sled sloshed back and forth behind. Bundled up and hot despite the icy wind, he raced up a steep, rutted, snow-packed dirt road while school chums dragged their sleds and fell behind. The boy reached an overgrown logging trail, then made a dash toward the crest of the hill.

"Beat you to the top," he yelled.

His chums sprinted after him. "No sir-ree," they hollered back, but they soon gave up the chase and trudged up the remainder of the hill.

Once he reached the top, the boy sat triumphant on the sled, his old brown overcoat flapped open. He pulled his kneesocks over his wool pants up to his knees, tugged at his galoshes and large woolen mittens, then slipped prone, head first, onto the sled.

"Slow pokes, slow pokes, work all day and still yer broke," he taunted.

He dug a toe into the snow, gripped the crossbars, and pushed off. As he soared down the snow- and ice-encrusted hillside, the sled hit a patch of ice, skidded out of control, and slammed with a thud into a small tree at the bottom of the hill. The boy was flung backward, then heaved forward, his head striking the tree.

A loud thud rang through the camp as American prisoners of war slammed a sledgehammer into the head of a water buffalo. The dreamer woke with a start, sat up, and slowly became aware of his surroundings. He had wandered away from Ward Zero the night before, to escape the dead and dying and spend the night in the open air, under the stars. The slamming continued. He listened to the voices of Japanese soldiers shouting orders, then crouched and crawled to the edge of the hillock and watched as the throat of the water buffalo was slit. Blood spurted fountain-like, forming ruby streams oozing onto the grass as POWs butchered the massive creature. The onlooker passed out and drifted back into the shadows of his childhood.

The boy sat slumped in a cracked brown leather Morris chair with a bandage wrapped round his head, sipping cocoa. Bundled up in a navy wool blanket, he felt increasingly hot. He squirmed and scanned his grandmother's living room and fixed on a calendar: December 1926. A garish graphic of rosy-cheeked youngsters

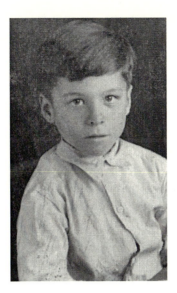

Franklin "Porky" LaCoste as a boy
Courtesy LaCoste/Thurber family

enjoying a winter sleigh ride was topped by black block letters advertising Mahoney's Garage, Athol, Massachusetts. His grandmother readjusted her beige shawl and busily worked in the adjacent kitchen. She poured and stirred blood drippings into a hot skillet on a cast-iron stove, then crossed to a thick-planked oak table. Nimble fingers peeled and sliced a potato, then sprinkled it with salt and pepper. Turning toward the living room, she smiled.

"How's my little soldier? How's Grandma's perfect little boy? Feeling better?"

"Naw. My head still hurts," he whined.

His grandmother carried the sliced potato to him and peeled off the bandage. "This should help."

The boy pushed her hand away.

"Aw, Grandma . . . I don't want no potato stuck to my head."

"Franklin, keep still," his grandmother snapped as she examined his wound. "Hmm, looks like you're healing. A potato poultice will draw the pain out, and in case you've got an infection, that too. It's the best I can do," she said as she applied the potato and rebandaged his head.

"Oh, Grandma, my head hurts. My head hurts," he said, snapping his head from side to side.

"Be still, or you'll fret yourself into a fever. Now, I'm fixing some blood sausage. And you'll eat it, like it or not. You need to get your strength back."

He made a nasty face. "I hate blood sausage."

"If you're not better by tomorrow, I'll call Doctor Bassow." She ignored his behavior and examined his head with her hands.

"Maybe you cracked your skull."

"I don't want to see no doctor. My head's not cracked, it's bumped. I want to go out and . . ."

She slapped his hand. "No. No. You sit there quiet and let the poultice do its job. Your head got swelled up, and that isn't good."

"Billy and Everett are going skating. Can't I watch?"

"Not 'til you're better," his grandmother clucked. "You were out cold when they brought you home. You were so bad I not only called the doctor, I called the priest. Franklin, you need to get your strength back, which means you'll eat what I tell you to eat."

"But I don't like it. It tastes . . ."

He made a face. "Ugh . . . ugh! Awful!"

"You've got no strength. I'm worried, I tell you. It's total bed rest for you until Doctor Bassow says you can go out. Now, close your eyes and rest, like Grandma's good little boy. Your ma will be home from the factory before long. She has plenty to worry about with your dad taking off to God knows where to find work. Now you be a good soldier and rest up and you'll be as good as new before you know it."

His grandmother kissed the top of his head as he handed her the emptied cup. He slumped back into the cushion and closed his eyes as his grandmother returned to the kitchen and placed the cup in the slate basin. She fretted for her husband to come home from the railroad yard. He was the section boss, and God only knew when he'd get home. She moved back to the doorway to check on the boy.

**Grandmother Rosanna LaCoste,
son Rosario and daughter Rose (Porky's mother)**
Courtesy LaCoste/Thurber family

"Your grandfather will know what to do. He'll be here any moment," she said softly, then returned to the washbasin to pump water.

Porky's grandfather, Ernest LaCoste, seated with daughter, Yvonne. Standing: daughter and son, Eva and Romeo.
Courtesy LaCoste/Thurber family

The Japanese soldiers shouted as the POWs butchered the carcass and carried it to the wood-framed barbed-wire gate. The young man woke and scanned the scene. He threw the towel around his neck, grabbed the pail and bamboo pole, and slowly moved down into the ravine. After greeting his fellow POWs, he gestured to the pail and blood.

"The blood there . . . Mind if I grab some to cook?"

The man with the sledgehammer said, "Sure. But grab it quick, while they're busy with the meat."

Blood from the massive body spurted from severed veins into the man's pail. Soon after, Japanese soldiers carted off the meat. The young man thanked his fellow captives and moved down to a sandy spot by a stream, grabbing scattered bamboo along the way for kindling. There he knelt, lit a fire, and stirred the blood in the pail until it thickened, removing it from the heat before it scorched. He grabbed his bamboo pole and a sharp stick lying in the sand and sat to dig out cooked rice he had stored in the hollow of the pole. He spooned the blood-sausage mixture into his mouth, popped in some rice, chewed slowly, grimaced, and swallowed.

"Dear, dear Grandma Rose, it still tastes like shit!"

Franklin, as his grandmother called him, was known as Porky to his friends back home. Although he was small, before the war he was muscular and compact. Now shrunken from starvation, he forced himself to eat, and then dug into the top pocket of his coveralls and pulled out a foil packet. Inside were sulfur tablets his medic friend Stickney had given him when he had come down with a mild case of dysentery, before the war. Stickney had chopped two of the tablets into fragments. Choosing the tiniest piece, he popped it into his mouth and swallowed, then carefully refolded the tinfoil and stuck it back into his pocket. Medicine available to prisoners of war was "scarcer than hen's teeth," he knew, remembering an expression his Gramps had used so long ago, in another time, another place. That small packet was worth its weight in gold and then some. Porky grabbed the pail and bamboo stick and walked back toward the barracks through knee-high grass thick with flies. A Japanese soldier approached—a teenager recruited from an isolated mountain village who was familiar with the ways of poultry.

"Egg for flies? Catch in can? Flies in can for egg?" The Japanese soldier handed him a soup can and a small piece of mosquito netting.

"OK. OK." Porky took the can and netting, bowed, and set out into the deep grass to catch flies. He slipped the netting along the grasses to gather the insects, then brought them to the stream, drowned them, dumped them into the can and went back for more. Spotting a frog, he snagged it with the net, cut off its head and toes and plopped it into a pouch tied to his waist. The Japanese soldier returned to find a can filled to the brim with flies.

"Good. Very good. Good for chicken. Chicken food."

The guard produced an egg from his pocket. The prisoner beamed with joy and bowed.

"Thanks."

He bowed again, "Thank you very much."

The Japanese soldier sauntered off with his flies as the POW quietly walked to the bamboo huts tipping with age. They served as barracks for Ward Zero. The bodies of dead and dying American servicemen, little more than flesh and bones with bloated bellies, were naked and visible as he passed. The burial detail (slightly healthier American POWs) arrived to remove bodies for burial. Porky passed by in silence and headed toward the "mess" shed. He picked up a beat-up frying pan and wiped it clean with his towel. As he passed the barracks, the last of the dead were brought out and "fresh POW arrivals" brought in. He checked them over to see if anyone else had arrived from his division, but they were all strangers. He wiped his face with the towel and slapped it back around his neck and moved on.

Disheartened, Porky made his way back to the stream to start a fire from the remainder of the dried bamboo he had gathered earlier and tossed the dismembered frog and egg into the frying pan. He shielded his eyes from the glare of the sun with his free hand as he cooked, and then ate from the pan with makeshift chopsticks. Afterward, he cleaned the pan in the stream and filled it with water and placed it back onto the open fire. Removing a pouch from his coveralls, he pinched out a few tea leaves and dropped them into the pan, then took a Japanese "dope" pipe from his breast pocket and stuffed it with tobacco. A metal cup hung by a string from his coveralls. He untied it and poured in the steaming liquid and settled back to enjoy his pipe and cup of hot tea. Though a prisoner of war, he had survived to settle in. For the moment, his spirits lifted and were as free as the breeze, the swaying grass, the sky, the sun, and the wandering spirits of his lost companions.

Athol Factory District 1914 panoramic
Courtesy Library of Congress

Chapter 2

Athol, Massachusetts
Saturday, September 21, 1940

Athol, on this bright September day, was one of the larger towns in Worcester County, Massachusetts, with nearly eleven thousand residents. Though times were tough, it was flourishing in comparison to other Depression-era communities. Many had kept their jobs even through the worst of times, and the majority of Athol's families owned their own homes, including the family of Franklin "Porky" LaCoste.

Athol was named after its founder in 1762. Tradition states he was the youngest son of the Duke of Atholl, from the Highlands of Scotland. Young Atholl was known for his spunk and determination, traits still prized by locals. From the beginning, Athol residents put their shoulders to the wheel, figuratively and, at times, literally. By the mid-1800s, personal property was valued at about a quarter of a million dollars. By World War I, combined property values were closer to a cool one million dollars, with a peak reached in the 1920s at over $2.5 million. Even after the stock market crash in 1929, the 1930 valuations had declined only slightly. But by 1940, after a decade of erosion, property values had plummeted by $2 million. Nevertheless, Athol wasn't licked. There was still work to be had. Not necessarily the type of work that was attractive to young men looking for adventure, but if you scrambled, there was work.

The industrial heart of Athol was the L. S. Starrett Tool Company, which was styled "the largest plant in the world wholly devoted to making fine mechanical tools." The company was a vast complex of interlocking, multistoried, red brick and white wooden buildings along the Miller's River. Hundreds of its windows overlooked the town, like so many eyes keeping watch in all directions. Driving east along the river toward Gardner, you passed the massive Union Twist Drill that manufactured gears and cutting tools. According to salesmen passing through, catalogue books from both companies were found throughout the country with illustrations of tools and machines manufactured in Athol. This was a source of great pride to residents—over the age of thirty.

Though Starrett and the Union Twist Drill drove the economy, earning Athol the nickname Tool Town of America, they were not the only game in town. Athol had nearly a hundred farms and a rail system that transported other locally manufactured goods to markets near and far such as shoes, toys, pocketbooks, assorted wood products, thread, straw hats, pumps, cradles, combs and other "celluloid" goods, as well as meat choppers and cigars. Porky thought of his grandfather whenever he passed the rail yard. Long since dead, Grandpa LaCoste had made his salary as a supervisor there but also turned a profit by trading in houses. Since landing a job as a salesman at the Sports Dugout, Porky suspected he was a chip off the old block.

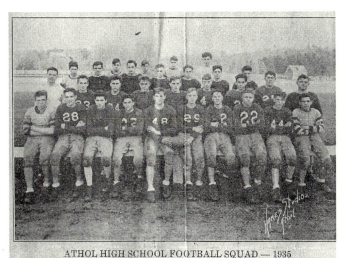

Athol High School 1935 Football Team
Porky, front row, 4th from left,
Fran Robichaud, third row, 2nd from right
Photo credit: Hames Studio, published by The Little Red Schoolhouse

Despite the country's woes, Porky didn't have a care in the world on this bright Saturday morning. He had taken the day off to have fun. Gray cotton pant legs flapped against his calves as he walked from his grandmother's house to the Athol Fairgrounds. The weather was glorious, barely seventy degrees, and clear with a touch of a chilly breeze; but he was snug in a cable-knit sweater his aunt Yvonne had knit for him. A cold snap the week before had turned the leaves from green to brilliant yellows, orange, and crimson. Porky inhaled deeply and was filled with a joie de vivre, as his French Canadian relatives would say. The town's football grandstand was now in view. In fact, it was the dominant feature of the fairgrounds' thirty acres, with its goalposts and four-inch-wide white field marks and wooden bleachers overhung by a wooden roof. Over breakfast, he had scanned the sports section of the *Athol Daily News*. One headline in particular caught his attention, a "Strong Athol Grid Team Awaits Ware." He agreed with smug satisfaction, based on what he had seen so far.

Even with the breeze, Porky had worked up a sweat as he entered the fairgrounds. He took off his sweater and rolled the sleeves of his white shirt to his elbows as he approached a high school senior setting up a card table a few feet away from the entrance to the field. The table would serve as the ticket booth for the afternoon's game. Helping him was a tall gangly junior wearing round wire-rimmed glasses. According to the badge clipped to the collar of his sports jacket, he was a reporter for the school newspaper, *The Little Red Schoolhouse*. Porky fished in his pockets for change. The ticket taker, who was decked out in the school colors—white slacks and a red V-neck school sweater—informed him that the sports council had just hiked the price to thirty-five cents. "But for you, it's free," he said and waved him through. Porky was well-known to the undergraduates, who regarded him as a hero of games past.

Porky walked toward the bleachers and looked about, searching for familiar faces. Thumbs on jawbone, he interlocked his fingers over the top of his brow to scan the scene and shield his eyes from the glare of the sun. He spotted a few friends and waved before relaxing to watch the hometown team in their Saturday pre-game warm-up.

A freckle-faced red-headed young man in khakis and a long-sleeved polo shirt was standing on the far side of the bleacher, watching the team practice. Phillip Dower, a.k.a. Pinky, had grown up on the right side of the tracks on Riverbend Street, not far from Athol High. He spotted Porky and approached from behind.

"Hey, hotshot. What're you doing here?"

Porky swung around, nearly knocking the head of his fellow gatecrasher with his elbow. "Why, Pinky Dower, fancy meeting you here! Haven't you heard? It's a free country." The young men laughed and shook hands.

"Thought you were avoiding Coach O'Brien."

Porky winced. "Aw . . . by now, he's gotten over it."

"Like hell he has."

"Pinky, no one's that valuable."

At five feet eleven inches, Pinky towered over his five-foot-four-and-a-half-inch friend. "Yaw? You may have been the shortest player on the team, but you were one of the best. You sure packed some power holding the line."

Porky rolled his eyes at his friend's flattery. "Quit dreaming. Hey. Keep an eye on Number 41, Eddie Lefsyk. He's their new captain. He held up the backfield single-handed in Wednesday's scrimmage with Gardner."

"Aw, he can't hold a candle to you. You called the signals that made us champions, and no one was better diagnosing plays. The papers sung your praises."

"Eddie's doing just fine. Look, Roger Bartlett did some gritty playing last season. Admit it. And Hawkins is a fabulous tackle, and Doc Brouillet's about as dependable a guard as you'll get. He's damn good in my book. Most of these guys aren't half bad. The coach has got himself quite a team, a winning team. Believe me, Pinky, I'm long forgotten."

"You may be gone, but you're not forgotten. Why, I've been out for two years and they treat me like a celebrity whenever I drop by. And I wasn't half the athlete you were. The difference is I stayed on and graduated."

"So I'm a dropout, so what?"

"That was a dumb move. And you weren't that far from graduating."

"Hey. Life's tough. I've got more than homework and football to think about," Porky said, smarting from the criticism.

"Tell me about it."

"Don't you worry, I'll make it. I'll do OK."

"I never said you wouldn't, but I hear from my grandmother that—"

Porky's defenses were up. "Look, working at the Union Twist Drill may not have been hoity-toity—"

"Hey, there's nothing wrong with the Union Twist Drill. Remember, I work there too. But dropping out of school to work there?" Porky crossed his arms and waited for the lecture to be over.

"'Course I mostly run errands. But that's beside the point. You need to think of a future in something other than a sweatshop," Pinky said emphatically.

"You're right. It is a sweatshop, but haven't you heard? I've moved up and out. I'm at the Sports Dugout now—at the sporting goods store, uptown."

"Really? Wow. That's great!"

"Of course, it's only part time."

"I suppose we're both lucky we've got jobs," Pinky said, softening his stance.

"Hey, the Union Twist Drill's not half bad. I liked the guys and some of them machinists make top dollar to boot. And they were more than fair with me—I came in as a green kid and they were letting me apprentice. I got eighteen bucks in real dough each week. Not bad for a shop boy."

Pinky's interest was piqued. "Eighteen bucks a week?"

"I'm telling you, I made eighteen bucks," he repeated.

"So why did you leave? Eighteen bucks ain't bad." Pinky whistled threw his teeth. "Beats what I'm making, and I graduated."

"Maybe that's your problem. They think you think you're too good for them and that you're looking to leave," Porky countered, gaining the upper hand. "'Course production's dropped lately," he admitted. "That's why I started looking. Besides, I wanted some clean work for a change. Still it was something, and it's bound to pick up again. Don't worry about that."

"Naw, you've got the right attitude. There's got to be something better," Pinky said, shaking his head.

"Times are tough. Even though Uncle Rosario's been working overtime at Starrett, he's still sweating it. Between you and me, I think he's itching to get married. And poor Grandma Rose," Porky sighed. "With Gramps gone . . . Why, the last time she had a new dress, she made it out of one of them cotton-print grain sacks they've been buying to feed the pigs."

"Thought your grandfather was loaded. Didn't he leave her anything?"

"Gramps did OK for himself, but he's been dead for a long while. The money's spent, Pinky."

"Oh."

"The walking bank, everyone called him that," Porky said, chuckling. "Gramps used to keep his money in the top pocket of his coveralls and buy houses in cash! After supper he'd sit in the Morris chair and check out real-estate ads. If he liked a property, he'd say, 'Frank, let's go for a walk.' Mind, I was just a little kid, but off we'd go. 'Course they'd haggle over the price. If they agreed, he'd dig into the pocket of his coveralls and pay in cash."

"Your grandmother talks about him as if he died yesterday."

"That right? Pinky, Gramps died two years before the crash, in '27. He dropped dead of a heart attack. 'Course at her age, maybe it seems like yesterday."

"It must be hard without him," Pinky said quietly.

"Life goes on. But times are tough. I've been saving up and buying groceries too. My mom's out west with her new husband. And what am I supposed to do? Go around looking like a bum? If you want a girl, you have to look sharp."

"Ain't that the truth." Pinky nodded.

"Hey," Porky nudged him in the ribs. "Are you up for a night out?"

"What's up?"

"The team's headed up to the Acadia Dance Hall in South Gardner to razz them about Wednesday. You want to tag along?"

"No, I can't afford it. Porky, I'm not the man I once was," Pinky said with a straight face.

"And you're telling me to give up my job and go back to school?"

Pinky looked shamefaced. "To tell the truth, my grandmother made me promise if I ran into you to—"

Porky laughed. "I thought you were coming on a bit strong. What a nerve!"

"And to top it off, I've blown a wad at poker." Pinky turned the inside of his pockets out.

"You, broke? Ha. I'm not falling for that. You left your wallet home. Hiding from your poker debts, that's what you're up to. Brother, oh brother," Porky snorted as he laughed good-naturedly and slapped him on the back. "Pinky, come on along. I'll even foot the bill."

"Thanks for the offer, but . . ."

"Hell, maybe you'll be lucky in love."

A pretty cheerleader started across the field. "Or maybe I will. See you around, sport," Porky shouted over his shoulder as he trailed after her. Pinky laughed and walked back to the bleachers.

Later that afternoon, sixty-seven-year-old Rosanna LaCoste stepped off the back porch of her Swanzey Street home. Rose, as her family and friends called her, was dressed in a calf-length floral housedress and starched white apron, with her hair pulled back in a bun. Strands of white fell across her worn face which, at that moment, was distorted in pain as she gripped the wire handle of an old tin pail laden with vegetable peels and table scraps. She stopped by the small shed that served as the pigpen and dropped the slop past the chicken-wire fence into where the pigs wallowed, lolling around in the dark brown mud and caked earth.

"Come and get it," she called with barely a hint of a French Canadian accent.

The richness of the soil was a source of deep satisfaction to Rose. Next to the shed, she kept a small vegetable garden that yielded more than enough for summer eating and fall canning. The fertile soil was compost from the remains of a deep primordial forest that had once blanketed the area, before white settlers stripped it away for farms. Later, developers moved in to create housing for the immigrants who worked the dozens of factories and shops, large and small, that dotted the town.

Rose blew wisps of hair back and ignored the slamming of the back-porch screen door as fat pink snouts lifted in her direction and squealed back in greeting. Porky stood on the porch and watched, dressed "fit to kill" for the evening. He looked nothing like his childhood nickname. At twenty-three, he had slimmed down since his football days. He had a handsome, well-proportioned face and, though short of stature, was well built. He still bore the scar from a childhood sledding accident, but it was barely noticeable. For Porky, his clothes said it all. He was decked out in an ill-fitted gangster-style double-breasted zoot suit—the height of pop fashion.

"How do I look?" His grandmother turned her attention from the pigs to her grandson. She rolled her eyes and shook her head. "Foolish. I've never

L. S. Starrett Tool Company
Photo credit: G. Thomson Fraser

seen such gaudy, newfangled nonsense. If that's the style, far as I'm concerned, you'd look better wearing a rain barrel."

On this particular Saturday, the foundry where Rosario worked was busy, and as a longtime employee, he had first dibs at the extra jobs. He had left his home early in the morning in a perfectly laundered set of work clothes, but his coveralls were now dirt- and grease-stained. He shifted his lunch pail from right hand to left and lifted the gate latch to enter the backyard.

"Uncle Rosario, glad I caught you. So what do you think?" Porky asked, knowing perfectly well what his uncle would think. He loved to get a rise out of him. Porky turned around on the heels of his black-and-white wing-tipped shoes to deliver the full effect. Rosario shook his head in disgust. "Darn it, those aren't the new clothes you was all hopped up about, are they? What a waste of hard-earned cash!"

"I pay room and board and then some. I have a right to look stylish."

"But those are gangster clothes. Makes it look like you're up to no good."

"It's all the rage. Problem is you never go out to movies or read *Time* magazine or anything else up-to-date."

"I read the papers. I see what Al Capone and the rest of them gangsters wear. Hey, Capone's out on parole and living in Florida. Maybe you could hightail it down there and get a good-paying job."

"I'm not dressed like Al Capone or George Raft, for that matter. More like Mickey Rooney. Oh, you're both jealous. What do you two know about fashion? You never go anywhere."

Rose burst out laughing. Porky, stung, maintained his bravado. "Grandma, tell the truth. When was the last time you went out?" "Church social, wasn't it, Ma? And it wasn't that long ago," Rosario added.

"Two years ago last July. But you can bet your bottom dollar, Porky, if you showed up dressed like that—why, the pastor would turn you right out the door. No respectable person would show up looking like a thug."

"Don't worry. I'm not going to a church social."

His grandmother wiped her slop-stained hands on her apron, walked up onto the porch, looked him hard in the eyes, and patted his cheeks.

"Now, you be good. No liquor, you hear?"

Porky smiled broadly. "Don't worry. If I'm not good, I'll be careful."

His uncle grumbled a warning, "As long as you're under this roof . . ."

"Uncle Rosario, no need to blow your top. I'm kidding. With my luck, I'll be holding up the wall with the other guys. Fact is, if I got lucky, I'd faint dead away . . . Wouldn't know what to do," Porky said, throwing the full weight of his boyish charm toward his grandmother. "And you just keep it that way," she said as Porky kissed his grandmother goodnight. "I'll never find anyone as good as you, Grandma," he said as he searched her pale blue eyes for support.

"Oh yes, you will. If you're careful and respectful, the right girl will find you!"

"I'll keep that in mind," Porky said, knowing he was securely in her good graces.

Uncle Rosario grabbed the handle of the screen porch door. "Always running around, spending his hard-earned cash . . . ," he muttered to himself as he entered the kitchen, clunking his lunch box down on the counter.

"Oh, don't be so hard on the boy," Rose called after him. "Porky contributes what we ask him to, and if he's got some left over . . . Well, I guess he's earned a good time."

Rosario ignored his mother and headed to the front parlor to grab the Saturday afternoon paper.

"So, Porky, where are you off to tonight? And I want details," his grandmother inquired, attempting to sound stern as she stepped back off the porch to continue her chores.

"First stop, Bobby Doolan's house; then, downtown to the York Theater to catch a movie, then to the Acadia in Gardner. Jimmy Collins and the All Stars are playing tonight. Of course, the crowd might be unfriendly. We beat the pants off Gardner in scrimmage, and today's game against Ware wasn't a contest. I was embarrassed for them. The word is out. We're the team to beat!"

Rosario reappeared at the back door with the newspaper tucked under his arm. "We beat . . . what's this we beat? You were too smart for them, you had to quit . . . I told you I could support us, but no, you had to—"

Rose interrupted, "Bobby Doolan's a nice boy. Didn't he go to business college? Now there's a friend who might help you out. Once he starts working, maybe there's a job that—"

Porky stepped off the porch and walked to his grandmother. "Grandma, Bobby works at the Union Twist Drill, just like I did. 'Course, he's into clean work, gentleman's stuff. He's what they call a laboratory chemist. I wouldn't qualify with or without a high school diploma."

"But still, that's a young man I can approve of," she added quietly. Rosario sat on the porch steps. "Hang out with him and maybe you'll learn something useful," he said, snapping the newspaper open.

"Trust me, I do. I learn a lot, like how to dress up for the girls! Well, got to go." Porky scooted quick as a rabbit to the backyard gate. He was anxious to depart before any further discussion might delay his plans for the evening. He unlatched the gate, turned, and waved, then whistled as he walked down the sidewalk to his friend's house.

Rosario stood up, irritated. "Listen to him. Just listen to him," he said, shaking his head. "You come home at a decent hour, you hear me," he called out as Porky turned on his heels, saluted his uncle, and continued merrily on his way.

"Rosario, stop trying to be his father," his mother said. "Porky's a young man now. He'll do just fine." Rosario responded by walking back into the kitchen and letting the screen door slam behind.

The LaCoste family lived in the South Park section of Athol on the corner of Swanzey and Everett streets, just off Sanders Street, an area some referred to as the other side of the tracks. It was literally the other side of the tracks because you needed to pass under the tracks through the railroad tunnel to access downtown Athol. Here, many of Porky's friends had first met in the classrooms of the squat redbrick Sanders Street grammar school. The school is adjacent to Chestnut Street, a small portion of what once was the Great Trail that Native Americans had traveled. According to the commemorative marker near the school's playground, the trail had been a mere eighteen inches wide but hundreds of miles long, stretching from Connecticut to Massachusetts to Canada, and locally from the Miller's River to the South Athol Road. For the more adventurous, tales of the Great Trail—of Indian warfare and territorial battles—implanted a desire to wander from the secure confines of this small but thriving mill town to see where their own trails led.

Porky was filled with wanderlust as he walked though South Park to Bobby Doolan's house. The stroll was pleasant enough, despite the surroundings—a blue-collar neighborhood with men tinkering on cars and women carting in groceries and laundry. He passed well-maintained multistoried houses along elm-, maple-, oak-, and chestnut tree-lined sidewalks. An assortment of evergreens stood tall in the less developed area beyond. The section had once been home to farms just outside of Athol proper, but by 1895, local bankers were promoting the area as *the best* and safest investment near the business center, churches, post office, and stores. "Outlay for Rent is Money Ill-Spent," read the headline to a well-placed advertisement in the local paper. "Every dollar should go toward your property—not your landlord's! It is easy to do," it counseled. "Decide now and let us show you how to do it." Inserted in the middle of the ad was a map of Athol with a giant circle, which used the Pequoig House Hotel as the center. The priciest lots, which went for between $500 to $1,000, were within the circle. South Park was outside and far more affordable.

The LaCoste home was a modest two-story dwelling with a backyard and porch and, according to the 1895 map, was technically within the inner circle of Athol residences, but along the extreme outer edge. The family was respected, hardworking, and for the most part sensible. The Doolan family was admired for the same reasons and many more. Bobby Doolan's father, Frank, was the proprietor of the Athol House Hotel, a fashionable hotel located near the train station that was central to the flow of trade and tourism in and out of the region. Porky was proud of his friendship with Bobby, whom he saw as part of Athol's upper crust. But he knew that the French Canadian LaCoste family as well as many of the Lithuanian, Polish, Irish, Italian, German, and other recent immigrants were the newcomers to this community and would be viewed as such, no matter what their accomplishments, for decades to come.

Athol's prominent names during the eighteenth and nineteenth centuries were still well-regarded in 1940. They included the Hamilton, Humphry, Smith, Sawyer, and Southland families as well as the Hutchins, Hunts, Cobbs, Fletchers, Williams, Starretts, and Fays. The fruits of their labor could be seen in the Italianate-, Colonial-, and Federalist-style buildings that were prominent along Main Street and the village squares and fashionable streets of Athol, on the other side of the tracks from where Porky lived. *The Doolans are not a family that keeps pigs in their backyard, Depression or not,* Porky thought as he crossed onto Exchange Street. But despite his background, Bobby was a regular guy, and Porky was particularly impressed by his mother, Eudora. Always fashionably dressed and dignified, she had a knack of making him feel at home.

Eudora Doolan was born a Fay, with a pedigree dating back to arrival in Central Massachusetts a decade before the American Revolution. Fays from Athol had attended Harvard and served as teachers, lawyers, bankers, gentlemen farmers, and lawmakers. Solomon Fay had been in the state legislature in the seventeen hundreds; Lysander and Beriah were elected in the mid- and late-1800s. And in 1914, three years before Bobby was born, Levi Fay was the Republican nominee for Congress. The sizeable mansion Levi inhabited on Pequoig Avenue had turrets as well as bay windows and later became the headquarters of the American Legion Post. The Doolans lived one street up, on the Wallingford Avenue hill, in a comfortable L-shaped Victorian. Across the street was a stately redbrick Colonial. The homes overlooked a manicured park, rooftops, and church steeple below and the forest-covered Chestnut Hill beyond.

Porky's gait slowed as he approached the Doolan home. He liked to make a good impression on Mrs. Doolan. Their large front porch, with its posh wicker furniture and spotless white floor, railings, and ceiling, was the way a porch should look, he thought—not strung over with clotheslines and laundry as they often were in his neighborhood. He always checked the soles of his shoes before he set foot on their porch, concerned that he might leave a trail of dirt or, once inside, soil the elegant oriental rugs. Porky rang the doorbell and straightened his tie.

Eudora answered the door dressed smartly in a tailored powder blue dress and a white cloth belt that accentuated her trim figure. Artie Shaw's hotel dance band played "Begin the Beguine" softly on the 1937 Zenith set next to the couch across from the fireplace. The cabinetry featured burl veneer, Japan trim, and parquetry inlays with a big black Magnavision dial. Bobby was in his bedroom, getting dressed for the evening. "Bobby's expecting you," she said after exchanging hellos.

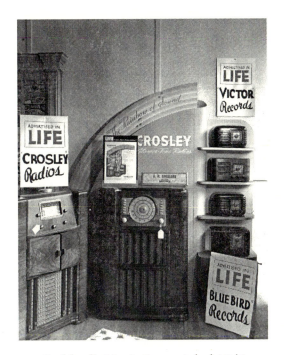

Goddard's Music Store, Athol 1940
Photo credit: Hames Photo Shop
Courtesy of Richard Chaisson

"I like your taste in music," Porky commented.

"One of my little treats . . . I adore Cole Porter. Frank and I used to love to go out dancing, but with the children and the hotel, it seems there's no time left. But there's always the radio . . ."

As the music ended, three chimes sounded, then the staccato of a telegraph. Porky and Eudora stood momentarily frozen as the radio announcer began, "An economic boycott of Japan was considered in U.S. House committee this week. News of Japan's intentions are not good. The question of whether an embargo of oil would push Japan into Dutch East Indies is now moot. They're going to march in there anyway . . ."

Mrs. Doolan moved to the couch and sat transfixed, listening to the news. As she leaned toward the radio, her attention was so rapt she appeared to stop breathing. The radio announcer continued, "Just off the wire, CBS reports from London that German raiders were driven back by the RAF. Invasion ships were given another pounding by the RAF as they continued to attack communications from Germany. More on last night's attack by an incendiary bomb as time bombs continue to go off in the morning . . ."

"Where do these Nazis get off anyway?" Porky remarked. Eudora shook her head in agreement.

"And in other news . . . Following the resistance to German bombing put up by the RAF, Hitler announced that he was postponing his planned invasion of Britain until further notice. But the mayor of London chose not to take the führer at his word and today Londoners were given permission to use the Underground as an air-raid shelter. Before this they were forbidden, but many people got round this by buying a ticket and staying put . . ." Eudora remembered she had a guest and looked up, smiling. "That's quite some fancy suit, young man."

"Gee, thanks," Porky said, then remembered why he was there and bolted upstairs.

Eudora watched him disappear into the upstairs hallway and her smile faded. She feared her sons and their friends would soon be forced into a nightmare similar to what her generation had experienced during World War I. Her greatest pleasure was in watching her boys be boys and encouraging their lighthearted amusements—within reason.

Eudora settled back into the couch, closed her eyes, and listened as the staccato of the telegraph sounded again and the subject changed to a reminder that this was the second anniversary of the hurricane that had struck the New England coast two years before. "The storm rapidly crossed Long Island, New York, and New Haven, Connecticut, and then moved through Massachusetts and Vermont. The storm caused massive forest damage, widespread flooding, and coastal damage. Over six hundred deaths were attributed to the storm," the announcer continued. Moments later, Porky opened Bobby's bedroom door and poked his head in. "Are you decent?" he asked.

Bobby stood in his boxer shorts in front of the large oblong mirror, suspended on dowels, attached to a mahogany dresser. He powdered his upper body before putting on his undershirt. "Sure, come on in, but close the door, will you? I don't want a peep show for the family." Porky surveyed the lineup of men's talcum bottles neatly displayed on the bureau. There was a green-and-cream Palmolive Talc tin; a milk-glass Old Spice bottle with a blue sailing schooner and a gray metal concave disk for dispensing; a gold-and-green Stern's Violet Talc bottle with a Basket-of-violet logo; a soft green Avon Gentlemen's Talc tin featuring an oval with the portrait of a mustached, leather-vested Gay 90's man in a bowler hat; a red Mavis Talcum tin sporting a golden-wreathed cupid and jet black lettering; Fitch's Talc, a cream-and-navy box with a profile cameo of a young man; and a green striped Mennen Talcum for Men tin.

Porky picked up the Mennen's and began to read from the back. "Neutral tint. Won't show on your face."

"Porky, that's an aftershave. You use aftershave, don't you?"

"Old Spice," Porky responded. "But this is like a face powder, like what women use." He surveyed the directions. "Apply before shaving to absorb the excess moisture. You'll get a smoother, cleaner shave. Apply after shaving to avoid face shine."

"You've never used powder, I take it," Bobby said, applying talcum to his back.

"Only Zanol Mosquito Powder," Porky stated as a matter of fact. "Uncle Rosario uses Sykes Comfort Powder when he gets boils. That's a healing powder," Porky said. "I suppose my mother used talcum when I was a baby."

Porky pointed to the talc Bobby was using. "Nice tin, what's that?"

"Trade Winds. Check it out for yourself." Bobby tossed him the can.

Porky examined the trademark graphic—palm trees and an ocean scene. "Made in San Francisco," he read. "What I wouldn't give to be there." He smelled the top of the can, dumped some of the powder into his hands and rubbed them together.

"What's keeping you from going?"

"Money, a job, not wanting to live like a bum. What's your excuse?" Porky tossed the tin back to Bobby.

"I'm happy right where I am, for now," Bobby responded with a grin. "Hey, I'll get you some talc for Christmas. Women love it, trust me," Bobby said, continuing to dress.

Set in the corner by the bureau was a horseshoe-shaped yellow Danish upholstered chair where Bobby had haphazardly tossed a magazine and a powder-blue tin with black Gothic lettering. "What's this?" Porky asked. He grabbed the tin, pulled off the cap, and sniffed. "Talc de fle . . . ? It's in French!" he blurted, unable to decipher the label.

"Trust me, Porky, that isn't baby powder. Smell it. It's a man's scent." Bobby adjusted his gold cuff links and tiepin as he examined himself in the mirror. He grabbed a bristle brush and began smoothing his hair back. "My brother's one of them Ivy League types. He's at Dartmouth. But whenever he's in Boston, he picks up a couple of boxes at Jordan Marsh." Porky rolled his eyes. "Relax. Movie stars use it. Clark Gable, Claude Rains . . . lots of them." Bobby smiled a dazzling smile, checked his teeth, and then affected a phony French accent. "It adds to zee sex appeal."

"So I'm a hick. So shoot me."

"I'd rather educate you. Trust me. Real men use talc. My father does, and he's a very successful businessman. You should use talc too," Bobby insisted, grabbing a light blue sports jacket and navy trousers out of his wardrobe dresser.

"Not on my side of the tracks. The guys I used to work with at the plant would beat me up. And the fellows who drop by the Sports Dugout—why, they'd think I was queer."

"Do you want to stay on your side of the tracks?"

Bobby moved so Porky could join him at the mirror as he smoothed his hair back with his hands. Porky shrugged and checked himself out alongside his friend. They looked like Mutt and Jeff. But here "Mutt" wore a zoot suit and "Jeff" looked like he had stepped off the pages of "*Esquire*—the Magazine for Men" Bobby had been reading earlier, which now was spread open on the chair.

"Here, check this out," Bobby said, grabbing the magazine and thrusting it into Porky's hands. "That's what you need to aspire to. Sit down. Take a load off while I straighten this mess up."

Porky sat and leafed through *Esquire* while Bobby neatly folded and put away shirts and ties he had tried on before deciding on his outfit for the evening. *Esquire* presented the latest in gadgets, fashion, automobiles, clothing, jewelry, and travel. Bobby was a young man on the go. He liked to stay ahead of the pack and thought he might head a company someday—perhaps hire a few of his old buddies, like Porky, groom them, and bring them along. He had a head for science as well as business and was particularly intrigued by this June 1939 edition, which he had saved, earmarking a full-page ad that announced, "NEW YORK GIVES ITS APPROVAL TO TELEVISION—RCA Victor Television receivers share in applause as newest scientific wonder clicks with world's most sophisticated public * Now New Yorkers know!" The photo layout featured television shots of tennis, baseball, horseracing, a live band in performance, and a television drama. Porky scanned the ad. This was a world unlike anything he knew. He wondered if he would ever belong. He felt suddenly downhearted and slightly foolish in his getup.

"Don't be so self-conscious," Bobby insisted, believing his friend was still anxious about the talcum. "Think about the girls you'll slay. Say, there are less-perfumed brands. I'll drop by Woolworth with you and help pick something out. In fact, I'll buy it. Hell, why wait for Christmas? It'll be a belated birthday gift. How's that for a friend?"

"Good enough, I guess," Porky admitted, closing the magazine and putting it back on the chair.

Bobby grabbed the green-and-cream Palmolive tin. "Here, smell this," he said, handing the talc to Porky, who unscrewed the top to sniff.

"Not half bad," he said as Bobby changed his tiepin to a New York 1939 World's Fair "I Was There" pin.

"I need something to spark myself up. I look flat next to you," Bobby said and winked. "Buddy, we're a great team."

"Like Mutt and Jeff," Porky commented.

"Funny, that's what I was thinking," Bobby said, suppressing a laugh. The two mugged it up, trying to outdo the other with poses and expressions until they burst out laughing. Bobby rested an arm on Porky's shoulder and turned toward him, suddenly serious. "I want you to promise. We'll be buddies until the bitter end."

Porky shook his hand. "Sure enough," he said and laughed. "Hey, how's this? You corral the sophisticated types, I'll corral the others."

"Great. Let's go."

As Bobby and Porky descended the stairs, Mrs. Doolan sat transfixed, listening to the radio. A basket of yarn was next to her on the couch, but the knitting needles were idle in her hands.

"According to an article in this week's *Nation*," the announcer stated, "with Axis hopes for quick decision in the Battle of Britain fading, there is a growing prospect that its chief effort in the coming winter will be directed toward ousting the British from the Near East. No doubt air attacks on England will continue, and strong forces be held in readiness to suggest an invasion, with the object of keeping the bulk of Great Britain's strength pinned down in England. In the Near East, Alexandria and the Suez Canal represent the heart of the British position. If they can be seized, Palestine will become untenable, and the road will be opened to the Iraq oil fields . . ."

Downtown Athol on a Saturday night was mostly filled with teenagers and people in their twenties. Hot rods and late-model Chevys and Fords paraded up and down. Bystander conversations were loud and in competition with honking horns. Porky and Bobby sauntered down the street toward the York Theater, waving at friends and giving the high five to the football players decked out in casual attire and eager to be noticed. Walking toward them were their high school buddies, Fran Robichaud, Billy Freeman, and Herman Hausmann. Fran and Herman were sharply dressed in beige linen pants and V-necked sweaters. Billy wore a cap and was conservative as always, in a brown suit and matching necktie.

Fran had grown up on the end of Sanders Street closest to town, not far from where Porky lived. His machinist father had done well at his trade and bought a three-story brown Victorian with large bay windows. Porky and Fran met as children at the Sanders Street School. They sat in the same classrooms, had the same teachers, and played in the playground adjacent to the Great Indian Trail. Their friendship was based on familiarity, shared experiences, and the South Park camaraderie that stuck up for its own. Fran attended every dance during his high school years, according to the 1937 Athol High School yearbook. Yet he had a serious side. "Hope is the yeast and the bread of life," was the quote under his class photo.

Herman lived on Hapgood Street in a wooded, somewhat secluded area on a hill overlooking a forested embankment. The Hausmann home was a large L-shaped converted farmhouse in one of the oldest sections of town, not far from the Uptown Common that had once served as a major stagecoach stop. His father was a carpenter and made steady improvements when work was slow, so it was one of the more attractive homes on the street. Despite the Depression, he had earned enough to send his son to the Boston Conservatory of Music with hopes he'd be picked up by a big band or might start a band of his own. But for the present, Herman worked in a sweatshop like most of the other guys and waited for his big break.

Billy lived on the other side of town, on Union Street, not far from Fish Park where President Woodrow Wilson had once spoken following World War I. He lived in a large gabled Victorian with a glassed-in sun porch on the south side. His home was not far from a bend in the road that followed the path of the Miller's River and was a favored fishing spot for young anglers.

Billy was known for his remarkable bass voice, which he used to great effect in the choir of the Immaculate Conception Catholic Church. He had a squeaky-clean image and was known as the Brain. Not only was he highly intelligent, he was private, rarely sharing what he was truly thinking. And though he enjoyed the gang, he had a life quite separate from theirs. For instance, his buddies were unaware that he had fallen for a young woman from Greenfield, about thirty miles due west. He intended to keep it a secret too, or the questions and innuendos would have been endless.

"Hubba-hubba, whooie wow!" Herman playfully slugged Porky on the shoulder. "Ask me, did I meet a sweet thing last night at Woolworth's! She promised to show up tonight with a couple of female-type pals." Herman inserted himself between the two friends, placing an arm around Porky and Bobby.

Billy looked sideways at Herman. "Why didn't you go pick her up at her house?"

Fran stepped ahead, turned around, and walked backward. "Are you afraid her parents won't approve of you, hotshot?" he said, jabbing Herman in the ribs.

"To tell the truth, she thinks I'm a wise guy," Herman said, grinning. "Don't know how she got that impression. But she thinks I'm cute anyway. Her friends are for protection."

Bobby shook Herman's arm off his shoulder. "So what's her name? Where's she from?"

"She's not from around here is all I know. And that's good enough for me," Herman answered.

"A woman of mystery? I like her already," Fran said, slamming into a couple walking ahead.

"Hey, watch what you're doing," the man said as his girlfriend screwed up her face in disgust.

"Sorry. I beg your pardon, Miss," Fran said as he turned back around to walk next to Porky.

"Hey, you guys, if you don't like what I have to offer, then get your own chicks!" Herman countered.

As the group approached the York Theater, couples dashed across the street to join the line formed outside the theater. The poster announced the feature, *Test Pilot*, starring Clark Gable and Myrna Loy, Spencer Tracy, and Lionel Barrymore, which had been released the year before but was just now making its way to outlying theaters. Most people who had read the review, as Bobby and Billy had, knew that Gable played a test pilot by the name of Jim and Tracy was his best friend, Gunner. They meet Ann, a college-educated farmer's daughter, played by Loy, during a test flight across country when the plane lands in Kansas in her father's field.

As the friends waited in line, the man Fran had bumped into was describing the movie to his date. He quoted Loy's line to Gable, "It was a thrill to see you come out of the sky; it will be a greater one to see you disappear in it."

"Hey, some of us haven't seen the movie yet. We don't need a play-by-play," Herman commented loudly.

The man rolled his eyes, as he whispered to his date, "It would be a thrill to see *them* disappear!" She nodded in agreement and then turned to stare straight ahead, quietly fuming.

The line grew by another half block as they waited for the theater doors to open. "Hey. I forgot. I've got to run a quick errand for my grandmother," Porky said suddenly. "I'll see you inside."

Porky dashed off as if headed toward the back of the line, then turned right down a side street that led to the back of the block and made his way to the fire escape of a building adjacent to the York Theater. After checking for an open window, he looked around quickly to see if he was being watched, and then stepped back, took a flying leap, grabbed hold of the bar-handle end of the fire escape, and forced it down. He climbed the fire escape, maneuvered to the roof of the building, and walked along the length of the roof. After jumping onto an overhanging attachment to the theater building, he braced himself along the outer edge of the third floor, carefully feeling for the casing of the open window as he inched along. Luck was with him. He grabbed hold of the window casement and pulled himself inside without breaking a sweat. Once in, Porky straightened up, brushed himself off, and exited to the balcony of the movie theater. Looking relaxed and totally in control, he descended the carpeted main staircase to the mezzanine and then down to the main lobby.

Porky spotted his friends with the young women he presumed were with Herman's date, and then edged to the back of the lobby as if he were just entering. "Hey, Bobby . . . Herman . . . Wait up, you guys," Porky yelled, waving until the group saw him.

Later that evening, with Porky on the passenger side and Fran and Billy in the rear, Bobby drove along Route 2 toward Gardner.

"Hey, let's check out the Edgewater," Fran shouted from the rear.

"I'm sure Herman can amuse himself with his harem while we check out the scene here."

Bobby squeezed his family's 1938 Plymouth Road King into the only spot left just as a drunken, disheveled teenager stepped outside and vomited all over his jacket and onto the grass. Just then a police car pulled up, sirens screaming and red light flashing.

"Where the hell did he come from?" Porky asked, checking to see if the officer was anyone he knew.

"Forget this," Billy piped up. Bobby agreed and backed out and onto the road.

A jitterbug contest was winding down as they arrived at the Acadia dance hall, which was secluded among tall pines next to a millpond. Several couples were outside lighting up. Hip flasks flashed silver in the moonlight as whiskey was added to ginger ale and rum to Cokes. Booze was strictly prohibited inside but flowed freely under the stars in the great outdoors.

Bobby parked the family car next to a roadster whose windows were open. Inside, the shadowy figure of a man was hunched over a woman, whose white bobby-socked foot wiggled as it rested uncomfortably on the doorjamb. Her two-tone saddle shoe sat sideways on the pavement below. The Acadia was one of hundreds of dance halls that had sprung up in Massachusetts since Prohibition was lifted. The most popular were secluded but within walking distance of lakes and ponds and camping sites. The halls that catered to adults served liquor, but many others were popular with high school and college students and young adults, and area towns made a show of prohibiting liquor from these establishments. The Puritan ethic still prevailed—at least on the surface.

Porky and his friends sat in the car and watched as a young man in suit and tie held the door open for his date to enter. She wore a tightly fitted buttoned-up sweater and pleated skirt.

"Nice boobs," Fran commented.

Streamers and balloons were strung from the light fixtures, and couples jitterbugged below to the tune "Hot Mikado."

"Let's go," Bobby said and opened the door to exit.

Dozens of couples congregated to the sides to watch dancers wiggle, jump, and jive. Several of the men dancing wore zoot suits, Porky noted with a tinge of pride. A loud cheer arose spontaneously from the crowd. This was definitely the place to be, the friends thought, as they forked over their dollars at the door, then wandered through the crowd to the nonalcoholic punch and soda bar.

After the jitterbug contest ended, the crowd parted for the bandleader, who presented a golden crown to the new king and queen. When the applause died down, the band swung into the ballad, "I Don't Know Why I Love You Like I Do."

Porky pointed to Herman, with his mystery date. "There's Herman," he said as he waved him over.

"Aren't you going to introduce us?" Bobby asked Herman. "Or are you afraid of the competition?"

Herman laughed and introduced his date, Louisa, and signaled for two of her friends to come over. "These are the guys I was telling you about. Porky LaCoste and Bobby Doolan, meet Mary Reilly and Carol Lane."

Porky gestured to Mary, "Can I get you something?"

Bobby had his wallet out and handed over a couple of dollars to the manager of the dance hall, who occupied himself serving the drinks. "Please. It's my treat."

As the women chose their refreshments, Herman turned to Porky. "This band's a drag. I'm going to liven things up. Louisa claims she can sing. Nothing like the present to check out her pipes." Louisa took a quick sip of her ginger ale and laughed as Herman escorted her to the stage.

Porky nodded to Mary. "This should be good."

Bobby and Carol moved to the window to look out at the waning moon and soon became engrossed in conversation. Porky stretched to see over the crowd, but couldn't see. He grabbed Mary's hand and pulled her to the front just as Herman was bent over, talking into the piano player's ear. "Herman went to a fancy music school in Boston," Porky bragged to Mary. The pianist got up. Herman took his seat and was soon joined by Louisa at the microphone.

"You think Herman's good. Wait till you hear Louisa!" Mary countered.

Herman straightened his tie, nodded to Louisa, and struck up the introduction to "Between the Devil and the Deep Blue Sea."

"I don't want you, but I hate to lose you," she sang.

Billy spotted Porky and walked over. "She's good," he whispered.

"You're next," Porky said.

"I sing in the church choir . . . Trust me, no one here wants to listen to me. I'm boring," Billy said, excusing himself.

Bobby joined his friends. "Billy, you're up for the next slow number. Now don't be bashful." The guys slapped Billy on the back.

"Sing 'Danny Boy.'"

Billy made a face and shook his head as Herman transitioned into a boogie-woogie swing number. He spotted Fran talking to a girl and wandered over to join them, just as the crowd headed back onto the dance floor and lost all inhibitions as Herman quickened the tempo.

Bobby leaned in and shouted into Porky's ear. "Now's the time to have fun. Carol tells me that FDR just signed that damn Selective Service Act into law. I was hoping he'd veto it."

Carol moved in between them. "I didn't say it's official. Nothing's been set up yet. No one's about to be drafted."

"What's the difference? The handwriting's on the wall. Sooner or later, it's bound to happen." Porky shook his head and looked at Mary, who looked downcast.

"I'm afraid you're right. And I have three brothers to worry about," Mary added.

"Oh, it's official all right. But that doesn't mean we'll be drafted anytime soon. It's just a precaution. It doesn't mean we're going to war. It's a scare tactic for German consumption," Bobby stated emphatically then turned back to Carol. "What the hell, let's dance."

Porky and Bobby maneuvered their dates for the evening onto the dance floor, elbowing Fran in the process.

"Hey, that hurt," Fran said, good-naturedly winking at his date.

"Move over, buddy. This dance floor's not big enough for both of us," Porky teased, gently shoving his friend for the hell of it.

Billy bought a ginger ale and leaned against the wall to watch the others having fun. He had hoped going to the dance would cheer him up. Instead, it reminded him of what he was missing. After a while, he slipped into the hallway to a pay telephone and rang up his girlfriend, who was working the night shift as a nurse's aide.

Athol YMCA 1940
Photo credit: Hames Photo Shop
Courtesy Richard Chaisson

Chapter 3

Saturday, One Week Later

Porky scanned the aisle at the Liggett drugstore. He paused at the Vicks VapoRub before plucking the black DeWitt's cough syrup package off the shelf for his grandmother, and Smith Brothers Cough Drops for himself or, as the guys would say, Sniff Brothers. His grandmother had found a crushed pack of Chesterfields carelessly left out on his bed. He had been catching hell ever since. A five-cent box of black licorice cough drops was the perfect way to cover up a tobacco smell, he knew, though he actually preferred the cherry flavor, which tasted more like candy. He was on his way to the YMCA, where he had a weekend janitor position and where he also held court with his buddies. For Porky, the Y was strategically located to maximize his social life. It was on the corner of Main and Traverse, with its front entrance across the street from the library, where young women dropped by to pick up novels, and high school and college students hung out, working on term papers. The back entrance of the Y faced the Doolan family's Athol House Hotel. A half-dozen coffee shops and soda fountains were also nearby.

Porky checked out the shop window at Woolworth's five- and ten-cent store, which showcased BACK-TO-SCHOOL notebooks, pens, pencils, and art supplies. He then moved on to O'Laughlin Brothers, where the "Rich Colors of Scotland in smart new worsteds and tweeds" were featured in men's wear, and the fall dresses selling for $5.95 to $13.95 included crepes, velvets, and wools. He checked his watch before pausing to read the marquee at the York Theater. "*Beau Geste* co-starring Gary Cooper, Ray Milland, and Robert

Preston opens Sunday—the story of three gallant brothers in the French Foreign Legion who endure danger and hardship because of their loyalty to one another," Porky read. He checked his watch again before hurrying on past Dr. Muzzy's dental office and Hames Photo Shop and finally scooted up the two flights of stairs at the Y, two steps at a time.

Porky soon busied himself with an assortment of odd jobs, sporting his trademark towel around his neck. He dusted, emptied ashtrays, and swept under and around the orange-cushioned easy chairs, card tables, folding chairs, and Ping-Pong table that filled the game room. He was headed to the maintenance closet to put away the broom and dustpan when he glanced out the window and saw Pinky Dower skip past a couple of bobbysoxers with schoolbags slung across their backs. Pinky dodged traffic as he crossed the street and bounded up the steps of the Y. *What's up with him?* he wondered.

"Where is everyone? The town's nearly deserted," Pinky blurted out as he burst into the room.

"Don't ask me, I've been working," Porky replied, depositing the broom and dustpan in the closet.

"What I don't get is why you're working here, seeing that you left a good-paying job at the Union Twist Drill to go to the Sports Dugout." Pinky was at it again.

Something's up, Porky thought. "Look, it's a good deal; earns my membership and a little extra," Porky responded coolly, closing the closet door. "So what's up?"

Pinky eyed his quarry. "Forget the odd jobs. I've got a better deal."

"Oh, yaw? Doing what?" Porky gestured to an easy chair. "Have a seat. You're a paying customer."

"I'm too wound up to sit. Porky, I've joined the service. And I've talked Pint Lawson into signing up too. Told him they've got baseball teams. You must know him. He's that big, blond Swede from Orange."

"Are you crazy?" Porky sat in a folding chair, resting his arm on the Ping-Pong table.

"Like a fox. I'm going to Hawaii!" Pinky pulled Porky's towel from off his neck and wrapped and tucked it around his waist. "Hoola-hoola, Boola-boola," he sang, dancing around, swinging his hips.

Porky rolled his eyes and laughed as Pinky plucked on an imaginary ukulele. "I swear. You've gone nuts!"

"I want to go back to my little grass shack in Ha-Ha-Ha—Hawaii." Pinky swung his hips in Porky's face.

"Dream on," Porky said, trying to grab his towel back.

Pinky outmaneuvered him and positioned himself between Porky and the Ping-Pong table. "I'm not kidding. Look. It's a job. Good, steady employment. And the money's not bad. All this, and heaven too!" Pinky swung his hips and danced on the other side of the room. "I want to go back to my little . . . ," he sang even louder, swinging over to Bobby Doolan, who had just entered.

"Hey. What's all the racket about? I could hear you halfway down the street," Bobby sputtered, escaping to the other side of the room.

"Glad you're here. Just in time. I need someone to help grab him and haul him away to the nuthouse," Porky said, shaking his head.

"Why? What's up?" Bobby asked, laughing at the sight of Pinky dancing away from Porky as he tried to grab back his towel.

"I'll be vacationing soon in Hawaii!" Pinky answered, nearly out of breath as he continued to dance and sing.

"Courtesy of Uncle Sam—he joined the service," Porky explained. "The Army Air Corps to be exact," Pinky added, handing the towel back to Porky.

"I told you he's crazy." Porky made a loco sign, rotating a finger near his head.

"I'm crazy? Why wait to be drafted? Why not sign up now, before the action begins?" Pinky said, collapsing in the easy chair. "That is, if it ever begins. By the time I'm out, I'll be trained for a good-paying job, and there's no real danger. The action's in Europe, not in Hawaii. I've heard from other guys it's the 'Life of Reilly' with lots of rum, women, and song. And after hours, you're free to lazy around on the beaches, shooting craps. If anyone's crazy, it's you guys for hanging around here. Nowheresville, USA."

"You may be right," Bobby nodded in agreement.

"Well. When you put it like that . . . ," Porky said, sitting next to Pinky. "No fooling, you're going to Hawaii?"

"I'm not only going. I'm going to have the time of my life!"

"Going to Hawaii. Gee. That does sound good," Porky admitted. "Sounds good to me, too," Bobby added.

Porky thought for a moment and then asked in complete sincerity, "Bobby, you mean to tell me you'd sign up too? But you just graduated from business school. You could name your ticket."

"Don't you understand? I can be drafted like anyone else. And consider this; your room and board's all paid for. Your wages are yours to keep, or send home if you like."

"I hadn't thought of that." Porky looked from one friend to the other and laughed. "Hawaii . . . Just think—a chance to really see the world." Pinky nodded in agreement. "Don't think of it as the service. Think of it as the world's biggest poker game."

"Hey. What are we waiting for? Let's go find the rest of the guys," Porky said, linking arms with Bobby and Pinky as they headed out the door.

Tuesday, October 2, 1940
Springfield, Massachusetts

Springfield, Massachusetts, where the local recruitment station for Athol and Orange residents was located, was home to the Springfield Armory, which George Washington had ordered constructed in 1777 for use as a major ammunitions and weapons depot. By 1794, the armory was manufacturing muskets. It continued to create weaponry for the military for the next 150 years. One of its most famous designs was the Springfield rifle, which was the principal U.S. infantry weapon used during the First World War. In 1936, it was replaced by the Garand (M1) rifle, which was also designed at the Springfield Armory. The M1 allowed the United States to enter World War II as the only army having a semiautomatic rifle as standard issue. But in the autumn of 1940, with Europe at war and America slowly gearing up for the inevitable, small arms ordnances were in short supply. Despite FDR's declaration of a state of emergency one year earlier, the production of military-issue rifles was still pitifully inadequate.

Porky and his friends were determined to beat the rush so they would have a pick of where they would be sent. Two weeks after they enlisted, the Roosevelt administration announced the first registration day for the peacetime draft. Despite scattered protests, more than sixteen million men signed up. By the end of October, compulsory conscription was put into effect. But the training facilities as well as the armaments for a large conscript army did not exist. Men enlisted, but there was nowhere to send them. One year before the bombing of Pearl Harbor, *Life* magazine reported, "The first draft call brought about the *summoning* of only 18,700 men . . ." Porky and his buddies were to be among the chosen few who got to pick their poison.

Bobby drove his family's Plymouth past the movie theater, where an Eleanor Powell movie was featured on the marquee, to the parking spot in front of the U.S. Army Recruitment Center. The celebrated Broadway and movie star, who danced her way into American hearts as her publicity boasted, was born in Springfield and was about five years older than Porky. But what struck the men as a particularly good omen was that Powell's latest film, which costarred George Burns and Gracie Allen, had been shot in

Robert Doolan 1940
Photo credit: Hames Photo Shop
Courtesy Richard Chaisson

Honolulu and featured a Hawaiian tap dance. It was more than a coincidence, they reasoned, and reiterated their pledge to stick together and push for an assignment to Hawaii.

As usual, Porky sat in the front seat; but this time he was crowded between Bobby and their friend from Orange, the Big Swede, Pint Lawson. The other recruits—Fran, Herman, and Billy—were squeezed into the backseat. Bobby pulled up to the curb and parked between a flat-topped army jeep and a farm truck with muddy tires. The car was still coasting into position when Fran swung the door open, nearly ramming the jeep.

"Gee whiz, Franny, try to be careful. The old man won't appreciate my coming home with a three-door sedan," Bobby shouted as Fran hopped out.

"And the army won't be pleased if we bang up one of their jeeps," Porky added.

While his friends climbed out of the vehicle, Fran read the posters plastered inside the window, next to the painted letters spelling, "U.S. Army Recruitment Center" on the plate-glass storefront. One featured a cartoon of Uncle Sam pounding his fist on a table laden with books. "This country must not succumb to the conditions which produced dictators in Europe," the notice read. The message was signed President Roosevelt. There was also a faded World War I portrait of Uncle Sam with a star on his stovepipe hat. "I need you," it stated simply. Another placard showed Uncle Sam kindly assisting a Chinese woman and her child. A Chinese soldier holding a rifle was positioned slightly ahead as if leading the fight. The statement said, "China is helping the U.S." It was an appeal for the United China Relief fund.

As the men filed in, an army recruitment officer looked up from his desk in surprise. "Are you men here to do your civic duty, or merely sightseeing?"

"We're here to enlist, sir," Bobby stated emphatically.

"We want to go to Hawaii," Porky declared. "One of our friends signed up and said it was quite a deal."

"Well, perhaps your friend was told if he was sent overseas to Panama, Hawaii, or the Philippines, in six months the army might send him back to the States to see if he qualified for pilot training. Is that what you men are geared up for?" The sergeant hoped he had scored.

"Flying an airplane—is that what you guys are after?" Porky looked from friend to friend. They each shook their head in the negative. "No, sir, we just want to go to Hawaii. By boat is fine with us."

"Why don't I get you men signed up and we can discuss details later," the sergeant said, revealing a tobacco-stained crooked-toothed smile. "The army offers the best in training opportunities, and we are recruiting for the South Pacific," he assured them as he took a second look at the men. "But we do have a few physical fitness requirements and height and weight standards, and if you boys pass muster . . ."

Bobby rose to his friend's defense, placing a hand on his shoulder. "Sir, Franklin LaCoste was one of Athol High's star football players," he said, concerned that he might be too short. Porky took the hint and stood as straight and tall as he was able. "And Winston Lawson, here, is one of the finest baseball players the town of Orange has ever seen," he said, pointing a thumb at Pint, concerned that he was too tall. Pint took the hint and slouched a bit. "As for the rest of us . . ." Billy also took the hint and tried to look inconspicuous. He had dropped out of school early because of illness, though he graduated a year later, in 1938, and had worked out on a regular basis to regain his strength and muscle tone.

"Yes, I can see that you all appear to be physically fit," the sergeant said, handing out forms for them to fill out. "Now if one of you lads would like to volunteer to step back into the examination room," he said, pointing to a door in the rear of the room. Herman was confident that he was exactly what the army wanted and stepped forward to volunteer.

One hour later, the recruitment office door opened, and one by one the men exited to the sidewalk and grouped around Porky, who was downcast. The height difference between the others and Porky was obvious. They were of average height, or taller; Porky was only five feet four and a half inches tall.

Bobby patted him on the back. "Come on. Cheer up. As the sergeant admitted, just because you're too short doesn't mean you can't get in."

"Don't you remember, Pork, he said he needs to get the OK from New York," Herman added. "He's placing the call right now. Turn around, look!"

Porky glanced back. Herman was right. He was placing a call. "He could be calling his girlfriend, for all we know," he shot back.

"Porky, it's just a formality. Didn't he say, if you don't get approved right away, you can work for the WPA while you wait. That's a government job too." Bobby said, pasting on a false smile.

"Aw . . . Don't sweat it," Fran insisted, brushing the whole thing off with a gesture of his hand.

"I just squeaked by myself," Pint added.

"I don't think so, Pint. He nearly offered you starring position on the baseball team," Porky countered, managing a weak smile.

Bobby was resolute. "We're a team and we're going to stay a team, even if I have to pull strings to . . . ," he trailed off, ashamed that he had let the cat out of the bag.

"And that includes you too, Pint, even though you're from Orange."

Porky and his aunt Yvonne
Courtesy LaCoste/Thurber family

Chapter 4

Long Island Sound
Monday, November 18, 1940

Tugboat horns blasted through the morning mist as the ferry chugged away from the dock. The green recruits from Athol and Orange had traveled by train from Springfield, Massachusetts, to the New Rochelle, New York, depot and now stood at the ferry's bow dressed in civilian jackets and overcoats, felt-brimmed hats and wool caps. They were chilled to the bone, but the experience was a novelty and their excitement served as an intoxicant, which brought about highs and lows as they traveled to their first assignment as soldiers.

Porky felt lost in the fog, not quite able to get his bearings. The truth was, except for brief trips to Boston, Springfield, and Worcester, he had never strayed far from home. "Are we ready for this?" he asked.

Herman fancied himself a sophisticate in comparison, having studied piano in Boston at the New England Conservatory and attended opera at Carnegie Hall in New York City. "Keep your mind focused, Porky. So what if we're going to the Philippines and not to Hawaii."

"I feel cheated," Porky whined. "How was I supposed to know the Philippines were islands out in Brooklyn Harbor?"

Bobby laughed. "You are kidding, right?"

"No," Porky said, feeling quite annoyed.

Bobby bent over laughing, and nearly choked as he blurted out, "That's right. I'd forgotten. You flunked geography."

53

Fran put an arm around Porky. "My friend, the Philippine Islands are located in the Pacific, not the Atlantic Ocean. Fort Slocum is located on an island in Brooklyn Harbor, which is where we are at this exact moment."

"This is Brooklyn Harbor? Are you sure?" Billy asked.

Herman cupped his hand against the wind, struck a match and lit a cigarette. "Close enough," he said between puffs.

"Actually, we're in Long Island Sound," Bobby stated once he had regained his composure.

"What the—? I thought we were in New York," Porky said, more confused than enlightened.

"I thought so too," Pint added.

"We are in Westchester County, which is in the state of New York. Sorry. I confused you," Bobby bellowed above the foghorn.

After the blast stopped, Porky pointed to Fran for further clarification. "So what you're telling me is the Philippines are in the Pacific, near Hawaii?"

"Close enough," Fran said, tired of the discussion and wanting to be let off the hook.

Billy couldn't take anymore. "Close enough? The Philippine Islands are near Japan. Don't you guys know anything?"

"The Philippines are better than Hawaii," Bobby said, hoping to placate his friend.

"How's that?" Porky asked with a note of skepticism.

"Hawaii's too civilized," Bobby continued, painting the verbal picture he hoped Porky wanted to see. "There are too many American officers, but worse than that, they're there with their wives. The difference between the two is, in the Philippines, the women still go native."

"So what's that supposed to mean?" Porky asked.

Bobby smiled. "The women wear skirts, but that's it. They are barefoot and topless. Haven't you checked out the *National Geographic* magazines at the library?"

With the exception of Billy and Pint, who were known for their straightlaced attitudes, Bobby's comment was well received by the men, who quieted down for the remainder of the ride. Porky was lost in a happy daydream as they approached the dock. Painted on the roof tiles of a long rectangular building were the words *Fort Slocum*. Fortunately, the ferry was equipped with rubber tires on the front that helped to cushion the impact as they slammed into the tires attached to the dock, which further cushioned the shock. The jolt propelled the men forward into the railing and into one another.

William Freeman—October 1940
Photo credit: Hames Photo Shop
Courtesy Richard Chaisson

Fort Slocum is located on the eighty-acre David's Island in Long Island Sound. During the Civil War, it was the site of the De Camp General Hospital for federal soldiers, the training ground for the Fourth U.S. Colored Infantry, and a detention center for Confederate soldiers. The site also served as coastal defense for New York City. Renamed "Fort Slocum" in 1896 after Maj. Gen. Henry W. Slocum, hero of Antietam and Chancellorsville, the fort served as the largest recruiting depot east of the Mississippi during World War I and II. But on that chilly morning in late autumn, 1940, as Porky and his friends stepped onto the gangplank to disembark, aside from the remains of Civil War battlements and the sight of soldiers in uniform, Fort Slocum could easily have been mistaken for an Ivy League college. They followed a group of men off the pier and into the grounds. They passed a number of buildings built of wood, but many more were constructed of red brick with white wooden trim, a style architecturally inspired by the Greek Revival movement of the pre- and post-Civil War era.

The main entrance to the receiving barracks was a three-story octagon with a wide-arched entrance and eight-sided pyramid-style domed roof. The single-storied wings to the left and right featured dozens of medium-sized arched windows. The mess hall was actually two connecting halls, with the front entrance a long one-storied rectangle with French doors and large white-trimmed Palladian windows. But the postal exchange was the real gem. This two-storied redbrick building featured a portico entrance reminiscent of a Greek temple with a dozen Doric columns posted on six pedestals and topped by a wide triangular gable, with heavy Greek molding. Unfortunately for the men, the exchange did not feature scantily clad marble Greek goddess statuary to accompany the rest of the décor.

Far more pedestrian were the two large wooden houses with wide verandas that housed the military personnel and, for the married men, their families. They straddled the edge of the parade ground along with rows of barracks for the enlisted men. Officer's Row on the east side of the parade field was built in 1893 and served as quarters for the senior officers on post. Temporary barracks had also been erected for the expected influx of recruits. There was a gymnasium and an officer's club and an administration building. The flagpole was at the upper end of the parade field, just south of the infirmary. An oval track along the edge of the drill and athletic field had been the training grounds for the 1920 U.S. Olympic team. Altogether, there were nearly one hundred structures on the post. But despite the grandeur of some of the architecture, the scheme of things was quickly apparent. The general complaint was that the fort was ruled over by nitpicking, and some would say senile, lieutenant colonels left over from World War I who controlled their domain by barking out directives to a bunch of wretched sergeants out to pick a fight with the newly enlisted men.

Except for a few privates returning from leave, most of the new recruits were not in uniform but wore civilian winter apparel and carried suitcases and canvas carrying bags. Despite the early hour, others arrived long before the ferry that had carried Porky and his buddies. As the morning progressed, the sun burned through the fog so that the ocean was visible between the buildings, and the cold air gave way to unseasonable warmth, despite being close to Thanksgiving. As the sun grew hotter, Porky and Pint attributed the mild temperature to their being far south of their Massachusetts home.

The early arrivals had not yet been assigned barracks but had visited the quartermaster post to collect their gear and uniforms. Men were scattered about along the parade ground, exchanging civilian wear for government issue. The friends got in line and soon entered the building to receive their uniforms. Counters and shelves were visible at the far end. The recruits chatted amiably, despite a stock-control officer barking orders to the soldiers distributing the outfits. They, in turn, yelled at the recruits. Pint was the first up to the counter and was taken aback when the GI shouted out, "Size?"

Pint stood mute until the soldier screamed, "Are you deaf? I asked, what size?"

The soldier next to him said, "Give him the largest boots you've got." The soldier reached back and grabbed the largest size available and shoved it forward. Pint turned red as he scooped up the boots but managed a respectful, "Thank you, sir," before moving along the counter for the next item. Later that afternoon the men settled into their assigned quarters and were allowed a few hours' peace before the bugle call announced the supper hour. Porky had been assigned a different barracks than his friends but eventually located Bobby, who was seated on his bunk writing a letter.

"Touch my forehead. I don't feel so good," Porky said in a weak and scratchy voice.

Bobby touched Porky's forehead. "Wow. You are hot," he said, yanking his hand away.

Throughout his childhood, Bobby had friends and relatives who had caught a case of influenza followed by pneumonia. One of his childhood friends had died. He also remembered his parents speaking of deaths following the influenza pandemic in 1918, the year after he was born. He hoped Porky had nothing more than a cold caused by excitement and getting chilled on the ferry ride to the island, but now was not the time to take chances.

Bobby put his writing materials on the bed. "Let's go find the sergeant," he said. Bobby led Porky through the barracks to a sergeant standing in the doorway, who provided detailed instructions on how to get to sick bay.

The next day, after roll call, Porky and Bobby walked back to the infirmary. "Bobby, I'm getting worse and worse. I wonder if it has anything to do with that shot. Look, I know they're going to keep me this time. So why don't you go back to the barracks?" he said softly.

"OK. But I'll check back tomorrow," Bobby assured him.

Early the next morning, the men gathered in ragged formation on the parade ground. There was little to buffer them against the chilly wind. Visibility diminished as clouds rolled in from the ocean and deposited a light snow. Sergeant Bass, a tall rugged Southerner, barked out a short-order drill to a couple of hundred freshly uniformed men wearing drab green-brown wool uniforms and overcoats. Fran, Billy, Herman, and Bobby marched in formation as part of the platoon. But they didn't mind. The exercise helped them to stay warm.

Francis Robichaud—October 1940
Photo credit: Hames Photo Shop
Courtesy Richard Chaisson

After lunch at the infirmary, Porky was released to his quarters with orders to rest. He stripped to his tee shirt and boxer shorts and spread out on his lower bunk, his head propped up on a folded pillow. To amuse himself in the sick bay he had scoured old magazines, passing up *Life* and *Time* for a stack of *National Geographic* magazines. The nurse on call had been impressed by his choice of reading and gave him permission to take the magazines out.

Porky's reverie was interrupted as his bunkmates entered the barracks, swearing and shivering from the cold. His hometown buddies, concerned for his well-being, followed close behind. They found Porky smoking and reading a *National Geographic*, his trademark towel wrapped around the back of his neck. Billy took off his heavy wool overcoat and approached Porky.

"Have you got the life!" Billy ribbed.

"What do you mean? I'm an invalid," Porky said, glancing up.

Fran approached, scolding, "An invalid? Porky, you're a goldbrick!"

"Hey. Back off, guys. Poor Porky's been suffering," Bobby mocked.

"Yaw. So we all noticed," Fran continued. "And when that SOB drill sergeant gets hold of you tomorrow . . . That's when you'll find out what it really feels like to be an invalid."

Porky maintained a poker face as he flipped over the *National Geographic* to share what he had been viewing—a picture of a half-naked full-busted woman bent over a stream, washing her child.

"Knock it off. I've been researching," Porky said, attempting to look studious. The guys crowded around to see. Pint turned red with embarrassment. Billy shook his head in disgust. Fran, Herman, and Bobby laughed and cheered. Just then the whistle blew.

"Chow," they shouted. All conversation stopped as Porky and his bunkmates dressed for supper, and his friends tumbled over one another heading to their bunks to change.

Franklin D. Roosevelt and Eleanor
Courtesy FDR Library

Chapter 5

Two weeks later Porky and Bobby took the ferry to New Rochelle wearing their "government issue" attire. They were decked out in olive-drab four-pocket wool service coats and trousers, mustard flannel shirts with pink ties, low boots, and garrison caps. Despite being allowed to wear civilian clothes while on pass, off duty in town, the plan was to show off as servicemen. They strolled past lampposts and buildings still littered with signs from the recent campaign between Wendell L. Willkie and the incumbent Franklin Delano Roosevelt, who had made a successful run for his third term. As they boarded the train for the short ride into town, they noted that it went all the way into New York City.

During the teens, twenties, and thirties, New Rochelle had been home to a number of celebrity artists who preferred the so-called simple life in New Rochelle to the high life of New York, where they made their living. Luminaries such as illustrators Norman Rockwell, J.C. Leyendecker, and Frederic Remington took up residence among an elite artist's community in town. With a population of around fifty-four thousand, New Rochelle also enjoyed the highest per capita income of any city in the early 1930s. This fact translated into storefronts that not only displayed an opulent lifestyle but had a flair that transcended mere wealth. As the men walked down the street, their hands in their trouser pockets, Bobby displayed a confidence that was at home in these environs. Porky was the tourist as they surveyed storefront mannequins in evening dress and furs. Porky stopped in front of what he termed a "high-class" lounge and peered through the window.

"Don't look now, but I've spotted one. You were right on the money," Porky said, nudging his buddy.

Bobby would rather be caught dead than appear to be gawking through a window. He moved to the other side of the door, leaned nonchalantly against the building, and lit up a cigarette. "OK. Tell me how he's dressed."

Porky was convinced he was a staff sergeant. "Well, for openers, he's wearing a belted service coat."

"OK. So he's an officer."

"And I see three-chevron tan OD stripes."

"You're right. He's a staff sergeant."

"Yaw. But do you think he'll talk?" Porky asked, checking his watch. "We've only got three . . . huh . . . with any luck . . . three and a half hours before we have to hightail it out of here. Or else—you know the rules—our goose is cooked."

"We won't miss the boat. Are you kidding? I know this pass is gold. If we blow it, we won't see life in New Rochelle or anywhere else for a long, long time," Bobby said, knitting his brows.

"Then what are we waiting for . . . Let's go!" Porky said, grabbing the door handle.

Porky and Bobby stepped into the lounge and headed for the cigarette machine. Staff Sergeant O'Toole sat alone at the bar, nursing a whiskey. He felt inundated as more and more green recruits had been assigned to the base. He now grabbed every opportunity he could find to get off base and enjoy the comfort of a quiet bar. But his mood had turned melancholy. He turned to see who entered. "Boys," Sergeant O'Toole called as Porky and Bobby popped in coins and pulled on the knob for Chesterfields. "Why don't you come over here and I'll buy you a drink." Porky looked up and grinned as he fished along the tray for the cigarette packs. "Why not? That is, if you let us buy you one after." Bobby approached the sergeant and extended a hand, "That's real nice of you. Thanks, sir," he said, shaking hands with the sergeant. "What are you having?" O'Toole said, dropping a bill on the counter.

"Couple of beers," Porky said as he sat to the left of the sergeant, Bobby to the right. The bartender grabbed the dollar and popped it into the cash register then busied himself at the tap as the golden brew spilled out and over the mugs. "This is real nice of you, Sarge . . . taking in a couple of greenhorns like us." The bartender dropped the change on the counter in front of O'Toole and the beers in front of "the boys."

"We sure are a couple of greenhorns. We would never have guessed that the service would be like this," Bobby said, grabbing a mug. "Not that we're complaining," he quickly added, downing half the beer in one long swallow.

"Where are you guys from?" O'Toole asked. "Massachusetts," Bobby said. "But trust me, you've never heard the name of the town." "It's called Hicksville, USA. Where are you from?" Porky asked between sips.

"The Midwest. And where I'm from is even smaller than Hicksville," O'Toole said, finishing his drink.

"Here, this is my round." Bobby fished in his pocket and threw change onto the counter.

"That's real nice of you," O'Toole said, sizing up his companions. Porky downed the remainder of his brew to pluck up his courage. "Say. Not that it's any of my business, being a greenhorn and all, but are there any special-duty jobs? My friend Bobby and me are trained to do a number of things."

The staff sergeant paused, polished off his whiskey, then smiled, "Oh, like what—typing, filing, general office?"

"Sounds good to me," Porky blurted out. "I was a crackerjack typist in high school. And my friend, Bobby here, is a business college graduate."

Bobby sensed they were making headway. "Sarge, you ready for another?"

"Nope. This one's on me. And don't worry about your eleven o'clock curfew. I'll get you back to the base. Don't worry about a thing." He turned to the bartender. "Another round," he said, sliding the change in front of him back toward the bartender. "So while we're still sober . . . Hey, bartender, could I have a scrap of paper and a pen?" he added, taking a closer look at Porky, then at Bobby. "I want your names and service numbers. I'll keep you in mind."

Bobby smiled and nodded. "Thanks," he said, taking the pen and paper from the bartender.

"That's swell of you," Porky added. "Hey, while we're on the subject, what do you know about the Philippines?"

"What he's really asking is, tell us about the women?" Bobby confided to the sergeant. The three men laughed and continued drinking.

The following morning as the sun rose over the barracks at Fort Slocum, the sound of a long, loud whistle was followed by a loudspeaker blaring, "Private LaCoste, Private Doolan, report to headquarters." Both Porky and Booby had overslept. They were overwhelmed with panic as they hurriedly dressed. The men met up at the service records office, yanked open the door, and sluggishly walked up to the second floor, yawning as they ascended the stairs. Staff Sergeant O'Toole stood at the top of the stairs, waiting to escort them into the office. "Rough night, wasn't it?" he commented as the men nodded in agreement. "Look. I've got a couple of openings here you might like."

Porky and Bobby looked at one another, stunned that their little scheme had worked. They followed the staff sergeant as he walked them around the office to where a half-dozen GIs sat, working at various desks. "As you can see, we've got a lot of work to do, and it's about to get a lot worse," O'Toole began. "Next week we're expecting another one or two hundred green recruits. As you've probably heard by now, Fort Slocum serves as the shipping point for all army troops going overseas to the Pacific—to Hawaii, to Guam, and the Philippines."

Porky and Bobby grinned from ear to ear, barely able to contain their excitement. They quickly wiped the grins off their faces as the sergeant turned back to face them. "And as you can imagine, we don't fly recruits," he continued, "even to the first stop, which is San Francisco. Everyone gets shipped by boat. It may not be the fastest, but it's the cheapest for Uncle Sam."

"Sarge, so how long would it take to get to, say—the Philippines?" Bobby asked.

O'Toole looked stern. "You still harping on the Philippines? Forget the native girls. Your job is here. And trust me, it's all for the best. We're not shipping out replacements anymore," he added with a warning in his voice. "We're shipping out reinforcements!"

O'Toole's point went over their heads. "Sure. But for the sake of argument, how long would it take to reach the Philippines?" Porky asked, attempting to bluff the officer. O'Toole saw right through them as if they were schoolboys.

"You really want to know? OK, I'll give it to you straight," he said, beginning a lecture to young men he now understood were incredibly naïve. "How's this? Try forty-five grueling days at sea. And we're not talking about the President Lines. Trust me, these are not luxury liners. They're refurbished World War I troop boats. And though you gripe about being frostbitten here, wait 'till you hit South Carolina. That's the start of a heat wave that lasts about thirty days. Have you ever been to the Panama Canal, boys?" O'Toole asked, eyes bulging.

Porky and Bobby answered in near unison, "No."

"And you don't want to," O'Toole stated with a condescending tone to his voice. "Not only do you sweat your fanny off, you're moving in canals across land. And the mosquitoes look like bees, and the bees are as big as birds. The only thing that's good about it is while you're on the boat, you won't be bunking down with the iguanas, and the tarantulas can't get to you," he said with a sadistic grin. "Are there any other questions, boys, before we get down to your assignments?"

Franklin "Porky" LaCoste
Courtesy LaCoste/Thurber family

Chapter 6

One week later, Pfc. Franklin J. LaCoste, in full dress uniform, traveled by rail from New Rochelle to Long Island's fabled, two-hundred-room Garden City Hotel, replete with Victorian elegance designed by the preeminent architect of the Gilded Age, Stanford White. The railroad station was directly across from the hotel. Porky disembarked and stood in awe as he watched the moon rise over the rooftops of the historic village and hotel. Cap in hand, he approached the landmark and watched a parade of elegantly dressed glitterati visible through the lobby window. Several women in satin evening gowns were seated on a plush circular red couch in the center of the reception area. The crystal chandelier above their heads lent sparkle to their jewelry and cast a shimmering reflection against the frosty windowpanes.

Porky took his prearranged place by the shoeshine stand to wait for his date, Arlene, a girl he had met back home at the Brookside Park Dance Pavilion in nearby Orange. The elevator doors opened, and Arlene entered the lobby dressed in a light brown wool coat with an attached mink stole collar. Three couples exited along with her friends Charlie, Sam, and Cathy.

Porky approached with a big smile. "What's a nice girl from Puritan Massachusetts doing in a swanky place like this?"

"Making beds, dusting, plus a little of this and a lot of that," she said, kissing him on the cheek. "Porky, allow me to introduce you to my friends. This is Charlie." She placed a hand on Charlie's arm. "Charlie's a bellhop. And Sam, here, is our ever-popular bartender. Cathy works with me cleaning the rooms."

"Charlie Denison," Charlie said as he shook Porky's hand. "Franklin LaCoste. But my friends call me Porky."

"Sam Cohen, pleased to meet you."

"Likewise." Porky shook hands with Sam then turned to shake hands with Cathy. "Nice to meet you, Cathy."

Cathy looked from Sam to Charlie. "Hey. If he's going to be hanging out with you guys, fess up. Don't blindside him. He's too nice a guy. Besides, he's Arlene's friend."

"Whatever do you mean?" Charlie asked with feigned innocence. "Porky's more than welcome to play."

"Look out, Porky, they're high rollers. So be on your guard."

"Along with tending bar, I'm a bookie. So what's to tell?" Sam asked.

"High rollers. Count me out," Porky said, digging into his pockets to display a couple of dollar bills.

"Don't worry about a thing. These guys are loaded. What about treating my friend and me tonight?" Arlene asked, looking from Sam to Charlie.

Sam turned to Porky. "It's fine with me. As far as I'm concerned, you're on the house."

"Why thanks, that's real nice," Porky said.

"Might as well enjoy it while you've got it, boys," Arlene said. "The military pay is lousy from what Porky tells me."

Charlie walked to a side door that led down to the garage below. "You think I'm afraid of the draft? Hell, the army's the biggest crap game in the world! By the time I'm out, I'll be a millionaire," he boasted as he opened the door to the staircase. "After you, my friends."

Moments later, the group was in the garage following Charlie, who weaved through expensive late-model sports cars and sedans until he came to his '38 Ford. He took out his key and opened the door on the driver's side, then leaned over to open the passenger door. Cathy pushed the back of the passenger seat forward to allow Porky, Arlene, and Sam to pile into the back. She slipped into the passenger side and closed the door as Charlie inserted the key into the ignition, revved up the motor, backed up, and exited onto the street. Charlie turned onto New York Route 25 and soon approached the Entering New York City billboard. Cathy wrapped an arm around Charlie's and snuggled close as she twisted the rearview mirror with her right hand to check for lipstick smudges. She noticed that Arlene looked squeezed and somewhat uncomfortable between Sam and Porky in the back seat.

"How's the weather back there?" Cathy piped up.

Just then they spotted the neon sign of the Jamboree Nightspot, a dance hall and former speakeasy and gambling den that maintained its appeal long after Prohibition ended, along with its gangland ties. He turned into the parking area and handed the key to a valet.

The group entered the club and walked to the cloakroom. A hatcheck girl waited for the men to assist the women with their coats before scooping them up and handing out the numbered checks. Inside the club, the dance floor was surrounded by terraced seats with plush chairs and small candlelit tables, barely large enough to hold drinks. A popular nightclub band played the swing ballad, "A Tiskit a Tasket," as their vocalist, a svelte blond in a backless black gown, belted out her version of the Ella Fitzgerald hit.

Porky surveyed the scene. A few men were dressed in zoot suits, but most had on a double-breasted suit or a sports jacket and tie. A few were dressed in elegant tuxedoes. The ladies' outfits ranged from ballroom gowns to cocktail dresses. This was definitely not a bobbysox crowd! "This is swell," he blurted out. For Porky it was like living a scene from a movie.

Arlene grabbed Porky's hand and pulled him out onto the dance floor. "Let's show them that a couple of hicks from the sticks can mean business," she whispered in his ear.

If only I had brought my zoot suit, Porky thought as he grabbed Arlene's hands and pulled her toward him in a jitterbug cuddle position. They moved on to a side step and then to a triple-step shuffle. Meanwhile, Sam, Charlie, and Cathy spirited past the dancers to the back wall, which was painted black. They ascended a staircase along the back wall to a balcony overlooking the ballroom. As Sam and Cathy watched the action below, Charlie quietly knocked in coded rhythm on a barely visible black door. After a moment, the door opened and Charlie, Cathy, and Sam disappeared into the room.

Arlene and Porky walked to the sidelines. "Hey, where did everyone go?" he asked.

"They're where the real action is. Upstairs," she said, nodding her head in the general direction.

"Shouldn't we join them?"

"You want my opinion? They think we're a drag! Hey, forget them." She grabbed his hand and pulled him back out onto the dance floor as the band played "Deep Purple," and the mood turned romantic.

Later that evening, Charlie drove out to Jackson Heights, Long Island. He pulled over to the curb to drop Porky and Arlene off. Porky put an arm around Arlene's waist and escorted her up the walk of the three-story brick Dartmouth College fraternity house. As the sedan sped away, Porky suddenly felt awkward and removed his hand from her back. "Say, that was swell of them, giving us a lift."

"Yaw. They're all heart." Arlene grabbed Porky's arm and spun him around to face her. "Look, get with it. They were thrilled to dump us. Sam and Charlie are businessmen. For them, the night's young."

"Do you remember Bobby Doolan from Athol?"

"Handsome dude, rich too as I recall. Don't tell me he's here," she said, brightening.

"Naw. His brother's at Dartmouth. This is his brother's fraternity, their New York City headquarters. He let me borrow his key," Porky said, producing a key from his pocket.

"Nice, real nice. Seems to me, you've got it all figured out," she said with a slight shiver as the wind picked up to deliver a cold blast. "Here you are in the service. And though everyone else has to drill, from what you tell me, you and Bobby got desk jobs. And you visit the city at least once a week. And now you've got free digs. Haven't you got the life!"

"Well. You're not doing so bad yourself—with your fur stole and fancy French perfumes," Porky said, his breath vaporizing in the cold.

"The coat's borrowed and the perfume is a sample. My roommates and I trade clothes; and I've got a friend over at Macy's," she said, shivering between words.

Taking the hint, Porky hurried her up the walkway to the double-door front entry. "Still, it seems to me you're living the high life too. With your looks, bet you'll marry a millionaire," he said, inserting the key. He opened the door and whispered, "Better be quiet, in case anyone's sleeping."

The couple gingerly entered the fraternity on tiptoe, hoping to soften the sound of the creaking floorboards, and moved into the main reception area. As their eyes adjusted, they spotted dozens of couples either bunked out on the few existing beds or making out on the floor. Porky whispered, "It's a bit crowded, but we'll find a spot. There are two more floors. The stairway is in the back."

Porky grabbed her hand to pull her forward to a section of bare floor between swelling blankets. Arlene resisted and whispered fiercely, "Are you kidding? This is kid's stuff."

Porky drew close and griped, "But I can't afford a hotel. And if we go back to your place, I won't be able to get back to the base on time. I'll be AWOL."

Arlene pulled away and headed back to the door. "Porky, let's just call it a night," she said quietly.

A man's voice piped up from the floor, "Will you two shut up. Some of us are trying to sleep."

"Sorry," Porky said as the couple exited back into the cold outside. "Sorry about that. You want me to get a cab?" he asked apologetically. "On nights

I'm in the city, I stay with a girl friend in the Village. Hey, the subway's up the street. Trains are still running. Don't worry, I'm a big girl," she said. The couple walked toward the subway stop, which consisted of a railing, a large A Line station sign, and a steeply descending staircase.

"Look. I'm sorry," Porky said, taking her hand.

"Don't be. It was swell seeing you again. Kinda like being back home." They walked the rest of the way in silence. At the subway station, Porky kissed her on the cheek.

"Maybe we can do this again? I don't think we're going anywhere soon."

"Hey, take care of yourself," she said, returning the kiss. The sound of an approaching train nearly drowned out her voice. "I've got a train to catch. See you around." Arlene waved and ran down the stairs. He watched until she was out of sight.

Porky pulled the collar of his army overcoat up and stuck his hands into his trouser pockets. He cut a lonely figure as he walked back to the fraternity; shoulders slumped, shivering, as a harsh wind blew a chill down his back. The sound of metal hitting metal was magnified in the chilled stillness of the night, as he reinserted the key by the light of the waning moon. He pulled the door open and entered as quietly as possible. After gently closing the door and pushing it shut with his back, he stood in the foyer for a moment before gingerly stepping back into the crowded floor. Philip "Pinky" Dower made his way over and whispered, "Back so soon? I was picking my way over the bodies when you disappeared. Where's Arlene?"

"She scrammed," Porky answered. "Where did you come from?" "Bobby ran me down. He and his date are upstairs, in first-class accommodations. There's a spot over here. Afraid you have to bunk down with the swine," he said with a laugh, then covered his mouth.

"As the song says, anywhere I lay my hat is home," Porky said softly.

The two men picked their way through the mass of bodies to a clearing and scooted down on the floor to bunk down for the night.

Philip "Pinky" Dower
Photo credit: Hames Photo Shop
Courtesy Richard Chaisson

Chapter 7

The army clock above the doorframe read 1700 hours—five o'clock civilian time. Porky and Bobby straightened out the papers on their desks and made a dash for the door. As they crossed the parade ground on their way to the barracks, Pinky waved and headed toward them. "Hello, suckers!" he yelled.

"Suckers? That's a nice way to greet your buddies," Bobby yelled back.

"Hey, you're the guys who have to work for a living," Pinky said, catching up with them.

"Look. If it wasn't for our hard work, you wouldn't be going anywhere," Porky shot back. "I'm the sucker who typed out your shipping orders."

"Then you know all about it?" Pinky was taken aback.

"So you're on your way to Hawaii. Don't rub it in," Bobby said, hitting Pinky on the shoulder.

"That's right. I told you so way back when. See. Everything's going according to plan."

"What's so great about Hawaii? I hear it's nothing but a great, big whorehouse," Porky said, faking disgust.

Pinky smiled. "I'll drop you a line and let you know."

The friends burst out laughing. "Of course, you two have nothing to complain about—pushing papers. By the way, how's Pint Lawson—now that he's joined up with you guys?"

"The big Swede's doing OK. Bobby and I take him out for a beer, and he orders a Coke and pastry."

Pinky doubled over with laughter. "Imagine Pint in Hawaii? He blushes at the thought of a girl."

Bobby shrugged. "Pint's Pint. He's all wound up worrying about how drilling with a rifle will foul up his ball playing. He's afraid it will ruin his pitching arm. I'll tell you something—it hasn't hurt my hitting average," he boasted.

"Tell him, if he makes it to the Philippines, there's a great ball team on base," Pinky advised. "Of course, you two have probably forgotten all about the Philippines—now that you've finessed duty as a couple of goldbricks."

"Goldbricks?" Bobby threw a fake swing as Pinky ducked. "Hey, we're the ones doing the real work around here. What does everyone else do? Prance around all day trying to look like a soldier."

"We are soldiers," Pinky spat out as he punched the air.

"Yaw, well, how many breaks do you guys get a day? Every time I look, I see you loafing!" Porky said, adding his two cents' worth.

Pinky jabbed at Bobby's gut as Bobby countered, "You got that straight. And before long I'll be loafing around in the sun and sand, drinking rum and Coke with hula-hula girls."

The friends relaxed and laughed. "Hey. Life's good. What can I say?" Pinky walked away whistling and then turned, cupped his hands round his mouth like a megaphone, and called out, "So long, suckers!"

December 24, 1940

Christmas Eve was unusually busy in the service records office at Fort Slocum. Christmas holiday and New Year's greeting cards were Scotch-taped along the wall, near the file cabinets, and an occasional clerk would hum or whistle a holiday tune. One private, who was particularly tone-deaf, sang "Jingle Bells" so out of tune Bing Crosby wouldn't have recognized it.

"Will you knock that off? You're driving me nuts," Bobby shouted across the room.

"Where's your Christmas spirit?" Porky admonished.

"Buried in a foot of work," Bobby said through clenched teeth.

Staff Sergeant O'Toole dropped a thick envelope on Porky's desk. "Cut a copy of this list of men," O'Toole ordered. "The dates and time of departure are on the outside of the envelope. The instructions are inside. There are two ships and a barge. Four hundred men are involved, so make sure you get the ships straight."

"But there are barely four hundred men on the base!" Porky pointed out.

Season's Greetings from the Philippines
Courtesy LaCoste/Thurber family

"Those are the orders," O'Toole barked back. After the staff sergeant left the vicinity of Porky's desk, Bobby quietly approached Porky.

"So what's up?" Bobby quizzed.

"See for yourself." Porky turned the envelope over so both could read, Philippine Reinforcements.

Bobby scoffed, "What do you want to bet, we're both left behind tending the office!"

Porky opened the envelope, pulled out the orders, and ran his finger through the stack, which was arranged alphabetically. "Let's see—A, B, C, D—Doolan," Porky said, looking up at Bobby, who was literally breathing down his neck. "You're moving out, buddy." Without uttering a sound, Bobby made a fist and threw his arms up over his head in a victory salute. "Now, who's next?" Porky checked through the stack and paused at the letter F. "Billy Freeman's on his way. It's about time he found out what life has to offer," he said with a wink. "G, H—Herman Hausmann—if there's a piano, everyone there will be happy. LaCoste . . . LaCoste," Porky said, his hands trembling slightly. "I'm going. I'm going," he whispered to Bobby and kissed the card with an audible smack. "Hello, baby, come to Daddy. Whoeee," he said, flinging his head back. Bobby slugged Porky's shoulder and laughed quietly. "L—Lawson—M, N, O, P, Q—Robichaud. Hail, hail, the gang's all here! We did it, buddy!"

Porky rose from the chair and slugged Bobby's shoulder. Bobby returned the punch. They doubled over and laughed quietly until they choked. Once their spasms calmed, they embraced and then shook hands. "Buddies to the bitter end," they said in quiet unison.

"The Philippines! Pint, get ready to play ball! Athol, Athol, rah—rah—rah—," Porky whispered and slapped a hand over his mouth to keep from laughing out loud.

"From here on out—the world is our oyster," Bobby said with a wink.

Both men grinned uncontrollably as Porky handed Bobby a portion of the work. "Here. Let's get this done fast," he said.

Porky and his friends arrived in Brooklyn Harbor by barge, in the company of hundreds of other soldiers from Fort Slocum. They docked next to the transport ship, the USAT *Leonard Wood*, which was to be their home for the next stage of their adventure. Built in 1922 by the Bethlehem Shipbuilding Company, the vessel was purchased by the War Department in 1939. Once known as the Nutmeg State, it was renamed after one of their own, Maj. Gen. Leonard Wood, a medical doctor who won the Medal of Honor from the Geronimo Campaign of 1886 and ended his career as the U.S. Army Chief of Staff, where he reorganized the War Department and prepared the army for the challenge of World War I.

Manned by the Coast Guard, the *Leonard Wood* was 535 feet long from stem to stern, with a 72 ½-foot beam. Her troop capacity was nearly 2,000, and she typically employed over 650 crewmen. She had speeds of up to 17.5 knots and weighed in at 21,900 gross registered tons. For the servicemen from Athol and Orange, the *Leonard Wood*, in terms of population, was about the same size or larger than the small towns that abutted their hometowns. But the population distribution was totally askew. There were no children present, and the ratio of men to women was near zilch. But that was due to change, they hoped, as they cheerfully ascended the ship's gangplank on that frosty January morning in the Year of Our Lord 1941—a year that had a date with infamy.

As Bobby and Porky grabbed the rope, they looked up to see Staff Sergeant O'Toole standing at the top of the gangplank, holding a box of service records. Another box was set on the deck rail beside him. "You two jackasses have got to be crazy to think you want to go on this assignment," O'Toole said to his clerks when they reached the top. He pulled two folders partially out of the box and lowered his voice. "Look. All I have to do is pull these two folders out. You two will step aside and the three of us can leave here after the ship is loaded. I'll reassign you to my office, and within three months you'll both be sergeants," he bargained.

The gangplank and dock below were filled with men waiting to board. Porky took a quick look back. "Thanks anyway, Sarge, but we're going to follow through with our original plan."

O'Toole shook his head. "I can't talk you out of it?" he pleaded. Porky and Bobby shook their heads, "No."

"Then good luck to you both," he said sarcastically. "You'll need it!"

Two days later, many were green from seasickness as they maneuvered gingerly along the open deck. Others sat in groups on deck, talking. Below deck, soldiers better adjusted to the circumstances played cards. Bobby, Pint, Billy, Fran, and Herman stood around the ladder well, surveying the scene. Porky was nowhere in sight.

Billy turned to Bobby, clearly concerned. "When did you last see him?"

"Isn't he on some kind of special duty?" Pint offered.

"Special duty?" Herman scoffed. "He's slicing bread."

"I checked out the mess. He's not there," Bobby said, taking the matter seriously.

"Last I saw of him, he was upchucking over the side," Fran added.

"Maybe he fell overboard," Billy said with genuine panic. "The sea's pretty rough."

"Someone would have spotted him," Fran said, attempting to reassure himself as well as his friends.

Bobby snapped his fingers. "I bet he's in the john."

The men fell over one another as the ship swayed from side to side, then stumbled forward as they proceeded to the ship's head. They shielded their noses in the crooks of their arms and opened the hatch. Porky was at the far end of a long line of urinals, braced against the compartment wall. The towel wrapped around his neck swayed to and fro with the ship rolls.

"We thought you were claimed by the sea," Billy griped. Porky looked up, moaned, and wiped his face off with the end of the towel.

"I wish I was. I wish I was dead," he whined. "I thought we were heading out on a ship. This is nothing but a rotten old junk heap. Talk about second-rate."

Herman sang along with the rhythm of the heaves, "You're in the army now. You're in the army now. You're not behind a plow. You're in the . . ."

Porky was not amused, "Herman. Shut up. That goddamn duty I've got is killing me."

Pint was stunned. "Killing you? All you're doing is slicing bread." "It's the fumes," Porky moaned. "I can't get away from them. The boat's rocking and I'm smelling this goddamn stench and—"

"Thought you were tougher then that, Pork," Bobby said sharply.

"Is this the hero of Athol High's football squad? I know guys that are afraid of you," Herman mocked.

"Knock it off."

"So what's wrong with bread? The yeast is a little strong but—," Pint asked in genuine confusion.

"Bread? The bread? You jerks, there's an oil leak in the kitchen. The boat's rocking, and if you guys don't get off my back and get outta here—" The boat heaved. Porky lurched toward them. "Don't blame me if—," Porky said and grabbed his mouth. "Oh, god—" The guys exited as Porky puked into a urinal.

Four days later, the friends leaned against the ship's railing as the *Leonard Wood* steamed past the Morris Island lighthouse into Port Charleston, South Carolina. They passed the customs house and the lighthouse depot yard to dock on the east side of the Ashley River. Straight ahead was the two-story redbrick Captain of the Port Building. The structure was also used as the headquarters of the Coast Guard's Mounted Beach Patrol. Since a Nazi submarine had surfaced off the coast of Maine in October of 1939, members of the Coast Guard had patrolled on horseback, with trained dogs, along deserted stretches of the eastern coastline. Constant surveillance was deemed necessary due to concerns that Nazi vessels might drop off agents to gather intelligence for the Third Reich. But when the gangplank was lowered, Nazi sightings were the last thing on the soldiers' minds as they rushed forward to disembark.

"This is the life," Porky commented as they crossed the street.

The friends strolled through the historic district, past the piazzas of the one-room-wide "single houses" as they were called. "Tradd Street, then a left onto Ashley, and then hook a right onto Broad Street," Bobby directed, looking at a city map. "Broad's supposed to have great places to eat, and according to the ship's crew, there's lots of action on Broad Street."

"Here we are in the dead of winter and it's balmy," Billy noted.

"How much of Charleston can we see in a couple of hours?" Pint wondered.

"Enough to forget our troubles for a while," Bobby said.

"Troubles? I've got no troubles. I haven't been seasick in three days," Porky confided.

"Next stop—the Panama Canal; and then on to San Francisco," Fran reminded them.

"If it weren't for the uniforms, you'd think we were tourists," Herman said, lighting a cigarette.

"And when we hit Panama, we're in for a special treat," Fran said, warming to the subject. "One of the guys was saying the canal is lined with whorehouses on both sides."

"Ugh. That's disgusting." Billy made a face and stated flatly, "If you're making a pit stop, count me out!"

"Hate to sound prudish, but that goes for me too," Herman said as he blew smoke rings into the humid air. But Pint was the most disturbed at the thought of casual sex.

"Whorehouses! They're filthy, diseased, dangerous," he lectured. "That's nothing I want to get tangled up with."

"Oh, don't believe everything you hear," Bobby said, attempting to sound worldly. "It's those army scare-tactic movies. They'd have you believe your 'whatchamacallit' would fall off on the first try. Use a rubber and your dick will be safe enough."

Porky stared straight ahead as he added, "I hear experience is a great teacher."

"Then call me Professor Robichaud," Fran said as he turned to whistle at an attractive woman in a tight skirt and heels. She smiled but kept walking. "Hubba-hubba. I'm in love." He took off his cap to fan himself.

Bobby smiled. "Nothing's like a Southern belle." Fran smirked and exchanged looks with Bobby as several women exited from a shop, outfitted in floral dresses.

"Stunning! Clingy on top, tight below, oh yes . . . very nice," Fran said, leering at the female shoppers.

"Remember, guys, in the Philippines, the ladies wear the same style except for one detail," Bobby said, waiting for his friends to fill in the blank.

"The tops are missing! Hubba-hubba," Porky, Bobby, and Fran shouted in unison. Billy, Pint, and Herman fell behind, pretending they had nothing to do with the no-class morons walking ahead of them.

The no-class threesome duly noted the snub, linked arms, and yelled at the top of their lungs, "Hubba-hubba!"

One afternoon as the ship approached the Panama Canal, Porky and Pint arrived on deck, having completed their chores in the mess hall. Billy stood in work dungarees and tank top, half blinded by the sun, as he squinted and peered through the viewfinder of his Kodak box camera. Herman sat basking in a regulation tee on a ribbed, non-skid platform with boom-and-winch gear, deck cranes and thick coils of rope as a backdrop, while Bobby and Fran sat on the deck, naked from the waist up. "Hey, Charlie," he called to a man he had befriended from Palmer, Massachusetts. "Would you like to join us for a group shot?"

"Sure. But why don't you let my friend here take the picture," Private Drexler said, grabbing the camera from Billy.

"Not that I'm decent," Billy added. "Aw, what the heck." He spotted Porky and Pint nearby. "Come on, guys. Join in."

Not to be outdone, Porky tore his shirt off and posed in back with Herman. Pint's shirt was open and his sleeves rolled up. He started buttoning up when Bobby intercepted. "Aw, Pint, don't be a Puritan. Your folks back home won't faint if they catch a glimpse of your hairy chest." Only Charlie remained fully clothed and would pass muster if the photo made the rounds back home.

Billy positioned himself in front between Bobby and Fran. "Don't worry, Pint. I've been sending pictures home to my brother Robert. He's keeping them safe for when I get back. Trust me, this'll never see the light of day," Billy assured him. "It'll be stuck between the leaves of an album."

As fate would have it, eventually the photo was placed in an album, but not before it appeared under four-inch deep headlines on the front page of the extra edition of the *Athol Daily News*, dated Sunday, December 7, 1941.

To transverse the Isthmus of Panama, from the Atlantic to the Pacific, may have been the dream of explorers from colonial days to the turn of the twentieth century, but the men aboard the *Leonard Wood* cursed the day the Army Corps of Engineers ordered the first pickax struck on the project. Since leaving Port Charleston, the weather had grown progressively warmer as they traveled south along the Atlantic coastline toward Cuba and the Caribbean Sea, with only brief bouts of relief from an occasional squall.

At first, Porky and his friends were exhilarated as they stood topside, cruising into the mouth of the canal at Colon in Limon Bay. Here they began the slow mount, lock by lock, into the man-made Gatum Lake, eighty-five feet above the ocean channel, created by the damming of the Chagres River. But as they began the descent into the Pedro Miguel Lock down to the Miraflores Lake and Locks to the Gulf of Panama beyond, the tropical beauty of the landscape and excitement from the experience was soon outweighed by the equatorial climate. Diseases that had plagued the work crews who built the canal resulted in thousands (some claim tens of thousands) of deaths from

Aboard the Leonard Wood—January 1941
Front row, left to right: Booby Doolan, Billy Freeman,
Fran Robichaud. Top row, left to right: Pint Lawson,
Herman Hausmann, Porky, Charles Drexler.
Courtesy LaCoste/Thurber family

accidents, malaria, and other tropical diseases. Some on the *Leonard Wood* wondered if they were next.

The friends from Athol and Orange were soon overcome by heat. While waiting for the remaining locks to fill, they speculated if the mosquitoes they swatted had first visited the malaria- and syphilis-infested whorehouses they imagined dotted the landscape. Mostly, they saw jungle. But then suddenly shanty huts would appear through clearings in the jungle landscape. Women in long black skirts and blousy white tops fanned themselves as they prepared food at outdoor ovens. Scrawny children in ragged clothes played beside them in the dirt. One particularly plump woman in a multicolored floral dress sat on a wooden bench and appeared amused as the *Leonard Wood* floated by. She beamed a broad toothless smile and waved at the men who watched from the passing ship. Only Pint had the heart to wave back.

"Holy smokes. Let me out of here," Porky commented, wishing he were somewhere else.

One week later, the ship was cruising through the fog toward Mare Island, their docking point. Once again, all the soldiers were topside as they

Balboa, Panama 1941
Courtesy LaCoste/Thurber family

passed under the Golden Gate Bridge and seemed to head straight toward the tiny island of Alcatraz, home to nationally known criminals: Al Capone, "Machine Gun" Kelly, and Robert "Birdman" Stroud. Veering to the left, the transport passed Alcatraz, then maneuvered between the steep hills of Angel Island, which housed Fort McDowell, a point of embarkation during World War I, and Treasure Island, a U.S. Naval Training Station. Both were in San Francisco Bay, with a clear view of the famous city. However, Mare Island was due north-northeast, in San Pablo Bay, adjacent to the city of Vallejo, California. From there, the men were to be transferred to a smaller ship, the USS *Grant*, which was docked alongside the island.

Though the men felt they deserved some rest and relaxation, the stop at Mare Island did not include R & R, though there might have been ample opportunity, given the hundreds of buildings on site. Mare Island was home to the first United States naval base on the West Coast, established in 1854. It also housed the Mare Island Naval Shipyard where, as the troops drilled the following morning, the *Leonard Wood* was checked over and fitted out for its next duty while the USS *Grant* underwent final preparations for its long Pacific journey. It was raining heavily. The troops marched up and down the muddy training field, and Porky began to cough.

"Bobby, Bobby, I tell you, I'm sick," Porky said, attempting to catch his breath.

"You're always sick," Bobby complained. "Why don't you relax and enjoy yourself. Remember, you're only a tourist. Just think," he said pointing out into the harbor, "over there is Alcatraz! Alcatraz! Think of all the movies we've seen about Alcatraz. Isn't it amazing—George Raft or Jimmy Cagney might have been here. Didn't you see the benches and picnic table by the bluff? Maybe they came to have a picnic with some gorgeous star, like Jean Harlow. Hollywood is just south of here."

Porky coughed and spit up phlegm that got pressed in the ooze of the mud as the men marched.

"We've only seen places like this in the movies," Bobby added, not missing a step.

"Forget the movies," Porky spit out in anger. "We might as well be in Alcatraz," he said, coughing in heavy spasms as he trudged on. "And somewhere over there, through the fog, is the Golden Gate Bridge. Wasn't it a glorious sight? Oh, count your blessings, Porky," Bobby pleaded. "Would you rather be sweeping floors at the Y? Look, it's a matter of willpower. Keep your mind off being miserable and you won't be."

Porky coughed violently as he tramped. "I'm dying, I'm telling you," he wheezed. Perspiration intermingled with raindrops and dripped off the tip of his nose.

"Think of Hawaii. Think of the Philippines. Keep your chin up," Bobby counseled.

"I've got to go on sick leave," he said, hacking. "I can't take this anymore."

Bobby started to sing as he marched. "Somehow I think I've heard this song before. It's from a familiar old tune. I know it well, this melody."

"You think you're funny," Porky moaned.

"Hey. You're the one with the *National Geographic*," Bobby shot back.

"I can't take another step. I'm beat. I'm drenched to the skin. I swear, Bobby, I've got pneumonia. Please. I beg you. Take me to sick bay," Porky pleaded.

Bobby stepped out of formation and pulled his friend aside. "OK, buddy, if that's what you want." He put an arm around Porky and helped walk him back to the wharf where the *Leonard Wood* was docked. They moved up the gangplank, crossed the deck to a staircase, and climbed up to the infirmary, a compartment at the top of the vessel.

Bobby returned to visit after evening mess. As the sun set, lights from the city of San Francisco sparkled through the infirmary's large plate-glass window. Porky was sprawled out on a hospital bed, a towel wrapped around the back of his neck.

"Good to see you, buddy," he said mournfully.

"Thought I'd drop by in case you wanted anything," Bobby said. An orderly approached and stuck a thermometer in Porky's mouth. Porky sat up, looking forlorn. "The doctor—," he said, trying to pronounce words despite the thermometer.

"Private, keep your mouth shut, please," the orderly implored.

"I see you're surviving. I'll check on you later," Bobby said, waving goodbye as he exited. Porky returned the wave and then lay back down, feeling more forlorn then ever.

"The doc will be along any minute, now," the orderly said, pulling the thermometer from Porky's mouth. He checked out the reading and swished the thermometer back and forth, looking at it again. "You've got a slight fever, nothing to write home about."

Once the orderly left, Porky closed his eyes. Tears escaped from the corner of his eyelids and ran down into his ears. He sat up again and leaned against the window to watch troops boarding the ship. "Dear, dear Grandma Rose, your good little soldier misses you," Porky whispered to himself. Tears streamed down his face. He grabbed a tissue, blew his nose, and finally relaxed. At last, a smile played across his face. *Only two more weeks; two weeks, and then the Philippine Islands*, he thought to himself as the doctor entered the room and grabbed his chart.

**Crossing the International Date Line
February 1941 party aboard the USS *Grant***
Courtesy LaCoste/Thurber family

Chapter 8

The USS *Grant* was a steel-hulled steamer, built in Germany in 1907 as a transatlantic passenger ship. Christened *Konig Wilhelm II*, the ship was seized after the United States entered World War I, but not before her German crew cracked her main steam cylinders with a hydraulic jack in an attempt to render her unusable. The U.S. War Department later acquired her and, after a major retrofit in 1922, the ship was renamed the USS *Grant* and became part of the Army Transport Service. Then her job was to haul passengers, troops, and supplies from San Francisco to the territories of Hawaii and Guam; Manila, the Philippine Islands; and Shanghai, China, to the Panama Canal Zone and New York.

Two weeks after the *Leonard Wood* docked at Mare Island, the USS *Grant* was loaded down with supplies and troops and steamed toward the Philippines aglow in a glorious Pacific sunset. Two naval officers, Corp. Vance Turner and Lt. Harry Rose, chatted on deck and were soon joined by Army Nurse Lt. Susan Waters.

Corporal Turner nodded and smiled and tipped his hat as the blond-haired, blue-eyed, dimpled Lieutenant Waters joined them. They had had a brief fling three months earlier, but he had dropped her for a redhead who later dumped him. Getting back into Susan's good graces wasn't easy. Hinting they should get back together sent her into a rage, so he had decided to slowly ease back into a friendship by treating her as a comrade, not a ditzy female for the plucking.

"Harry was telling me reconnaissance thinks something big is brewing with the Japs," the corporal began. "The question is, what's Washington doing about it? Can you believe, most of these guys think they're going to a resort," Harry added.

Susan shook her head. "I wish I had a nickel for every soldier who's 'informed me' that they're replacements."

"Are these guys stupid or are they oblivious?" Vance asked.

Harry pulled a pipe from his pocket, packed the tobacco down, and lit it. "It is beyond their comprehension. Some are straight out of high school. They're kids, out for a joyride," he said between puffs. "Course some are older and haven't had a full-time job in years. For them, the Army's a gold mine and they've struck it rich."

Susan rolled her eyes and laughed. "One bright light had this theory about the big brass being swell guys, so 'out of fairness,' they switch the troops around. Uncle Sam gives each of them a crack at 'fun in the sun.'"

"You are kidding." Harry sucked on the stem as he relit the pipe.

"Hasn't anyone had the common decency to inform them that they are not replacements, but reinforcements?" she asked Vance.

"Don't look at me. I'm not in charge. Besides, even if they were informed, I doubt that they'd understand the difference."

Harry leaned in and said in a loud whisper, "All I know is the USS *Grant* is the largest floating crap game in the Pacific." He looked intently at Susan. "I'm surprised you're only administering to the troops above the deck. It's the troops below that really need you."

"You can say that again," Vance added. "I dropped by last night. Sue, it must have been 105 degrees and climbing. But more cash was riding on the game than they store at Fort Knox, so no one was budging."

"Spare me the details," Susan responded in a tone that made it clear she was Lieutenant Waters to him. "Say, if anyone passes out from the heat or has a heart attack because they've lost their last nickel, please do me a favor—throw him overboard!"

Harry laughed, put an arm around her, and smiled, "My kind of lady; a real Florence Nightingale."

"Hey, I went down there a couple of nights ago, out of concern for the poor lambs. I took a look at one greenhorn who kept staring at me as if he'd seen a ghost. Next thing I know, he passed out. And no wonder. They're packed in like sardines. There's not a breath of fresh air. And the stench! A locker room's a rose garden by comparison," she said, screwing up her nose.

Vance leaned in closer. "I don't know which are worse—the gamblers or the dreamers. Not only do these guys think they're headed for paradise, but that's about all they've been trained for."

"They're in for a rude awakening," Susan agreed.

"Susan, if you need a hand, I'd be happy to—," Vance managed to say before he was cut off.

"Thanks. But as I've mentioned to you before, I can handle myself. See you later, guys," she said, winking at Harry, then headed back to the infirmary.

Moments later, Bobby, Billy, and Herman passed Nurse Waters as they scouted out a spot for the evening. Each carried a blanket. Bobby beckoned for the men to join him. "Here's a good spot," he called as he dropped his blanket not far from where the corporal and lieutenant stood chatting.

Billy took one last look around. "Good as any, I guess."

The tip of Herman's cigarette glowed as red as the sunset at their backs. He inhaled deeply, then blew out the smoke and tossed the butt overboard. "I'm so wound up I can't sleep. Imagine six guys from Tool Town, USA—Nowheresville, Massachusetts—about to dock in Hawaii. I feel like I've died and gone to heaven." Herman's smile was so broad he looked like the corners of his mouth would split. "I can't stop smiling."

"Quit smiling," Bobby cautioned. "Or one of those officers over there might get a notion to wipe it off."

Billy breathed deeply. "Who would have thunk it? After all, we're not millionaires. 'Course, this isn't exactly a luxury liner. But for me, it might as well be. And for the most part, we've managed to stay together. If the folks back home could see us now," he said, overcome with the wonder of it all.

"One for all and all for one," Herman said, dropping his blanket to the deck. "Buddies to the bitter end," he said with feeling, then shook Bobby's and Billy's hands.

"What a lark! So we put in our time doing a few push-ups." Bobby spread his blanket out on the deck. "If I wasn't doing it here, I'd be at the gym. So what's the difference?" he asked, looking up at his buddies. "Think of the poor slobs back at home—the adventures they're missing."

Turner and Rose stopped chatting to listen. Just then Porky, Pint, and Fran arrived, bearing gifts—bags loaded with bread, cheese, cold cuts, and bottled soda pop. Porky, as usual, sported his trademark towel around his neck, which completed the picture for the officers, who let out a short laugh when Porky yelled, "Party time!"

Pint noticed that the officers were observing them. He whispered frantically to Porky, "Keep it down or we might lose our special duty jobs."

Bobby had his back to the officers and was oblivious to anything but the food. "Hey. We appreciate you guys stealing this stuff for us," he said.

Pint tried to shush him, placing a finger to his lips. "It's not stealing. These are just leftovers," Pint said loud enough he hoped the officers heard.

Fran was also oblivious to all around him except his best buddies. "No. I stole. I set aside the best meats and saved them for us," he admitted proudly.

Pint whispered, jerking his head in the general direction of the officers, "Keep it down, guys."

"Who cares? Let's eat," they shouted, grabbing food and settling down to eat. The officers laughed and wandered off for a stroll.

As the men ate, darkness settled and flying fish began to land on deck. Porky picked up a fish that plopped nearby. "Let's get this slimy thing back in the water before someone breaks their neck." He walked to the railing and threw the fish overboard. "Last night, after I dozed off, one flying son-of-a-B hit me along the side of my face. I smacked Bobby trying to brush it off," he whined as his friends burst out laughing.

Not to be outdone, Bobby chimed in, "One landed next to me the other night and cuddled so close, I thought it was an old girlfriend."

Porky choked on his food. Herman slapped Porky on the back until he stopped choking. "Who did you think it was? Thelma? Remember the smell when she'd walk into class?" The men groaned. Porky started choking again, but this time with laughter.

Pint snuggled down onto his blanket. "Settle down, you guys. I need my beauty sleep. You know, some of us have jobs, we're not loafers like the rest of you."

"Loafers? We do calisthenics," Herman said in their defense.

"That's right," Bobby added, "for at least a half hour every day."

"This boat's so small there's no place to move," Billy complained.

"So that's your excuse for whacking me?" Porky asked.

Pint was tired of their perpetual cutting-up. "Shut up. I'm trying to sleep. Please." Before long he was snoring.

"How can I sleep with your snoring?" Porky asked in a loud whisper. Pint opened an eye. "Look, I'll make a deal. If you shut up and let me sleep, I'll introduce you to my sister, Helen, when we're stateside." Pint was serious. "Bet you'd like her. She's shorter than you, blond, and most guys think she's a knockout. But I'll introduce you on one condition."

"Which is . . . ?" Porky asked.

"You watch it with those native girls," he warned. "I won't introduce you if you get VD."

"Someone pointed her out to me, once," Porky recalled, "a long time ago, back in high school. I was coming out of the drugstore and she was across the street. Yah, I remember, even back then she was a blond knockout. She's gorgeous. Say, why should she go for me? Why, she could have anyone she wanted!"

"On my say-so," Pint said quietly. "I'll show you a picture of her sometime. She's prettier than ever and very sweet. After Ma died, she raised us kids. So the deal is—if you're good, I'll tell her about you," he added with a yawn and was soon sound asleep.

The stars were bright in the night sky. Porky lay back and looked up at the moon on the rise. He tingled with excitement as the men settled down. "Helen. That's a nice name." The thought of going out with her would be a dream come true. But that was just it. It was a dream, and he was headed to the reality of the Pacific Islands, *his* dream come true. "Look, don't expect me to be a saint," he whispered to Pint. "Why, anything could happen."

Herman had had it. "Will you two shut up!" he hollered.

By sunrise, men and flying fish were sprawled all over the deck. As light played across their faces, Porky and Pint woke up, yawned, stretched, and knelt to roll up their blankets. They packed them under their arms and headed for their jobs at the mess hall below deck. Not long afterward, the ship's bell rang and the rest of the men rose and headed below deck for breakfast, coughing and cussing as they entered the chow line. Breakfast consisted of scrambled eggs, toast, coffee, cereal, and oatmeal. As each man was served, he passed on into the dining area and began to eat. Suddenly, a loud explosion thundered through the ship. Men braced themselves against the tables, while others stood as if to flee. Private Blake sputtered, then cussed. "What the hell was that, a torpedo?"

"Blake, we're not at war. That was the ship. Something's happened," Sergeant Cranston shot back.

Within minutes, nearly all the men had scrambled on deck. Soon, two sharp whistles sounded and the loudspeaker began to crackle. "Now hear this. Now hear this. Now hear this. The loud noise you heard is the result of a problem in the engine room. Further information will be announced as soon as possible," the voice boomed.

This was not the first time that problems had arisen on the USS *Grant* since it was "rescued from the Germans" during World War I and retrofitted. Two years earlier, the transport had run aground on a dangerous reef as it approached the yet-to-be-completed Guam Harbor. Members of the U.S. Naval Insular Force and local stevedores worked for twenty-one hours to unload three hundred tons of cargo from the grounded steamer onto nearby vessels before she was able to lurch free. Since then, despite several overhauls, the crew had kept their fingers crossed.

Porky and Pint returned to the mess area to continue serving breakfast, still shaken by the misadventure. "I knew it was in the engine room," Porky bragged. "If it were a torpedo, we wouldn't be standing here. We'd be dead or scrambling for our lives."

"Could have fooled me," Pint said, still unnerved. Though most of the men had returned to the mess hall, Bobby and Herman were curious and milled around on deck with a few other stragglers. Soon after, the whistle blew shrilly again, followed by the crackle of the loudspeaker. "Now hear this. Now hear this. Now hear this. The cause of the problem has been located. The ship has blown a piston, which will be repaired in port," the announcement began.

"We should be docking at Honolulu within the next two or three hours, where repairs will be made. Troops will be housed at Hickam Field for approximately one week before departure." When the announcement ended, there was dead silence. Suddenly, a loud cheer broke out above and below deck. Not only had the "unfortunate" mishap resulted in a promise of a dream come true—an extended stay in Hawaii—but also the fabled Hawaiian Islands were now visible along the horizon.

Soon Bobby and Herman were joined by Fran and Billy. "Hickam Field. Isn't that where Pinky's stationed?" Bobby asked. "I wonder if he's started training to become a pilot."

"That is exactly where Pinky is. Great! He can show us where all the cathouses are," Fran said with a wink.

"As I've mentioned before, that doesn't interest me," Billy said, shaking his head in disapproval.

"Ah, come on. You're no longer a choirboy," Bobby teased. "Father Curran's thousands of miles away. Loosen up. Besides, you're our photographer. You need to capture this for posterity. Hey. Go get your camera. Take some shots you can send home."

"I'll be your photographer, but as for any extracurricular activities, you are strictly on your own," Billy scolded as he left to get his camera. Porky arrived on deck and nudged his way into the circle. "Is what's happening what I think is happening?"

"Hawaii. That's what's happening," Bobby said, attempting to appear nonchalant. "We're going to be holed up for one week," he continued coolly, then jabbed Porky in the ribs. "Paradise!" he hollered. "We did it, partner. We have arrived," he yelled, wild with enthusiasm, then shook Porky's hand. The buddies jumped up and down and cheered as GIs passed by, shook their heads, and made the circular loco sign with their index fingers.

"Those guys are definitely nuts," several commented.

Halawa Beach, Hawaii during the USS *Grant* stopover
Courtesy LaCoste/Thurber family

The soldiers had traveled nearly two thousand four hundred miles nonstop from the safety of San Francisco Bay to what they considered to be paradise. They were not alone in their assessment. Though Hawaii was still an exotic destination for most Americans in 1941, the tourist industry was warming up to the islands, which are below the Tropic of Cancer. There, weather conditions are considered ideal, with northeast trade winds mitigating the humidity.

The USS *Grant* anchored at the Honolulu docks, several miles east of Pearl City and the massive naval operations housed at Pearl Harbor. Lugging their gear, the troops disembarked from the ship and were soon boarded into the backs of trucks. They traveled west of Honolulu, beyond Fort Shafter, the Rodgers Airport, Pearl City, the outer edge of Pearl Harbor, and Fort Barrette to post headquarters at Hickam Field. The Army Air Corps had constructed the site a few years earlier to increase its air strength in the Pacific, and to provide a base for the Hawaiian Air Force.

The trucks stopped at the end of a row of tents set up approximately one thousand yards from the airfield, which comprised three landing strips shaped in a triangular formation. The soldiers jumped off the trucks and were instructed to count down by twelve, and then each group was assigned a tent.

Porky had barely entered his assigned tent when a sergeant entered. "Men, unpack your gear as quickly as you can. When you hear a whistle blow three times, fall out and we'll march to the hangar for further instructions." The sergeant left the tent to enter the next tent and repeat the same instructions.

Porky and his new bunkmates unpacked their gear then joined others in a march to the hangar. The soldiers seated themselves in an orderly fashion as the commanding officer, Major Briggs, stepped to the front. "Men, welcome to Hickam Field, your stopover until repairs are made to the USS *Grant*. First, you should know a bit about the man, Lt. Col. Horace Hickam, who commanded the Third Bomb Group in 1933 and 1934, and for whom this base is named. The Third Bomb Group was assigned to deliver airmail, a very important assignment when you consider how far and wide our American forces are currently scattered."

"Colonel Hickam understood the importance of training even for a task others might consider mundane—delivering the mail. But Colonel Hickam knew that individuals assigned to this job are sometimes forced to confront difficult and dangerous situations. In fact, Colonel Hickam protested loud and long that the Third Bomb Group was not properly trained. But he protested in vain. Colonel Hickam was killed in a night landing at Fort Crockett, Texas, on November 5, 1934. Hickam Air Field is named in his honor," the major said, hands behind his back. "Men, in honor of the memory of Lieutenant Colonel Hickam, I want to encourage you to take advantage of the educational opportunities, great and small, that wait when you get to Manila."

"As for today, after a brief instructional film, you'll be driven to Soldiers Beach for a swim. Following supper, I invite you to drop by the Post Exchange for a drink, and then head over to the rec center for a game of pool. Thank you for your attention." Briggs crossed to the back to shut off the lights as the projectionist closed the door to the hangar and started the film.

A soldier next to Porky groaned. "Not another educational film! What are they afraid of? That we'll leave here and line up at the first whorehouse in Honolulu?"

"Not a bad idea," Porky whispered back.

Weeks later, when the friends settled into their lives in the Philippines, they noticed a large tent set up outside the base. A procession of servicemen was habitually lined-up outside, each waiting his turn. After being "serviced" by a lovely lady, each man was handed a coupon he was to redeem at the base for a special chemical treatment to his "whatchamacallit." Along with a film and poster campaign featuring tough but enticing women that carried warnings such as, "She may be a bag of **Trouble**," and "Easy to Get—**Syphilis and Gonorrhea**," the military had instituted a practical and efficient way to deal with the issue of men being men who had forgotten their rubbers.

Halawa Beach and Pavilion
Courtesy LaCoste/Thurber family

In the afternoon, the men were brought, as promised, by truck to Soldiers Beach, a half mile down from a luxury hotel along Halawa Beach. One by one they hopped off. Pint, Porky, and Billy stripped down to their GI regulation bathing trunks and ran across the sand to the water's edge. Waves licked at their feet as Billy bent down, touched the water, and then tapped his forehead, chest, and shoulders in the sign of the cross. A wave crested about fifteen feet out and crashed down as they made their way into the foamy brine, hollering like school kids before diving into the sensual release borne by tropical waters.

Several days later, all six friends walked along the palm-lined Vickers Avenue to the Post Exchange. They headed straight for the bar, then to a nearby table and had just sat down when Pinky entered. Bobby spotted him first. "Over here, Pinky. Over here."

Pinky was all smiles as he approached his friends. He walked around the table and shook everyone's hand. "Great seeing you guys again. Have you been to Honolulu yet?"

Porky, Billy and Herman in Hawaii
Courtesy LaCoste/Thurber family

Bobby grabbed a chair from an adjacent table and gestured for Pinky to join them. "Not yet. Tomorrow."

"So how long are you guys here for?" Pinky asked. "Let's see. We docked four days ago. That means we'll be here another two or three days," Porky said with a grin.

"Great. I'll be by and bring you out to see the sights," Pinky promised.

"So, Pinky, you have to tell us. Is what you said before true? Is Honolulu a great big whorehouse?" Porky asked with a straight face.

"Well. I'll tell you," Pinky began, wincing. "We've only been here a couple of months, and the truth is, I haven't checked it out yet."

Billy sat back. "And if I were you, I wouldn't bother," he said in disgust.

"I know you guys laugh at those films, but you know, there really are diseases," Herman said, tapping down a cigarette on the tabletop. He held out the pack to Pinky, who waved it away, then offered a cigarette to the rest of his friends.

"Diseases or not, who's got the cash?" Porky conceded.

Bobby was shocked. "What are you guys doing? Backing out? I thought we joined the service to have fun."

"Yah, why get so prissy about it? The least we can do is go sightseeing," Fran added.

Pinky had promised, and he decided to deliver. "You're on, tomorrow at three. Sharp!" he said, slapping the table for emphasis. Porky saluted Pinky in mock seriousness. "Yes, sir, we'll be there, sir, tomorrow at three, on the double!"

Tent City, Hickam Field, Hawaii
Front row, left to right: Pinky, Billy, Herman
Back row: Porky, Bobby, Fran and Pint
Courtesy LaCoste/Thurber family

The following day, Pinky stopped by the tent and, before long, the men were walking along a sidewalk on the outskirts of town toward Honolulu center. Sailors were lined up along both sides of the street, waiting to enter bungalows and two-story pink-and-white stucco houses. Sailors lounged around in chairs and hammocks on porches. Cars filled with sailors pulled in and out of parking spots. Sailor's white jumpers, bellbottoms, and caps were as far as the eye could see.

"The cab and bus drivers are on strike today. What adds to the tragedy is that today's payday. So every fool within thirty miles who owns a car is making an extra buck, providing a vital service for the suckers," Pinky said as he pointed out the sights.

Bobby surveyed the scene. "You don't say."

Porky strained to see through the windows. "Too bad we can't get in on the action."

Billy was overwhelmed with embarrassment. "This is one experience I am not going to write home about!"

"Billy, hey, let me have your camera for a second," Bobby said, reaching across Porky for the camera.

Billy pulled the strap off from around his neck and handed it to Bobby. "If you want a group shot, count me out. I don't want anyone to know I was here."

Pint straggled behind. "Yah, me too," he said clearly and emphatically. "Fellows, I'm too straight-laced for this."

Bobby and Porky doubled over with laughter.

"Hey, Billy, you mean you don't want your girlfriend back home to find out," Fran said with a wink to the others.

"What makes you think I have a girlfriend?" Billy blushed.

"Your girlfriend's mother happens to be friends with my second cousin from Greenfield, who was visiting my mother, who sent me a letter that just arrived. You see, my friend, even you can't keep a secret forever," Fran said smugly.

"Some of us do care about our reputations. If she even suspected I was near a place like this, why she'd—," Billy pleaded, hoping against hope that his friends would keep their mouths shut.

"You guys are no fun," Bobby teased. "Billy, relax. You look like you're afraid to breathe. No one's going to tell, and what would they tell? You aren't doing anything anyway. And you can't catch VD like you would a cold!"

Porky sputtered trying to speak; instead, he choked with laughter.

"If nothing else, it's quite a sideshow," Herman sighed urbanely.

"Guys, I hate to tell you. These sailors aren't the sideshow. We're the sideshow," Bobby observed. "You guys are the oddballs."

Pinky assumed command of the troops. "Wise up, guys. You're in the Army now!"

Several Hawaiian women walked past, with long black hair that swished along bare shoulders and the backs of their clingy, strapless floral sarong dresses. Bobby and Porky whistled coolly.

"I guess that's about the only action we're going to see," Porky said, waving a hand back and forth over his face as if to cool off.

"That's about all I want to see," Billy commented. "Next stop—the Philippines, where the real action begins."

"Baseball!" Billy and Pint shouted in unison. Porky and Bobby groaned.

"That's some action," Porky added absentmindedly as he fixated on a sailor slowly pulling up a woman's skirt while they made out on a hammock. "Not that I have anything against baseball. I trust you caught the headlines in the *Athol Daily News* sports page, a week or two before we enlisted," Bobby boasted. "I still lead the Athol Community Softball League with a .526 batting average."

"La-di-dah, my friend, have you got a case of swelled head," Porky said, sticking Bobby in the ribs with his elbow.

"Oh, Pint can give you a run for your money, if anyone's in a mood to bet," Fran offered. "Didn't you lead the Orange League, Pint? And in high school I wasn't half bad."

Pint made a gesture as if to zip his lips.

"Hey, I'll serve as bookie. Who wants to wager?" Porky put his hand out for cash. Bobby pushed it down.

"Gee, you guys, let me finish. Despite my *remarkable* achievement, I'd rather be a connoisseur of fine liquor and fine women. So shoot me!" Bobby shouted.

"And I'd rather be a connoisseur of fine tobacco," Porky said as he grabbed one of Herman's cigarettes from his breast pocket and lit up. Fran grabbed one of Porky's cigarettes from the pack in his breast pocket and lit up off of Porky's cigarette. They threw random punches at one another, stuck a leg out to trip Pinky up, sang Athol High football songs, laughed uproariously, and continued their trek to the center of Honolulu, looking for adventure.

All too soon, the privates from Athol and Orange were saying their good-byes to Pinky and Hawaii and mounted the gangplank to continue the voyage. One week later, as the friends hunted for a place to bed down for the evening, crackles from the loudspeaker were heard, followed by the now familiar ear-piercing whistle.

"Now hear this. Now hear this. Now hear this," the announcement began as a flying fish landed at Porky's feet.

Startled, Porky jumped back. "Damn. I'll never get used to these GD fish."

The piercing whistle cut once again through the noisy chatter, followed by, "The captain wants to inform you that we will be anchoring outside of Guam. Tomorrow, all officers and nurses are invited to join in the native celebration of a special feast day that will take place in the capital city of Agana. All other military personnel will be dinghyed ashore to spend a day touring. Before dark, all personnel must report back to the ship."

Approaching Guam aboard the USS *Grant*
Courtesy LaCoste/Thurber family

The men cheered. "Good deal," Bobby said with a thumbs-up.

"I like the Army," Fran said with gusto.

The next day, Porky, Billy, Bobby, and Fran climbed up from Apra Harbor to a coral beach road, on the west side of Guam. Off to their left, turquoise bay waters sparkled in the sun as proa outrigger canoes bobbed among the waves, manned by Chamorros natives. They fished as their ancestors had for hundreds of years, long before the Spanish arrived in the seventeen hundreds. As the friends walked, they passed a graveyard on their right, with a Spanish-style arched entrance. Copper-skinned, barefoot boys in white shirts and tan shorts flew kites. They ran and skirted between grave markers while two little girls in clean white dresses watched and held a black umbrella between them for protection against the sun.

As the men continued along the road, packed coral turned to sand. The occasional palms offered scant shade, but they were once again on dry land. To have solid ground securely underfoot was a relief, following an oceangoing adventure that had spanned an additional three thousand three hundred miles since chugging off from the Honolulu dockside. According to the ship's crew, there was a village ahead.

"Am I crazy, or do I hear music?" Porky asked.

"Food; I definitely smell something tasty," Fran said, sniffing at the shifting wind currents.

Children from a Guam village
Courtesy LaCoste/Thurber family

GIs congregate on a Guam village road by Nipa huts
Courtesy LaCoste/Thurber family

Moments later, they crested the hill. Straight ahead was a field full of nipa huts, with a lone barroom jam-packed with native Chamorros and GIs. A wood-sided pickup truck passed them and pulled up to the barroom. Two native men appeared from the bar to help unload cases of bottled rum. Soon, nearly everyone streamed out of the barroom into the field and ran over to the truck to buy bottles of rum before supplies ran out. Billy straggled behind on the edge of the crowd, while Porky, Bobby, and Fran ran ahead and were among the first to arrive at the truck. But they were quickly boxed in. Rum sold for sixty-five cents a bottle. The bar workers broke into the crates while the driver of the truck put out one hand for the money and grabbed a bottle of rum from the crate with the other. Porky and Bobby made their purchases, then fought their way out of the crowd, but Billy was nowhere to be seen. They sat down under a palm tree, unscrewed the tops, savored their first sip, and waited for Fran, who had stayed close to the truck, trying to edge back in to buy a few extra bottles. Suddenly, above the din, "Beat Me Daddy, Eight to the Bar" boogie-woogie reverberated from one of the huts.

"Is that what I think it is?" Porky asked, cocking an ear toward the hut. "That's not a recording. That's a piano!"

"I bet that's where Herman wandered off to." Bobby stood up, stretched, and headed for the nipa hut. "What are we waiting for? Let's go!" True to form, Herman was hunched over an old Victorian-era mahogany upright, left over from earlier missionary days. The piano was graced with ivory inlays in the soundboard panels and carved-scroll front pedestals. But instead of playing hymns to be sung by the faithful, Herman switched from the Andrew Sisters number to Cab Calloway's hit from the early 1930s, "Between the Devil and the Deep Blue Sea."

A native woman, wrinkled with age and sun, was the owner of the hut. She stood facing Herman and yelled at the top of her voice. "Please, I told you a hundred times, please leave. Please to leave, please. Too many people, I tell you—too many people!" she pleaded.

Herman looked up and begged without skipping a beat. "Just a few more songs, I'm just getting warmed up."

The old woman screamed and clutched the bodice of her white cotton dress. "I was good to you. Let you in to play. Now too many, I tell you. The hut fall down, too many people."

Porky and Bobby pushed their way into the crowded room as the owner plowed through sweat- and booze-stench bodies to the open door. She shrieked red faced, but the crowd continued to enter. "Stay out. Stay out. Too many people, please too many, I tell you!" She blessed herself with the sign of the cross and held the palms of her hands out, hoping to stop the crowd. Fran was on the outskirts but managed to sneak in by crouching down and worming his way through wherever he saw an opening.

Billy was already inside, wedged in between two bare-chested sailors, whose sweat was quickly absorbed by his short-sleeved dress shirt. Porky spotted Billy and pushed him toward Herman as Bobby and Fran maneuvered to the side of the piano nearest the open window. Billy yelled above the din, "How'd you find the piano?"

Herman hollered back, "One of the natives tipped me off."

Pint seemed to appear from nowhere. "Billy, sing one of your songs."

Fran pushed through and joined them, unscrewed the bottle, and took a long, slow swig of rum.

"Not here. I'd bore everyone," Billy said modestly. "My stuff's too slow."

Fran put an arm around Billy. He reeked of rum. "For me, Billy, please sing 'Danny Boy.' I've heard you sing it before. They'll love it. Such a beautiful song," Fran pleaded, drunk as a skunk. He looked into Billy's eyes while tears welled up in his own.

A freckle-faced teenaged soldier stood next to Fran. "He sings?" "He could have been an opera star, but he can sing anything," Fran slurred. "You should hear his 'Danny Boy.'"

"My name's Sullivan, Jim Sullivan," he said, shaking Fran's hand. "'Danny Boy.' There's nothing I'd like better."

"Is it my imagination, or are you from Boston?" Fran asked, amazed.

"South Boston Irish. My parents are from a small village outside of Dublin," he told Fran, then crossed to Billy. "Soldier, can I shake your hand?"

"Don't see why not," Billy said, shaking hands.

"Can't I talk you into singing?"

"Aren't you afraid I'll make you homesick?"

"We're already homesick," Pint said, butting in. "Please Billy, don't be shy."

"Honest. It would mean a lot to me, and I bet to a lot of other fellers here," Private Sullivan said with obvious sincerity.

Herman swung into the intro. Billy was trapped. He cleared his throat, breathed deeply, and began in a basso profundo that seemed to emanate from the depths of his being, "Oh Danny boy, the pipes, the pipes are calling, from glen to glen and down the mountainside."

As Billy sang, the crowd quieted down. To everyone's surprise, even the old woman, whose home had been invaded by a hoard of uninvited American servicemen, quieted down, and a peaceful look settled over her face.

"The summer's gone, and all the roses falling. 'Tis you, 'tis you must go, and I must bide." As Billy continued, the faces of the GIs turned inward. The room was silent except for the voice of Billy and the piano accompaniment.

"And if you come, when all the flowers are dying, and I am dead, as dead I well may be, you'll come and find the place where I am lying, and kneel and say an 'Ave' there for me."

Bobby looked out the window to the field and nipa huts, and to the sea and sky beyond.

"And I shall hear, tho' soft you tread above me, and all my dreams will warm and sweeter be, if you'll not fail to tell me that you love me, I'll simply sleep in peace until you come to me."

Billy ended in the highest octave in his range, repeating the refrain, "I'll simply sleep in peace until you come to me." His face was angelic as the last dying notes drifted into silence.

Courtesy LaCoste/Thurber family

Dusk descended, and Apra Harbor grew noisy. The dock swarmed with soldiers climbing into dinghies headed back to the ship. As they arrived on board, the occasional thud of a rum-filled coconut smashed onto the deck and reverberated along the metal byways of the transport vessel. Officers grabbed the contraband and threw it overboard as the deafening sound of the ship's whistle broke through the intoxicated stupor of the troops.

"Now hear this. Now hear this. Now hear this. All men are to report to their quarters for roll call. Any man caught smuggling liquor on board will be punished," the loudspeaker blared. The harbor soon resonated with the sound of bottles and rum-filled coconuts splashing into the briny waters and smashing alongside the ship, and the air hung heavy with the stench of liquor.

Porky and some of his buddies
Courtesy LaCoste/Thurber family

US Army Transport *Grant* docked in Manila
Courtesy William Patrick Mungo Photographic Collection [mungoA0032], D.H. Ramsey Library Special Collections, University of North Carolina at Asheville

Chapter 9

After traveling one thousand seven hundred nautical miles from Guam, the USS *Grant* skirted the northern tip of Luzon and headed south into the South China Sea, past the Bataan Peninsula and then east-northeast into Manila Bay.

As the ship entered the Port of Manila, it passed Fort Drum, which was shaped like a battleship, and Caballo Island, with its massive fourteen-inch coastal guns and twelve-inch mortars. But what most impressed the soldiers gathered on deck was Corregidor Island, with its three-story, mile-long barracks, said to be the longest in the world. Excitement grew as they caught a glimpse of the famed city of Manila, the Pearl of the Orient, whose Spanish *Intramuros*, or Walled City, was begun in 1571. The transport headed for the South Harbor docks, bypassing the smaller North Harbor, which was used solely for inter island shipping. Both harbors were protected by breakwaters and separated by the Pasig River.

The USS *Grant* docked at Pier 7, on the south bank of the Pasig River where most of the governmental buildings and hotels were located. Attached to the port-of-entry building was a large sign: Manila, PI. As the soldiers disembarked, officers' wives boarded the ship from an adjacent gangplank. Soldiers carrying luggage, large sea trunks, and cardboard containers filled with household items entered the vessel via a gangplank farther down.

"That's strange," Bobby noted.

"Yah," Porky agreed. "Just when we arrive, the top brass decides to send their women home? What are they . . . afraid of us? We're bad, but not that bad," he joked.

Pasig River, Luzon PI
Courtesy LaCoste/Thurber family

But Pint was not in the mood for horsing around. "Maybe it's not us they're afraid of, but the Japanese," he said with an edge to his voice. "Why? What's happened?" Porky asked naively.

"It's not what's happened," Bobby said as he dropped his gear on the sidewalk. "It's what they're afraid is going to happen."

"Don't worry. Uncle Sam will take care of us," Porky reassured his friends. "Remember, we're reinforcements. And there's going to be more and more reinforcements. We're here to scare the Japs! Remember, we're the strongest power in the world. No one's going to push us around. No one's going to take us on," he said to his friends as they joined the rest of the GIs standing in line, waiting to hop onto the trucks that would take them to their next destination, the U.S. Army Air Corps post headquarters at Nichols Field.

One week later, the men lay on their cots in the predawn hours and awoke to the steady drum of rain on the tent tops. Nichols Field was two miles south of Manila along the Pasig River. Rainy season in the Philippines was not the "fun in the sun" they envisioned, but still, they had arrived. Their home was wherever the Twentieth Air Group took them. And it had taken them to their dream come true. As the last note of the bugle call ended, the morning gun was fired, the flag raised, and the men assembled for morning roll call. Bobby Doolan's mind drifted to thoughts of home. It was 6:00 a.m. here, but back home it was what? *There is somewhere between an eleven- and*

Main Street, Tent City—Nichols Field, Philippines
Courtesy LaCoste/Thurber family

twelve-hour time difference, he reasoned. *If the Philippine Islands are ahead, then it's dusk back home, time for retreat. We're observing reveille, raising the flag, and they're lowering it,* he thought. Soon the breakfast call was sounded, and Bobby forgot about home and regrouped with his friends to enter the mess hall.

Following breakfast, the soldiers drifted back to their assigned eighteen-man tents. By 10:00 a.m., the newest arrivals marched to a nearby field for close-order drill and training, while other GIs exited the barracks to their jobs in truck, machine, and carpentry shops. Company sergeants and other personnel walked by with folders tucked under their arms and headed to office buildings. By 11:00 a.m., the morning drill had ceased, which was about all Porky and Bobby could stand. They joined Pint, Billy, Fran, Herman, and dozens of other men on their way to the athletic field.

Porky turned to Bobby with a puzzled look on his face. "All the classes are full. So what are we supposed to do? Just hang around?"

"Yeah, sounds about right," he said, then caught sight of someone that made his flesh crawl. "Holy cow, look who's here." Porky glanced in the direction of Bobby's horrified gaze. "Staff Sergeant Bass from Fort Slocum," Bobby muttered, then turned to Porky, serious as all get out. "The game is over. He's sure in hell going to get us this time!"

Porky walks back to his tent, Nichols Field
Courtesy LaCoste/Thurber family

"Are you kidding? He'll never remember us," Porky said, feeling safe as the staff sergeant turned his back and started to walk toward a group of men at the far end of the field.

Suddenly, Bass stopped dead in his tracks, turned on his heels, and with a face that looked like a pit bull about to attack, bellowed, "Hey, you two," with a thick Southern drawl. He thrust out an index finger, which pointed straight at Porky and Bobby. "You two over there, you didn't drill under me at Fort Slocum, did you?" he shouted like the Grand Inquisitor.

Bobby and Porky approached and saluted. "No, Sir, we were on special duty in headquarters, Sir," Bobby responded with as much respect as he could muster.

Staff Sergeant Bass put his hands on his hips and shouted into their faces, "Special duty? Doing what? Pushing pencils?"

Porky and Bobby remained at attention. "Sir, we did drill at Slocum—when we first arrived, Sir. And then we got special orders to-," Bobby sputtered.

Bass cut him off. "Special orders? Don't give me that crap! Couple of goldbricks, that's what you two are," he screamed, then blew his whistle. "Fall in," he commanded, then lowered his voice. "I'll be watching you two closely," he said in a menacing tone.

The soldiers who had been scattered about quickly "fell in" and began to drill. Bobby was in good form, but soon Porky fell behind. Bass pointed to Porky. "LaCoste, you're a disgrace. See that infield, over by the ballpark?

I want you to run around those bases 'til I tell you to stop," he yelled, then turned his attention to the others. "Men, forward—March."

A half hour later, Bass blew his whistle. "Men, fall out. That's all for today. Check the bulletin board for tomorrow's assignments." The men had built up a sweat as the midday heat approached peak temperature. Several pulled out white cotton handkerchiefs and mopped their faces as they gathered to talk. Bass sauntered to the ball field and addressed Porky, who was still running. "Over here, LaCoste." Porky stopped running, approached the sergeant, saluted, and stood at attention. "Look," Sergeant Bass began, "I've got to get you in shape. That desk job did you no favors. A month with me and you'll be a real soldier. Disss . . . missed!"

Porky gasped and relaxed. "Yes, Sergeant," he responded, knowing in his heart that Bass had sized him up correctly.

"Because of the climate hereabouts, we can only drill in the morning," Bass explained. "Check the bulletin board at company headquarters for your assignments. The rest of the afternoon, you're on your own time. That is, unless you get a special duty job, which is what you're accustomed to."

Porky and Pint and a friend, Nichols Field
Courtesy LaCoste/Thurber family

By noon, men were clustered around the bulletin board in front of the company headquarters. Bobby searched the assignments, then turned to Porky and Pint. "Well, guys, it looks like this is the parting of the ways, at least for now. I've been transferred to Clark Field, Third Pursuit Squadron—part of the 24th Pursuit Group under Claggert."

Porky's heart sank when Bobby announced his departure, but he changed the subject to his own situation. "Sergeant Bass must be a prophet. Looks like I've lucked out again. I've got a special prison detail. There's twenty Filipino prisoners assigned to me."

Bilibid Prison, Manila (1925)
Courtesy C&GS Collection (NOAA)

Pint was startled by this announcement, "Prisoners? I'm not sure I'd like that."

Porky decided to have a little fun at Pint's expense. "Yeah, what am I suppose to do with twenty prisoners?" Porky continued. "This isn't exactly pushing pencils. Bobby, what do you make of it? What do you think these guys did?" Bobby shrugged. "Maybe they're murderers?" Porky asked, laying it on thick. "What happens if they riot or run away? What am I supposed to do? I know I'll be armed. But what if they come after me?"

Pint thought for a moment. "Well. Shoot 'em!" he blurted out.

"Don't talk so big. Your name's on the list too," Porky said with a smirk.

"Prison detail! Let me see that list," Pint said, muscling in for a closer look. "I thought I was on the baseball team."

"Don't talk to me. Talk to the sergeant," Porky shot back.

"I think I will," Pint said.

Several trucks arrived and stopped in a small field not far from the headquarters building. They watched as prisoners jumped off the back of the truck. Pint looked scared and started to hyperventilate. Porky took pity on his friend and pulled him aside as Bobby moved close to eavesdrop.

"Don't worry. I got the lowdown on this job," he whispered. "In fact, I got tipped off we were going to get assigned. My spies tell me it's a good deal for a lazy guy."

Pint relaxed as Porky continued. "First off, they're thrilled to be prisoners. Look, Pint, these aren't hard-core murderers and rapists. The real criminals are sent to the Davao Penal Colony. These guys are in for petty shit. Bilibid Prison's like a hotel for them. They get two square meals a day, good clothes, and a decent place to sleep at night. Ta them, this is a racket! And all we have to do is figure out who's the headman, the honcho, and bribe him with a couple of cigarettes. He'll run the detail and keep everything shipshape!" Porky explained, then covered his mouth to suppress a laugh. He glanced back at Bobby, who was rolling his eyes.

But Pint was too straightlaced to associate with prisoners, no matter how harmless. Pickpockets and hucksters were hard core in his moral lexicon. "I'm still going to complain," he said, screwing up his face in disgust. "Where's the sergeant?"

As Pint headed off to complain, he was stopped in his tracks by the sergeant, who pushed him aside. "Men, the procedure for prison detail is that each of you has been assigned a number. Twenty prisoners have also been given that number. Check out a spot on the field, then stand there and holler out your number," the sergeant shouted.

Bobby whispered to Porky, "Now, don't be too rough on those poor prisoners, just because they're smaller than you." Bobby burst out laughing at his half-baked humor, walked away, and then turned back around to shout, "I'd say, good luck, but you've already got it."

Porky grinned and waved good-bye to his longtime buddy, then walked to a nearby tree and yelled out, "Number three."

Twenty downtrodden prisoners wearing large, white caps, black-and-white striped slacks and long-sleeved shirts walked toward Porky. He looked them up and down, which confirmed to him that they were more to be pitied than scorned. He also knew that Bobby was right. He had lucked out again.

Pint Lawson made the team and played shortstop at
Rizal Baseball Stadium in Manila.
Courtesy LaCoste/Thurber family

Pfc. Libby in Hangar #3, Nichols Field
Courtesy LaCoste/Thurber family

Chapter 10

One week later, Porky was stationed outside of a hangar. He sat on the ground, his back against the structure, dozing, with a rifle between his legs. A Filipino head honcho stood nearby with a cigarette dangling between his lips, a gift from Porky. He took a deep drag and pulled it out, spewing smoke as he barked orders. Porky's honcho spoke Tagalog, the most widely used language of the eighty-seven spoken by the Filipino people. Porky thought he spoke "Philippinese." The honcho yelled for the prisoners to cut brush and pick up trash around the hangar, but to be careful not to disturb their American "guard."

Technical Sergeant Hall, middle aged, with excess layers of gut hanging over his belt, exited from the company's headquarters and made his way toward the hangar. He stopped to watch his "prospect at work" before sauntering over to Porky, who snored unaware that the stocky figure was approaching.

"LaCoste! LaCoste," Hall shouted. Porky opened his eyes, but it took a moment for his brain to process his predicament.

At last, Porky jumped up and saluted. "Yes, sir, Sergeant," he shouted back as beads of sweat popped out on his forehead and dribbled into his mouth.

"LaCoste, don't call me 'sir.' I work for a living," Hall stated with a smirk.

"Yes, Sergeant," Porky said as he lowered his arm and stood at ease. Hall continued with only a shade of sarcasm, "Do you think you could spare a moment?"

"Of course, Sergeant," Porky said, unsure of where the conversation would lead.

"Good. I'd like a word with you."

Porky was now fully awake and somewhat shaken, hoping he wouldn't find himself locked up in the brig.

"Sure, oh, sure," he said with a touch of humility.

Hall smiled, hoping to relax his quarry. "I was checking through the service records up at headquarters. I'm looking for a soldier who can type. I noticed you took high-school typing."

"Yes. Yes, I did, sir," Porky said, nearly stuttering.

"You see, I've got a problem," the tech sergeant continued. "Last year, I was supposed to have put out a report, but I couldn't find anyone to type. Would you be willing to help me out? I'll get you assigned to my office."

"Sure. Oh, sure. There's not much of a future here in prison detail," Porky added, desperately hoping to erase the image of a lazy good-for-nothing.

"Report to Hangar Number 3, tomorrow morning at 7:30 a.m. sharp," Hall said, saluting.

"Yes, sir!" Porky responded, returning the salute with genuine enthusiasm.

The next morning, Private LaCoste arrived at Hangar Number 3 at 7:30 a.m., sharp. Inside the hangar was a flight of stairs that opened into an office cut into the roof. As Porky entered the office, he looked around for Technical Sergeant Hall, but instead a lieutenant was standing by the desk.

Porky wasn't sure what to say. "LaCoste, reporting for duty, sir, to Technical Sergeant Hall," he ventured.

"Lieutenant Murphy here. At ease, soldier. I need to report to you that Technical Sergeant Hall has been reassigned to General Claggett's office. And Sergeant Smith, second in command, has also been reassigned. That leaves just you and me," he said as the phone rang. The lieutenant picked it up.

"Lieutenant Murphy. Yes. So what's your problem?" Murphy asked as he grabbed a pad of paper and started writing. "That's six light bulbs out at the mess hall. I'll have the electrical department send you the bulbs right away," he said and hung up. Murphy checked a number in the rolodex, picked up the phone, and dialed. He held up a finger to Porky to wait a minute, then—"Hello. This is Lieutenant Murphy. Send six light bulbs to the mess hall, on the double." He looked back to Porky as he hung up. "Do you think you can handle this?" he asked.

"I thought I was supposed to type a report," Porky blurted out. The lieutenant shook his head.

"You've been reassigned. You're now in the technical maintenance department."

Nichols Field Mess Hall
Courtesy William Patrick Mungo Photographic Collection
[mungoA0025], D.H. Ramsey Library Special Collections,
University of North Carolina at Asheville

Once again the phone rang. "Hello. Lieutenant Murphy." He balanced the receiver on his shoulder to rest against an ear as he grabbed the pencil, sat, and wrote. "Plaster down in the dining hall. That right? Much of the ceiling is gone," he repeated, then paused to listen. "Whew, it's that bad! We'll try to get to it as soon as possible. Give me your phone number and the exact location," he said, writing in bold print as he spoke, "Twentieth Air Group dining hall." He paused to listen again, then added, "Look, if you get stuck, feed them in the tent. I'll be back in touch."

Porky beamed. "So this is where the action is!"

"You've got the job, soldier, if you're fast. Think you can handle it?" The lieutenant needed to size him up, pronto.

Porky was confident this was the job for him. "I'll give it a shot," he said as the phone rang.

"No time like the present," Murphy said, nodding at the phone. Porky answered, "Private LaCoste. Yes, sir, speaking. Can I help you? Yes, sir, Lieutenant Johnson. And how can I help you, sir?" he asked as he grabbed the paper and pencil and began to write. "You need a two-ton truck to move equipment to Hangar Number 1. I'll get to it right away, sir. Can I have your phone number?" Porky asked as he jotted down the number. "Thank you, sir." Porky hung up the phone and pointed to a list that was typed, with a few numbers that were crossed out and written over.

"I take it these are the numbers and the departments? I noticed the machine shop, truck shop, and carpenter's shop on my way over."

The lieutenant sighed in relief. "You've got the job down pat, already. Congratulations! There's only one problem, LaCoste. You're a private. And no noncom is going to take orders from a private," Murphy said as Porky hung his head in disappointment. "Listen, I trust you to handle yourself as best you can. I'll skip over to headquarters and talk to Sergeant Rumford. When you finish up at 1130 hours, stop in at the Post Exchange and buy yourself some corporal stripes. Then bring your uniform over to the tailor. At 7:30 a.m. tomorrow, I want Corporal LaCoste to report to duty!"

Porky was in a state of shock. "Yes, sir," he said as he saluted his mentor.

"Give me four more months and you'll make sergeant," Murphy said as he descended the stairs.

Sea Wall along Dewey Boulevard, Manila
Courtesy LaCoste/Thurber family

Porky was flabbergasted. His mind was racing, "Corporal! That means $64 a month. My pay's doubled!" Porky also knew that the work day was from 7:30 a.m. to 11:30 a.m. "Easy street, here I come. What a life," he thought, wishing Bobby was around so he could brag to his best friend. He'd imagined bringing him down a peg or two with some good-natured wisecrack. But thoughts of Bobby soon morphed into home and family. *Grandma Rose, your soldier boy's going to make you proud*, he thought with pride as the phone rang.

Two weeks later, Fran and Porky, wearing white casual slacks and shirts, rode into Manila on a *carromata*, a donkey-drawn wagon driven by a native Filipino. The air was hot and sticky, but they could smell the flowers and harvested coconuts and see the *bancas*—the fishing boats—at a distance in Manila Bay. Porky pulled a couple of cigars out of his left-hand breast pocket, offering one to Fran. "Finally, the 'Life of Reilly,'" he said, puffing at the cigar as Fran held a match to its tip. "A Filipino boy polishes our boots, takes care of our laundry, cleans our wall locker, makes our bed—and anything else you want. And all for forty-five cents a month, a few pieces of fruit, and a pack of cigarettes a day. What a life! Now this is class!"

Swimming Pool at Nichols Field
Courtesy LaCoste/Thurber family

Fran blew smoke and watched it trail behind as they slowly moved forward. "You're forgetting the rec hall: a swimming pool, an air-conditioned bowling alley; cheap drinks, easy women, dance halls everywhere," Fran said as he began to cough. "You know, Pork, I never could get used to cigars." He pushed the glowing tip of the thickly rolled tobacco into the wooden rail. "All we need are some sharp-looking clothes," he added as Porky too put out his cigar and grabbed a pack of Lucky Strikes from his right-hand breast pocket. Fran grabbed a smoke and lit up. Up ahead was a familiar figure, swaying in front of a liquor store, half-cocked from cheap booze. He was attempting to barter with a Chinaman for gin in exchange for cigarettes. The broad-faced Chinaman wore traditional silk garments and sash and stood behind bushel baskets filled with watches, cameras, cigarettes, and pint bottles of rum and gin. The Chinaman wasn't buying. Five cigarettes did not equal a pint of rum or gin.

Pasig Barber Shop—Pasig is on the eastern border of Manila
Courtesy LaCoste/Thurber family

"Isn't that O'Malley—one of the guys from 'Southy' we met at Guam? From the looks of it, he's a regular 'peck-a-gin' guy, a real boozer," Fran commented.

"Yeah, too bad, he's not a bad sort," Porky said, hoping that none of them would suffer a similar fate. The two men leaned from the carromata to wave to Private O'Malley, who waved back with a drunken grin. Porky wondered if he recognized them or was responding as a child might respond to the friendly gesture from a stranger.

"I hear half the uptown shops are owned by GIs. Now there's the racket," Porky said, leaning back as the wagon bumped along. "Work in the a.m. for Uncle Sam, and you've got afternoons and weekends to run your own business and to party. As a matter of fact, I've started a loan business. Even the officers need money for their hunting trips. I've been using my military chits. Do you realize, I'm pulling in 20 to 50% profit on those loans," Porky said with pride.

Fran burst out laughing.

"What?" Porky looked hurt.

"Sorry, buddy. Look, I'm proud of you. But remember, not long ago you were sweeping floors at the Y, and now you're a banker. If I tried doing what you do, with my luck, they'd welsh out on me. Porky, you've got the technique. With you it's a gut instinct. You just know how to do things naturally," Fran said with genuine admiration.

"You're probably right," Porky said, relaxing. "Now don't tell Pint, 'cause he wants me to meet his sister. But between you and me, Franny, I've found my home. I have no intention of leaving this place 'til I retire. Have you noticed the White Russian women? They're gorgeous."

Courtesy LaCoste/Thurber family

Party time at Legaspi Garden, Manila
Courtesy LaCoste/Thurber family

"The pretty little Filipino ladies aren't so bad, either. And now that I'm working at headquarters, my chances for advancement are looking better by the hour," Fran added.

"We get thirty days' vacation a year. Why, in a couple of years, we could take a trip back home and take our time—spend months. I have to pinch myself when I realize I'm a corporal, and at the rate I'm advancing, I'll make sergeant in three months. I wish I were a fly on the wall, to hear what's said when my grandmother gets the letter."

The friends leaned forward as the carromata approached a men's clothing shop with display mannequins outside, sporting white linen and sharkskin suits.

"This is the spot. Driver, stop," Fran shouted above the street noise. "Here's eighteen centavos . . . eight cents," he said as he exited.

"Maybe I'm a cheap Yankee, but in my book that's a great deal. A carromata may be slower than a taxi, but it's a hell of a lot cheaper," Porky commented as he stepped out onto the sidewalk. "And besides, what's the hurry?" They watched as the driver slowly maneuvered the donkey back into traffic—older-model Ford trucks laden with produce, a late-model Chevy roadrunner, an occasional taxi, pedestrians, and an endless parade of carromatas.

The smell of *ensaymadas*—a doughy sugar, egg, butter, and cheese treat—emanated from a small bakery down the street. "Hungry?" Fran asked as Bobby Doolan passed by waving in a carromata, with a beautiful Filipina, dressed in red satin, by his side. Porky and Fran stood in stunned silence as Bobby pulled the woman onto his lap for a passionate kiss, which was partially obscured by the flow of her long, black hair. The friends took a deep breath and exhaled simultaneously, "Hubba—hubba," before entering the bakery.

**Billy Freeman—
Army Reconnaissance**
Courtesy LaCoste/Thurber family

Chapter 11

The Army Air Corps Air Warning Service facility was located at Nichols Field, along with an intelligence branch assigned to survey the Philippines and beyond for any unusual activity. One Sunday afternoon in early November, Porky was alone as he sat on his bunk, writing a letter. Billy Freeman ducked under the raised flaps to enter. He was dressed in his Sunday best in slacks, shirt, and tie.

"How was church?" Porky asked, putting aside the paper and pencil.

"The chaplain has me singing in the choir. And Herman plans to volunteer if their organist can't make it," Billy said. "It almost feels like home."

"I'm writing to my grandmother," Porky said with a big grin on his face. "Any message? While I'm at it, I could write to your girlfriend. What's her address?"

"Yeah, like I'm going to trust you. Hey, have your grandmother send my love and tell them I haven't written because they've got me working seven days a week."

"Seven days a week? Doing what?" Porky asked with more than a hint of incredulity.

Billy hesitated a moment then sat on the bunk next to his friend. "Don't write this down, OK? Look. They've assigned me to G-2, the Intelligence Branch," Billy said, lowering his voice.

Porky scoffed, "The Intelligence Branch? Well, excuse me for living. What's that supposed to mean? You're brighter than the rest of us?"

Billy put a finger to his lips and kept his voice low.

"I'd like to believe that. But I think it's because I'm an amateur photographer. As a matter of fact, Mr. Smart Aleck, if you're not doing anything, why don't you come with me? Sunday afternoons they leave me alone to mind the shop."

Catholic Church frequented by GIs
Courtesy LaCoste/Thurber family

'Course anything you see, you have to keep to yourself," he added, turning suddenly serious. "And I mean that."

"My lips are sealed," Porky said, picking the letter up off the bed to fold it. "I'll finish writing this when we get back. Let's go."

Porky followed Billy as they walked past row after row of tent barracks, aircraft, and ground installations to the secured rear entrance of the headquarters building. Billy signaled for Porky to remain silent as he rang the buzzer. They heard the sound of clicking metal gears, and then an enlisted man opened the door. "Oh, hi, Billy," the guard said.

Billy appeared relaxed. "I've got a friend of mine here, Corporal LaCoste. I thought I'd show him around."

The guard looked Porky over and then stepped aside to allow them to enter. The men walked down the hallway to the G-2 office, which took up three rooms. Each of the rooms had large counters that were attached by hinges from the walls. Stools were scattered about. Billy grabbed a stool and brought it to one of the counters. Dozens of large photographs were scattered over the counter. Others leaned against the wall. All the photos had a common theme: islands covered with aircraft of the Imperial Japanese Army and Navy Air Service bearing the insignia of the Rising Sun.

"Guess where these islands are?" Billy asked, inspecting the photos. "In Japan, I hope," Porky replied with a shudder.

B-18 Aircraft, Nichols Field

Porky and Herman at Nichols Field
Courtesy LaCoste/Thurber family

"Guess again," Billy said.

"Not nearby, I hope," Porky grimaced as he looked over Billy's shoulder.

"Let's say, two hours away, tops," Billy responded with the utmost seriousness.

"Are these the islands that aren't supposed to have any planes or weapons on them?" Porky ventured.

"What's supposed to be and what is are two different stories," Billy replied grimly.

Porky put a hand to his forehead. "Holy smokes! I thought we were here to party."

"If I were to guess, I think the party's just about over," Billy said, catching the scared look in Porky's eyes.

"Still, Uncle Sam knows about this. You've got proof. You've got the photos," Porky reasoned in an attempt to reassure Billy as well as himself.

"Sure," Billy countered. "We've got the photos. As to what they plan to do about it, your guess is as good as mine."

"You know," Porky said, suddenly connecting the dots, "maybe that's why the new second lieutenant from the thirty-first infantry's been brought in. For a while, I was getting out of doing anything much. I had one day of drilling and that was it. And now they have all of us, including me, going through basic training again."

Billy nodded his head and tried to make light of the situation. "That's right. Finally, even you have to act like a soldier."

"But how is basic training supposed to help if the bombs start falling?" Porky asked. "Oh, who knows, maybe the top brass has something up their sleeves. Aren't we expecting a couple more shiploads of men?"

"Yes. But remember, they're reinforcements, not replacements," Billy countered emphatically, adding new meaning to the phrase they had heard repeatedly but had never fully comprehended.

"That's right. But before we know it, there'll be thousands more GIs on these islands. Before long the islands will be filled with all kinds of planes and equipment," Porky maintained with patriotic defiance as he clutched at straws.

"You think so? Porky, we haven't got the runways. We haven't got the hangars," Billy insisted quietly.

"Don't worry. If I know Uncle Sam, supplies will come in and we'll build them," Porky said, attempting to reassure his friend.

"We'll see," Billy answered as he grabbed photos to reorganize them according to location.

One week later, Lieutenant Murphy suggested that Porky visit the quartermaster depot, located in the Army Port Area of Manila to get a better understanding of supply operations for the island bases. Fran tagged along for the trip to Manila Harbor. The weather had turned from glorious to cloudy, with scattered rain showers and thunderstorms. Moderate to strong

Sightseeing in and around Manila
Courtesy LaCoste/Thurber family

winds were blowing from the northeast, which created rough seas, but the water was relatively calm within the protection of Manila Bay. The talk was that most American goods were in short supply, so every effort was made to obtain items from local contractors, especially food. But despite the shortages, large quantities of food supplies and other items had been shipped from the United States and were being stored as reserves at various strategic locations on Luzon and Corregidor.

Pier 7 in Manila Harbor
Courtesy Lacoste/Thurber family

Porky and Fran watched from the second story of the quartermaster building as army supply officers and enlisted men supervised Filipinos, who carted goods off ships, unloaded them into ox carts, or dumped them in heaps along the pier. As a large cargo ship approached the harbor, a tugboat maneuvered the ship away from the pier, which allowed a large presidential liner to approach. The liner was filled with two thousand troops from an army dive-bombing outfit. As the liner docked and men disembarked, soldiers swarmed over the pier to greet the reinforcements. Fran thought he recognized an acquaintance from home. "Porky, look over there, isn't that Franklin Bachelder? His brother runs an insurance agency," Fran said, pointing him out in the crowd.

Porky searched the faces. "Oh, the guy over by the post. I think you're right. I know that face. Wasn't he a couple of years ahead of me in school?"

"I think so. Hey, there's another one. What's his name? Wow, this is old home week. Isn't he Doc Musson's son?" Fran asked. "Come on, you know. What's his name?"

"I don't know. I never could remember it. Bet he's a second lieutenant. I can see his gold bar from here," Porky said, scrutinizing him a bit.

Fran tapped on the window glass. "Hey. What's that cargo ship doing?"

Porky dropped his jaw and grunted in shock. "That's funny. It can't be leaving. It just got here. This is the only pier it could possibly dock at. Am I right?"

Fran was starting to sweat. "Now, why would the brass drop off a couple of thousand troops, but not food and equipment?"

"Maybe it's not equipment," Porky speculated.

"Not equipment? Then what the hell is it?" Fran was mad. "Let's see what the boys down below know," Porky recommended.

They walked down the flight of stairs and exited to the dock below. Fran was about six inches taller than Porky, so he took the lead in maneuvering through the crowd. But it was Franklin Bachelder who spotted them first.

"Hey, Musson, look who's here—a couple of guys from Athol," Bachelder said, waving Fran and Porky over. Porky grabbed Bachelder's outstretched hand and began the reintroductions.

"You may not remember me, I'm Franklin LaCoste from Athol, and this guy here is Francis Robichaud," Porky said with a smile. "Good to see you. Your dad runs an insurance company in town, right?"

"You betcha. Hey, I'm a Franklin too. But my friends call me Batch. You're Porky, Athol's star athlete, if memory serves me." Porky smiled and shook his head as if dismissing the comment. "You must remember Ralph Musson," he said as Fran and Porky shook Musson's hand.

"Doc Musson's son, right?" Porky inquired. "Hope he's doing well." Ralph nodded yes.

"We spotted you guys right away. Good to see you," Fran said, grinning from ear to ear. But soon Musson and Bachelder were pushed along by the troops.

Batch talked as he walked. "You guys stationed here at Nichols Field?"

"You bet. At least for now," Porky replied, keeping step beside him. "We're headed over to Fort Mills," Batch commented.

Fran maneuvered to the other side of Musson. "Fort Mills is about a couple of miles down the road. Wait 'till you hit Manila. You've never seen anything like it, especially the women."

"So we've heard," Musson said with a grin.

"Tell me. Why did the cargo ship take off?" Porky asked, attempting to appear nonchalant.

Musson bit his lower lip. "Yaw. It's kind of weird. Batch and I were wondering about that too. I can't figure out where the hell it's going. What I know is that *all*, and I mean *all*, our equipment is on board. So what the hell they're doing is beyond me," he said with a shrug. "Maybe the liner needs to move to let a cargo ship enter. It'll come back," Porky suggested.

Fran had resigned himself for the worst. "If it does, that'll be a first," he responded cynically.

The men exchanged knowing looks before Bachelder and Musson were forced to move on. "Hey. Great seeing you guys!" Batch called out. "Give us a call once you're settled," Fran called back.

Fran and Porky stepped aside to allow the others to pass. "There's only one place that cargo ship is headed, and that's Australia," Porky said bluntly.

"Do you get a funny feeling something's about to happen?" Fran ventured as he watched Musson and Batch blend into the two thousand troops ahead.

Porky walked to the edge of the pier and spit out into the water. "If it does, then they value the cargo more than they do the men."

Fran leaned against a post. "Well, maybe some brass at the top's pushing the panic button," he said, hoping against hope.

"It's tough to figure," Porky said, grabbing his pack of cigarettes. He slapped the bottom to pop one out for Fran.

"Yaw, when you think about it." Fran cupped his hand to shield the flame from the wind. "According to the pilots, the B-18s are decrepit. All we've really got here are P-35s, P-36s, and they're considered obsolete. 'Course, we just got in the B-17s but they're so big, looks to me like all they're good for is transport." He took a drag and exhaled, "The P-40s aren't so bad . . ."

"The talk is, those P-40s were never meant for us. They were bound for Finland or Denmark. But they were afraid they wouldn't reach their destination, so they're on their way to Australia," Porky said, coughing and spitting into the bay.

"Yaw, I heard the dashboard controls are in Danish," Fran added. "But the point is, they were afraid they were going to be intercepted."

"Yaw. So we've got ten P-40s. But maintenance tells me we've got no equipment or coolant for them," Fran added.

Porky pulled a cigarette from the pack. "Yesterday I took a hike down to the runway to check things out. A couple of civilians approached me. They said, 'It's going to happen.' They were wondering what our plans were to stop the attack." Porky looked Fran straight in the eyes. "You know what I'm driving at?"

"That's not a good sign," Fran responded with a hint of fear in his voice. "What did you tell them?"

"Nothing. I said nothing. I just listened and shook my head." Porky placed the cigarette between his lips. "What could I say?" His hands shook slightly as he lit the cigarette against the wind. He took a deep drag and exhaled slowly. "But I'll tell you something else, if you can keep it to yourself. There's a dozen or so B-17s at Clark Field. Despite what you say, that's the biggest bomber we've got."

"That's reassuring," Fran responded sarcastically.

"At least they can keep the Japs occupied while we duck for cover!" Porky replied, trying to make light of the situation.

"Before any attack begins, I'm heading for the hospital. I've got a growth on my foot that needs attending to," Fran said, pointing to his right foot.

Porky laughed. "Franny, hasn't anyone told you? You can't goldbrick your way out of a war?" Fran put an arm around his buddy's shoulder as they headed back to the Quartermaster Depot.

"And maybe you need to get that cough attended to. Tell them you've got malaria. Maybe they'll ship you back home," Fran ventured.

"Hey, Australia wouldn't be bad," Porky said.

End of Part 1

Lake Taal in southwestern Luzon

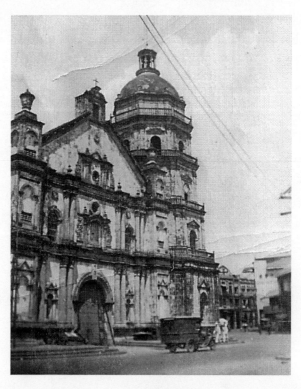

Binondo Church (Manila) 1941

Pasig 1941—Before the war
Courtesy LaCoste/Thurber family

Pre-war Barrio carnival, Manila. Even the children look apprehensive.
Courtesy LaCoste/Thurber family
Tondo District of Manila

Tondo before the Great Tondo Fire of 1941
Courtesy LaCoste/Thurber family

The Great Tondo Fire of 1941 served as a precursor to the devastation of 1945. Courtesy LaCoste/Thurber family

Tondo Funeral 1941
Courtesy LaCoste/Thurber family

Part 2

Athol, Massachusetts
Photo credit: Hames Photo Shop.
Courtesy Richard Chaisson

Chapter 12

Early in the afternoon on Sunday, December 7, 1941, the *Athol Daily News* received an Associated Press report from Washington. Japan had declared war on the United States. The newswire was a transcript of a broadcast from Honolulu, which claimed some 104 soldiers were reported dead and 300 wounded at Hickam Field, with numerous casualties at other locations. The wire also contained a report from the White House that Manila was attacked by Japanese. But the information was false, though it proved to be a prediction of things to come later that evening. A joint session of Congress was hastily being scheduled for Monday, December 8, according to the AP.

The editor gathered his staff together and began a mad scramble for additional stories. Perhaps Athol men were already dead or were among the wounded, they conjectured. For over a year, the paper had reported on local men who had joined the military and were to be stationed in the Pacific. As the staff hunted through files to gather names of the soldiers, the editor reminded his reporters to be extra sensitive as they made calls to family members and friends. Within hours they had their story, complete with photos.

Five-inch deep headlines read: "EXTRA EXTRA—JAPS DECLARE WAR ON U.S.; BOMB HAWAII, GUAM; 104 SOLDIERS DEAD—PRESIDENT TELLS ARMED FORCES TO CARRY OUT SECRET DEFENSE PLAN—DOZEN LOCAL MEN IN COMBAT AREA."

Beneath the headlines was the photograph taken in January aboard the USS *Leonard Wood*. The caption read, "Six of the Army Air Corps privates shown above lolling on the deck of an army transport en route to Manila now are in service in the Philippines with the forces which will be the first to fight back after the surprise Japanese attack before dawn Monday." Left to right, starting from the back row, the names listed began with Winston Lawson and ended with Francis W. Robichaud. A bare-chested Porky was shown next to a tee-shirt clad, normally dapper Herman Hausmann. In the front row, Bobby was half naked and happy, Billy Freeman was smiling but thin, and Fran appeared to have gained a few pounds.

There was a photo below the caption: "One Athol youth, Philip J. Dower of 159 Riverbend Street, is stationed at Schofield barracks, Hickam Field, where a bomb made a direct hit on the barracks." What was not reported was that Pinky had survived the attack. The headline of the article that accompanied the photos read: "Dozen Local Men In Combat Area".

Captured Japanese photograph taken aboard a Japanese carrier before the attack on Pearl Harbor, December 7, 1941.
Courtesy National Archives

As the paper was hitting the streets, it was still pre-dawn in the Philippines. The Japanese had planned an early Monday morning attack on Manila, but the planes had been delayed due to inclement weather. By 11:00 p.m. on Sunday, December 7 in Athol, it was approaching noon on Monday, December 8 in the Philippines, which is when Japanese planes approached. Bobby Doolan was an eyewitness as the American bombers stationed at Clark Field were strafed repeatedly and utterly destroyed. But Porky and the others at Nichols Field were spared this first onslaught.

Destruction at Hickam Field, where "Pinky" Dower was stationed.
Courtesy National Archives

President Roosevelt signs Declaration of War against Japan
Courtesy FDR Library and Museum

Chapter 13

In the predawn hours of Monday, December 8, Porky was sound asleep in his bunk. Weeks before, he had moved from the eighteen-man tent he had been assigned to as a private to a two-story barracks more befitting his status as corporal. Approximately 140 army bunks were in the room. Suddenly, the men were awakened by a loud whistle, followed by the crackling sound of the loudspeaker: "Now hear this. Now hear this. Now hear this. We have just received news that Pearl Harbor has been attacked by the Japanese. President Franklin Delano Roosevelt is preparing to address Congress to request a declaration of war against the Imperial State of Japan. All men report to headquarters for further instructions." Following the announcement, pandemonium broke loose as men scrambled to dress.

Several hours later, the soldiers had eaten and stood by the bulletin board, scanning the skies, waiting to read their assignments for the day. Headquarters had reassigned men based on the emergency preparations now underway. After reading his assignment, Porky was more confused than ever. "Where the hell is the ammunition dump?" he asked a nearby soldier as he pushed his way out of the crowd. "It says here I'm supposed to report to the ammunition dump."

The soldier was as confused as Porky, "All I know is—it's thataway," he said, pointing to the far left of the headquarters building. "I'm supposed to pick up a shovel and start digging a trench. Oh boy, I wish I was somewhere else," he said, turning from left to right, trying to get his bearings.

"Yaw. Well, good luck to you," Porky said, patting him on the back. "I guess we'll all need it."

Porky crossed the field and entered the ammunition bunker, which struck him as nothing more than a tractor shed minus the farm equipment, where hundreds of boxes of .50-caliber shells were stacked. A red-faced sergeant began screaming at Porky as well as the three men who trailed behind him.

"Grab them boxes of belts," he ordered, pointing to a stack of boxes. "They're for machine guns. Then come over here and I'll demonstrate how you put the bullets into the belts."

Porky and the others did as they were told.

"How many of you have worked with machine guns before?" the sergeant demanded to know.

The men stood in mute attention, afraid to speak.

"None of you, I bet. Well, my name is Dynamite Dunn, Sergeant Dunn to you. And I didn't get my nickname playing horseshoes," he said, then pointed to Porky. "Hand over one of them guns, a belt, and some ammunition, Corporal," Dunn ordered.

"Sir, before this, the closest I'd come to a machine gun was watching movies," Porky said as he grabbed the gun, belt, and ammunition. "Well, soldier, get used to it," Dunn snapped as he began to demonstrate. "The first thing to remember is to get the right ammo for the right gun. Trust me. Before the day is over, you men will know all you need to know about machine guns."

"LaCoste, Smith, pick up a box of guns and fill the back of the truck out front." Porky and Private Smith began loading the truck. "And you two—Jones and Granger, start loading the other trucks." Porky and Smith completed the initial assignment and reentered the shed, followed by the other men.

"Men, we've got foxholes being dug all around the base. Each of them holes is being given a number. Your job is to drop two guns and ammunition at each hole. Then come back and do it all again till the warehouse is empty. Yaw got that?" Sergeant Dunn asked gruffly.

After the first truck was loaded, Porky jumped behind the wheel as Smith opened the door to the passenger side. They took off, heading for the outskirts of the base, starting at the hangar line. As they rode, they saw men hard at work digging holes around the base. Porky pulled the truck up to a foxhole. They jumped out and began to unload machine guns and ammunition belts. A sergeant barked out orders to the soldiers nearby. "I need three men per hole," he said, pointing to three privates. "You three—grab that equipment the corporal's handing out and man this foxhole."

Later that evening, the soldiers gathered inside the headquarters mess hall. As they sat down for supper, it crossed Porky's mind that this might be their last meal together. He was exhausted. His arms and back ached as they had never ached before, but the pain was nothing compared with the disturbance that was growing in the pit of his stomach. He closed his eyes briefly and took a deep breath. He began to snap to when he scanned the faces of those around him. They were every bit as afraid as he was and just as exhausted, he thought as he watched men, elbows propped on the table, drop their heads into their hands and then onto the table to rest. His mood lightened when the KP approached with the food—bread, cold meat, and coffee. After supper, the men exited the mess hall and grouped outside around a sergeant who was giving out further orders.

"Men, go back to barracks," the sergeant instructed. "Grab blankets and a few personal belongings, then report to your assigned foxholes to bunk down for the night."

Porky hurried to the barracks, along with hundreds of other men. As he walked down the aisle to his bunk, he overheard two lieutenants chatting as they gathered their blankets and gear. "Hell. The foxhole's nearby. I can come back and get the rest of my stuff later," one bragged.

"Lucky you," the other replied as he tossed his blanket over his shoulder and tucked pictures of his family into his breast pocket. "I haven't got that luxury."

Porky grabbed his blanket then exited the barracks and wandered in the dark to a nearby trench. He was the last man in. As the others welcomed him, the sound of a small plane was heard overhead, followed immediately by the sound of machine-gun fire. Tracers lit up the sky like fireworks. "Doesn't that sound like a Piper Cub? How do they know it's the enemy?" Porky asked, concerned that it might be one of their flyers out on a scouting mission.

Private First Class Slater was a tall thin man who looked particularly cramped in such small quarters. "How do we know it's not the enemy?"

Porky offered him a cigarette. "Smoke?"

Slater relaxed and smiled, "Sure. Thanks."

The men lit their cigarettes and looked up at the star-studded sky. "Despite it all, it's a nice night," Porky commented as he maneuvered his way to a comfortable spot and spread out his blanket. He put out his cigarette in the dirt and pocketed it back into the pack. Just in case they became a luxury item, he thought as he collapsed in a heap onto the blanket. Within minutes he was fast asleep.

Barracks at Nichols Field, Porky's living quarters prior to the Japanese attack. Courtesy LaCoste/Thurber family

Chapter 14

On December 9, the men awoke as dawn's dim light stole into the trench. Breakfast was taken outside the mess hall, in case there was a need to quickly break for shelter. The soldiers were back to their assigned tasks when they heard the drone of approaching planes. They rushed to the foxholes as the base was strafed with bullets. But soon the planes were gone, and an all-clear signal was sounded.

Two days later, in the predawn hours, a warning shot was fired from a five-inch cannon to alert the men to a bombing raid. As the attack began, Porky and his foxhole companions awoke to see the field alive with soldiers carrying other soldiers in stretchers toward the base hospital. "Where are they bombing?" he asked.

"Seems to me they're aiming at the hangars, maybe hit the barracks too," Slater said, squinting into the darkness. A loud explosion lit up the sky as planes continued to circle like vultures over the base.

"I hope that wasn't the ammo dump," Porky offered with a trace of fear. He braced his back against the wall of the hole. "And I hope the officers followed their own orders and bunked in the foxholes for the night." He ran his hand through the dirt, searching for his half-used cigarette butt. He wondered how Bobby and Pint and Herman and Fran were doing. *Where's Billy?* he wondered. *He knew, he knew, he knew.*

"Goddamned fools," Slater sputtered, thoroughly disgusted, then slipped back down next to Porky. "Get this. Last night I spotted a couple of pilots heading toward barracks. Supposedly they were dropping by to pick up their belongings. But some of them ain't so used to camping. I'm sure they wanted to get a little shut-eye in comfort, like the rest of us poor slobs."

"Holy shit," Porky muttered.

"I never saw them come out," Slater confided. "They're goners for sure."

"You sure in hell got that straight," Porky said as he watched the smoke from his cigarette waft up out of the trench.

December 10, 1941—Nichols Field Bombed and Burning
Courtesy National Archives

As daylight broke, the bombing ceased and the drone of planes grew distant. Fire trucks rushed toward the hangars and barracks, ablaze in brilliant gold and red against the pastel hues of the dawn. As the men poured out of their foxholes, it became apparent that several buildings had been totally obliterated, while others suffered serious damage. The men headed toward the mess hall, which had miraculously been left standing. Once again, tables were set up outside. The KPs were busily setting out food and drink on the tables for the waiting men.

Porky grabbed a couple of biscuits and coffee and sat next to several other men he had never seen before. The events of the last few days had been so horrifying it was almost painful to hang out with his childhood friends. But he searched through the crowd, spotted Pint and Fran at a nearby table, and waved. They pointed to a table at the far end of the field and shouted, "Herman and Billy are over there."

Porky flashed the A-OK sign, hoping that Bobby had also made it through, and then sat back down to eat. "It's not much, but it's better than nothing," he said to the men as Private First Class Slater joined them.

"Well, Corporal, I wonder what's for lunch," Slater asked sardonically.

"Hopefully, the Japs haven't barbecued all our steaks and hot dogs. 'Course, even if they're a bit overdone, might not be that bad. I'll eat anything," Porky said through bites.

A sergeant approached the tables. "Men, when you're through eating, start heading toward Fort McKinley. Emergency headquarters are being set up over there."

The soldiers finished breakfast and began to cluster in groups for the short walk to the army base, adjacent to Nichols Field. But a few preferred to walk alone. Porky caught up with a group walking ahead.

"Do any of you know what's going on? For one thing, who's in charge?" Porky inquired, hoping perhaps he had missed a communication and that he alone was out of the loop.

"If Major Davis survived, I suppose he's in charge," a private responded. He was about Porky's height and appeared to be a Mexican American based on his accent.

"Corporal LaCoste," Porky said, shaking the man's hand. "And you are?"

"Private First Class Jose Martinez, sir," the private responded.

"Well, Private, I guess my next question is—in charge of what? We left all our machine guns in the foxholes," Porky said, knitting his brows.

"The only gun I've handled is a Springfield rifle. Maybe I'm wrong, but frankly, I don't think that'd be much help against a bombing raid," the private said as he walked a bit faster to catch up with his companions.

"From the look of the barracks and hangars, the machine guns weren't of much use either. How many of our planes did we lose, I wonder?" Porky continued.

"The question is, how many do we have left?" Private First Class Martinez snapped back as a truck pulled up alongside them. Major Hyde was in the back.

The major leaned out of the truck and shouted, "I need you men for a special detail."

Sergeant Hill was leading the men to the fort. "Sir, we've been ordered by our commander to head toward Fort McKinley," he shouted back.

The major ordered the driver to pull ahead of the men and stop. He stood, towering over the men from the platform of the truck bed. "I don't care if you disobey orders. If you don't hop onto the back of this truck, I'll see to it that every one of you is court-martialed," he yelled back, red-faced with anger.

Major Hyde jumped off the back of the truck and scrambled into the passenger side of the cab. Every soldier, including Porky and the sergeant, hopped into the rear of the truck. Moments later, they were headed off to the City of Manila. Once inside the downtown area, the truck turned onto a side street and minutes later stopped in front of a large nightclub, the Shangri-la, which had a wide veranda and portico entry.

The major got out of the cab and walked to the rear of the truck. "Your job is to guard this building."

"But it's a nightclub. It's off-limits to the men," Sergeant Hill protested.

"You've got your orders! Hop to it, sergeant," the major insisted. Sergeant Hill jumped off the back of the truck but resisted by turning his back to the major and walking a short way down the sidewalk. He stopped after a few moments, took out a cigarette, and lit up. He stood silently staring into the roadway, fuming, feeling utterly stymied by the arrogance of this so-called superior officer. The soldiers looked at one another and then one by one jumped off the back of the truck and quickly entered the club. Inside, the lights were dim but the men could see that there were three bars and an enormous polished dance floor.

The major knew he would get nowhere further with the sergeant, so he followed the men inside. "Jesus Christ," he yelled. "Where are your brains? Outside, you bastards," he ordered. "You guard outside. No GIs are allowed inside. Didn't you hear the sergeant? No GIs are allowed inside," he ranted, shoving them out the door. Once outside, he regained his composure—somewhat. "Your orders are to protect the building in case anyone tries to loot the place. Make sure no one enters unless they're authorized." He grabbed the cab handle, yanked it open, and jumped back into the passenger side as the driver took off toward Fort McKinley. The soldiers exchanged looks, shrugged, and positioned themselves for guard duty.

Porky approached Sergeant Hill. "I wonder how long we're here for."

"Your guess is as good as mine, Corporal," Hill replied, still hot under the collar. He walked back to join the men. "I hope you guys have money for food, because I'm sure it's not going to be supplied," Hill informed them, straining not to take his anger out on the soldiers.

"Is this legal?" Martinez asked. The sergeant spit onto the sidewalk. "I've got a strong feeling it's not regulation. But he's a major, so he could make a lot of trouble if we don't comply." Hill's moral victory was that it was the major who had given the orders, not him.

Moments later Japanese bombers were spotted approaching the base, followed by the sound of warning cannons, which echoed throughout the

P35 Pursuit plane, the US Army Air Corps' first modern production fighter with all-metal construction, enclosed cockpit, and retractable landing gear. Courtesy Department of Defense

city. The men watched as bombs were dropped on Nichols Field, which was soon enveloped in smoke. The Japanese bombers disappeared from view, followed by flight after flight of Japanese pursuit planes that appeared from the southwest and began strafing the base with machine-gun fire. Several American planes took to the air. Soon, a dogfight began a quarter of a mile away, which for the men seemed right before their eyes. They stood and watched in horror, frozen in place as the drama unfolded. "I wonder what's happening at Clark Air Base," the sergeant ventured, fearing the worst.

"Do we really want to know?" Porky replied, choking back tears as he remembered Bobby. Several American planes dropped from the sky and exploded as enemy planes continued to strafe the airfield, the rising sun insignia bold against the blue and smoke-filled sky. At last, the battle ended, but victory was theirs. As the drone of the planes faded, the sky was shrouded in smoldering haze and silent. Soon afterward, a Filipina approached from the restaurant across the street, wearing a pale blue sarong and a worn-out look on her face. She carried a tray of food, which she offered to the men. Within moments, three more women spilled from the restaurant, bearing food and drinks. Sergeant Hill was delighted to see them. He dug in his pocket for some change and attempted to hand it to the women.

"No thanks. This is for you—free. You help protect," the woman in the blue dress insisted. Her soft smile caressed the stricken men.

"That's awfully kind of you," Porky said, his voice cloudy with emotion. He grabbed roasted pork from the platter and smiled in gratitude.

Sergeant Hill walked from platter to platter, grabbing bites from each. "This is the best food I've had since the bombing started. Ladies, you are wonderful!"

"Funny, I didn't feel hungry 'til I saw the food. It's amazing how a few bombs can make you forget about food—and your friends, for that matter," Porky said, downing freshly prepared lemonade.

"Yeah, it's tough," Martinez agreed. He scuffed at the dirt on the road with the toe of his boot. "But better eat up now, 'cause who the hell knows where our next meal's coming from. By the way, where are we supposed to bunk down, on the sidewalk?"

"Hell no, there's a porch. Take a look—a couple of the guys have already bunked down, not that the major would approve." Porky waved to Private First Class Slater, who was making a show of relaxing on the veranda as if he were living in the lap of luxury.

"Hey, come on over and join us," Slater called, his hands clasped beneath his head. "It's not so bad here. The bamboo floor's got a little give to it. 'Course, it's a bit bumpy in spots."

Porky thumbed his nose at Slater, who cracked up laughing. He then turned his attention to Sergeant Hill. "To think, I wanted to spend the rest of my military career here. As a matter of fact, I was ready to stay for life!"

"If the major has anything to say about it, you will," Hill quipped, lowering his tall frame down onto the cement curb. Porky joined him for a smoke as the rest of the men bunked down on the porch.

Porky buys a Sunday newspaper, Downtown Manila (pre-war 1941)
Courtesy LaCoste/Thurber family

Chapter 15

The morning sun rose over the rooftops of the shoe shop, bakery, and restaurant into the Shangri-la veranda and warmed the soldiers sprawled every which way across the bamboo of the porch floor. The street was quiet except for chirps of a few mole crickets swimming around in a nearby puddle as they tugged at a few grains of rice. A sailfin lizard crawled out from under the porch and was sunning itself on the curbstone as a truck pulled up. A slim, long-nosed Lieutenant Green got out from the passenger side and slammed the door shut, hoping the sound would wake the men. The men opened their eyes to find the lieutenant standing on the porch, peering down at them.

"Men, jump in the truck," Green said briskly. "You're headed for another assignment." He walked back to the cab of the truck and hopped in as the soldiers scrambled onto the back of the truck. They were headed off to Quezon City, northwest of Manila. The city was founded by and named after Manuel Quezon, who dreamed that Quezon City would one day replace Manila as the capital of the Philippines. Quezon was a noted politician and the first nationally elected president of the country. He was also an important American ally who had been reelected by a landslide a month earlier.

The truck drove to the southeast outskirts of Quezon, to a manufacturing area that bordered Manila, and pulled up to the curb next to a former Japanese-owned bicycle factory, a large U-shaped brick building. The lieutenant stepped out of the cab and walked to the rear of the truck.

"This is it, men. Look it over and I'll be back with some food. And I mean just that," the lieutenant cautioned. "Look it over before you touch anything. It could be booby-trapped." The soldiers jumped off the truck and reassembled on the sidewalk. "The Philippine army has a supply base nearby. I'll get enough food to last us a day or two," Lieutenant Green continued. "While I'm gone, check out the basement. That's where the machine shop is. We'll need it. See if you can get some locals to help. After you've checked out the basement, I want you to check upstairs; later, we'll start cleaning. That's where our living quarters will be."

The lieutenant saluted the men then stepped back into the truck and signaled his driver to move on. Sergeant Hill instructed the men to follow the lieutenant's orders, enter the building, and begin operations to clear the debris. As they moved from sunlight into the shade of the enclosure, the soldiers behaved as if they were walking on eggshells until they spotted a 1928 Model-A Ford at the rear of the building. It was a standard black, two-door sedan with a running board, a rectangular flat top, and spoked wheels. Seeing something familiar, a car that their grandparents drove, made them feel at home. They relaxed but still approached the vehicle with caution. One of the GIs, Pvt. Hank Mosley, slowly opened the door to the driver's side. Everyone else scattered, concerned that the car might be rigged to explode. It didn't, so they moved on to find tasks that looked harmless, like sweeping up and picking scraps of metal, gears, and chains from the trash and sorting them into piles.

Hank grew up on a subsistence farm in the Midwest where survival dictated that one improvise with vehicles and equipment. As a soldier, he was valued as a crackerjack mechanic. He checked in the ashtray, found the key, inserted it into the ignition, but it wouldn't start. He pushed up the hood from the side, which peaked like a roof, checked the engine, and then slipped under the car for a quick inspection. Following that, he ventured down a flight of stairs and returned with welding equipment. Hank was soon engrossed in welding a five-gallon can onto the fender. That finished, he grabbed copper tube from a shelf and ran it from the can to the carburetor.

Porky was supervising the nearby cleanup but turned to watch Hank while his buddy, Private First Class Martinez, swept up debris. "What's he doing?" Porky asked.

Jose leaned on the broom for a moment. "Can't you see? The gas tank has a leak. He's improvising," he explained with a laugh and continued sweeping.

"That's smart," Porky admitted. He waited for Hank to shut off the welding implement and then approached. "Look, Private. I've got twenty-five bucks in the YMCA bank. What do you say we drive down to Manila? I'll draw it out and then we can pick up some beer. The lieutenant's getting us some food. We'll need something to drink," Porky suggested.

"Sounds like a deal to me," Hank said as he poured gasoline into the newly improvised "gas can." He turned to Porky and smiled, then hopped into the Model-A to check it out. The car started right up.

Porky reached in through the open window to shake the mechanic's hand. "Corporal LaCoste."

"Private First Class Mosley, sir."

"Hank, is it?"

"Yes, sir."

Porky walked over to the passenger side, opened the door, stepped onto the running board, and slid in as Hank maneuvered the vehicle out of the garage into the driveway. He turned left onto the road and headed toward Manila.

"Let's head back to the base before we go to the Y. I've got some things I want to get out of my footlocker," Private Mosley suggested. Porky couldn't think of a reason not to go. Catching flack from the Jap Zeros was a matter of bad luck. Hadn't they done enough damage to the base? Nowhere was safe, he reasoned. Besides, it was a beautiful day and they deserved a chance to take a relaxing drive back to their old headquarters.

Dewey Boulevard, Manila
Courtesy LaCoste/Thurber family

After a while, they came to a crossroad. The private swung to the left again but this time headed straight for Nichols Field. As they approached the base, the full extent of the damage became apparent. The place was utterly devastated, left in ruins.

"Jesus Christ Almighty," Hank muttered as he pulled up to the barracks.

Porky was speechless. He felt numb. The barracks were completely strafed, riddled with bullet holes. As they got out of the car, the warning cannon fired. Japanese dive-bombers could be seen approaching fast from the east. The men jumped back into the Model-A. As they drove past the hangar line, bombs began to drop nearby. Porky leaned over and yelled into his ear. "Hank, stop the car. Let's head into the swamp before they blow us to hell."

Nichols Field stream and mud flats
Courtesy LaCoste/Thurber family

The private pulled the car to a stop. They jumped out and splashed into a stream, thick with mud. Bombs dropped onto the hangar less than a hundred yards away. The whistling of the bombs was deafening. Porky blocked his ears with his fingers and pushed his head into the muck to escape the noise. Before long, the planes continued on to the other end of the field.

Porky and Hank pulled themselves up out of the marsh and slowly approached the car. Mud clumped and stuck like glue on their hair, faces, and hands, onto their uniforms, and oozed into their boots. They wiped off as much as they could and got back into the car and headed back to the barracks. They bolted out of the vehicle into the former sleeping quarters, afraid that the bombers might double back. Once inside, they stood silent in a state of complete shock. Beds, clothes, and footlockers had been so thoroughly strafed that everything was totally destroyed. They left the barracks in silence and jumped back into the car. Hank swung the car around and headed back to Manila to the YMCA, while Porky kept a watchful eye on the sky and checked for bombers.

Intramuros—The Walled City—Manila
Courtesy LaCoste/Thurber family

The car swung onto a boulevard and headed toward the Intramuros, the medieval Spanish section of Manila. There were two YMCAs in Manila. One was for civilians and located behind Manila City Hall. The other was built in Intramuros to service the U.S. Army. This Y was an imposing three-storied structure, salmon colored and constructed of reinforced concrete in a neoclassical style with large Palladian windows, wide overhangs, and a red-tiled roof. As the men entered the ancient walled section of the city, they relaxed. Manila had not been bombed; at least not yet.

"You know, at one point during the bombing, I thought we wouldn't make it," Porky admitted. "The whistling from the bombs was so loud I thought, 'This one's coming for me.' And then know what happened? All the sins I've ever committed flashed through my mind. Not that I intend to stop committing them," Porky said with a short laugh.

"Yaw. It was close. But I knew we were OK," Hank said as he turned a narrow corner and approached the Y.

"And you were right," Porky said, shaking his head as if it might wake him from a bad dream.

Santos Tomas University patio inside the Walled City
Courtesy LaCoste/Thurber family

Hank pulled up to the curb but decided not to shut off the ignition. "I'm afraid to turn off the motor. We'll never get it started again. So make it snappy," he said as Porky jumped out of the vehicle.

Porky responded with a thumbs-up then turned and walked up the steps, swung the wide, heavy door open, and entered. It was cool inside. The ceilings were high and wide and felt more like the entryway to a basilica than to a recreational building. Porky's muddy boots had dried but left small clumps of dirt on the polished tile floor as he walked through the hallway toward the teller's cage. Traces of mud were still stuck to his neck and hair, and his clothes were damp and discolored with dirt.

"I'd like to withdraw all my funds," Porky said to the clean and tidy Filipino clerk as he handed over his bankbook. He noticed that his hands were still dirty. He wiped them along the sides of his pants as the clerk looked him over.

After a moment, the clerk busied himself with the task at hand. He perused the account book, then opened the cash drawer and proceeded to count out the money. "Five hundred pesos," he said, handing over a variety of Philippine bank note denominations.

Porky smiled and inquired, "Would you happen to know where I could buy some beer?"

"There is no beer." Porky's smile faded. "There's no liquor available anywhere. Everything's locked up tight."

"Why? Are they afraid of looters?" Porky inquired.

"My guess is, the longer they wait, the higher the price!" the clerk said with a knowing wink.

"So what are we supposed to drink?"

"The store at the corner is open. They've got soda pop and milk," he offered.

"Milk?" Porky was flabbergasted. What would his fellow soldiers think of him?

"Yes, sir, white or chocolate. Now if you'll excuse me," he said as he drew the shade down on the window.

Porky wasn't sure if he was closed for business or anxious to get rid of him. "Chocolate milk. Say, that's not half bad," he said to himself as he walked down the long corridor and exited outside to the waiting car. "I've got pesos to burn, and there's no beer anywhere. Do you think the men will be disappointed if I pick up a couple of cases of chocolate milk?" Porky asked Hank as he slid back into the passenger side of the Model-A.

**Taft Avenue, Ermita District outside the Intramuros
During the 1945 Battle of Manila, much of Ermita was destroyed.**
Courtesy LaCoste/Thurber family

The drive from Manila back to Quezon City was pleasant and peaceful. Porky leaned back in the cracked leather seat. He thrust his hand out the window as if to grab the sunshine and warm and cool air currents and let them pass through and reenergize his body. He savored the view. The lush landscape and floral gardens surrounding the stucco and bamboo homes along the way were gorgeous and very upscale. "This has got to be one of the richest neighborhoods in Quezon City—probably in all of the Philippines. I wonder who lives here."

"Politicians and bankers, I suspect," Hank responded as he turned onto a palm-tree-lined boulevard, which led to the commercial and industrialized area.

"Beautiful day," Porky said, staring into the clear blue sky.

Hank pulled up to the bike factory and turned to Porky. He pulled the hand brake and opened the door. "Well, here we are. It's a wonder we made it."

Lieutenant Green and several soldiers were seated on the curb, legs stretched out in front of them. They had been waiting patiently for their return.

"Chocolate milk. Come and get your chocolate milk!" Porky shouted through the open window. He grabbed the milk bottles and stepped onto the curb. Lieutenant Green walked up to the car to help Porky.

"Chocolate milk? Hey. What happened to the beer?" he asked as he grabbed a few bottles and cradled them in his arms. The soldiers who had been sitting with Lieutenant Green laughed and headed toward the car. They planned to rib Porky unmercifully. But instead, an explosion was heard from what seemed to be the back of the factory.

"Goddamn booby traps," Lieutenant Green yelled, handing the milk back. Glass clinked upon glass as Porky carefully placed the bottles onto the floor of the passenger side and pushed them under the dashboard to shield them from the glare of the sun. He closed the door with care, trying not to rattle them further, and then ran to join the soldiers who were making a mad dash toward the building.

The bike factory was U-shaped, with a small courtyard in the middle of the complex. The structure comprised a large rectangle, which housed a machine shop in the basement, and two smaller buildings attached to either end. The plan was to secure the use of the machine shop to help the U.S. military operations. Filipino civilians had been employed to search out booby traps. Following the explosion, the building and courtyard filled with smoke and two of the Filipino workers ran from the basement tunnel, situated within the main building, into the courtyard. The men's clothes had been blown off, their eyeballs hung from their cheeks, and their skin was shriveled and bloody.

"Help me. Oh God, help me," the men screamed.

Porky and Jose grabbed the men, threw them over their shoulders, and raced toward the Model-A. Hank jerked open the door and pulled the seat back while Jose and Porky carefully sat them in the backseat of the car. As he pushed the front seat back in place, Porky's eyes fell on the chocolate milk. The bottles clanked as his bloodied hands grabbed to unload them once again, carefully placing them along the sidewalk away from the curb. Hank hopped into the car and sped away with the critically injured men to the hospital.

Porky and Jose reentered the factory to investigate the extent of the damage. They were joined by several marines who had been assigned to other areas of the factory. The machine shop where the explosion occurred was totally destroyed, with tire molds, rubber bike tires, machining equipment, and shards of metal and chain strewn about. A marine major and a young lieutenant lay dead on the floor.

Marine Sergeant Kelly was the first to approach. He dropped to his knees to examine the bodies. "Oh my God, what a mess," he said, fighting back tears. "Major Hannigan had just introduced us to his son—not ten minutes before the explosion. It looks like it's too late for an ambulance." Porky stood stunned. "His son?"

The bodies were so mangled the sergeant had trouble pointing out which was the father and which the son.

"Major Hannigan is dead there next to his son, 2nd Lt. Ralph Hannigan. This is unbelievable. They died together. Can you imagine?"

"I'd hate to be the one who informs the family," Porky said, struggling with the weight of the tragedy.

"That's odd. Both their right legs are blown off," Jose said, then averted his eyes.

Soldiers who had been scouting out the grounds entered and gathered around the carnage but were soon overcome by the horror of the situation. They stared in silence at the corpses. Lieutenant Green made his way down a flight of stairs, waded through the debris, and stopped to examine the bodies.

"All men are accounted for, Lieutenant," Sergeant Kelly reported. "Two have been taken to the hospital. As you can see, Major Hannigan and his son are dead."

Lieutenant Green was visibly shaken. "Terrible, just terrible," he muttered, fighting against breaking down. Green's mind was spinning. He stood in silence with the men as his thoughts turned to the events of the last few days. He feared they had been sucked into a maelstrom of unimaginable consequences. His job was to keep things as sane and orderly as possible until help arrived, but he feared the Hannigans' deaths were a harbinger of things to come. If help didn't arrive soon, all hell would break loose.

"I've checked out the rest of the factory. The old living quarters upstairs are still structurally sound. Corporal LaCoste, get a few men together and go upstairs. Clean up the quarters; at least make it livable," the lieutenant ordered. "We don't know how long we'll be here, but we'd better make the best of it. I'll deal with matters down here."

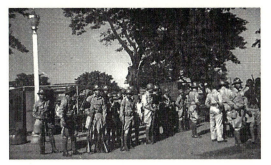

Philippine Army squadron (pre-war photo)
Courtesy LaCoste/Thurber family

Chapter 16

In 1898 following the Spanish-American War, the United States took possession of the Philippine Islands at the insistence of Britain because the British Empire's resources were already stretched to the hilt. Annexation of the Philippines meant control over the sea lanes going to China and also ensured access to three of the greatest ports in the world: Manila, Cebu, and Davao.

Following World War I, a strategy was developed in case the United States was ever at war in both the Atlantic and Pacific simultaneously. Pursuant to War Plan Rainbow, potential enemies were assigned code colors. Japan was Code Orange. The plan included a buildup of U.S. naval and army defenses, as well as the creation of Philippine scout regiments serving as U.S. forces. Later, when the Commonwealth of the Philippines was formed, the United States Congress passed a bill mandating the creation of a 100,000-man army that initially would be under U.S. control. In 1935, with President Roosevelt's approval, Philippine President Manuel Quezon hired General MacArthur—who had completed his tour as Army Chief of Staff—to supervise the creation of a Philippine Army and serve as its Field Marshall. MacArthur served in this position until he was recalled by President Roosevelt into active military service as concerns grew about a possible war with Japan.

On July 26, 1941, MacArthur was appointed commander of the U.S. Army Forces in the Far East (USAFFE). Soon after his appointment, he revised earlier war plans and requested vast shipments of men and equipment to the Philippines to shore up defenses and supply the fledgling Philippine Army. Washington agreed, and plans were underway to transport the desperately needed supplies at the time the Japanese attack occurred. On December 3rd, U.S. and Philippine forces were assigned to Northern and Southern Luzon, Visayan-Mindanao and Harbor Defenses, but no mention was made of holding the beaches.

Shortly after the bombing of airbases on the main island of Luzon commenced, Japanese Imperial Forces under the command of Lt. General Masaharu Homma landed and easily overpowered U.S. and Philippine resistance. But the bombing of Pearl Harbor had rendered any plans to rescue the Philippines a hopeless dream. By Christmas Eve the Japanese had successfully completed the first stage of their invasion and U.S. Army and Navy planners in Washington admitted that the Philippines were now indefensible.

Courtesy Department of Defense

Manila was declared an Open City on December 26th, and all military forces were asked to leave by the 30th. Despite this attempt to spare the lives of the civilian population, Lt. General Homma ordered that Manila be bombed on December 27th and 28th. As a result, hundreds died. At this stage, elements of the earlier Code Orange war plan were implemented. These included abandoning the bases around Manila and other areas throughout

Luzon to retire into the natural jungle fortress of the Bataan peninsula, where they would make a united stand. The coastal artillery stationed at Corregidor would protect the rear, but hopes were that the Navy would come to their rescue with food, equipment, and fully armed carrier battleships was an abandoned dream.

####

Porky hummed a boogie-woogie tune Herman had often played as he helped out in the factory living quarters. He was busy covering a partially eaten twenty-pound round of cheese with the wrapper it came in while guessing at its current weight. Others organized food the lieutenant had secured, boxing it for transport. Lieutenant Green walked upstairs to inform them that the convoy would be arriving any minute.

"The Twenty-seventh Material Squadron—that's my unit. I haven't seen the guys since the war began. When was that now, five or six days ago? No. Let me think now. Can it be two weeks?" Porky asked, genuinely confused by the rush of events.

"I don't know. I've lost track," Lieutenant Green admitted. "Look, when we join the convoy we're moving on to Bataan."

"Bataan," Porky repeated with a shake of his head. "Never heard of it. Where the hell's Bataan?"

"It's on the other side of the island. It's a peninsula that juts out into Manila Bay. From the tip you can see Corregidor," the lieutenant explained. A soldier entered and announced the arrival of the convoy. The men grabbed the food and exited the building. Several tractor-trailers as well as smaller trucks had entered the driveway that circled the courtyard. The commanding officer, Captain Stewart, stepped out from one of the trucks and pointed to a group of GIs.

"Men, hop onto the back of the truck," the captain ordered. "Corporal, jump into the tractor-trailer," he said to Porky. "I want you to assist Sergeant Dunn."

Sergeant Dunn. Yes, it was one and the same, Porky thought as he lifted himself into the passenger side of the big rig. Sergeant "Dynamite" Dunn was at the wheel. "Morning, Sergeant."

Dunn maneuvered them out of the courtyard into the road. "Good to see you again, Corporal," he said with a nod.

"Dynamite Dunn! I never thought I'd see you again," Porky said with a short laugh. "How the hell have you been?"

"No complaints. We're eating and breathing. But who the hell knows what's going to happen next?"

"Did you get a chance to get back to the base?" Porky asked. "Nope. We just went down to Fort McKinley and now we're on a run to Bataan," Dunn said with a grunt.

"Well. I made it back," Porky shared. "The ammo dump and where I worked are all blown to bits."

"A tractor shed makes a great target," Dunn said, careful to keep his eyes on his driving. They were moving slowly through the city but if the trucks ahead came to a stop sign, or orders were given to halt, he had to react fast because his rig was slow to stop. "Hey, wasn't your office right by the runway?" he asked.

"You got it."

"Our planes were the first thing hit."

"I'm not surprised."

"Porky, do me a favor. Stick your head out the window. I need you to keep a sharp eye out for Jap planes. We're a perfect target."

Porky grabbed the window rim and pulled himself half-ways out. Blue skies ahead, above, and behind, with a scattering of clouds and birds in flight was all he saw. Before long the convoy pulled alongside the road.

"LaCoste," Dunn yelled. "Haul your ass inside." Porky pulled himself back inside, stretched, and relaxed, happy to be seated comfortably once again. Dunn steered hard to the right and slowly applied the brakes as he straightened out the wheel. "We're pulling over so the brass can bring us up to date on whatever the hell it is they think they're doing."

"You think they know?" Porky quipped.

"We'll soon find out. Look. I have to walk up to the front of the convoy for instructions," Dunn explained. "When the convoy moves out, bring the tractor forward to wherever I am. I'll hop in then."

Dynamite Dunn jumped down from the cab and walked to the front of the convoy. Porky grabbed the steering wheel and pulled himself over to the driver's side to practice shifting so he could drive the trailer once he received orders. Porky pushed his foot down toward the pedals, but he was unable to reach them. At five feet four and a half inches, his legs were too short. Now he understood why the army had hesitated to accept him. He was perfect for a desk job, but the obligations of war were another matter, he thought as he broke out in a sweat.

Porky attempted to move the seat forward, but it wouldn't budge. He rocked back and forth, trying to move the seat, but that wasn't working either.

He looked around the cab and then got on his knees to check out what might be stored in the back of the seat. *At least I've got brains*, he reasoned as he fumbled to grab hemp bags stashed next to a tool kit. He grabbed a bundle, shoved it against his back, and readjusted himself in the seat. This time he was able to reach the pedals, but was barely able to see over the dashboard. Just then, the convoy began to move. Porky turned the key and the motor revved up. He pulled out slowly, keeping the vehicle in first gear as he strained to see ahead. He came to a stop by Dynamite Dunn, who howled with laughter as he opened the door.

"Jesus Christ! What are you—a midget?"

"Pretty near. I'm so short, I had to pull strings to get into the service," Porky said with a smirk.

"In other words, you could have beaten the rap?" Dunn said, shaking his head in disbelief.

"Hell, what did I know? I thought I was heading to paradise," Porky admitted, then stuck his head out the window to search for enemy planes.

Fighting Filipino
U.S. War Department Poster
Courtesy of Department of Defense

Chapter 17

The convoy began to spread out and gain speed as they left the city limits for the open road. Dynamite and Porky relaxed as they drove along the main road leading from Manila through the river delta area of the Bulacan region. Rice paddies and swamps seemed a pastoral retreat from the urgencies and noise of war. They were headed thirty-five miles north-northwest to San Fernando, in Pampanga Province. San Fernando was the chief connecting point for all the troops stationed in Luzon. There was some concern that

Filipina girls gathering coconuts
Courtesy LaCoste/Thurber family

enemy planes might take advantage of this fact if they anticipated MacArthur's directives.

The convoy passed through San Fernando without incident, stopping briefly to allow the senior officers to confer about details of where each unit would encamp and the latest word on the advance of Japanese battalions. From there they would take a sharp left, almost a U-turn, and head southwest for about twenty-five miles until they came to the top of the Bataan Peninsula. Then the convoy would head south along Highway 7, down the East Road, a route that would place them on the opposite side of Manila Bay. Midway they would be directly across the bay from the capital city by about twenty-eight miles. At the southernmost tip of Bataan, Corregidor would be in view. It was here that General MacArthur retreated once he abandoned his Manila headquarters. He had set up Corregidor as a fortified military headquarters where he would command the strategic defense of the Philippines, which for all practical purposes now meant the defense of Bataan.

Lt. Gen. Masaharu Homma, 14th Army Commander, Japanese Imperial Forces comes ashore at Lingayen Gulf, 24 December 1941
Courtesy Department of Defense

Shortly after the war began, enemy forces had landed on the northwest coast of Luzon at the Gulf of Lingayen and further up at Vigan as well as at the northern tip of the island at Aparri. Porky remembered Bobby saying if you continued north from San Fernando, you would eventually arrive at Clark Field, where he was stationed. A shiver passed through him. Clark Field would have been heavily bombed at the outset of the war and later as the battalions of Japanese headed down from Lingayen in light tanks, on horseback and, as was rumored, mounted on bicycles. The Japanese forces would have passed through the base as they fought their way to the capital city. The Southern Luzon divisions urgently needed to cross the San Fernando River before the Imperial forces reached it. Once the remaining tanks crossed the bridge, it would be blown up, just as the bridge over the Pampanga River had been destroyed earlier. But the most daring gambit involved safe passage over the bridge at Calumpit, just south of San Fernando, where Highway 3 from Northern Luzon to Manila joined with Highway 7 leading into Bataan. The Northern Luzon troops were charged with holding the enemy back from San Fernando and the Calumpit bridge until the Southern Luzon forces had passed. They then moved on to join the Americans at Bataan to prepare for the siege that would soon follow. If they hadn't succeeded, MacArthur

Philippine Scouts. "Bataan was defended by 62,000 Filipinos and 12,000 Americans. The Filipinos did most of the fighting and dying on Bataan. The Filipinos death rate on Bataan was 30 times higher than the American death rate. Their death rate on the Death March and in Camp O'Donnell was 10 times higher than that of the Americans." (Federico Baldassarre 2007) Courtesy Department of Defense

would have lost more than half the forces he needed to defend Bataan and Corregidor.

The courageous men who accomplished this feat were the Filipino troops whose service was invaluable throughout the battle and the occupation.

As the afternoon wore on, the convoy slowed as it entered the narrow eastern Bataan road at Layac. The Malasimbu Mountain and steep jungle forest confronted them on their right. They were about to join what would soon become the seventy-four thousand American and Philippine troops distributed over two hundred square miles of Bataan. For the most part it was relatively safe at the moment; most of the enemy's efforts were still north of Bataan. However, the troops holding the trails and interior pockets of resistance fought bravely when the enemy advanced. Once entrenched, the advantage they had was the nearly impenetrable nature of the thick jungle cover of this mountainous terrain and the fact that the maps were unreliable. As confused as the troops were, the Japanese were new to the region and even more confused. Most dug in, as had their U.S. counterparts, and waited.

Porky strained his neck, looking up at the steep terrain of Mount Natib. It rose 4,220 feet above sea level. Ahead was Mount Bataan that topped Mt. Natib at 4,660 feet. Both had 4-mile craters at the top. Between the two volcanic mountains is the Pilar/Bagac Road, a pass that transverses the peninsula from east to west. At the southern base of Mount Bataan, carved into the foothill below, was Mariveles Airfield; below that was the Mariveles Naval Station on the southwest tip of the peninsula. Mariveles was the final stop on the East Road overlooking Manila Bay and the beginning of the West Road, which headed north overlooking the South China Sea.

The convoy continued with plans to reach their destination before nightfall. They passed through the towns of Limay and Lamao, drove past the Bataan airfield and the airfield at Cabcaben, adjacent to the village. Ahead was a small roadside stand with a Coca-Cola sign. Dynamite Dunn knew they were close to their assigned encampment so he pulled the big rig into a paved parking area to the side of the stand. Porky opened the door and jumped out onto broken pavement. A pretty young Filipina with her hair pulled back in a ponytail appeared at the open window. Porky asked for four Cokes and then dug in his pocket for change.

"Twenty centavos, please, for four Cokes," she said in perfect English as she handed the bottles over.

"Twenty it is," Porky said with a smile. She didn't smile back. He wondered if she was the proprietor's daughter and had been warned about American men. Her father must guard her with a shotgun, he thought, then realized with a shudder that once the Japanese landed, a shotgun wouldn't help much.

"That's a nickel apiece in American money," he said as he grabbed the Cokes. *If her father is the owner, I'm sure she knows it's a nickel apiece in American money.* Porky blushed with embarrassment, hoping he hadn't offended her. *She must think I'm a moron*, he conjectured as he walked back to the tractor-trailer and handed the Cokes to Dunn. He pulled himself back into the truck cab and the sergeant drove off. Ahead were two hospitals—one for civilians and the other for base personnel. As they rounded the edge of the southern tip, headed for Mariveles, MPs standing alongside the road directed each outfit to a designated location. Dunn pulled the big rig over and braked to a stop. The men popped off the caps and drank the Cokes. Porky turned to Dunn. "Have you got any money on you?"

"A few bucks."

"What I'm thinking is we should have bought a couple of cases of Coke back there to share with some of the other guys."

"Good idea," Dunn agreed. "Let's unhitch the trailer and head back with the cab."

The soldiers jumped from the cab, unhitched the trailer, and headed back down the road to the stand. Porky realized this might be his last chance to talk with a pretty girl for a while. He hoped her mother or father wouldn't be there instead. Dunn pulled the truck cab over to the same spot they had parked before. Porky jumped down from the cab and approached the stand. He was disappointed. This time a young man appeared at the window.

"I'd like to buy a couple of cases of Coke," Porky said, digging into his pocket for Dunn's money and the few pesos he planned to contribute. "Twenty-four bottles to a case. That makes forty-eight dollars please," the clerk said as he turned to pick the cases off the back shelf. "Forty-eight dollars?" Porky was in shock.

"Yes. Ninety-eight pesos for two cases," he responded.

"But a half hour ago I paid a nickel apiece—twenty centavos for four Cokes." Porky was flabbergasted by the steep change in price.

"The price has gone up. Lots of GI want lots of Coke. The price is now one dollar a Coke," he replied sternly. Sergeant Dunn had been listening to the exchange.

"Forget it," he shouted out to Porky.

Porky climbed back into the cab, thinking that he should have kept his big mouth shut when he bought the Cokes from the girl. They drove back to the Twenty-seventh Material camping area in silence. As Porky and Dunn got out of the truck, a soldier approached.

"Follow me through the woods. That's where we'll be eating. We have to be careful about cooking. If they spot smoke, next thing you know, we'll be bombed."

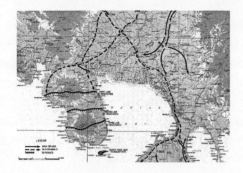

Courtesy U.S. Army Center of Military History

Chapter 18

We're the battling bastards of Bataan;
No mama, no papa, no Uncle Sam;
No aunts, no uncles, no cousins, no nieces;
No pills, no planes, no artillery pieces.
. . . And nobody gives a damn.
—Frank Hewlett, 1942

The forest the troops were using as cover was at the southern tip of the Bataan peninsula, facing Manila Bay. It was rugged terrain. The jungle was thick with palm and banyan trees and indigenous hardwoods—mahogany, apitong, yacal, lauan, camagon, ipil, white and red narra, and mayapis. This was a wilderness where orchids, bamboo, cinnamon, and clove grew wild; where monkeys, bats, rodents, shrews, and snakes slithered, climbed, and flew. Dwarf deer and the mongoose foraged succulents along with tusked boar. Colorful parrots, owls, button quail, cuckoos, and monkey-eating eagles perched and chatted and dived among the trees. Mosquitoes thrived too; and so did malaria, dysentery, typhoid, jungle rot, and a host of parasites.

Porky and Dunn were guided along a path through a grove of trees and ferns. They crossed a moss-bottomed stream and came to an open area where soldiers, sailors, airmen, and marines were scattered about, sitting on the ground or leaning against palm trees eating sandwiches and drinking coffee. For all practical purposes, they were all in the army now, whether or not they ever shot a gun. Their guide pointed to an area where food had been prepared.

"Orders are to grab something, then scatter," their escort informed them. "I guess they don't want us congregating in case they start dropping bombs."

A captain in the marines was seated, talking to the cook under the thicket of a large banyan tree. He rose and approached Porky. "Corporal LaCoste, grab some food and then set up guard duty. Sergeant Dunn, I'd like a word with you."

As Dynamite Dunn sat with the captain, Porky made his way to the food, then selected eight men to circle the camp. They followed him as he assigned positions. He continued on to the edge of the forest cover. Ahead was a fifty-foot embankment. As Porky surveyed the scene, the sound of a plane was heard in the distance, making a fast approach in his direction. A soldier who was standing by a clump of tall ferns watched as Porky took cover behind a boulder. "Relax. He's one of our own," he said. Porky turned, startled he hadn't spotted him earlier. "That's Mariveles field up there. The Cub flies back and forth to Corregidor. It's the only point of communication we've got with the island," he said, pointing to the military base some called the Rock.

One of the tunnels at Corregidor
Courtesy Department of Defense

Porky dusted off his knees as he stood. "Corregidor. So that's Corregidor. I spotted it at one of the sentry positions. They say it's laced with tunnels. We have everything we need there to fight a war for the next ten years, is what I hear. Problem is, how do we get there? Swim?"

"It's only two miles out," the private said.

"Maybe we could have the natives build us canoes," Porky suggested.

"Or maybe we could sprout wings," the private said with a grin.

The soldier looked younger than his years. He was freckle-faced, with ears that stuck out and looked too large for his face. *Maybe his ears are wings*, Porky thought callously. Instead, he asked, "Tell me about the airfield. Are there many planes left hidden?"

"You've got me. The Japs seem to think so. They fly over once or twice a day, taking pictures," the soldier said, his ears dipping slightly as he spoke.

"Photo Joe himself," Porky offered, consciously deciding to forget about the poor man's ears.

"It's a wonder he doesn't crash, he gets so low," the soldier said. Porky surveyed the scene again. He studied the embankment and the grassy edges along the top. "If they know nothing's there, why do they keep coming back?"

"There are sandpiles up at the field. That could look very suspicious. So they make their morning rounds and start bombing away."

This guy's a good soldier, Porky thought. *He keeps a sharp eye out, and he's observant.* "How close do they get to us?" he asked.

"Hey, we're still alive! No one from our unit has been lost yet. Good luck, Corporal," the soldier said as he turned to walk back to the squad camp.

"Good luck to you too, soldier," Porky replied with a lump in his throat. *We're all in this together*, he thought, wondering where his school chums were hiding out and praying they were all alive and well. He lit a cigarette and watched a salmon-pink sunset until the last rays disappeared and then turned toward the jungle to make the round of sentry positions for the night.

Daybreak found Porky seated, leaning against a palm tree, a pistol holster on his hip and a Springfield six-shot rifle propped against the tree. As he stared straight ahead, his eyes slowly began to close and he nodded off into a light sleep. He woke to the sound of a low-flying aircraft and watched as the giant shadow of a plane moved along the ground. Glancing skyward, he saw bombs dropping along the edge of the airfield from the plane overhead. The nearby cliff resonated with the sound of explosions. Porky's body shivered involuntarily and slammed against the tree. He wet himself and jumped up, stunned.

Map of Japanese Landings on Bataan
Courtesy Department of Defense

Chapter 19

From one day to the next, no one knew what to expect. In mid-December, Admiral Kimmel was replaced by Rear Admiral Nimitz as commander of the Pacific Fleet, but that was small help to the forces stranded on the Philippines. The Japanese assault on American ships and planes in the Pacific had been so thorough the belief the men once held that help was on the way was fading fast, despite reassurances from General MacArthur. Adding to their pessimism was the news of what had long been anticipated. Four days after the attack on Pearl Harbor, Congress declared war against Nazi Germany and Italy, Axis partners with Japan. So whatever manpower and equipment might have been used for their rescue was now deployed for Europe. President Roosevelt had more pressing issues than sending resources to a lost cause.

By the end of January 1942, the battle for the Philippines had entered a new stage. The Associated Press reported that with Manila gone and the Cavite naval base abandoned, "a consolidated defending force north and northwest of the Philippine capital continued resistance to an increasingly furious Japanese onslaught." But for Porky and the fifty other men in his unit, "resistance" meant surviving and drilling in preparation for what might lie ahead. Several weeks after they arrived on the Bataan, the Battle of the Points was heating-up, a battle that saw combined American forces defeating two Japanese battalions.

One battle was centered on Longoskawayan Point, which faces the South China Sea along its western edge while jutting out like a half-closed gate into the North Channel leading to Manila Bay. Its beachhead was breached by Japanese amphibious forces, but to their surprise, the largest heavy-caliber

Japanese Light Tanks
Courtesy Department of Defense

American coastal artillery fire since the Civil War was waiting for them. Twelve-inch mortars lobbed sixty-seven-pound land-attack projectiles on the invaders. "After the fourth shot, the forward observer on Mount Pucot reported that such large fires had been started on Longoskawayan Point that he could no longer see the target," wrote Colonel Bunker, who died on May 16, 1943, in a prison camp at Kinkaseki, Formosa (Taiwan).

Despite the victory, there were heavy losses, but further up the coast at Quinauan Point, which was defended primarily by Filipino squadrons, even greater casualties were reported. However, poor seamanship and a lack of navigational charts led the bulk of the Japanese landing craft to run aground. Adding to their misery, the shoreline was dense with tropical forest and promontories that ascended up to a thousand feet, and the ragged coast confused all but the native population. And though some of the enemy forces managed to climb up through ravines and dried-up riverbeds to take up positions in the dense cover, most had been killed or driven back to the sea. Some were reported to have jumped off cliffs to their deaths. Others who straddled the beach faced machine-gun fire from American troops stationed above. But others had remained undetected, hidden out in caves that dotted the landscape, waiting for reinforcements and for the Japanese blockade to starve out the combined armed forces of the United States until they died or surrendered.

After the war was over, details of how the Japanese experienced the battle began to emerge. Apparently, some Americans survived because of dumb luck. Sailors with white jumpers and bell-bottoms had their duds dyed in iodine so they wouldn't be obvious in the moonlight. To the Japanese hidden out in the coastal regions, these men were clearly suicide squads attempting to smoke them out. There are reports of Americans in brightly colored pink to orange uniforms sitting out on promontories or along cliffs, casually smoking and talking loudly. The Japanese knew if they fell for the bait and shot them, their positions would be revealed.

As Porky finished the day's training with the new unit, a captain approached the lieutenant in charge. "I need twenty-five men from the outfit. They're being shipped up north for coastal defense. Three other units will be joining them. I want the men packed and ready to go on the double," the captain said, handing the lieutenant a list. "Here are the men I want on the detail."

Porky's name topped the list. The lieutenant, in turn, handed the list to Porky, who perused the names.

"LaCoste, gather the men together. I'll meet you back at the mess area. I want these men fed now. They'll be moving out after dark."

As darkness descended, a beat-up bus that had once served the city of Manila arrived at the squad camp. The cook reached into a large crate and passed out two cartons of cigarettes to each of the men as they entered the bus. Porky was the last to enter. "I thought there were P-40 engines in those crates," he said to the cook, who handed him two long white boxes stamped with the red-and-black circle Lucky Strike label.

The cook let out a short laugh. "There were, but Uncle Sam never thought to give us the planes. We decided the crates were more valuable than the engines."

"You dumped a million-dollar boondoggle and kept the fifty-cent crates?" Porky said, shaking his head in disbelief.

"How do you think we got the food and cigarettes here?" the cook shot back.

"Makes sense to me." Porky began to board and then turned to yell, "Hey, where's the food?"

"You'll be joining up with another outfit and all the supplies should be there," the cook yelled back with a wave.

The bus took the men north along the West Road, which had been carved through the rugged terrain above the South China Sea, ragged with inlets and bays, cliffs and jutting promontories. As the men slept, the bus jogged along white coral road by the light of the half-moon, through the village of Lusong, up the mountain pass until it reached the coastal road that led down to Luzon Point, across the wooden Agloloma River bridge to the Agloloma Bay side of Quinauan Point. They reached their destination, an embankment overlooking a large inlet, around midnight. The soldiers glanced out the window to what appeared to be an isolated area. They stretched, yawned, grabbed their gear, and disembarked.

As the bus rode off, a major appeared out of the darkness from the shelter of a cluster of coconut palms and introduced himself to Porky. "Follow me, men. But be quiet," he warned. "There could be Japanese about."

He led the men away from the embankment into the jungle. When they came to a clearing, he raised his hand for the men to stop. "Men, leave all your packs here where they'll be safe. We're about to climb up this embankment to a field where you'll be bedding down for the night." The men dropped their knapsacks and bags in a pile and followed the major, carrying only their guns and blankets. They arrived in a grassy field and bunked down for the rest of the night. At daybreak, they awoke to find the major gone, but two lieutenants had joined them, Lieutenants Day and Kirkpatrick.

"We're going back down to pick up your packs and then we'll be moving on," Lieutenant Day informed them.

The men clambered back down to the clearing and searched through the pile to locate their packs. One of the youngest men in the outfit, Private Gibbs, reached into the knapsack to grab a pack of cigarettes. He opened the flap all the way and spread out the opening to look. "What the hell! I must have the wrong backpack. My cigarettes are gone," he said to the man next to him, who checked his knapsack. The cartons were missing from his rucksack too. Soon all the men were searching for their cigarettes.

Porky was standing next to Lieutenant Day. "What's going on here?"

"I haven't got a clue."

Lieutenant Kirkpatrick walked around the cluster of men to Lieutenant Day. "There seems to be a bit of a commotion," he commented as several GIs approached the lieutenants.

"What's this about? All our cartons are gone," Private First Class Conte said and was soon joined by a chorus of voices.

"Yaw. What's the joke? Who stole our cigarettes?" they demanded to know.

"That goddamn major is what's up," Porky said, staring hard at the lieutenants. He wondered if they were in on it too.

"What a GD bandit!" another soldier shouted as he threw down his knapsack.

Porky addressed the lieutenants. "Those cartons were the most valuable thing we owned," he said, barely suppressing his anger.

"What major? What are you talking about?" Day asked.

"Varney. He told me his name is Major Varney. He ought to be court-martialed!" Porky spit out as he checked through his sack. He pulled out a towel and wrapped it around the back of his neck. "At least he didn't steal my towel."

Lieutenant Kirkpatrick stepped forward into the cluster of men. "If any of you men would like some cigarettes, I know where to get some. If you've got pesos, I've got cigarettes," he offered.

The men were suspicious they were about to buy their own cigarettes back, but were desperate for a smoke. Several reached into their pockets and handed money over to the lieutenant.

As the unit fretted over cigarettes, Second Lieutenant Smith approached from the path leading back to the roadway. He stood for a moment, watching and listening to complaints. "Men, forget Major Varney and forget about your cigarettes for a moment, please. We've got bigger problems than that."

"Don't tell me—your outfit packed the cooking equipment and food, didn't they?" Day asked, ready to explode.

"They packed it, but it's not here," Smith said, still hoping that the supplies were somehow momentarily delayed.

"We were told everything would be here," Lieutenant Kirkpatrick said, confronting Smith.

"Look, I know it's bad. We've got a hundred men, no food, and no containers to cook food if we had food!" Smith admitted, pushing his way past Kirkpatrick to Lieutenant Day.

"So what should we do?"

"The third pursuit outfit is down the road apiece. I'll check it out and see if they can help us," Day offered. The second lieutenant approached the troops, who stood in a cluster by their gear. It was early in the morning, yet they appeared exhausted, visibly shaken by the turn of events.

"Follow me, men. We've been here before and we've got some things planned out," Smith said, hoping to uplift their spirits. The men followed Lieutenant Smith as he descended into a ravine and gathered close as he attempted to give them the lowdown as they walked.

"The Japs were hiding in the cliffs and caves, but most—if not all—were driven out or killed by the Philippine Army at the beginning of the war,"

Smith explained. "I was talking to a Philippine officer about it. He told me the Japs have been in the cliffs and caves so long their equipment's all green and corroded. One day they spotted a Jap who ran out and tried to drink ocean water. They watched him go back up the path, under a big canvas, and disappear."

"Didn't they go after him?" Porky asked.

"Apparently, but for one reason or other, they couldn't find him. The point I'm making is that there still could be some Japs around," Smith said, pointing out possible locations where they might be in hiding. Lieutenant Day clambered down the ravine and caught up with the unit. He was carrying a ten-gallon cooking pot. "This is all they'd give me. This pot! Inside there's a big spoon."

The second lieutenant stood in a state of shock. "No food? Where's the food?"

"They couldn't spare any," Day said, feeling foolish holding the empty pot. "But there's supposed to be a supply truck along any moment. As a matter of fact, I think I hear it now," he said, suddenly putting a finger to his lips. "Keep it quiet guys 'cause you never know. We'll sneak back up if it's the supply truck—hopefully, for some chow."

The men climbed from the ravine back onto the jungle path and marched to the clearing. "Listen up, men," Lieutenant Day continued. "I've got orders concerning the food, when and if it arrives. We've got thirty-six pounds of rice a day, three pounds of sugar, three cans of sardines every other day, and on occasion, a can of corned beef. I know it sounds like shit, but it's food. And if you're hungry it'll be good."

Private Thomson stepped forward and addressed the group. "I'm from the Midwest, grew up on a farm. I've tasted woodchuck, rabbit, squirrel, and snake. If there's critters about—if I find any—trust me, they'll soon be in the pot."

"Good luck, soldier," Day said, clasping him on the shoulder. "The Japs have eaten everything that walks, crawls, or flies."

"Look, men, we'll get by," Smith interrupted. "But right now, I've got to hand out assignments. We'll have lots to do just to survive. A bit later, a runner will join you to signal it's time for chow." Smith pointed to a small path. "Conte, you take twelve men and head west along this trail until you get to the cliffs. Watch for any troop movement along the shore. We've got several radio hookups to pass info along. LaCoste, grab a dozen or so men and head south along that path," he said, pointing to an opening.

Porky chose Private Thomson and a dozen other men. They marched up a narrow dirt path for a quarter of a mile when Porky spotted what he thought was a familiar figure in the distance. As the men drew closer, Porky's heart sank. Bobby Doolan was fast asleep on a cot alongside the path. A bottle of orange juice was set next to his canteen beneath the cot. A mosquito net was strung above from the branch of a tree.

"Bobby, Bobby," Porky said softly, kneeling by his side. Bobby's eyes remained shut and his breathing was labored. "You know this guy?" Thomson asked.

"Sure I do. He's my best friend, Bobby—Bobby Doolan—from my hometown. There must be something wrong with him," Porky said. "He's got food. See the orange juice," he offered, pointing to the cup under the cot.

"On the way back, I'll try to talk with him," Porky said, brushing his knees off as he stood. "I bet he's got malaria."

Porky sighed and fought back tears as he continued on leading the men along a path through the jungle that led to the designated location—a steep cliff with an inlet below. The inlet was the only entrance to their position. Ten machine guns were set up along the cliff, pointed down toward the inlet. Porky stood next to one of the machine guns along the cliff to address the men. "Looking over the layout here, seems to me the Japs would have to come through the inlet and work their way through the jungle. If they come at all, they'll be coming from behind," he observed as a field phone in the center of the row of machine guns rang. Porky grabbed the call. "Lookout Number 7," Lieutenant Day was calling.

"Leave one man at the post and bring the rest down for chow."

"Got it."

Porky asked Private Conte to stay and then led the remaining men back until he came to Bobby's cot. "Men, I'm going to stop here and talk with my friend for a minute. Private Thomson, you can go on ahead. I'm sure the men are more than ready for chow." Thomson led the men as they descended down the path into the jungle.

Porky stood by the cot as Bobby had so often stood by him as he lay ill. Finally, he lifted the tent-like mosquito netting and entered, moving close to the cot. Overhead, birds screeched, darting from tree to tree to tree. "How are you doing, buddy?" Bobby opened his eyes and recognized Porky. "How are you doing?" he repeated.

Bobby nodded, struggled to sit up and then stand. Porky tried to help, but his friend pushed him aside, determined to stand on his own. "I've got some quinine left over from that case I had." He reached into his coverall pocket to grab the tablets.

"It's no use. I've taken pills, and they're not helping. I may have a couple of things. Malaria, dysentery, who the hell knows. I'm in bad shape, Porky."

"Bobby, I'm going down to get some chow. Want me to bring some back up to you?"

"Thanks," he said, managing a weak smile. "A couple of times a day my outfit brings food down to me, but I can't eat it," Bobby said, barely able to speak above a whisper. "We were at Iba at the time of the attack. I was just starting to get sick. I can't remember the last time I was able to stomach food." His hand shook as he pointed to the juice. "I can't even manage juice or water," he said weakly as he lowered himself back down to a sitting position.

"Well then, I won't bother bringing any back to you. Anyway, it's nothing but slop. But I'll drop by every morning and evening and we'll talk." Porky patted him on the shoulder. "Keep your chin up. You'll make it."

"OK." Bobby slowly lay back down on the cot.

He's so fragile, it's as if he's made of glass, Porky thought as he lifted the mosquito net to leave. He stood for what seemed like an eternity, staring at his closest friend on earth before stepping back onto the path into the jungle.

That evening, Porky set up a standard-issue shelter half, an olive drab tent made to fold into a small, lightweight square pack. Fraser Products Company, Manufactured 1940 was stenciled onto the top flap. With the war on, they must be millionaires, Porky conjectured. He strung the rope between two trees and put down pieces of plywood that had been left by the Philippine soldiers that had defended the area earlier. The plywood was a luxury. He had a roof over his head and a floor. "What more could I want?" he muttered and crawled in the shelter to sleep.

Later that evening, he awoke and got out of the tent to check his watch by moonlight. It was time to relieve the sentry stationed about two hundred yards away. He sat down on a log and placed a .45 pistol and a rifle on his lap. Before long he thought he heard three or four footsteps, then silence. He held his breath and heard several more footsteps, but from where? Porky slowly took his jacket off and used it to cover the .45 and rifle as he slipped off the safety. Once again, there was a sound. This time it was coming from bushes about a hundred yards away on his left. *Jesus. It's a Jap*, he thought. He heard breathing and finally the shadow of a form closing in on him. He drew his pistol and fired five times in the direction of the shadow. A wild pig shot out from the bushes, its wide snout covered with grass roots. Shocked, Porky took careful aim and fired once more, this time envisioning roast pork for dinner. The pig squealed bloody murder then disappeared into the foliage. Soon guns started firing throughout the jungle. Porky hit the dirt and muttered to himself, "Jesus Christ Almighty. I've started a friggin' war!"

Weeks later, Porky was stationed along the cliff outpost overlooking the inlet. He had set up his shelter half about thirty feet away from the cliff. It was midafternoon. As he listened to the pounding of waves below, he began to feel drowsy, so he leaned his rifle against the tent pole and crawled into the tent for a nap. Nearby, several men were seated on the ground by the machine guns. Down below, GIs were positioned by the inlet and across the chasm on the other side of the cliffs. All of a sudden, Porky was awakened by a strange sound. As he picked his head up to see, he saw a giant python slithering outside near the entrance to his tent. He began to scream as the giant snake maneuvered away and headed toward the cliff. "Snake . . . snake!"

Several soldiers rushed to Porky's aid, rifles drawn; among them was the farm boy, Private Thomson. "So where the hell is the son of a bitch? Just let me at 'im. He'll make a swell stew," Thomson boasted.

Porky crawled out of the shelter and pointed to a rocky area by the edge of the cliff. "He's slipped back into his hole. As far as I'm concerned, I don't want anything more to do with him," Porky said with a shiver.

"It's gone into a hole? Where?" Private First Class O'Brien demanded.

"I don't know the exact spot. He's somewhere over there, by the rocks along the cliff," Porky responded sheepishly.

"Over there? He's over there? Doing what? Visiting his friend, the pig?" O'Brien asked with a smirk.

Porky was red faced. "I swear to God," he said as several men laughed and walked away.

Private Thomson shook his head, peering down at the corporal. "Only you, Porky. Only you."

"Thomson, I swear to God. It was a man-killer, a giant boa constrictor. And the pig—he was snorting at me. I could almost feel his breath," Porky said in his defense as the private walked away. "He was so close, I could almost taste him," he added, talking to himself.

Filipino scouts and Marines strategize defense
Courtesy Department of Defense

Chapter 20

Another month passed. February had been relatively quiet as the Japanese withdrew to regroup and re-strategize. And though other units had seen action during the earlier Japanese advance, Porky's outfit was spared. But supplies were dwindling, and what supplies existed were increasingly hard to distribute to the scattered forces. It wasn't a matter of Washington refusing to ante up to purchase food and equipment—funds were allocated and plans were made to scour the Pacific to buy up whatever they could find. But breaking through the Japanese blockade was another matter. Few shipowners were willing to risk the loss of a ship and the lives of their crew for a suicide mission. And of those who did try only a fraction made it through. But despite the courageous efforts and success of the lucky few who outfoxed the Japanese, much of the produce had rotted by the time it reached Bataan and the edibles that had not spoiled were sufficient to last only about four days. By March, everyone was put on half rations, but even that strategy was not adequate to feed the eighty thousand American and Philippine troops, who were now joined by twenty-six thousand civilian refugees.

Bartering for food with the native village people became the course to survival. Bananas, papayas, and shrimp were traded for U.S. regulation long underwear and other items deemed nonessential. And though cat, dog, rat, and monkey were occasionally on the menu, some were fortunate and ate bits of chicken and rice or water buffalo. Horses and mules from the Twenty-sixth Cavalry were available for some, but most GIs were stuck with hardtack, canned salmon or sardines, and small portions of tinned beef.

Luzon's Last Stand
Courtesy Department of Defense

Simply put, the regiments were surrounded on land, by sea, and in the air. The trap had been sprung. They were snared and growing weaker by the day. During the month of March, President Quezon took flight from the Philippines for America and President Roosevelt ordered General MacArthur to abandon the Philippines for Australia. MacArthur turned his duties over to General Wainwright, who had been in charge of forces on Bataan. That meant Wainwright must be secreted off the peninsula to Corregidor. Once ensconced on the Rock, Wainwright then turned responsibilities for the men in the trenches in Bataan over to General King.

One morning, Porky stood on the cliff looking out across the bay when he spotted two six-man *bancas*, dugout canoes paddled by native fishermen. One of the natives threw a dynamite clip into the placid water, which was followed by a loud explosion. Three from each canoe dove into the water while the remaining men cast out open-weave rattan and bamboo baskets which were quickly snatched up by the divers.

Private O'Brien joined Porky to watch. "You ever see anything like this?" Porky asked O'Brien.

"Sure. They're dynamiting for fish."

Iba fisherman in a small banca
Courtesy LaCoste/Thurber family

The soldiers watched as the divers burst back onto the surface, hauling baskets now swarming with silver sea bass, codfish, and *bangus,* or milkfish. After the baskets were hauled in, the fish were dumped into the hull, and the divers handed back the empty baskets to gather more.

"I could do that. Jack, you know where they store the dynamite and caps. Why don't you cop some and we'll try our hand at it," Porky suggested. The next morning the tide was out as Corporal LaCoste and Private O'Brien walked along the exposed coral reef, searching for an opportunity. O'Brien was carrying two sticks of dynamite, blasting caps, and two small fuses. They came to a pool where a half-dozen large fish were swimming. The men stopped to watch. Porky's courage was faltering, but he gamely asked O'Brien for the explosives. His hands shook as he assembled the pieces. "OK. Light the GD thing and then let's run like hell!"

Jack lit the dynamite and Porky tossed it into the saltwater pool as they scrambled for higher ground. The dynamite exploded, causing a geyser to rise twenty feet into the air. The men took cover, then returned and dove into the pool to retrieve the stunned fish. Each held four large fish as they climbed up the trail back to their position at the top of the cliff.

Porky was triumphant. "Victory! Let's cook them here, now."

"Cook 'em. Why wait?" Jack countered. "Let's eat 'em raw," he said, baring his teeth.

"Better yet, let's get some banana leaves. We'll roast them on hot coals tonight," Porky said with excitement then suddenly went pale. Japanese planes were roaring directly toward them. The men hid in the bushes as a spy plane flew directly overhead, taking photos.

"Shit! I've tipped them off. Our goose is cooked," Porky whined.

"Hey, with any luck, they'll think we were natives. Ah, don't worry. We'll hide the fire under a tent and enjoy ourselves with a real feast tonight," O'Brien said, peeping out from the bushes.

Soldiers seeking cover in Lamao
Courtesy Department of Defense

Chapter 21

The Surrender

On April 3, 1942, Japan launched its final offensive on Bataan. For days, the air was thick with smoke and the sound of bombing raids and gun battles echoed throughout the jungle canyons. The violence climaxed on the fifth day, when all hell broke loose in a scene that rivaled the apocalypse. Orders were given to destroy the ammo dumps and anything else the enemy could use against those who survived. On the sixth day, things grew quiet again except for a few Zeros on bombing runs. On that day, General King rode along the East Road to a bamboo cabin in Limay to meet with Japanese officials. Two white flags were perched above the headlights of his car. He attempted to negotiate the use of American trucks to transport the sick and disabled to wherever the Japanese chose to keep them captive, but the enemy would hear none of it. They demanded to be brought to General Wainwright instead. Later, General King would travel to the provincial capital to pose for the requisite photographs, where he made it known that he alone took responsibility for his actions, based on the situation at hand. MacArthur and Wainwright had not been consulted. For MacArthur, surrender was out of the question. General King was concerned for the survivors.

Porky sat by his tent with a couple of men from the unit when the phone rang. "Lookout Number 7."

"Hello, sir," Porky answered.

Lieutenant Kirkpatrick was on the other end. "So it's you, Lieutenant Kirkpatrick. Are you calling about the cigarettes you owe us?"

General King Surrenders
Courtesy Department of Defense

"No. I'm calling to let you know that the war is over," Kirkpatrick answered perfunctorily. "But Corregidor hasn't surrendered, at least not yet. I'm going to try to reach Corregidor by boat. You and your men are on your own. I would advise you to throw your weapons over the cliff into the ocean."

"I suspect the men and I will probably want to try to make it to Corregidor too," he responded, though he hadn't a clue how they'd get there.

Lieutenant Kirkpatrick's voice softened. "Good luck in whatever you decide," he said and hung up.

Porky slammed the receiver down. "And good luck to you, you bastard!"

Private O'Brien stood. "What's up?" he asked, sensing that the inevitable had finally happened.

"Jack, get the rest of the men together."

O'Brien walked toward the center of the clearing to address the men, who were scattered about. "Everyone, get your sorry asses over here," he hollered. "LaCoste has an announcement."

The men gathered round and grew silent as Porky began to speak. "As you probably know, I just got a phone call. It was from that GD Lieutenant Kirkpatrick. The one who took our money and failed to deliver the cigarettes as promised."

"I bet he was in cahoots with that GD major who stole them in the first place. What's his name? Oh yaw, Major Varney," Thomson piped up.

Others agreed. "What's happened? Has he repented and we're finally going to get our cigarettes?"

O'Brien held up his hands to quiet the men. "Listen up, fellows; I suspect the corporal has something important to say."

"Men, the war is over. We've surrendered everything but Corregidor." Porky paused as he looked at the faces of the ragged troops. "Lieutenant Kirkpatrick's instructions are to throw all our weapons into the sea."

Several men swore as he continued. "Look, if we're caught with weapons, the Japs will kill us, no questions asked."

"We're dead meat now. We'll never make it back to our families," Private Ross confided to the man standing next to him. He was one of the older married men in the outfit who had enlisted before the draft, unable to find work back home.

O'Brien glared at Porky. "So what the hell are we supposed to do?"

"Lieutenant Kirkpatrick said he's going to find a boat and make a run for Corregidor. Maybe that's what we should do too," Porky suggested.

The men grew silent, contemplating what few alternatives they had. "OK, let's look at it this way. Chances are good we can't make it through the jungle alive. So we might as well head down the path to the beach road and maybe someone will pick us up."

"OK. That's an option. But where the hell is Corregidor?" O'Brien blurted out.

"Follow me, men. And while we're walking, try sprouting wings. Corregidor is on the south side of the peninsula, two miles out at sea," Porky said as he grabbed his rifle and tossed it over the cliff. The other men reluctantly followed suit, including Private O'Brien. After they broke camp and gathered up a few essentials, Porky led the men onto the path through the jungle. Private Thomson walked by his side to the front and O'Brien took the position at the rear.

A half hour later, the men came to the West Road. They had two choices: left or right. But it had been a lifetime ago that the beat-up bus drove them to their last position, and they had been asleep when they arrived. *How in hell do we get to the shore road, or is this the shore road?* Porky wondered. He turned left.

As the men marched north, a truck headed toward them. Seated in the passenger side was the captain of a hundred-man detail. He ordered the lieutenant who was driving to stop.

"What the hell's going on here? Do you men know where you're going?" the captain shouted out to Porky.

"We're headed due east, to the ocean, sir," Porky said, saluting the captain.

"The sea is to your west, corporal. Manila Bay is to the east, and there's a mountain in the way. What you want is to head back to Mariveles to the south. That's where we're supposed to meet up. Presently you and your outfit are headed north. You need to turn around," the captain explained.

"Sir, Lieutenant Kirkpatrick called. What I've been told is that we've surrendered. We're trying to reach Corregidor, which is what Lieutenant Kirkpatrick told me he was going to attempt to do."

"Yes. Lieutenant Kirkpatrick was given an option. He could join up with us and we'd try to reach Corregidor together. Or he could, as anyone can, try to make it on their own. Look. There are thirty or forty men a short ways back. Why don't I get them and we'll all go together."

The captain and lieutenant abandoned the truck and walked back to join the remainder of the troops. Porky and his outfit followed. Before long, they spotted the other troops standing along the side of the road. The captain signaled to one of the officers. "Lieutenant Cohen, would you join us? Corporal LaCoste and I want to have a word with you about the path down to the ocean."

"Yes, Captain," he said with a thick Bronx accent. The lieutenant had a pained expression on his face.

"My advice is to get everyone to take out a handkerchief and tie it around his neck. That way, it'll show up by moonlight. Trust me, it's no easy thing going down a hillside path in the dark. We're going to have to proceed single file. Each man's got to hang on to the shoulder of the person in front. After a while, we'll come to a dried-up riverbed. That will lead us straight to the seaside. You get the picture? But we'd better do it now, fast, while I can still make out the trail."

The captain and Porky joined Cohen in organizing the men and soon began the climb down the path as dusk descended. At midnight, the men listened as waves crashed against rock and pounded over sand below. It was the sound of the incoming tide as it funneled up the base of the Agloloma riverbed toward the troops, who stumbled down its bone-dry channel. By four o'clock, the tide was in retreat. Shadows of the troops could be seen as they inched onto the beach. One GI stood at the ocean's edge, attempting to send an SOS by flashlight. By dawn, the weary men were trudging along a seaside road when a truck driven by Japanese officers pulled alongside them and came to a stop. One of the officers spoke perfect English. "Hop on the back. There's room for fifty more."

The captain, Porky, and the rest of the men hoisted themselves up into the back of the truck and squeezed in among fifty or so other GIs. The truck started up and headed down the road. One of the soldiers sitting next to Porky was about to introduce himself when he spotted a gun partially concealed by Porky's jacket flap, tucked into his belt. "What the hell are you doing with that thing?" he asked, pointing to the pistol. "Are you trying to get us all killed?"

"Jesus Christ. I forgot," Porky said as he flung the gun out onto the beach.

Later that afternoon the truck pulled into Mariveles field. Thousands of men had already arrived, remnants of the battalions that had slowly disintegrated over the last few days when communication lines had broken down and the Imperial army had routed out the remaining pockets of American resistance. The field buzzed with activity as men wandered about; others sat off to the side or were lying down, eyes closed, attempting to shut out the chaos. They were disheveled and dirty, exhausted, hungry and thirsty, and feared what the future might hold. Porky and the captain stared at the assembly as the truck maneuvered toward the remnants of a bombed-out hangar. "Looks like Mariveles field is the central collecting point," the captain said.

"There must be thousands of GIs here," Porky agreed.

"Correction, Corporal. The men are no longer GIs. All of us are now officially POWs. Good luck," the captain said as he jumped from the truck.

"Good luck to you too, sir," Porky called out as the captain disappeared into a throng of men. Porky jumped from the truck and was soon followed by the rest of his outfit, who one by one dispersed into the crowd as he wandered toward the outer edge. There he spotted wreckage from what once had served as a hangar. It now offered shade from the sun. He sat down beside a young man, who appeared to be barely out of high school.

"I haven't had a bite to eat for days. What about you?" Porky asked the private.

"Here. I've got five cans of corned beef. You take one," the young man offered.

"You mean it?"

"Sure, I mean it."

"Thanks."

He passed a can of corned beef over to Porky, who yanked the key off the top and opened it. "You'll need this too," he said, handing him a spoon.

"Thanks." Porky managed a slight smile and then ravenously ate the contents without pause. "I swear to God, you saved my life. My name's LaCoste," he said, studying the young man's face. He wanted to remember him, in case someday he might be able to return the favor.

"Vincent Bowers from Swanzey, New Hampshire," he said, shaking Porky's hand.

"You don't say. Well, I'm very pleased to meet you. I'm your neighbor from up the road a piece—Athol, Massachusetts. And as a matter of fact, I grew up on Swanzey Road." With their bellies full, they forgot their troubles for a while. Both men laughed out loud at the coincidence and for a brief moment were transported back home. They were interrupted when Pvt. O'Meara, from Porky's regular outfit, poked his head through the crowd, guided by the laughter.

"Hey, Frenchy! Good to see you," O'Meara said, ambling over to him. "I swear your laugh would cut through a foghorn."

Porky rose and shook his hand. "Good to see you alive and well."

O'Meara lowered his voice. "Your buddy Swede Lawson's over there," he said, thrusting his thumb toward the southeast. "He's got a bad case of malaria."

"You say, Pint Lawson's here? Show me the way," he said, turning back to wave at the young man who had saved him from starvation. Porky and O'Meara pushed their way through throngs of men to the corner of the airfield where Pint sat, leaning against a tree, eyes closed. Porky knelt beside his friend and gently touched his shoulder. "See you later," O'Meara said and moved back into the milling crowd.

"Pint, it's me, Porky. How're you doing?" Pint's eyes fluttered until they opened. He was obviously weak with fever, but his voice was loud, forced.

"Porky? Oh, Porky, good to see you." He paused to cough and spit up phlegm. "My hearing's shot so you'll have to speak up. And I've got a case of malaria."

Porky shook hands with his friend, and then sat down to face him. "So what's new? Bobby Doolan's got a case too. But he's got it real bad." Porky felt more tired then he had ever felt before. He stretched out beside Pint and closed his eyes.

"I'm glad to see you, Porky. God only knows what's going to happen next," Pint said, his eyes filling with tears. He looked down at his friend, who had fallen sound asleep.

Japanese troops celebrate taking Bataan
Courtesy National Archives

American Generals in captivity
Courtesy Department of Defense

Chapter 22

The following day, the Japanese soldiers stripped the men of expensive watches and other valuables. They then separated the Filipinos from the Americans and organized them into groups of one hundred or more, four abreast, with one guard assigned to each group. Some reports claim that more than seventy-thousand Filipinos and Americans were on the march. Others claim that hundreds, if not thousands, of Americans escaped into the mountainous jungles to join guerilla fighters. Several thousand, including the nurses, managed to escape by boat to Corregidor.

The infamous Bataan Death March began as stern-faced enemy officers in khakis and visor caps barked out commands to foot soldiers who shouted and prodded prisoners with their rifles onto a dirt road. The march was to lead those who survived from where they gathered at Mariveles and Cabcaben to San Fernando, and then on to Camp O'Donnell. Porky and Pint were fortunate to be in one of the lead groups from Mariveles. Those in the middle, or who straggled behind, witnessed or were victims of many of the worst atrocities. Porky dug his towel out from his knapsack, wiped his face, and wrapped it around his neck. The scorching heat made each step harder than the next. Hunger, thirst, and fatigue began to take their toll. Some with malaria or other diseases began to falter. Overcome with exhaustion, they stumbled and fell. Such behavior was a death sentence. No one was permitted to delay the march. Japanese soldiers hit them on the head or slugged them on their backs as an encouragement to proceed. If the sick continued to hang back, they were shot or bayoneted. Others had their heads lopped off as sport, the cruel pleasure of brandishing swords against the defenseless. Prisoners walked

American GIs surrender to Japanese on Bataan
Courtesy Department of Defense

over the bodies of fallen comrades or faced a similar fate. The dead were tossed onto the side of the road and left to rot in the ditch.

As they walked, they passed trickling mountain streams, glittering like liquid silver in the sun. A few delirious souls broke from the march but were shot before they managed to taste a drop. They passed a well but were prohibited from filling their canteens though the Japanese guards made a show of relaxing as they drank luxuriously from the natural spring water. The one benefit afforded the men was a chance to relax as their tormentors indulged. In order to lighten their load, POWs began to shuck off extra clothing, backpacks, and blankets. As dusk descended, they came to a large field that lay between the villages of Cabcaben and Lamoa. The Japanese officers signaled for the POWs to enter the field and lie down. The weary mean collapsed. Some passed out on the spot. Soon the POWs and their captors faded from view into the darkness of the night.

Dawn filtered through the jungle into the clearing. Porky and Pint groaned as they left the comfort of sleep to awake to the harsh light of their captivity. They lay sprawled next to one another and arose, along with thousands of their companions, at the sound of Japanese commands and rifle shots. Trucks, tanks, and military equipment driven by enemy soldiers passed by on the road heading south as Porky and Pint stepped back into line.

"Don't you bet they're about to take on the Americans at Corregidor," Pint conjectured.

"The truth is, there is no escape," Porky admitted, resigned to their fate.

As the captured troops moved back into position, they were directed to head in the opposite direction—due north. "If they're going to Corregidor, where are we going?" Pint wondered.

"To hell, my friend, we're going to hell," Porky said bitterly.

The prisoners trudged on as trucks passed by with Japanese soldiers kneeling in the back, holding long bamboo poles used to strike at the tall Americans. Without warning, Pint got smacked on the head by one of the poles, which passed over the five-foot-four-inch Porky without coming close. Pint grunted in pain, stumbled, then fell to the ground. Porky grabbed his arm to help him up. Soon another truck passed and Pint was hit again. Once again, Porky helped him to rise and continue marching. "That's what I get for being so tall," Pint groaned in response.

"Look, keep marching, and when I say duck, you duck, and fast." His friend felt the welt growing on the back of his head and nodded yes. They continued in silence except for the steady crunch of shoe leather on the coral pavement. Before long, Porky spotted another truck with an outstretched pole approaching from behind. "Duck, now!" Porky yelled. Pint ducked, but an army sergeant several yards ahead got whacked instead. Porky and Pint marched on. The next day was even more grueling, yet tens of thousands of POWs covered with dirt and sweat continued on the long march north despite heat, thirst, and hunger. To their left they passed Americans—some covered with filth, vomit, and blood—passed out or dead alongside the road. To their right Japanese battalions marched south. A man several rows ahead opened his canvas belt, pulled it off, and threw it away with his canteen attached. Porky grabbed it before it hit the ground and looped the belt around his fist. After carrying it for several miles, he held it up for inspection. "What the hell am I doing, carrying this? It's just added weight."

Instead of concentrating on his misery, Pint had been playing out various means of survival. "Save it. You never know, at some point they might show some mercy and let us have a drop of water."

Porky tossed the belt but kept the canteen and attached it to his belt, as another man farther up the line threw off his backpack. "Pint, what the hell are you doing with that pack on your back? It must weigh a ton. Throw it away."

"But I have three cans of rations left. There's a piece of chocolate I think I can eat, and some hardtack. Why don't you take the hardtack?" Pint swung his backpack off and grabbed two twelve-ounce cans, handing one to Porky.

The friends used the moment as a distraction as they peeled open the smooth golden lacquered tins. Pint pulled out a dark chocolate wedge. Porky had a square cookie. As they tossed away the opened tins, Pint turned to Porky in deadly earnest. "Want to save the coffee?"

Porky thanked Pint for the treat with a sad smile, but anger was in his voice. "No. Why bother. Toss it."

Without considering any future regret, Pint tossed the small square can of coffee and heard a metal clunk as hands grabbed the tin somewhere in back of the line. "I'm so thirsty, I can't take it anymore," Porky said as he took a bite of the butter pecan cookie. He ate the treat slowly, with deliberation, relishing each morsel, but as the last crumbs stuck in his throat, he felt he had reached the end of his reserves. He stared intently at an enemy soldier about fifty feet ahead, marching in lockstep with his battalion, headed in the opposite direction. Porky unscrewed the cup off the canteen, and as they approached one another, he held the cup out to his enemy.

"Water, please, water," he said, pleading for compassion. The Japanese soldier unscrewed the cap off his canteen and poured a small amount of water into Porky's cup without missing a step. Porky drank it on the spot and quickly rejoined Pint.

"You've got a lot of grit. You could have been shot."

"To tell the truth, I don't care anymore."

"Don't take that attitude. We're going to make it. Keep plugging."

Porky thought for a moment and his face softened. "Along with feeling less parched, I learned one thing."

"What's that?"

"There's still some good left in the world."

Pint thought there must be a rational explanation for what he had witnessed. "I bet that Jap was American-educated."

"Or maybe he's an American and got trapped, just like us," Porky reasoned.

"Poor bastard."

"Yah."

But the enemy's kindness triumphed over Porky's anger. "Or maybe he's a Jap soldier who just committed an act of treason by having some pity."

"Poor bastard, maybe he'll be shot." As he spoke, Japanese soldiers in the rear of the march slammed rifle butts and plunged bayonets into prisoners who faltered or fell behind. Shots rang out and a fallen American was kicked to the side of the road, blood gushing from his mouth and back. A sword was unsheathed and a POW decapitated. His head dropped like a bloody ball onto the white coral roadway, eyes bulging and tongue swollen and protruding between the hairs of his beard. Soldiers kicked his head about like a football to the amusement of the officer who had decapitated him, while those who followed stepped over his lifeless trunk and limbs. The game was soon dropped, but the point had been made. Their lives were not worth the dust beneath the enemy's feet.

Beyond exhaustion, Porky nearly vomited but threw his canteen and belt away instead. The POWs continued their grueling trek as twilight approached, and the first stars shone as pinpricks of light in the emerging darkness. Finally, they were led to a field as before and collapsed wherever they stood. Porky sank into a kneeling position and froze in place, eyes closed. When he opened them, he noticed the outline of a man nearby, who appeared to be eating a potato. "Where'd you get that?" he asked, wondering if he had missed a guard passing out food before they all starved to death.

"Just kneel down and start digging. We're in some poor Filipino's field. We're trampling on his crop."

Porky dug around Pint's arm. There was little room to stretch out, so Pint lay on his back with his feet tucked as close as he could get them to his torso. His knees formed a bony pyramid pointing skyward. Before long, Porky located three tubers. He cleaned one off with the end of his towel and ate it. "Not half bad," he said, handing one to Pint. "Here, you try one."

Pint wiped the legume on his coveralls, sat up, and bit into it. "It's juicy."

"Juicy and delicious. You make sure you finish it, Pint. You haven't had anything to drink for three days. And nothing to eat except that chocolate."

"I hate to admit it, but I don't think I can take much more," he said as he struggled to chew.

"Like you said before, we're going to make it. Just keep plugging along," Porky lectured his friend, who was now in a fetal position, fast asleep. The night air was refreshing and uplifted Porky's spirits. He wiped off another legume and ate it slowly, savoring every morsel.

By day 4, enemy battalions no longer passed the POWs as they headed south, but the weary prisoners, their numbers ever decreasing, continued on despite exhaustion, starvation, and disease. Now even the ever-present Japanese guards were showing signs of weariness as the afternoon wore on. Ahead was a small village—a few Philippine huts on stilts, surrounded by jungle. One of the huts had a Red Cross flag displayed on the side, next to an open doorway. An American Red Cross worker stood in the opening, wearing a wide-brimmed panama hat, khaki shorts, and an open-collar shirt. He was middle aged, with a great handle bar mustache and tobacco-stained teeth, but he was muscular and trim and, though unarmed, had the bearing of a

Rest stop along the Death March
Courtesy National Archives

man who knew how to use a gun. The march came to a standstill. The guards disappeared into the nipa huts to demand refreshments for themselves from the locals. Seizing the opportunity, Porky approached the Red Cross worker with Pint. "My friend has a bad case of malaria," he said, appealing to the man for help. "We've got a hut full of crippled, sick, and dying soldiers. We're hoping against hope that the Japanese supply us with some transportation, but no guarantees. But your friend can stay, if he'd like."

A Japanese guard stepped out of a nearby hut and approached, gesturing for Porky and Pint to move on. "Pint, you stay here. I'll meet up with you later—wherever our destination is."

"OK," he responded weakly. The men shook hands, embraced, and said good-bye.

Porky walked toward the prisoners, who were reassembling, then turned to watch as the Red Cross worker placed an arm around Pint to help him into the hut. Porky was sick with loneliness as the march resumed. At the outskirts of the village, the guards moved them into a field and the men were commanded to sit. A guard carrying a pail of rice began to make the rounds, dumping rice into mess kits and waiting hands. Porky cupped his hands and received one spoonful of rice. Within moments, the rice was devoured. As the guards continued to hand out rice to the crowd, Porky began to sway. His eyes rolled backward, he passed out and fell into the lap of an Army Air Corps major.

The next morning, Porky awoke to discover his fellow prisoners had risen and begun to march back into the village. His bones ached so badly they felt broken, but he forced himself into a standing position and joined the group, grateful that the guards hadn't killed him as a malingerer. As the men filed past the Red Cross station, the march was halted momentarily. Screaming, moaning, and cries of agony emanated from inside the hut. Porky thought he heard Pint screaming for him to help when he passed out again.

Porky was still unconscious as the noonday sun reached its apex the following day. He was crammed into the back of a truck along with thirty or so sick and disabled men on their way to Camp O'Donnell. As they approached the entrance, the Japanese driver slowed, pulled into the camp yard, and came to a sudden stop. Porky jerked awake and was helped off by several slightly stronger men. Nipa huts were everywhere and came in a variety of shapes and sizes. Some were small, others long barrack-type huts. The huts that were to house the vast majority of the prisoners were damaged to some extent, with holes and pieces of broken bamboo meant to pass as walls, floors, and ceilings. Several leaned precariously close to total collapse.

Healthier POWs carrying gravely ill POWs
Courtesy National Archives

Filipino prisoners were congregated on one side of the road, American POWs on the other. The first building on the American side was the kitchen. Next to it was a shack with doctors seated on the porch. The barrack huts were scattered farther up in tall grass within an open field as far as the eye could see. Porky thanked the men who helped him off the truck, who pointed out the medical hut and wished him good luck. Gathering every ounce of strength, he managed to walk there on his own without further incident and approached one of the men seated on the porch. The man looked bone weary. He was smoking a pipe and wore olive drab slacks and a long-sleeved shirt that looked freshly laundered. His face and hands looked freshly scrubbed too.

"I was told you're a doctor," Porky said as if he needed one. He stepped onto the porch and leaned against the railing for support.

"Yes," the man replied. "I'm a doctor, but I don't have anything I can give you." Porky was stunned.

"We have no medicine, and it's highly unlikely we'll get anything in the future. Look, soldier, they're making rice in the kitchen next door. Why don't you go there and try to get some. There's a water spigot out there." The doctor pointed to a pipe sticking up from the ground, a hundred yards away. A faucet was visible on top. "You're going to have to keep a sharp eye out for when they turn it on. It's only on for a few hours, and there's no telling when."

Porky managed a faint smile and stepped off the porch. "Thanks for the advice," he said.

The doctor raised his hand as if to wave him on. Porky hobbled over to the kitchen hut, which was set on the ground instead of on stilts. Inside, several American cooks were stirring rice in a fifty-gallon pot over an open fire pit. Porky joined the crowd around the pot. All that was left were the brown scrapings on the bottom and sides. He gladly accepted his portion, moved away from the crowd, and started nibbling on the crunchy rations. He was feeling faint from the heat so he walked outside, surveyed the scene, and then walked over to a barracks where bamboo was scattered about on the ground. He picked up a piece that was split in half, dumped the remainder of his rice in it as if it were a plate, wiped his hands on an end of his towel, and sat down to finish eating. After savoring the last morsels, he got up to scout for a large unbroken piece of bamboo.

Hidden in the grass were three foot-long bamboo poles. Using the sliver of a broken stalk, Porky hollowed one out, carefully leaving a sealed end at the bottom. That task complete, he looked up and saw men headed toward the water spigot, but by the time he reached the end of the line to wait his turn, there were several hundred men ahead of him. Soon, hundreds more joined. Nonetheless, the line moved along quickly, so Porky felt privileged to be so close. As he drew nearer the waterspout, Porky turned to the man behind him, who looked more ragged and forlorn than he did, he thought. "Would you mind if I borrowed your cup to fill my bamboo pole?"

"Your bamboo pole?"

"Yeah. See, I hollowed this thing out—except for the bottom, of course."

"Very clever. Sure. Be my guest," he said, handing Porky his canteen cup.

Porky poured water from the spigot into the cup and then transferred it into the gouged-out bamboo pole without spilling a drop. He thanked the man, handed him back his cup, and then wandered over to a shady spot near one of the long huts to sit. He wanted to relax and forget his troubles for a moment as he savored each precious drop. After a few sips, he carefully rested the pole against the barracks, settled down on the bare ground, closed his eyes, and fell asleep. When he awoke, the sky had turned into a glorious pink sunset. He sat up to get his bearings, took a sip from his improvised water container, stood, then grabbed his bamboo "plate" and "water bottle" and headed back toward the kitchen.

As he approached the hut, he noticed two men carrying Bobby Doolan, one by his feet, the other by the shoulders. "Excuse me, that's my friend," he said, forcing the men to halt. "Bobby—Bobby—It's me, Porky. Bobby? Bobby!" Bobby hung limp between the two men.

"It's no use. This man's in a coma. We're bringing him up to the sick bay." Porky was overcome by grief, overwhelmed with fear that his friend was dying. He shouted and stroked Bobby's forehead, frantically pleading with him to wake up. "Bobby. Bobby, you can hear me. I know you can hear me. Bobby! Please, Bobby, open your eyes."

Porky sobbed uncontrollably as the men passed on to the sick bay and his friend disappeared from sight. There was nothing he could do, so he turned and walked back toward the kitchen. But he couldn't enter. Instead, he sat on the ground in a state of shock, so overcome with sorrow he felt numb. Men shuffled by him for their evening rations, not noticing his tearstained face.

"Buddies 'til the bitter end," he mumbled over and over to himself.

Porky watched the moon rise, large and full and luminescent, and the North Star appear in its position with the Big Dipper. Sorrow slowly released him from its vise. He pulled himself together, wiped his face with the end of the towel habitually draped around his neck, and entered the kitchen.

The cook's assistant who was serving the rice was burly, with tattoos etched onto his muscular forearms. Porky approached and announced, "I'll wait 'till you get down to the bottom. I prefer 'browned' rice."

"You and the rest of the guys," he said as he scraped rice from the side of the pot and dumped it onto Porky's bamboo plate. "Thanks," Porky said, grateful for his kindness as well as the generous portion. He emerged back into the open air and took a walk around to see what was happening. He ate as he walked and realized that though he had a "plate" and "water bottle," he now needed storage for extra food, so he could snack as he pleased throughout the day. Except for the light emerging from the fire in the kitchen, the only source of light was the light of the moon. After scouring the ground for a few minutes, he found the perfect bamboo shoot, hollowed it out, and stored the remainder of the rice in it. He wandered back to his sleeping area and leaned his water stick against the hut, then carefully poked back the rice at the opening of the bamboo and placed it on the grass.

The moon cast an eerie light on the POWs carrying dozens of bodies past the barracks. Porky looked about and noticed dead lying close to the shed, adjacent to the doctor's hut. He approached a corpse and picked up a canteen and cup by its side. Searching for something to tie them together, he stumbled upon a piece of rope, fastened the mess kit to the rope, and tied it around his waist, then wandered in search of anyone he knew, occasionally calling out names of his lost companions.

A billowy cloud passed in front of the moon and a soft rain began to fall. Porky faced skyward for the shower to wash over him. It soon passed. He wandered back to the area where he last saw Bobby Doolan. There were a dozen or so legs sticking out of the mud underneath the shed. He averted his eyes and called out, "Bobby? Bobby?" *They're all dead*, he thought.

Porky went back to the hut where he had his afternoon siesta, sat, and grabbed a handful of grass. He bunched and twisted it and stuck it into his water and rice sticks, then headed out into the tall grass of an open field where he hunted for a spot to spend the night—away from the death and confusion and disease of the camp. He fluffed his towel into a pillow, matted tall grass into bedding, lay down and pulled fistfuls more grass down across his small frame, and fell fast asleep as the moon climbed higher and higher, casting an ethereal glow over his slumbering form.

POW Camp O'Donnell Main Headquarters
Courtesy National Archives and Lewis Brittan family (Bataan Project)

Chapter 23

In surrendering Bataan, General King had negotiated the largest surrender of troops in United States history, but he did not have the authority to surrender the Philippines. Though under siege, Corregidor had not surrendered, nor had the remaining islands. As a result, there was confusion about the status of the Americans and Filipinos. Were they Prisoners of War (POWs), or hostages held captive by the Imperial Forces of Japan as a bargaining tool for the ultimate surrender of American forces in the Philippines? The question was moot because in either case, rules involving the treatment of prisoners under the Hague Convention of 1907 as well as the Geneva Convention of 1929 were not upheld.

Porky woke with the sun, rested but hungry. For a moment, he forgot where he was and why he was there. Then he spotted the rope with the mess kit and canteen he had retrieved from the dead soldier and flashed back to the last moments he had spent with Bobby. He tied the rope around his waist, shook out the towel and slapped it round his neck, took a few nibbles from his rice stash and a few sips from the water, put the stoppers back, and headed off to the latrine before moving on to the kitchen.

But there was a commotion at the straddle trenches. Everyone was talking about one poor sucker who had wandered over in the middle of the night to take a piss and had fallen in. He screamed for help, but his would-be rescuers were too weak to pull him out, so he slipped under the raw sewage and drowned. Porky looked down as he urinated, saw the putrid corpse of the tech sergeant who had given him his first job as a typist, and vomited into the latrine.

After morning rations were plopped into mess kits, he wandered back off into the open field to eat. It took all his powers of concentration to focus on the food. Thousands of fellow prisoners—most starved down to skin and bones—were scattered throughout the field, eating and resting. Meanwhile, an air force lieutenant was in the officer's hut, preparing an official announcement. Finally he emerged, papers in hand, and hunted for a box strong enough to hold his weight. He found something that resembled an old milk crate and mounted it to speak. Once the lieutenant began calling out names for work details, the men gathered their belongings and drew closer to listen. Across the way, on the other side of the road, dozens of Filipinos were already busily employed digging as others carried corpses in a burial detail.

"The following men will report for water detail," the officer shouted. "R. Smith, D. Blake, S. Greene, A. Dexter, F. LaCoste, J. Peters, L. Kelley."

Porky was startled to hear his name called. He had thought all the records were lost and they were destined to wile away their hours, occasionally joining in to help with tasks as they saw fit—until they starved to death, died of disease, or were rescued. He walked toward the kitchen hut, where his work crew was gathering, as the officer continued calling out names for other details. It occurred to him that though they were captured, as far as Uncle Sam was concerned, they were still in the military. They were down, but they were not yet out.

Once the group gathered, the officer in charge instructed the six men whose names had been called first to pick up long poles piled up not far from the left entrance to the kitchen. The remaining six were told to grab five-gallon cans that had been tossed haphazardly to the right by the cook and crew. The cans had been fitted with strong wire handles and were now suitable as buckets.

"Follow me, men," the officer ordered. The pail and the pole duty groups assembled behind the officer for the water detail. He marched them a half mile down the road to a broad stream where the men with pails were instructed to rinse out and fill the cans only half full with water.

Meanwhile, the men assigned to pole duty waited for further instruction as the officer watched to ensure that the bucket brigade was thoroughly cleaning the pails before refilling them. Porky dropped the pole by the bank of the stream and waded in to scrub his towel before slapping it back around his neck. As he bent over to plunge the towel into the water, he heard laughter, horses neighing, splashing, and conversation that seemed to come from behind the bushes in the middle of the stream.

Porky signaled for the officer to come and listen. He waded over and eavesdropped for a moment before pushing aside a branch for a better view. Half-dozen horses were being scrubbed down by Japanese soldiers splashing about in play. The officer returned to the men and whispered further instructions. They were to place two buckets on each pole then carry the poles, Jap style, one man at each end of the pole, back to the kitchen. Though the instructions were simple, the task wasn't. The men no longer had the strength of other men their age. They winced with pain as the poles were thrust onto their thin shoulders. The half-mile trek back was agony as the weight from the water in the pails dug the poles in and penetrated to bone.

For the next week or so, Porky rose each morning, gathered his belongings, and returned to the kitchen for rice, then wandered back into the field to wait for his assignment. Then one day Porky wondered if he had been passed by. The air force lieutenant had called out nearly everyone's name and still there was nothing when finally his name was called. This time he was grouped with ten others. They were instructed to report to the lieutenant's right—by a truck. Porky dropped his food stash by the barracks before heading for the truck to join the others. Along with his towel, the rice- and water-filled bamboo sticks were his most valuable possession, his reserves in case he got hungry or thirsty. He carefully camouflaged them behind a clump of grass, hoping no one would suspect.

The POWs gathered by the truck were met by an enemy soldier. He instructed them in Japanese while motioning for them to hop onto the back and be seated. Before long, they had cleared the prison-camp grounds and headed out on the open road. Thirty minutes later, they arrived at a village where hundreds of Filipinos were milling about in the streets. Most were young women dressed in colorful skirts and tops. Several of the prettiest were escorted by Japanese officers. The few Filipino males in the crowd were mostly old men and young boys, on hand as servants to the Japanese, who had converted the entire village into a giant brothel. The Imperial forces had scouted throughout the entire expanse of the Philippine island network and abducted the most attractive women they could find. As Porky jumped from the truck, he was struck by the beauty of the women but sickened realizing what they had to endure. They too were held captive, and their lives could be snuffed out on a whim.

The truck driver escorted them to a nipa hut and motioned for them to enter and be seated on the floor. Soon a guard was posted at the door. The driver returned to the truck and drove away. Not long afterward, a Filipino male entered with a pail full of steaming rice and another which contained soup broth. He too was a prisoner, based on the remnants of his uniform. He smiled and nodded and seemed to acknowledge them as allies as he ladled the soup and rice into their mess kits.

"This food ain't half bad," one of the POWs said between mouthfuls.

The man seated next to him laughed. "Finally, a cook who knows how to prepare rice!"

"The soup's real tasty," another said. "I wonder what's in it."

The Filipino sat cross-legged in a corner and rose to serve them whenever the Americans wanted more. Once they were full, he stood and addressed them in perfect English. "Your instructions are that tomorrow you will ride in the Japanese army trucks to keep the American guerrilla fighters from firing at the trucks—which is what they are doing now."

Porky's jaw dropped in astonishment. "So what you're telling us is our special detail is to serve as hostages?"

"At least you have been well fed. If you look in back of you, there are blankets. The elevation here is higher than at Camp O'Donnell. The nights are colder. Tomorrow I will return with rice and water for your breakfast and extra rice to put in your mess kits for lunch. You'll be gone on work detail all day and return for chow," he said, bowed, and exited.

The next morning, a ten-truck convoy lined up outside the hut. Each man was assigned to a truck. Their destination was a fertile plains area several hours from the village. They traveled without incident through forest and brush, over bridges, and past isolated native dwellings. The prisoners kept a sharp eye out for fellow Americans. On the one hand, they hoped they were out there somewhere but realized if they were attacked, they were as good as dead. Around noontime, the convoy pulled into an opening in a thick canopy of bushes. Ahead was a field. The trucks encircled the outer edges of the field and parked. The POWs were ordered off the trucks, then gathered together in the center of the field to sit and eat.

One of the drivers returned to his truck and grabbed a toolbox stored in back of the seat. He flicked open the metal fasteners. Inside, he had stashed sixteen-ounce cans of sardines. He picked out two cans and brought them back to the prisoners, gesturing for Porky to open the cans and pass the contents around as a sort of feast. As Porky dumped chucks of sardines into the mess kits, several of the drivers began to pick on the largest prisoner, a young man about six feet tall who had been a farm hand back in his native Georgia. They nudged him in a good-natured way, smiled, and laughed and forced him to stand.

"I think they want to wrestle with you," Porky said. The other prisoners looked down, intimidated by the antics. "Go along with it. We'll cheer you on. They want to prove how tough they are. Just make sure they win. Bow to them."

The would-be sumo wrestler shot Porky a look, then bowed and prepared for the onslaught. Soon, one of the larger Japs faced off his opponent and prepared to throw him onto the ground. The American resisted with every fiber of his being. Soon everyone was into the action—cheering, yelling, laughing. "Hey, don't let him trick you. You lose if anything but your feet touch the ground," a freckle-faced GI yelled. But the American, who had been weakened by months at war and the grueling death march, was toppled. The Japanese truck drivers doubled over with laughter as he lay on the ground, sweating and panting. Soon he popped back up in a sitting position, straightened a kink out of his back, stood, and approached the reigning champion in the American manner, with his hand outstretched. The enemies shook hands and bowed and everyone cheered.

Following the wrestling match, the men were instructed to hop back onto the backs of the trucks and the convoy snaked its way out of the field and back onto the open road. Before long, they passed clusters of Philippine women carrying baskets laden with rice and root vegetables, fruits and fish. They were headed to what had been a sleepy interior village but was now transformed into a bustling open market. The convoy pulled into the village square where the drivers were to pick up confiscated equipment. Everyone was ordered out and was free to roam about, except for Porky, who was asked to take two pails filled with the drivers' underwear and wash them out at the town pump, located at the far end of the village. For this he would receive a few cans of sardines.

As their captors bartered for food and military equipment confiscated from surrendered American and Filipino bases, the prisoners walked around, checking out the women and goods, and those with cash purchased bananas, hard-boiled eggs, green vegetables, and sweets. Porky was penniless as he wandered to the village watering pump. All the money he had was long gone, spent during the long siege on Bataan. But his belly was full, and he felt vaguely happy as he soaked up the color and gaiety of the scene, the most spectacular part of which was straight ahead at the village pump station.

Hundreds of pretty girls and young women who had been brought in and were forced to serve as prostitutes were congregated there, chatting and washing themselves and their clothes. When they spotted Porky, they went wild. Though he was a bit scruffy, with a bushy beard, and carried two pails of dirty laundry, here was a cute American with an adorable smile, sporting a white towel round his neck like an athlete. And he was just their size. He pushed through the crowd to the pump, which was spraying out water like a fountain, and commenced to wash his captors' underwear. But he needed soap. He turned to one particularly sweet girl in a yellow sarong and gestured to borrow her soap. She giggled, pushed back her long sleek black hair, looked seductively into his eyes, and handed him a long white bar. After he washed and rinsed and wrung out the boxer shorts, he handed her back the soap, which is when all hell broke loose, or from Porky's perspective, all heaven broke loose.

Several women grabbed Porky, stripped him naked, lathered him up, and cavorted with him under the spewing pump station until they all doubled over with laughter—including dozens of onlookers who too got splashed and were enjoying the spectacle. Then a thought crossed his mind. If a Japanese officer came upon the scene, he could be shot on sight. He grabbed his clothes, dried himself off with his towel, dressed quickly, grabbed the pails of sopping laundry, waved and smiled, and headed back. Before long, the Americans were ordered back onto the trucks to return to their positions as hostages, and the convoy moved out, headed back to the main village.

Back inside the hut, the men were served rice and soup as before, but this time, the Filipino POW left them to fend for themselves with the open pots. Porky spotted an opening. Several of the prisoners—the ones with the cash to buy the extra food—had left bits of banana and egg on their mess-kit plates. One looked as if he was about to doze off and had left more than the others.

"Would you like me to wash out your mess kit?" Porky offered.

"Sure. I'm feeling kinda lazy. Ain't that's the truth," the man replied with a thick Southern drawl. "The name's Savage," he said, shaking Porky's hand.

"Franklin LaCoste. My friends call me Porky, though some call me Frenchy." Porky grinned as he took Savage's mess kit and brought it with his own to the back of the hut. There, as he suspected, was a water pump. Before scrubbing the plates clean, he ate every morsel of garbage left on Savage's plate.

Porky returned to the front of the nipa hut and was about to enter when one of the Japanese truck drivers drove up and handed him a shaving kit through the open window. The driver smiled and gestured for Porky to shave. Porky bowed. "Thank you. Thanks a lot. You want me to shave?" Porky gestured as if shaving himself. The enemy soldier smiled and nodded and drove off before his act of kindness was spotted. "If only he had asked me before my laundry duty in the last village," Porky said to himself, then returned to the water spigot and primed the pump. He opened the kit and took a long look at himself as the mirror glinted and flashed in the late-afternoon sun. He was startled to see how grubby he had become. *Like a mountain man*, he thought. "Or a bum," he said out loud. "No wonder the girls tried to clean me up." There wasn't a speck of shaving cream, but the razor was sharp and did the trick though it tugged at his skin. He winced with pain, nicking himself a few times, but once finished admired himself in the mirror. "My, my, you are a handsome devil," he said then opened his mouth wide to check out his teeth. He scrubbed at his teeth and gums with a finger, cleaned off the razor, closed the kit, and returned to the front of the hut. Before long, the driver returned and Porky handed the shaving kit back to him with a broad smile.

"Thank you. Thank you, very much," he said with a deep bow. As he walked back into the hut, he was startled to see Savage sprawled out on the floor, wrapped in a blanket, shaking.

"Frenchy, is it cold in here? I'm goddamn freezing."

Porky knelt by his side and felt his forehead. "You've got a fever. I bet it's malaria."

"No, I doubt it," Savage said with a violent twist.

"You want some water?"

"No."

Porky sat cross-legged as Savage closed his eyes. "Let me tell you a little story. A few days before the war began, when we were at Nichols Field, I had a headache. One of the worst I've ever had. A friend wanted me to go downtown with him, but I told him I was feeling lousy, with a real bad headache. He said, 'Let's go up to the medics and get some aspirin. I know the guy on duty. I'm sure he'll take care of you.'"

"So we went over to the sick bay, and when I asked the corpsman if I could have some aspirin for my headache, a voice from the next room yelled out, 'Soldier, come in here.' It was the doctor. He took one look at me, felt my pulse, looked at my eyes and a few other things, and said, 'Soldier, you've got yourself a mild case of malaria.' The doctor turned to my friend and said, 'Can you take him down to the Thirty-first Infantry Hospital in Manila?' My friend said, 'Sure. I'm sure I can scout out a truck.'"

Savage began to shake more violently, so much so that he rolled loose from the blanket onto the bare floor. "Here. Let me wrap the blanket around you so you'll get the most out of it," Porky said. He rolled Savage back onto the middle of the blanket and then folded up the sides around him, tucking in the ends.

"Thanks," Savage said as Porky pulled his head up and forced him to take a sip of water.

"So anyway, my friend takes me to the hospital. They checked me over real good and signed me in as a patient. I got lots of quinine and sulfa pills from that visit. And wouldn't you know it, I've got several left over and they're in my coverall pocket. I think you need them more than I do."

A Japanese guard pointed his flashlight into the dark hut and spotted Porky huddled over by Savage. "Nanda—Nanda?" were the sounds Porky heard.

"Be-o-ki," Porky sounded out in pidgin Japanese. "My friend is sick."

The guard flashed the light onto Savage's face. Perspiration dripped from his forehead. Porky took a pill out and showed it to the guard before propping Savage up and slipping it into his mouth.

"Ah—ah." Savage swallowed and slowly sank back down.

Porky looked at the guard and extended his index finger. "Honcho—tobacco?"

The guard grabbed a cigarette from his shirt pocket, lit it, and handed it over to Porky. They shared the cigarette as they stood watch over Savage, who began to moan and attempted to pull himself back up. Porky knelt down to restrain him as the guard quietly exited, disturbed by the spectacle. After a while, Porky went outside and nodded to the guard. He was there to hunt for a shelter half he had spotted earlier outside the entrance to the hut. He felt along the outside of the straw siding until his fingernail snapped against the metal rope hole in the canvas. Grabbing the shelter half with both hands, he dragged it into the hut and wrapped it around Savage to help him sweat out the illness. As the night wore on, he removed another quinine tablet and later a sulfa tablet and forced the pills and water down his throat.

"Swallow, my friend. You'll be over this in no time."

Porky spread out next to Savage with the intention of maintaining a vigil throughout the night. As morning light filtered through bamboo slats into the hut, the Filipino cook entered with food. All the men were awake and seated, except for Porky, who was sprawled sound asleep and snoring next to his new friend.

Savage opened his eyes. "Frenchy. Frenchy?"

"Wha . . . ?"

"I feel good. No headache. I'm drenched to the bone and feeling weak, but other than that I'm doing fine."

Porky sat up and shook himself awake, then removed the canvas and blankets and helped Savage sit up. The cook approached. "No detail today. You can rest more. I hear you'll be going back to the main camp today."

Porky nodded at the cook and breathed a sigh of relief. "Savage, let's get you outside. You need to dry out in the sun," he said as he accepted the food from the cook.

Porky helped Savage outside. He blinked and jerked back from the full glare of the sun. So Porky took him to the back of the hut where they could sit in the shade to eat. Later that afternoon, the men packed into the back of one truck for the ride back to Camp O'Donnell. Porky helped Savage off and over to an open bay barracks to rest. He then wandered around, checking out the new arrivals to see if any of his outfit had made it to the base when he spotted a detail coming over a hill. Dozens of other men spotted them too, and they flocked to the new arrivals to see if they were carrying any merchandise or food to sell. Smack in the center of the detail was Pint Lawson, looking healthy and fit and carrying a bushel bag.

"Pint. Pint," Porky called loudly until Pint glanced over in his direction. A broad smile spread over his handsome face. He waved but kept on marching, for the detail was heavily flanked by Japanese guards. Once the detail passed, Porky followed at a distance. Finally they came to a halt. The guards dismissed the detail and Porky walked up to Pint and shook hands.

"You're looking good," Pint remarked after taking a good look at his friend.

"I should be. I just had a detail where I got all sorts of food," Porky added with a laugh. "So, my friend, what's in the sack?" By now, the two were surrounded with fellow prisoners anxious to see too.

"Yeah, what's in the sack?" the others asked as they pressed in closer.

"Candy," Pint whispered into Porky's ear. "You know them penny-a—piece candies we had as kids. I've got a sack full of boxes and boxes of them. If I have any more, it's going to kill me."

"Then sell it," Porky whispered back. "You can always use the money."

Pint opened the sack so the men could peer in. "Hey I'll give you five pesos for a box," one man shouted.

"No. No. No," Porky yelled into Pint's good ear. "Five pesos for a box is not good enough. You're not a salesman. Here, let me handle this." Porky reached into the bag and grabbed out a box. "Twenty pesos for a box," he barked out like a carnival huckster. He moved away from Pint and the crowd followed, outbidding one another on the boxes. He grabbed the money and a handful of candy from each box he sold and stuffed it in his pockets. Before long, the entire bushel of boxes was gone and he handed the money over to his friend.

"You keep some. You earned it," he protested.

"No. I've got what I want. Look at all the candy. I can either sell it or eat it. But I'll probably eat it."

"Good enough. See you in the morning," Pint said and turned to rejoin the men in his work detail.

Porky wandered back toward the field and made his way through the high grass to a roofless barracks where he sat and popped penny-a-piece candies into his mouth off and on throughout the night.

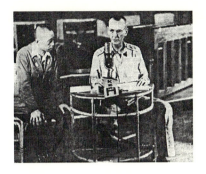

7 May 1942—Station KZRH
General Wainwright broadcasts
orders to surrender
Courtesy Department of Defense

Chapter 24

Cabanatuan
June 1942

The next day Porky was summoned to serve in a large detail and was later boarded onto a truck for transfer, along with hundreds of other men, to another camp—the main prison camp on the island of Luzon—Cabanatuan. His main regret was leaving Pint and his newfound friend Savage behind, and he hoped they were traveling with the convoy or would soon follow. What he did not regret was leaving the conditions created by Captain Tsuneyoshi, a rabid American-hater who had been in charge at Camp O'Donnell. Deprived of basic medicines, over one thousand five hundred men died at the camp under his watch. But would the situation at the next camp be any better, Porky wondered as they traveled to the east along the Pampanga River.

Cabanatuan, their next destination, was home to thousands of men captured when Corregidor and most of the islands fell the month before. By June 8, the last pockets of resistance had surrendered to General Homma. Now the combined American and Filipino forces were officially prisoners of war or, as some euphemistically referred to themselves, guests of the Japanese. Because a number of the newly captured were engineers, the camp had expanded beyond its earlier confines as a prewar Philippine Army installation. Irrigation ditches, septic systems, and latrines were installed, and larvicides and disinfectants liberally used, along with makeshift fly and bug traps. Medical personnel had directed that clothes be boiled and the men's hair shaved to discourage lice. Sleeping mats were aired out routinely and exposed to the natural mildew resistant sun's rays. The nurses who had once served the battalions were now in a civilian internment camp.

Porky was in no shape to travel the sixty miles to Cabanatuan. He was visibly ill and had the runs. Before long, the men nearby began to grumble. "This is horrible. Soldier, you need to get to the back of the truck. Peeyoo," they complained as they cupped a hand over their noses. As Porky moved to the rear, his fellow travelers cut a wide berth to let him pass.

The convoy bypassed Cabanatuan City, home to fifty thousand, and headed four miles farther to the camp that bore its name. The trucks passed through the main entrance and gatehouse and pulled to a stop. The men were asked to disembark and line up for barracks assignments. As Porky did what he was told, the men moved away from him, holding their noses and fanning their faces with their hands as they stepped away, so he stood alone. Each was given the number of his barracks, then told to "about face and march" to his new quarters. Porky did as he was instructed, then collapsed in a swan dive onto the dirt road. When he awoke, POWs were looking down at him. He turned his head and noticed he was lying on the ground, outside of a barracks. He passed out again. The next time he awoke, he was in a sick ward. Though it was now nighttime, he could make out the outline of the enclosure—a five-foot-high wall with a roof on top, but no floor, just the bare ground. The men around him were all groaning.

Porky stood up, walked out, and began to hunt for a water spigot to wash his clothes and himself. Before long he spotted the outline of a vertical metal pipe, handle, and spout. His palm bruised as he turned the handle, but when water began to pass over his parched body, rinsing off the fecal matter and stench, his pain subsided. He cupped his hands to receive the water, bent and lowered his face into the tiny pool, then splashed the water over his head, down his neck onto his chest. This was sheer bliss. He washed his towel then used it to sponge down every speck of skin, wash between his toes, and scrub his armpits, backside, and privates. He scrubbed his coveralls and shirt and shoes and put them on wet. He drank liberally from the water spigot before turning it off and heading out for a drying walk before heading back. But when he thrust his head back into his assigned ward, he saw that the men were naked and dying. Some were dead. He stepped back away from the death house and used a grassy area not too far away to bed down for what remained of the night.

As the sun rose over the Sierra Madre, the guards entered the sick ward to wake the men. Those who could get up were forced to march. Those who could not were placed in bamboo and canvas carriers and transported by other POWs into newly assigned barracks. The dead would be brought out later by the burial details. The POWs carried their charges to a ward that was isolated from the other barracks by a barbed-wire fence put up to keep men contaminated with transferable diseases from wandering and infecting others. These barracks would house the sickest of the prisoners. The name of the place was Ward Zero.

Porky got up and headed for the outhouse. When he exited, he saw where the POWs were carrying the sick and followed them. Several men lay outside the barracks, covered in dried mud. Those inside were bunked down toe-to-toe. Approximately one hundred men were resting on a solid wood floor. Porky crawled in and found a space, sprawled out, and fell into a deep, dreamless sleep. When he awoke, he was lying in what appeared to be a field of naked, shriveled dead, though he could hear groans emanating from across the room. He pulled himself into a sitting position and moved toward the barracks entryway when his eyes slowly focused on the men lying outside, half stuck under the barracks. One man looked vaguely familiar. He wandered outside and stared down at Dynamite Dunn, now gaunt, with bony protrusions visible through his uniform.

"Dynamite, Dynamite, it's Porky," he whispered hoarsely, kneeling down to check if he was alive or dead. Dynamite's face was ashen and his breathing shallow, interspersed with what Porky suspected was a death rattle.

The burial detail arrived to remove the dead and clean out the building. From the far corners of the ward, several of the seriously ill managed to get up and leave. Porky watched as a pail of rice was brought in for the few living who remained. He took one last look at his friend, then reentered the ward and grabbed something to eat and drink before passing out for the remainder of the day into the night.

At dawn streams of light filtered through the bamboo slats, illuminating the grisly scene. Porky slowly regained consciousness. Corpses were strewn about on the floor, with limbs contorted from their last moments struggling against pain. He stared up the enlarged anus of one carcass, averted his eyes, and curled up into a fetal position and found himself cheek to jowl with a familiar figure. Savage had snuck in under cover of darkness to bunk down beside Porky, a burlap sack propped beneath his head as a pillow.

"What the hell are you doing here? Don't you know this is the most contagious area in the camp? Why do you think they've got this barbed wire separating us from the rest of the camp?" Porky whispered.

Savage sat up and pushed the satchel between them to show off his booty. "I snuck in because I wanted to help you," he said as he pulled out bananas, tins of sardines, and a bag of sugar he had snatched.

"You are one crazy kid." Porky shook his head and pulled himself into a cross-legged position. But his scowl soon turned to a grin as he surveyed the foodstuffs.

"You saved my life. The least I can do is get you back on your feet."

"I'm not that bad off," Porky said as he reached into the sack for a banana.

"Then what the hell are you doing here?"

"I got hold of some candy and stuffed myself with it," he narrated, peeling the banana. "So I ended up with a bad case of the runs, and they thought it was malaria. They thought I was on death's door," he said, stuffing the banana into his mouth.

Savage covered his mouth with both hands and started to shake, which concerned Porky until he noticed he was stifling a laugh. "You crazy bastard," he managed between spasms.

"So how did you get this stuff?" Porky asked as he rifled through the sack.

"If you were a foot or two taller and your eyes were good enough, you could see up over that field," Savage drawled. "There's a small village there. I crawled under the barbed wire, two sets to be exact, and snuck through the field until I got to the village. Paid cash for everything, and did they have everything! Sardines, boiled eggs, rice, bananas—I grabbed everything I could carry that didn't need to be cooked."

"And then you snuck back in?"

Savage was very proud of himself. "Sure enough," he said, gently slugging Porky's shoulder.

"Did it ever dawn on you—you might have gotten yourself killed?"

"They'll never catch me."

Porky rolled his eyes and shook his head. "Well, my friend, thanks for breakfast. But I don't want you killed on my behalf."

"Frenchy, I've got to do something around here, or I'll go stir-crazy."

An American POW entered with a can half full of rice. He surveyed the scene and was about to exit when the faint cries of POWs in the middle of the corpses caught his attention. "Over here. We're alive over here." Two men struggled to sit up to be seen. The man on the breakfast detail covered his face with his shirt and brought the pail over. He dropped it by their side and stepped through the bodies of the dead as quickly as he could. Once outside he breathed deeply and hurried away into the fresh air and sunshine.

Porky and Savage made their way to the can and dished out rice into their mess kits. Lying beside the rice pail was a friend from Porky's outfit.

"Carroll—Carroll, what the hell are you doing here?"

Carroll opened his eyes and sat up. "It's a long story."

"Grab some food and let's get out of here. There's no one around so we can chat. Hell, everyone's afraid of this place."

Porky and Savage helped Carroll to his feet and plopped some rice onto his kit. Savage made his way back to the sack and grabbed a tin of sardines, three boiled eggs, and three bananas and exited to the outside as Porky helped Carroll meander through the corpses. Once outside, they relaxed and made their way to the water spigot to drink before sitting down to eat.

"So, Carroll, when did you arrive at the morgue?" Porky asked between mouthfuls of rice.

"I snuck in last night," Carroll said sheepishly.

Savage sprawled out on the grass to relax. "It's a popular place, ain't it?"

Porky was perplexed. "So what brought you here? Savage snuck in to keep me company and nurse me back to health. What's your excuse?"

"The food. I came for the food, the quon. In the barracks you get quon for fifty or sixty guys, but here—who can eat? They're all dead or dying."

Porky was confused. "Quon, quon—that's a new one on me."

"Where have you been? We've been using that expression for a week or so. Quon—it means anything you can digest; anything you can put in your mouth and stand to swallow."

Savage picked up the rice with his spoon and wrinkled his nose. "Even this garbage?"

"Hey, it's a meal," Carroll snapped back.

Porky put down his tin plate. "I think both of you guys are nuts. There's a reason people don't come here. The place is contaminated. The place is crawling with germs. I passed out, and they brought me here. If it were up to me, this is the one place I wouldn't be caught dead in."

Carroll stood and looked down at the men. "Look at it this way. We're all dead men. We're being slowly starved to death."

Savage opened the big can of sardines as Porky stood. "Hey, give me your cups. I'll get some more water. What else do you have for us, Savage?"

Savage stuck his hands into his coveralls and pulled out the booty. "I've got some hard-boiled eggs, fruit, and some sugar to stir into our water for energy."

Carroll sat next to Savage. "Wow, a feast!"

Courtesy National Archives

Chapter 25

As the summer wore on, Porky, Savage, and Carroll were still in Ward Zero. They slept in an area nearer to the opening of the entrance where they could get fresh air and separate themselves as much as possible from their highly contagious roommates. In the early mornings, as sunlight spread across the floor, a POW would rush into the barracks with a rice pail and hurry out before he could be stopped by anyone begging for help. One morning, as several men rose to painstakingly make their way to the bucket and Porky and his friends slowly sat up, stretched, and yawned, Porky leaned over to his friend, Savage. "Let me have some of that sugar," he requested. "The guys seemed to like it stirred into their rice the other day."

Savage pulled the bag of sugar from the sack and tossed it to Porky, who gingerly walked through the corpses toward the few who managed to hang onto life during the night.

"Here, let me sprinkle a little of this onto your rice."

"Thanks, Frenchy. It's not half bad with some sugar on it. All we need is some milk and it'd be like something from home."

"Yah, a rice pudding like your gray-haired ma would make."

The sickest of the POWs smiled weakly. "You're a great guy, Frenchy."

"It's the least I can do. Catch you later," he said as he rejoined his friends. "Let's get out of here," Porky whispered as he led the way out to the water spigot and sat down on the ground.

Savage pulled out a wad of bills from his coveralls. "$5 . . . $20 . . . $50 . . . $90. Whew. It's amazing, the amount of cash you can get for just about anything. Problem is, I'm getting real low on supplies. I've got to make a dash for it."

"I thought you snuck out last night."

"I did, but the Filipinos in the village told me they were low on supplies too. They told me to come back in the morning."

"In broad daylight?" Carroll gasped.

"Now I know you are crazy," Porky said.

"Are you kidding me? Haven't you noticed there's no one stationed here? Even the Japs know enough to stay away. It's a wonder anyone comes by at all. After all, we're all supposed to be half dead."

"What surprises me is no one from the main camp has found out you're missing," Porky said, concerned about the game they were playing.

"Do you honestly think they know who's here?"

"Well, Savage, I think they're beginning to get a handle on who is who and what's what. Haven't you noticed the work details? It's the Jap guards who call out the names now. They've started to figure it out, and fast."

"Then I've got to make my move before they do miss me. I'm going to get these supplies come hell or high water, then hightail it back to my regular barracks."

As Savage finished talking, a Japanese guard walked past on guard duty between the two barbed-wire fences. He came uncomfortably close to the seated men, which made Porky wonder if he might have been listening to their conversation.

"This is it. I'm gone," Savage whispered, then turned and crawled underneath the wire into the tall grass before Porky and Carroll could stop him.

The path that Savage had used night after night was clearly visible in the light of day. As Savage maneuvered toward the second fence, the guard turned round and raced back to catch Savage halfway through, hidden in the grass. He armed his rifle and stuck it at his head. Porky and Carroll remained seated but spun their bodies away from the action while attempting to watch from the corner of their eyes. After several minutes, the guard motioned with his rifle for Savage to crawl back under the fence into the enclosed area. Savage maneuvered the sack beneath him and slowly backed out from under the wire, stood, and returned to the barracks without glancing back at his friends. After the guard went back to his rounds, Porky and Carroll slipped back into the barracks to join Savage, who was visibly shaken, but still clutched the supply sack in his lap.

"Jesus Christ, that was close," Porky exhaled.

Carroll was shaking with fright. "Didn't I tell you, you're crazy!"

Savage took a deep breath and looked squarely at Porky. "I'm still leaving. I've got to."

Porky was beyond exasperated. "Savage, you are crazy!"

"Don't worry. I've forgotten all about the village."

"Look, Savage. You've proven you're brave. And hell knows you're lucky. But don't press your luck because it's bound to run out."

"I'm surprised he didn't sho . . . shoot you," Carroll said once he stopped shaking.

"Tonight I'm taking no chances. I'll sneak under the barbed wire back to the work area. No one patrols there."

Just as Savage finished talking two Japanese guards entered. The men froze, terrified that Carroll's and Savage's cover had been blown. Instead, two well-dressed and shaven Army Air Corps sergeants followed behind, accompanied by a Japanese officer and an American POW doctor.

"They want you to stay here," the doctor explained to the sergeants. "See those guys over there," he said, pointing at Porky and his friends. "They're less contagious," he explained, then left the barracks with the Japanese.

The army officers took a hard look at the seriously ill men strewn about among the emaciated remains of the dead and shuddered. "So I guess we get to call this home for a while," one said to the other, who seemed to be having a hard time absorbing the shock.

They picked their way toward Porky, Carroll, and Savage, carefully stepping over the POWs, who were groaning, coughing, and thrashing about. "Jesus Christ Almighty. Where am I? This is horrible," the second sergeant burst out. "Jesus," he said and sat down next to Porky.

"You're in Ward Zero. So what happened? Did you two get shot down?" Porky asked coolly.

"Yah, something like that," the first sergeant said. "Ward Zero—what does that mean?"

Porky dropped his voice, not wanting to further upset the men struggling for life around him. "Only one man has been discharged in the past two weeks; in fact, since I've been here," he stated flatly. Several POWs entered with bamboo slats to carry out the dead, followed by another POW, who hosed down the area while yet another POW knelt down to squeegee the sites where the captured American servicemen had died during the night.

"At least they clean the place up after . . . you know," Savage ventured in a bizarre attempt to offer some Southern comfort, if not hospitality. "They push the crap out the door. Of course, then they leave it there in a heap to fester."

"Jesus," the second sergeant said.

"Ah, you'll get used to it," Porky assured in a hopeless attempt to cheer them up.

Just then, the doctor reentered and looked around for his new charges. Carroll and Savage turned their backs and quietly slipped out the entry as the doctor's eyes slowly readjusted to the spectacle. "How are you two doing?" he asked the sergeants.

"I'm doing great, except for these stomach pains." The first sergeant seemed to be adjusting better than his companion; he stood as the doctor approached. The second sergeant remained seated and appeared to be completely disheartened.

The doctor glanced from one to the other. "Look, men, I could examine you, but there's nothing I can do for you. I haven't got an aspirin I could give you. My advice is to eat the rice, as lousy as it is, and to drink enough water, or else you'll dehydrate. And if you show any signs of malaria, for God's sake stay out of the sun. Talk with Frenchy, here. He's been through it. He knows what to do. So, Frenchy, how are you doing?" the doctor asked.

Porky managed a smile. "Good," he said. "I'm doing much better."

"Glad to hear it." The doctor turned his attention back to the officers. "Look, I'll come back and check on you," he said, then scooted down to speak directly to the second sergeant. "Keep your chin up, sergeant."

"I'll try," the sergeant said, then doubled over with pain. "Jesus Christ, what's wrong with me?"

"I suspect you've got a touch of dysentery. The straddle trench is out back in case you have to go."

"Thanks, Doc." He grabbed the doctor's arm and struggled to get up, then maneuvered to exit to the john.

"Frenchy, I'll see you later," he said, following the sergeant to be sure he made it to the latrine.

Porky looked at his new companion. "If the folks back home could see us now."

The next morning, there was a vacant place where Savage had bunked down the night before. The sack was gone too. Porky woke to hear Carroll moaning. The two sergeants were close by.

"You OK?"

"Not really."

"I told you not to stay." Porky noticed a bulge in his coverall pocket. He stuck his hand in and brought out a wad of bills. "Jesus, where did this come from?"

Carroll rolled over and propped himself up on an elbow. "It's a present from Savage. I saw him slip it into your pocket before he left."

Porky felt a lump in his throat. He remained silent for a moment, afraid that he might cry. "He's quite a guy. I hope he made it back OK."

"I didn't hear gunfire, so maybe he's safe."

Porky turned to the Army Air Corps sergeant close by. He had covered himself with a blanket, which made Porky wonder if he had come down with malaria. The first sergeant got up and headed to the latrine. "Boy, he's still out like a light," Porky said, drawing closer.

"Maybe he's got the blanket over his head for a reason," Carroll said, looking concerned.

Porky mouthed the word, "Malaria."

Carroll nodded in agreement. "He needs the sleep," he said as the POW kitchen detail ran in with the pail of rice and ran out again.

"Yah, but as the doctor said, he needs food too. If he's not up to it, I'll go and get him some water. You want some water too, Carroll? Or can you take care of yourself?"

"To tell the truth, I feel weak. Yah, I could use some help."

"Hey, that's what I'm here for."

Porky stood and crossed over the sergeant. "Rise and shine. Room service has come and gone," he said with a wink to Carroll. "Breakfast is here." The sergeant didn't respond. Porky gently poked him, but he still didn't move. "Jesus, I'll bet he's passed out under that GD blanket."

"Well then, for Christ's sake, give him some air," Carroll whispered hoarsely.

Porky began to lift the blanket. "Sorry to wake you, but . . . holy shit! Oh my God. Jesus!"

"Why, what's wrong? Is he all right?" Carroll struggled to maneuver himself into a sitting position.

"Jesus Christ, Carroll, there's blood everywhere. He's dead."

"Oh my God," Carroll slid back down on the floor.

Porky pulled back the blanket, exposing the scene. The sergeant's face had turned marble white, with eyes and mouth wide open. "It looks like he got a razor out of his duffel bag and slit his wrists," Porky said as he threw the blanket back over the corpse.

POW Camp Cabanatuan
Courtesy National Archives

Chapter 26

As autumn approached, Porky became increasingly active, tending to a variety of ventures. At times he slept in an open field, not far from the rim of the plateau where water buffalo grazed below, hoping that the fresh air would ward off further contagion. One day a POW kitchen helper showed up with canned milk for the men. This led to Porky's bright idea, which he went over with the man, hoping he could add some pointers. The experiment involved Porky pouring his ration of canned milk into his mess cup, placing a mosquito net over the top, and setting it out in the sun. With any luck, he hoped it would turn into a sort of whey or cottage cheese.

"Hey, tell me. Did it work?" the mess detail asked.

"Looks good," Porky said, taking a whiff. "I hope it tastes as good as it looks."

"I've got some more milk today. Things are looking up in terms of rations. There are rumors about Red Cross packages. Christmas is a comin' so keep your fingers crossed."

Porky entered the barracks along with the kitchen help, grabbed some rice and milk, and headed over to Carroll. "So how are you feeling?"

"Not so good. But I'll make it."

Porky handed Carroll his breakfast and watched with satisfaction as he drank the milk down in one long gulp. They listened as the sound of a truck grew closer and backed up to the barracks. Japanese guards entered with bags of sugar.

"I wonder what this is about," Porky whispered to Carroll, who had propped himself into a reclining position, a rolled blanket serving as a support.

223

"Anyone want to buy sugar?" one of the guards asked with barely a trace of a Japanese accent.

"How much?" Porky inquired.

"Three dollar," he responded with an unexpected smile.

"Three bucks, you've got a deal," Porky said, handing him over the money. He suspected he was being sold supplies intended for the POWs. *So what else is new?* he thought cynically. The guard turned and examined the dollar bills in the light, then handed over a twenty-pound bag of sugar. After the guard left, Porky plopped the sack down and pulled the string at the top to open it.

"Hey, guys, any of you want some sugar?" Porky yelled.

Suddenly some of those who appeared half dead a moment before came to life. "Sure," several responded.

"OK, those of you who are able to get up, go outside and fill your cups with water and I'll put a tablespoon in."

Three men propped themselves up on bony hands, stood, and managed to get outside without help. Porky hoisted the bag back up, but to his chagrin, sugar began spilling out. "Damn it! What am I going to do now? Aha, I know," he said to himself as he put the bag back down and exited. Once he disappeared, several men snuck up to the sack and grabbed handfuls of sugar. Outside, Porky was intent as he hunted through the ever-expanding pile of discarded clothing from the dead, who were stripped before burial. He examined several pairs of pants and finally chose a pair that appeared to be free of holes. He washed them out thoroughly at the water spigot and hung them out to dry on protruding pieces of bamboo along the elevated edge of the barracks.

In the afternoon, Porky returned to the pants, tested them for dryness, and then tied the bottom of the legs off and headed back to the barracks. He carefully transferred the sugar into the pant legs, guiding the small white granules into the two leg compartments and partway up the torso. He inserted a piece of rope into the belt loops, pulled and tied the top, then slung it over his shoulder like a saddle pack

"This should work," Porky said as he picked his way through the maze of invalids back to Carroll. "Hey, guys, get some water and I'll get you some more sugar." Everyone who was able to stand lined up for the sugar.

Porky was spooning the sugar into cups when the doctor entered. "What's this?" he asked.

"Sugar detail," Porky answered brightly.

"Well, the detail is coming to a close, because you're being shipped out."

Two days later, Porky and five other Ward Zero patients deemed healthy enough to leave were housed in a bamboo barracks by themselves. It was a sort of halfway house. They were separated from Ward Zero but not yet within the confines of the main barracks area. As the men stood around a rice barrel, they chatted about the new "assignment."

"I wonder how long they'll keep us here."

"Long enough to see if we drop dead or stay alive," Porky said sardonically.

"At least it's an improvement. It's clean for starters."

"Yah," Porky agreed, "but I'm getting bored. I'm going over to shoot the breeze with Carroll. I'll send him your regards."

Porky was disease free as far as he knew, and though he was still feeling a bit weak, he'd been in far worse condition. Compared to many others, he was in great shape, he thought. Though the day was hot, there were a few puffy clouds in the sky, and he thought he detected a slight breeze as he wandered toward his old digs. He realized he almost felt happy as he entered Ward Zero and glanced over to where they had been staying, but Carroll was not there. He walked into the center of the barracks and searched through the crowd. *He couldn't have been released, he was too sick*, he thought, then began to imagine the worst.

"Where's Carroll?" Porky asked a patient.

"Frenchy, is that you?" a thin voice called.

Carroll had been moved to the far right, toward the rear—over to the "sick side" of the ward. Porky maneuvered through the men to Carroll's side. "How did you know it was me?"

"I recognized your voice. What are you doing here?"

"I came to visit an old friend. Are you up for a cigarette?"

"Sure, if you could prop me up."

Porky bunched up the blanket Carroll had tossed aside and gently pushed it under his head, but Carroll never looked at Porky. Instead, he stared up at the ceiling.

"If you can wait a sec . . ." Porky said as he pulled a cigarette from his pack and a wooden match. He struck the match against the bamboo floor and lit up. The smoke filtered across the room like incense. "Here you go," he said, holding the cigarette above Carroll's face.

Carroll reached out with his bony hand and waved it in the air. "You're going to have to help me out, Frenchy. I can't see. I'm blind."

"Oh sure, no problem. Glad to oblige," Porky said, grateful that Carroll could not see the tears rolling down his cheeks.

Carroll slowly propped himself up. "Where's that cigarette? It smells great."

"Here, let me put it in your mouth." Porky gingerly placed the cigarette between Carroll's lips. He reached out and grabbed it by instinct.

Porky sat by Carroll's side until the cigarette was nearly gone, and then gently took the butt from Carroll before he burnt himself. "I'll be back," Porky promised.

"Thanks, Frenchy. I can always count on you."

Porky left Ward Zero as downcast as he had been cheerful before he entered. When he returned to his new digs, he noticed a crowd had gathered on the other side of the barbed-wire fence. They were haggling over the price of a piece of fresh fruit. Along the edge of the crowd was someone who looked familiar but was so bedraggled he couldn't be sure. He walked up to the barbed wire for a closer look. Sure enough, it was Herman Hausmann, once a spiffy dresser, now reduced to looking like a bum. "Hey, Herman, how the heck are you?" Porky yelled as loud as he could.

Herman turned and looked around.

"Hausmann, how the hell are you?" Porky yelled again. Finally, Herman spotted Porky and burst out into a wide grin.

"Hey, Porky, how are you?" he responded as he cautiously approached the barbed wire.

"Not too bad. Hey, don't worry. I don't think I'm contaminated, at least not anymore."

"Glad to hear it."

"Herman, Christ, don't you have anything to wear? You're the worst dressed in the crowd."

"I had some decent clothes, but I traded them for food. From what I hear, you sick guys at least get to eat."

"Sorry. I shouldn't have mentioned it."

"I suppose you didn't hear—Billy passed away a few days ago. He's been over here in the malaria ward. I have a touch too, but it seems better."

"Billy's dead too?" Porky paused, too choked up to speak. "His poor family . . . and his girlfriend," he said softly. "You know about Bobby?"

"Yah, Pint told me."

"Pint's OK?"

"Sure."

"Good."

The two men stood in silence united in pain, facing one another across the barbed wire. "Herman, I have to get back now. But why don't you meet me here tomorrow, sometime late in the afternoon, and I may be able to help you out with some clothes."

"Gee, thanks, Porky. I'll be back."

The old friends turned and went their separate ways. But Porky was not one to stand idly by while a friend was in need. He walked past his barracks and headed straight for Ward Zero, picking up a stick along the way. As he approached the pile of clothes in the back of the barracks, the stench was so bad he backed off for a moment, but then, holding one hand over his nose and mouth, he averted his face and began poking through the extremely soiled discarded clothes with the stick.

"This is worse than I remember, or maybe I was too sick to notice," he mumbled to himself. Finally, he located a decent pair of army regulation suntan pants and a shirt and a large pair of shoes. He carried each item, one at a time with the stick, over to the water spigot and began the arduous task of cleaning each item as thoroughly as possible, and then hung them on the barbed-wire fence nearby to dry. The next day, Porky met Herman at the designated spot where they had met before.

"This is real swell of you, Porky," Herman said as he reached over the fence while Porky held the clothes and shoes up as high as he could reach.

"That's what buddies are for. Catch you later," Porky said with a salute.

For the next week, Porky visited Carroll religiously, careful to wash himself down thoroughly after each visit. But on the eighth day, he was gone. He had died during the night and had been removed by the burial detail. On the ninth day, the day after Carroll's death, Porky was in the open-air barracks he now called home, looking out, when he noticed a large tent in the distance. He had never spotted the tent before, so he left the barracks to investigate. A corpse of a man emerged from the tent and reached out to Porky as he walked. He moved his mouth to speak, but no sound emerged. Torrential rains began to fall. The man stumbled and fell face down. Porky ran to help, knelt down, and turned him over. He was wide-eyed, dead. Just then, the tent collapsed. Porky jumped up and ran back to his barracks.

By the beginning of November 1942, Porky had graduated from the halfway house to the other side of the barbed wire—the malaria section, which consisted of five barracks. It was about a hundred yards from Ward Zero, but still within an expanded barbed-wire area, designed to segregate them from the healthier men.

Porky walked about his new confines wearing one of his cleaned-up suntan specials: a light army summer shirt and pants and a good pair of army shoes, scrounged from discarded clothing, stripped from the bodies of the dead. He walked about, checking out the scene with his saddlebag "sugar" pants over his shoulder and wandered into the open area between the barracks. There he found Herman Hausmann, dressed like a tramp once again in tattered shorts with no shirt and pieces of wood with leather straps for shoes. But this time he did look clean and he was shaven.

"What the hell happened to you?"

"I'm sorry, Porky. I got hungry again."

"Well, there's not much I can do about that now. I'm not in a position to get you any more clothes."

"I am sorry, Porky." Herman was crestfallen, extremely dejected.

He hung his head down and avoided meeting Porky's eyes and kept glancing back at a group of men standing by the barracks that he was staying in.

"Ah, forget it."

"I don't know what's wrong with me."

"Really, it's OK," Porky insisted, hoping that Herman hadn't become suicidal.

"Poor Billy. Look, I have to get this off my chest."

"Why, what's wrong?"

"The day Billy died; he took off his black onyx ring. You know the one—a gold band with a small diamond set in the onyx."

"You don't mean the one his mother gave him when he left for boot camp."

"Yeah, that's the one."

"So what happened to it?"

"Not long before he died, Billy asked me to take the ring off of his finger and put it on mine. He gave it to me outright, but I told him, 'Look, if I'm ever rescued, I'll make sure your mother gets it.' That was before I realized how desperate a guy can get when he's hungry . . ."

"You didn't—"

"He knew I might have to sell it to survive. But I told him to forget that; I was going to make it, and I'd bring it on back home. But then . . . ." Herman's eyes were moist with tears. "Look, this guy spotted the ring on me a few days ago and offered me two cans of sardines and a hundred American bucks. I know I'm weak willed, but let's face it. If I starve to death here, I am never going to make it home, and that'll be the end of the story. And Billy knew the score. He knew what we were up against. He gave it to me for a reason. He knew my survival might depend on it, but . . ." Herman broke down and wept. "Besides, I had already traded the clothes I got from you. Porky, I was starving," he managed between sobs.

"Well, there's nothing I can say. What's done is done."

"But the guy never came through. He never paid me."

"Never paid you? OK, let us go find the bastard."

"I know exactly where he is—in Barracks Number 4."

Porky and Herman strode over to Number 4 and entered. Herman pointed out the man, who was seated on a "bamboo bay," a bed against the edge of the wall.

Porky approached and glared at the POW with a menacing stare. "Hey, you, where's the diamond ring this man sold you?"

"I don't have it. I sold it to a man who's supposed to pay me, and that is how I was supposed to pay him." He pointed to Herman.

"I'll give you two days. Either you hand over the money or give back the ring, or I'll work you over like you have never been worked over before," Porky threatened.

"OK, OK, I'll take care of it."

A week later, Porky was working on another of his special projects near the back entrance to the malaria section, not far from the water spigot. He ripped open a gallon-size tin can at the seams, stomped on it until it was flat, and folded the edges. Next, he filled a small can and his mess kit cup with water, then sat cross-legged to fashion discarded wire to suspend the can. The fire was no problem—bamboo scraps were everywhere. He lit a small pile and hung the can. As the water came to a boil, he untied one of the sugar pant legs and poured out small quantities into the boiling water. Spooning up the boiling mixture, he placed a drop into the cup of cold water.

The sun was hot overhead and Porky was frustrated. Sweat dribbled down his face, but he kept experimenting until he got it right. Finally, a drop of the mixture hardened in the cup. He burnt himself as he took the heated can off the fire. He quickly placed the can on the ground, unbuttoned his shirt, folded it into a kitchen mitten, then grabbed the hot can and poured the mixture into the flattened pan.

"Doesn't look like much, but give it some time," he muttered to several guys who had come for water but stayed to watch as he measured along the sides of the pan with his fingers. "Let's see, if I get forty-four squares at ten sen a piece, that is four hundred forty sen, not bad. That is forty yen and forty sen," he said with a smirk to his prospective customers.

Later that day, Porky sat out in the open area between the barracks with his freshly hardened "fudge" by his side. A rather gruff-looking tall man walked by, wearing a discarded sailor's outfit several sizes too small. He paused, then turned around and walked back to Porky.

"Hey, what are you going to do with that stuff?"

"Sell it. Do you want to buy?"

"I don't have any money. What if I help you sell it? Would you give me some?"

"Sure. Here, take a couple of samples. See how it goes," Porky said, handing him five pieces of the candy. Porky sat back to relax as the man scurried off to sell the wares. Not long afterward, the gentleman returned. "A fellow wants to buy all of it."

"So much the better," Porky said. "There's about thirty pieces left. You already have the sample. Keep them, and I'll give you five more. You just take me to the guy who wants to buy it all."

The two men headed off to the barracks. But Porky's excitement turned to shock when he was escorted to Herman Houseman, who sat on the edge of the bamboo bay, eating the samples. Porky handed the middleman the five pieces he promised and grabbed the two remaining samples from Herman and handed them to him too. Herman and Porky looked one another over without saying a word, but the guy in the sailor suit sensed that it was best to leave the negotiations to the men involved, and so made his escape before anyone grabbed his candy back.

"I see you must have gotten paid," Porky began.

"Yeah. Right after you left me, the guy came back."

"No ring?"

"Sorry, the ring is long gone. It's passed through several hands by now."

"And now you want this candy?"

"Sure."

"OK, I'll give you a break. It will cost you thirty yen and five sen."

"I've got it right here," Herman said as he peeled off the yen from a wad of bills and dropped them, along with the sen, in Porky's outstretched hand. "And don't think I'm not grateful."

"Look, Herman. I'm flattered that you like my fudge. But if you eat too much you'll make yourself sick. Trade it for an egg, or bananas, or cash."

"Porky, I'm a grown man. Don't tell me—"

"OK. See you later, chump," Porky said and exited back to his barracks.

Liberated Cabanatuan POWs January 1945
Courtesy National Archives

Chapter 27

December 1942-Spring 1944

Despite steady improvement to his health, as Christmas 1942 drew near, Porky still called the malaria barracks his home. He had slowly adapted to his new lifestyle and spent little time immersed in self-pity. Instead, he roamed about the enclosure freely, chatted amiably, or became engrossed in sympathetic conversations with those who were not coping as well, or whose condition was far worse than his own. Some of the men had developed wet beriberi, which caused their balls to swell to the size of grapefruits or larger. At times the cries and groans of some of the men in the malaria ward were even more intense than in Ward Zero. Here, many still had the strength to shout in agony.

One day in mid-December, after he had taken an early morning stroll, Porky returned to find a friend—a man named Johnson from his old outfit—assigned to his barracks. The place he was now housed in was little more than a bamboo floor on stilts with open-air elevated bunk bays and carrying posts topped by a roof. Johnson sat inside on the bay with his legs hanging outside to air. His legs were swollen, with large purple marks on his thigh—an obvious sign of gangrene. Porky took one look and knew his fate but disguised his reaction with camaraderie.

"Jesus Christ Almighty. Look what the cat dragged in."

"Not Frenchy! Jesus, why the hell did they stick me here?" he joked as the men shook hands and laughed.

"So, Johnson, how's it going?" Porky asked as he crossed over to his bunk.

"Not too bad. Did you hear, Dynamite Dunn died. Cerebral malaria."

"Is that what got him? I wasn't sure."

Porky sat on his bay and tried to blot out the image of Dynamite in the throes of death. Smith, a navy man and fellow malaria patient, crossed over to Porky and sat. "He's going fast. Did you notice—the gangrene has moved up to his thigh?"

"Yeah, poor guy!"

"So what do you want to wager? I'll give him two more days," Smith whispered.

"Na, he's in good spirits. I'd give him three," Porky whispered back.

"How much do you want to bet?"

"Two American cigarettes."

"You're on."

Porky got up from the bay and crossed to Johnson. "I wonder if the rains will be starting up again."

"It's supposed to be rainy season, but it looks pretty sunny to me. Of course, I shouldn't have my legs out in the sun. They're starting to split open again."

"I can see that."

"I have gangrene real bad, Frenchy. Say, I have no need for these flying glasses," he said, pulling a pair of aviator glasses out of his duffel bag. "I'd like you to have them. I don't have much time left."

"Na, you don't look that bad to me," Porky said, flushed with shame at having bet on the death of an old friend.

"You're right. I'll live forever. The good die young and all that crap." Johnson struggled against his pain and smiled at Porky as he handed him the glasses.

"Gee thanks, that's real nice of you." Porky was close to tears as he tucked the aviator glasses into his shirt pocket.

The officer in charge of the malaria unit entered. "Guys, listen up. I have an announcement about the Red Cross packages. This is not a rumor. They just arrived. Each barracks will be notified in turn when to come down to the main building."

"Come down, I can't even walk," Johnson retorted, trembling as another wave of pain wracked his body.

"Don't worry. We're assigning the strongest to pick them up for the rest of you."

Porky spoke up. "Hey, I'm not that bad. I'd be glad to oblige. Do you want me to tag along?"

"Thanks anyway, but these weigh eight pounds each."

The officer had slapped Porky across the face with the hard truth. Despite his size, Porky had always been known for his strength and as a star athlete. But since the war, Porky's muscles had atrophied from hunger and disease. "Eight pounds. I wonder what's in them?" Porky mumbled as he got up from the bay to head back to his bunk. The morning's activities had tired him and he was ready for a nap. He turned and shouted back to Johnson, "Don't worry. I'm sure you'll get yours." Two hours later, a truck entered the malaria area and men lined up to receive their boxes. Porky got up, exited from the barracks, and headed into the crowd. "I need two," Porky explained to the distribution crew. "I have a buddy who can't carry his own."

"Don't worry, soldier. We'll carry it for you."

"His name's Johnson. He's got gangrene running up his leg."

Porky grabbed his box and headed back to the barracks. He was able to handle the eight pounds, but the officer was right. He was barely able to handle one package, let alone two. As he approached the ward, Porky saw that men had not only opened their boxes, the trading had begun. Each box was made of cardboard and was two by two feet square and eight to ten inches deep and labeled with the American Red Cross logo.

"I'll give you two packs of cigarettes for your quarter-pound cheese," one man announced loudly as Porky entered.

"If you give me four packs, you've got a deal," Porky countered.

The man grabbed four packs of cigarettes from his package as Porky dropped to his knees to rip open the container. The cheese looked tempting, but he knew that four packs of cigarettes could buy him much more that that.

"Here you go," he said, handing the gentleman the quarter pound of cheese.

"But it's moldy," he protested.

"That's what makes it so good," Porky countered. "Don't you know anything? I suppose you're one of them city boys. Look, do what the farmers do. Cut off the mold. That's how they make 'aged' cheese. It's much better for you."

"You sure?"

"Cross my heart," Porky said, crossing his heart the way he used to as a kid.

The exchange complete, Porky returned to his friend. "Sorry, Johnson, I didn't have the strength to carry two. But there'll be someone along in a moment with yours." Porky collapsed back on his bay and reopened the box. Along with the four packs he had just bartered for, there were eight packs of American cigarettes neatly stacked in the carton. There was also a can of

Spam, a two-ounce can of coffee, hardtack biscuits, a chocolate bar, sugar, and powdered cream. "A no-fooling treasure chest," he said out loud, remembering that his childhood dream was a treasure chest filled with gold.

For the next few weeks, Porky bartered enough Spam, fresh fruit, and cheese to be noticeably improved. Throughout the spring of 1943, he slowly regained his health so that by the time summer came, he was assigned a work detail in the farm area. He was now part of an irrigation crew in a large field where row after row of sprouted corn and other vegetables could be seen in all directions. But the vegetables were not destined for them but for their Japanese overlords. Of course there were exceptions, such as when there was so much extra produce if it weren't used, it would rot, or when spoiled produce was given to the Americans to see what they could salvage.

Things had changed since his early confinement. The camp had enlarged and was better organized. By midsummer Porky was part of a five-hundred-man crew carrying five-gallon pails to a nearby stream. Each man filled a pail one-quarter full, headed back in line into the field, and poured the water onto the parched crops. Eight to ten Japanese guards directed rifles at each group of POWs to keep the operation moving. Porky enjoyed dipping his hands in the stream and wiping his hot face with water before returning to the field with the pail, but only if the guards weren't looking.

One day in August, as he watered a row of sprouting plants he felt like he was burning up. Suddenly, a sharp pain grabbed at his guts, and his stomach felt like it was undergoing contractions. He collapsed onto the ground, spilling the water over himself. As he thrashed about, a Japanese guard rushed over. Porky groaned and writhed in pain, clutching at his stomach. The guard, who was dressed in regulation khakis and canvas sneakers with ribbed rubber soles, kicked Porky in the chest and side, turned him over with his foot, and then kicked him in the back, all the while shouting orders and swearing in Japanese. Porky moved into a fetal position. Frustrated, the guard ordered Porky to get up and move over to a nearby shed to sit. Porky slowly rose but remained hunched over. He clutched at his stomach and gagged as he hobbled toward the bamboo enclosure. The guard screamed out orders for a fellow POW to help Porky. At first the POW froze, unsure of the guard's directive until the man's flailing gestures convinced him that he did indeed intend for him to accompany his fallen comrade. The POW braced Porky against his own spare body and put an arm around his thin waist. They reached the shed just as Porky collapsed back down onto the ground, groaning and crying out in agony.

"Sorry, pal. I've got to get back before I'm beaten senseless," his fellow prisoner said as he turned to head back to the water detail.

Eventually, the pain subsided. Porky moved back into a fetal position and rested on the ground until the work detail ended. As the men gathered to return to camp, Porky dug his hands into the dirt to brace himself into a sitting position. He paused until his head cleared, then slowly rose, dusted himself off, and rejoined the detail, which headed back to the base.

The next day, Porky took the aviator sunglasses from the breast pocket of his suntans and headed to the sick bay. Johnson had died two days after the Red Cross packages arrived, as Smith had predicted, but he had cigarettes to spare. So he didn't mind forking over the wager. Initially, he planned to keep the gift and enjoyed walking around the malaria section with his trademark towel around his neck, sporting the sunglasses. But now he had made it into the main camp and had no intention of returning to what he thought of as the death-camp area. And work details were no place to sport around wearing aviator sunglasses. His health depended on getting what he could for them and getting medicine by hook or by crook. So he opened the shades and positioned them on his nose, careful to throw his shoulders back as he walked to look self-confident—at his very best. "Thank you, Johnson, from the bottom of my heart," he said under his breath as he cast his eyes about, hidden by the deep greenish tint. He wondered if anyone was checking him out. *Whether or not anyone admits it, I know I look pretty goddamn sharp*, he thought to himself.

Finally, someone tapped him on the shoulder. Porky turned and there was his old drinking buddy from before the war, Francis Hoctor, from Biddeford, Maine. Since the war, they had been on a few details together.

"Howdy, Sport!"

"Well, as I live and breathe. Mr. Hoctor himself. How's it going? You're looking swell."

"And what about you. I'd have thought you were stateside, training to be a pilot."

"You like these?"

"You bet."

"What have you got to trade?"

"Try zilch."

Porky laughed. "I'm planning to do some horse-trading if the doc can't give me some pills. I've had a couple of bouts of malaria. And now I've got this stomach thing."

"Tell me about it. But I'm doing OK compared to the rest of the guys, I guess. Rotgut liquor killed everything. Sterilized my bloodstream, kidney, and liver, I suspect. Why, I'm such a tough old bird, the germs are afraid to land."

"Wish I could say the same."

"Say, I'm starved. I'm on my way over to the kitchen. Want to join me?"

"Later. I've got to tend to business first," Porky shouted as he continued on to the infirmary.

"You hear Canadian Red Cross packages have arrived?" Hoctor shouted back.

That was great news. Perhaps things were looking up.

Porky entered the sick bay and found Stickney, a medic from his old outfit, talking with the doctor. The men glanced in his direction and continued to discuss the prognosis of a particular patient, an air force lieutenant who seemed to be pulling through but had suffered a setback. As they spoke, Porky took off the glasses, folded them, and carefully placed them back into his shirt pocket. Finally, the conversation ended and the doctor turned to Porky.

"Doc, I don't know what's wrong with me. I get these terrible, terrible pains in my stomach. They knock me right off of my feet, and I'm afraid I may be getting a touch of malaria back. The headaches and sweats are starting to return."

"Look, we can give you a few aspirin to help with the malaria, but as for your stomach pains, there's nothing we can do. Nothing's changed—there's no medicine or surgical equipment. You have to live with that, soldier." The doctor pushed past Porky and stepped outside for a smoke.

Porky checked around before he spoke. He trusted Stickney, who grew up not far from him across the border in New Hampshire, but there were spies everywhere, he had learned. "Isn't there some way I can get some real medicine for this malaria?" Porky asked, lowering his voice.

"Got anything you can trade? What about them glasses? Are they flying glasses?"

"Yeah, Johnson gave them to me before he passed away."

"I can't give you more than four or five quinine or three or four sulfur pills, but hang on to the quinine. I'm not so sure you have your malaria back, and someday you may need it. And maybe you better hold on to the sulfur tablets too. Meet me here tomorrow and I'll get you some real food. What do you say about a couple of eggs?" Porky pulled off the glasses and handed them to Stickney, who examined them for scratches or other defects and then put them on. "I'll see how much cash I can get thrown in to sweeten the deal. These are a hot item." He modeled the glasses for Porky. "How do I look? Pretty sharp?"

"Pretty sharp? Wow, you look like a million bucks! But if you can't come up with a million, I'll accept less."

"As I said, I'll see what I can do," Stickney said, opening a drawer in the table set in the rear of the room. He took out a shaving mirror and admired himself.

"Just parade around wearing those aviator glasses and the suckers will start lining up." Porky said with a thumbs-up and wink as he exited.

As Porky neared the third-year anniversary of his enlistment, he became despondent, thinking about how things used to be when Bobby and Billy were alive. And despite the medicine, his stomach problems would crop up on occasion and render him useless, and that added to his woes. One day, as he wandered over to the kitchen, he ran into "Tiny" Smith, the six-foot five-inch two-hundred-forty-pound chief cook. Tiny was the third in command in the kitchen, which was run by an army major and a captain. He was also an old friend from Nichols Field before the war. Payday had been the day the biggest crap game was held on base. Porky made money during crap games, not by gambling, but by serving the sandwiches, soda, pie, and beer that Tiny provided, for seventy-five pesos per game.

"What the hell are you up to, Frenchy?"

"I'm looking for a detail. Growing season's coming to an end."

"Want to work with us? We need a fireman in the kitchen. You look like the right size for the job," Tiny said, towering over him. "If you don't mind hanging out with me and think you'd like it, just go down to notify whoever is in charge of your barracks."

Porky knew a good deal when he saw it. The kitchen hut was the center of life at a camp that had seen too much death, much of which might have been avoided if their nutritional needs had been met. Several days later, Porky rose with the sun and walked over to the kitchen. Inside there were two cooks who showed him what to do—Bill Young and Pappy Kroll. Bill was also from his old outfit. But Pappy Kroll was from a different division; he was also a legend. He had served in every post in the United States for thirty years as a "do-grabber"—a GI who works for an officer. He had made it to tech sergeant, but his claim to fame was his cooking. He was the best. He knew all there was to know about cooking under any situation. Pappy was muscular. He stood midway between Porky and Tiny, smiled and joked around a lot, and had a set of teeth that were all there but worn down like those of older natives in the Filipino villages.

Porky was kept busy as the rainy season began. His job was to tend fires both inside and outside the kitchen. He'd grab handfuls of wood chips and throw them on the hot coals in the firebox. Wood was also placed in a fourteen-inch-deep trench that had a steel plate on top, where two fifty-gallon pots plus a smaller *kawali* pot were typically set. He'd grab a five-gallon can and fill it three-quarters full of rice, dump it in one of the fifty-gallon pans, get some more rice and dump it in the other, and then fill the pans with water. The wood was set ablaze, and before you knew it, things were popping. Months before, one of the earlier firemen made wooden covers, which Porky dutifully placed on top of the cauldrons. But the covers banged about as they were pushed up by the bubbling water and steam. Other times, burlap rice bags were placed on top, which allowed some of the steam to escape. But then he got smart and put the steam-saturated burlap on top of the wooden covers for added weight. The problem was if the burlap dried out, it'd catch fire if the flames licked up too high and spread to the covers, which were wood, and then they'd catch fire. There was a lot to do to keep everything under control.

The kitchen operation was dependent on the wood detail—two hundred men who also rose at the crack of dawn and marched to a forested area where a few of the men hacked away using dull axes. A West Point officer, who had his own axe and kept it razor sharp, would split the wood. Members of the detail hoisted the wood onto their shoulders and marched to the kitchen where they dropped stacks nearby. Part of Porky's job was to make sure that once the fire was started, he fed the flames with four-foot logs he grabbed from the nearby woodpile.

Christmas 1943 came, and along with it Red Cross packages filled with cigarettes and cheese and Spam, coffee, hardtack, cookies, and canned fruit. There were also crate loads of items for the kitchen. So all in all the men's diet improved, if only briefly. New Year's Day 1944 was rainy, but at least they had made it to the new year. To celebrate the holiday, Pappy Kroll made pancakes out of rice flour cooked in pig fat and smothered with syrup from boiled-down sugar and water. Yes, the kitchen detail was the best detail of them all.

Several months later, Porky was grousing to Pappy, who was busy grinding rice to make flour for bread, cakes, and pies. "Those GD bamboo lice," he complained after pushing a log into the red-hot coals. He stood upright and scratched his chest. "It's spring and I'll be damned, they're coming out in force," he said, grabbing a wooden spoon to scratch his back. "I thought I took care of them. Last night, I ran all of my bamboo slats through hot coals."

"Hell, that's not going to work," Pappy shouted back, pulling a forty-pound bag of rice from a nearby pile. "You'd have to throw the entire barracks through hot coals to get rid of them," he said as he slit open the bag.

"In other words, burn the place down and start over again. Those GD lice!" Porky scratched his chest again as Pappy braced the rice against the wall and grunted in response. He was headed out to talk with the major about the evening's dessert he planned for the officers.

Porky put the wooden spoon down and walked to the open fire pit outside to check on a fifty-gallon barrel full of water he had set on stones. Though the barrel had been heated for about an hour, it had not begun to boil; instead, wisps of steam wafted across the surface like fog on hot pavement after a rain shower. Porky walked to the woodpile, bent over, and grabbed another log, but just as he reentered the kitchen hut and was about to toss it into the firebox, he doubled over with pain. "Jesus Christ Almighty, I don't know what's wrong with me," he said, dropping the log.

Bill was slicing native tubers a member of the wood detail had unearthed on the advice of Filipino villagers, who believed they were full of nutrients. He got up from the table and was about to dump the pulp in the pot when he spotted Porky on the floor, writhing with pain. "Frenchy, what the hell, if you're hurting, go lay down. I can take care of the fire," he said, tossing the vegetable in along with the rice.

Porky made his way outside and lay down on the ground, not far from the fire pit. He tried to lie down and stretch out but was soon curled back into a fetal position, clutching his stomach. Tiny had just left the officers' barracks and was headed back to the kitchen when he spotted Porky.

"Frenchy, what's your problem?"

"Tiny, I'm sorry," he said, pulling himself into a sitting position. "Things were going great. I really like the job, but this started up again. This is the second attack I've had. It knocks me right off my feet, but don't worry, it won't last."

"I'll get someone else to work as fireman. I want you to work with Pappy Kroll for the rest of the afternoon. Pappy will find something for you to do. Something easy." Just then, Pappy approached from behind and quickly sized up the situation.

"Tiny, don't worry, I'll take care of him."

"Thanks, Pappy. We take care of the officers. There's nothing to say we can't take care of ourselves too." They helped Porky back onto his feet, into the kitchen, and onto a short bench by the table.

"I'll give you a slicing detail," Pappy told Porky as he fetched a cup of water for him to drink. "You can slice the rot from the vegetables and sweep up around here once you're feeling better."

Two Japanese soldiers approached, carrying two large buckets from the Japanese officers' quarters across the yard. They stopped at the fence and a major walked over to see what they had to offer. One of the Japanese soldiers spoke briefly to the major and handed him the buckets, which were full of scraps. The major bowed in thanks, then turned and headed for the kitchen. Pappy met him at the entryway. "So what do we have this time?"

"Looks like pork scraps," the major said, entering the kitchen area. "He said something about some parts of the pig being taboo. Apparently, one of the officers made a fuss."

"That's mighty nice of them," Bill said as he stirred the rice with a large wooden spoon. "Of course, maybe they're hoping that whatever curse might have befallen on them if they ate it falls on us instead."

"You think you can fix this into something decent?" the major asked.

Pappy examined the contents of the buckets. "There's plenty of food here. And I can make fried rice with the fat. What do you say, I'll fix up something for the officers, and the rest goes to the kitchen crew."

The major turned to Porky. "Enjoy it while you can, soldier, because you'll be shipping out by the end of the summer."

"Where to? Another POW camp nearby?"

"Hell, no. We're shipping out to Japan. I understand all those who can walk will be headed back to Manila, to Bilibid Prison first," the major said, then sauntered out of the kitchen as if he didn't have a care in the world.

"Oh, brother!" Porky shuddered as a chill ran down his spine. Pappy and Bill shook their heads and continued cooking. There were thousands of men who needed to be fed, and only God knew what lay ahead.

Sgt. James Baldassarre testifying at the Manila War Crimes Tribunal in February 1946. Baldassarre swore he spotted Lt. General Homma riding in an "official" car along the Death March route. The sergeant's testimony placed Homma at the scene of the crime. Consequently, he was sentenced to die by firing squad. Courtesy National Archives and Federico Baldassarre

POW rescued from sunken Japanese transport "Hell Ship"
Courtesy National Archives

Chapter 28

Athol, Massachusetts
November 17, 1944
Friday Noon

Thanksgiving was in the air as passengers boarded and exited from the Athol Train Station. Children in wool coats, mittens, and caps held hands with ladies in fur hats, wool coats, and leather gloves. Businessmen in overcoats and galoshes walked this way and that. They all skirted past twenty-eight-year-old Pvt. Francis Hoctor from Biddeford, Maine, as he stood on the sidewalk, waiting for his fellow soldiers to join him. Hoctor's gaunt features were accentuated by the heavy olive-drab overcoat he wore over his army uniform. The bus he and the other soldiers from Fort Devens were riding on had broken down, but they had somehow made it to the Athol train yard. The soldiers were going home for the Thanksgiving holiday and had just dropped off a soldier in Belchertown before heading back along Route 202, which would take them into Rindge, New Hampshire. From there they were to travel on to Manchester and Portsmouth before turning north on Route 1, into Kittery, Maine.

But something had started smoking under the hood. The bus driver knew the area and had headed to the train station to call the company mechanic. It was a convenient location. Hoctor carried his duffel bag in case they had to transfer to the train. "Athol, Massachusetts." Who did he know from Athol? He had journeyed to hell and back and was recuperating from malaria, dysentery, shellshock, and living on an island full of cannibals before being rescued by a U.S. submarine. He had always enjoyed a stiff drink and a good laugh, but since his return stateside, he had begun to drink heavily, but so too had his fellow passengers, who planned to join him in search of the nearest bar.

As the soldiers made their way across South Street, they waved at Hoctor, who waved for them to follow the crowd onto Exchange Street, where blasts of icy wind pushed them along. The crowd continued on to Main Street, but Hoctor stopped at 98 Exchange, the Café Royale. Hoctor was thirsty. Across the street was a barbershop. He put a hand to the stubble on his chin but decided that securing a drink was of greater importance. But one of his companions decided he needed a shave.

Next to the barber was Gabarino's, a grocer with a storefront stocked with fruit and vegetables and a sign announcing Liquid Refreshments Available in the Rear. But Hoctor needed nonmilitary companionship as well as booze. He needed to reestablish contact with the workaday world of civilians before he returned home. Way too much water had passed under the bridge for him to face his family cold turkey. One of his buddies had a different opinion and dropped into Gabarino's to purchase a few pints for the long bus ride home.

Café Royale today—Athol, Massachusetts
Photo credit: G. Thomson Fraser

The Café Royale was located in a narrow three-story building sandwiched between two larger buildings that housed a furniture shop, a hardware store, legal and insurance offices, and a shoeshine parlor with a cobbler below. One of the soldiers wanted a shoeshine and another needed a heel replaced on his boot. Hoctor looked up above the café at a false balcony that extended from the second story and served as a marquee and protective awning for customers. A young woman in a blue sweater stared down at him from the window above.

The building had once housed a millinery boutique that peddled locally manufactured lady's hats in the late-nineteenth and into the early twentieth century. The awning still carried remnants of its past along its fringe. But as Prohibition laws were passed, the millinery closed to cater to more pressing needs—bootlegging, gambling, and a speakeasy. Betting on horses and the numbers racket were popular pastimes for mill workers, but as Prohibition came to an end, the speakeasy went legit. A common victualler license from the state was acquired in 1936, and the Café Royal reemerged under the ownership of Ernest Cucchi, who transformed the bar into a café that served food as well as drinks. Cucchi had insisted on procuring a common victualler instead of a tavern license because in the early post-Prohibition era, taverns strictly prohibited women and he preferred a mixed crowd.

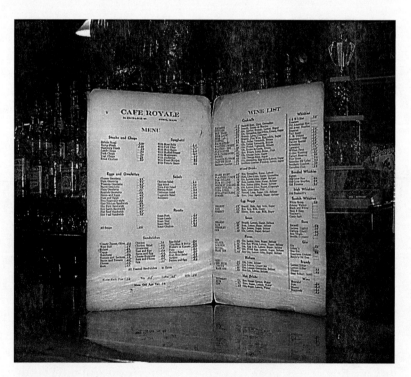

Photo credit: G. Thomson Fraser

Hoctor sized up the café as he peered through the steamed pane-glass window. The breakfast crowd had vanished and the lunch crowd was trickling in. Already several tables were full, and workmen in coveralls were seated at the bar. Posted next to the door was the menu. He examined it in detail: steaks and chops, fourteen styles of omelets, eight varieties of spaghetti dishes, dozens of sandwiches, seven salads, and five different roasts. The menu cover sported the Pabst Blue Ribbon girl in a wide-brimmed red hat trimmed in blue ribbon with a large blue bow tucked under her chin. Inside he spotted a colorful poster of the Ballantine Ale girl tacked to the wall. The so-called Wine Menu was posted on the other side of the door. He was amused to note that it failed to list any wines but instead featured fifteen types of cocktails, nine mixed drinks, three eggnogs, four sours, five fizz gins, three hot drinks, five rums and five brands of gin, nineteen straight whiskey brands, plus Old Bushmills Irish whiskey. From what he could see Ballantine, Anheuser-Busch, and Pabst were on tap, and more varieties were stashed in the cabinets. The well-stocked bar was displayed under a five-foot-long mirror as well as in the cabinetry beneath.

Hoctor took a closer look at the dozen or so people scattered about the tables eating, elbows propped onto the red-and-white checkered oilcloths. Additional chairs were scattered about along the left-hand wall. Perhaps he could sit there and wait for his buddies. He wished his friends would finish their business and join him. In the center of the establishment was a four-foot-high divider that separated the eating section from the bar. The divider was mandated by the state so that the family fare might be kept separate from the boozing. But a three-foot break in the divider allowed customers and waiters to move freely from one section to the other; and the bar stools were high enough so that customers were swiveled round in their stools engaged in conversation between the bar and the tables. It was the kind of place where everyone knew everybody. He feared he'd stick out like a sore thumb and was about to join his friend in Gabarino's when his eyes fell on the twenty-foot polished oak counter that dominated the narrow room no matter where you sat. He hadn't sat at a bar like that since the war began.

He had been deserted by his friends, Hoctor reasoned, so he decided to go in alone. The air in the Café Royale was blue with smoke. He took off his army cap and tucked it under his arm. There were ladies present, and at heart he was a gentleman. As he made his way to the bar, he noticed a serviceman at one of the tables and wondered if he had spent time in the war too. At least he could relax and maybe strike up a conversation and make an attempt to enjoy himself.

"I'll have a beer. San Miguel, if you've got it," he said to the bartender. He spoke loud enough to be heard over the chatter. No one offered to pay, which was his secret hope, so he dipped into his pocket for change. "Bartender, where am I? What town is this?" he asked, trying to keep his hand steady as he forked over the change.

"Athol. You're in Athol. How's tap. Pabst OK? We ain't got San Miguel. Never heard of it," the bartender said as he stuck a chilled mug under the spigot and then handed the drink over to a waiting customer.

"It's pretty common in the Pacific—even parts of California."

"Oh yeah?" the bartender feigned interest as he grabbed a chilled mug from the icebox.

"Athol, Athol! That's right. That's what the sign at the train station said. A buddy of mine used to live here."

"That right?" The bartender filled the mug and slid the brew over. "What's his name?"

"LaCoste. Frenchy LaCoste."

The bartender gave him a closer look. His uniform looked clean enough but his overall appearance was disheveled. He wondered if he was drunk. Of course, half the guys who stepped out of his joint were. Still, there was something about him he couldn't put his finger on.

Photo display in downtown Athol typewriter shop window: "They Died"
Photo credit: Burton Newton. Courtesy Richard Chaisson

"Sam," he called out to one of the customers seated at a table. "What's the name of the guy who's being buried today? Isn't there a Mass up at the Immaculate Conception?"

Sam left his seat and crossed to the bar. "Yeah, the LaCoste kid got killed a couple of weeks back. There's a big display up at the Athol Gas and Electric. He's on some sort of honor roll. Nice kid. It's a shame."

The bartender grabbed a pad of paper and a pencil and wrote in large block letters: Our Lady of the Immaculate Conception. "It's up on School Street, not far from the high school. If you hurry I bet you can catch the service."

Hoctor chugged down half the beer in a long gulp. "I don't believe it. Not Frenchy. That's impossible. I only saw him—what was it—a couple of months ago?"

"Look, I'm sorry. He got killed and he's being buried. War is hell. What can I say?" Sam blurted out.

"So what happened?

"I don't know. Maybe it was an explosion, or . . ."

"I bet he was on a Jap transport that got torpedoed. That's what happened to me."

The bartender handed him the name of the church and the directions. "It's within walking distance. Don't worry, you won't get lost. Anyone can point out where it is. I'm sure his family will be happy to see you."

"Geez, I don't think I can make the service. We're out of Fort Devens—headed home and the GD bus broke down. We're leaving after it's repaired."

"Who's we?" Sam asked.

"Me and the rest of the guys."

Sam looked around. "The rest of the guys?"

"Yeah. They'll be along." Hoctor slipped out a pack of Lucky Strikes from his hip pocket, tapped down a cigarette, and lit up. "Frenchy was doing great the last time we talked. I can't believe it. 'Course a lot of the guys died onboard them GD transports. See, they're unmarked. The one I was on, the *Shinyo Maru*, there were 750 of us guys stuffed down in the cattle holds for nineteen days; barely anything to eat and next to no water. I swear, half the guys were already dead when out of the blue the torpedoes hit. Broke the ship apart. Still those GD Japs were gunning for us. Threw a grenade down the hole. I missed that one. 'Course the water's pouring into the hole. Thought I was a goner. Thought I was going to drown but somehow I made it out and dove off the deck into the water. You'd think with all we went through they'd give a sucker an even break. But not them bastards. The Jap boats were everywhere—blasting away. It's a wonder I made it. Out of 750 guys, only 81 of us lived to tell the tale. Imagine being hit by one of our own, out to sink the Japs. Imagine surviving Bataan, the Death March, Camp O'Donnell, Cabanatuan, and Bilibid Prison only to die like a rat on a stinking Jap transport ship."

The bartender filled Hoctor's drink to the top and slipped his change back. "Here. This one's on me. Would you like a sandwich, spaghetti—name it, you've got it."

"Club sandwich, if it's not too much trouble." Hoctor swiveled in his barstool to face a nearby table. "So where are you headed, soldier?" The private looked up at Hoctor.

"I'll be shipping out from Fort Devens in about a week," Private Landry answered. "I'll be going to Georgia, an armored tank division, then on to England and maybe France or Germany."

"Oh yeah, I just shipped out of Devens." Hoctor closed his eyes and appeared to be in danger of falling off the stool. "But this time I'm headed home," he said, suddenly opening his eyes. "And despite all I've been through they won't discharge me." The bartender dipped mugs into soapy water, and he kept an eye on Hoctor.

Private Landry turned back to his friends. "So, Harry, how come you're still here?"

"Me drafted? I'm too fat, too old, and I've got too many things wrong with me. Or so Sally tells me. So I work in a shoe shop, but it's a living. I don't envy you guys."

Sally looked up at Private Hoctor. "Getting drafted is bad enough, but we had a bunch of guys that thought they'd escape the war. Joined up in 1940, thought it was going to be a lark, a vacation in Hawaii, with room and board supplied by the U.S. Army," she said, pulling a compact out of her purse to reapply her lipstick.

"Yeah, and the day they bombed Pearl their mugs were plastered all over the paper," Harry added. "God knows what happened to them. They're all listed as missing in action. Most folks here figure they're dead," he said, shaking his head.

"Sounds like the guys I knew from Athol. Poor Frenchy."

The three looked at one another. "Frenchy? That could be half the town. You're sure his name is LaCoste?"

"Harry, the guy who's being buried is about 20. He couldn't have signed up in '40. What's the name of the guys who took off for Hawaii?" Sally asked.

"I can't remember who went where," he answered, slightly annoyed. "And there's been so many since. Hey, Ernie," he yelled up to the bartender. "How's Eddie doing?"

"He's quitting school to join the Navy. Wants to head out to the Pacific."

"Thought you talked him out of that."

"Fat chance," Ernie retorted.

"I was in the Pacific," Hoctor commented. "Just got back from an island full of cannibals. If it weren't for the American resistance, I would have been in a stew on the island of Mindanao. Who's Eddie?" he asked the bartender.

"My boy, who thinks he knows everything. I own this joint and need him around here, for Christ's sake."

"Ah, don't worry. The war will be over before he sees any action," Private Landry reassured him.

"I made it out of Manila in one of them unmarked Japanese freighters," Hoctor interjected. "You know, cargo ships with holds that are supposed to carry crates of sugar, rice, salt, that sort of thing. But instead, they stuffed hundreds of us down each hold. Packed us in real tight—pushed and shoved us down the ladder with rifle butts. Not that we weren't used to that sort of treatment, but this was no wide-open prisoner of war barracks. The space was so small you could put your hand up and touch the ceiling. I'd say it was about fifty feet wide and ninety feet long alongside the hull. It was so blasted hot there was no air, so guys were suffocating. Others died of thirst. But it wasn't like some fellow just dropped dead. We were packed in so tight they didn't fall down like you'd expect, but were squeezed up next to you and rotted there, days on end. Every once in a while, the Japs would open the hatch and we'd pass the dead over and they'd dump the corpses overboard. The good thing was when they came for the bodies, the hatch was open longer than usual so we could breathe. Then an American sub torpedoed the boat," Hoctor added, grabbing the mug and downing the remainder of the beer. "Did I already mention that? Sorry if I'm repeating myself."

"You didn't get any food or water?" Sally asked.

"He's talking about them Hell Ships. You've heard about them?" Harry asked Private Landry, who shrugged.

"Yeah, I guess that's what they call them. Hell Ships so blasted hot you thought you were in hell," Hoctor spit out.

"But you're OK. So how did you survive?" Sam asked as Ernie busied himself behind the counter, listening to a story that echoed the deepest fears he held for his son.

"Hate to say this in mixed company."

"Hey, I'm just one of the guys," Sally said, batting her eyes at Harry.

"We pissed into our cups and . . ."

"I've read about throats being slit and men sucking out their blood," Harry whispered.

"Ick! That's even worse," Sally said, wrinkling her nose.

"That's nothing I did. Every once in a while, they'd drop down a bucket of putrid water and half-cooked rice, loaded with maggots—for protein, I guess."

"But you survived," Sally said, attempting to add a cheery note though she was starting to feel queasy.

"Yeah, a torpedo hit and then another. It was one of our own subs. Hell, a Japanese freighter hauling supplies to the enemy is fair game! We knew we were doomed. There was a hole in the side, and we were taking on water. A lot of men drowned then and there, but one of the guys got the hatch to pop. Some Jap threw a grenade at us and everything went orange. I was far enough away that I was OK, and then I crawled over the bodies to the opening so I managed to get out. It was awfully slippery with the water pouring in, and the Japs were there shooting, but we kept coming. I managed to crawl up and fight my way out. Slugged this one Jap so hard we both fell on deck, then the ship started to roll sideways, and we landed in the ocean. We were strangling one another. Wonder we both didn't drown. I don't know where I got the strength, but I killed him. Somehow I managed to grab his knife and slit his throat. But I didn't drink his blood," he added, staring at Sally.

"Good for you," Sally said.

"Jap machine gunners kept shooting as we swam. Those goddamn bastards were firing even as the ship was going under. Goddamn fools. Then it was their turn to try to make it to shore."

"I thought you were way out at sea," Landry said, casting doubt about the authenticity of the story.

"We were not more than a mile or so out from an island."

"That was convenient," Landry said with a smile.

"And it was full of cannibals."

Private Landry downed his beer. "This is a tall tale. Right?"

"It's easy to laugh when you're stateside, Private," Hoctor said, his temper rising. He wanted to punch his lights out.

"Hey, I believe him. Knock it off," Harry reprimanded, glaring at his friend.

"Fortunately, the cannibals liked Americans who had treated them well but hated the Japs. They hid us from the Japs, and any they caught, they beheaded and—"

"Look I believe you, but I'm not sure I want to hear any more details," Sally said, squirming in her seat.

"Aw, let him talk," Sam insisted. Private Landry made a gesture as if to button his lips.

"There's not much more to tell. Around eighty other guys made it ashore too. There were some American reconnaissance guys on the island and they radioed Australia that there were survivors and they contacted a nearby sub, and so that's why I'm here. About eighty-one POWs out of over—I don't know—about 650-660 died one way or another."

"I'm glad I've missed the action," Harry said.

"So that's what the Japs are up to—shipping the prisoners off to Japan to work so that their men can fight, packing POWs like sardines into hellholes, locking them in—some suffocate, some starve, some die because they're so weak from years in prison camps they're on their last legs. But Frenchy, I always thought he'd make it. He'd be OK," Hoctor continued, staring into space.

"It is odd that he'd come so far, only to be—" Harry stopped in midsentence.

"The hardest part was the stench. There's nothing quite like the smell of rotting human flesh mixed in with the stench of human waste. There were only about two or three buckets for the latrine. And it was dark, pitch-black. That's what really got to you—total darkness. And the heat so insufferable men were going mad. Nonstop screeching and hollering and clawing over one another." He closed his eyes for a moment, then opened them wide. "Aw, forget it. I'm on my way home and no one wants to hear this crap."

"So what if this Frenchy guy from Athol isn't the one they're burying?" Sally asked.

"Sally, I doubt that Private . . . sorry I didn't catch your name—"

"Hoctor."

"If Private Hoctor—"

Harry put a hand up to interrupt. "Hey, it's worth a shot. We know that this Frenchy guy is named LaCoste. Do you think you can remember the names of the other guys?"

"Try me. I didn't know all the other guys, but he'd talk about them."

"Let's see, there's Franny Robichaud. He grew up not far from me on Sanders Street. Bobby Doolan's parents owned the Athol Hotel, next to the train station," he said, counting each man off on his fingers. "Let's see, Pint Lawson is a ballplayer from Orange. Hell, Landry, you knew a few of the guys."

"Billy Freeman lived not far from me. His mother's a wreck," Landry admitted. "She's still hoping against hope."

"Porky, Porky—what's his last name? He grew up on Swanzey Street," Sally said.

"Porky was a first-string center for Athol. He was the smallest guy that ever played center, but he was tough," Harry added. "You know, he was so short, he had to get special permission to get into the Army. But from all accounts, he's dead, whether or not he's the one they're burying today. Didn't he die when they bombed Nichols Field? That's the name of the place, isn't it, Sally?"

"I don't remember," Sally said, scratching her head. "I just remember it was in Hawaii."

"Nichols Field is outside of Manila," Hoctor explained.

"Yeah. Like I said, it's in Hawaii."

"You mean the Philippines."

Harry interrupted. "The guy's right. Pinky went to Hawaii. Everyone else was in the Philippines. That means Nichols Field was in the Philippines."

Sally blew smoke in his face. "So you think you're smarter than me. Hawaii, the Philippines, what's the difference? It's on the other side of California. So you grew up not far from him, smarty-pants. So what's his name?"

"LaCoste, Franklin LaCoste. He's a LaCoste too, but everyone called him Porky."

Hoctor stepped down from the barstool and steadied himself on the partition. "Porky? You don't mean Frenchy LaCoste." By this point, everyone in the café was eavesdropping on the conversation.

"Yeah, maybe. Do you know him?"

"Yeah, we're buddies. He's not dead. At least the last time I saw him, he wasn't. He got me a mess kit—a spoon, a canteen, and some clothes. We were at a prison camp together, at Cabanatuan," Hoctor said, falling against the partition.

An older man, dressed in a cable-knit sweater, wool trousers, and cap was sitting at a table by the window, reading a paper as he ate a bowl of beef stew. He had looked up when he heard the name Porky mentioned and was watching Hoctor when he noticed him slip. He quickly rose to lend a hand. "Steady there. Look here, they've got room at the table, haven't you, Harry?"

"Of course," Harry said as his girlfriend and Landry adjusted their chairs to make room.

"Let's say you and me join them." The older man maneuvered Hoctor through the divide and over to the table, grabbing an extra chair in passing. "Ernie, where's that sandwich you promised?"

"Coming right up," Ernie said, wiping his hands on his apron as he stepped into the kitchen.

"My name's Lionel Smith," he said, grabbing Hoctor's hand in a hearty handshake. "I know Porky real well. I'm a friend of the family. You're telling me that Porky is not dead?"

Hoctor looked up, bleary-eyed and confused. "What's this, November?"

"Yes. November 17, 1944," Smith added, not sure if this man even knew who he was, never mind Porky.

"Frenchy was alive a few months ago. He made it to corporal before the war. I got torpedoed on September 7. But he could have died a month ago. I don't know. I don't know what to say."

"Porky made it to corporal," Smith confirmed.

"He was working in the kitchen at a POW camp, the last I knew. Before that, he tried to sell me a pair of aviator glasses. I remember one time he asked me how I was doing, and I said, 'Frenchy, I've been sober since they bombed Pearl Harbor and I made it through Bataan.' He laughed like hell, then slapped me on the back and asked me what the fuck I was doing in rags." Hoctor paused and his eyes watered. He fought back tears and continued, "Frenchy helped me out, got me a clean set of suntans and shoes, a mess kit, the whole shootin' match. I was wearing rags and he helped me out. He was like that. Everyone likes Frenchy."

"And you say he's alive?"

"He looked about as good as anyone at Cabanatuan. Of course, we were all starving, and with them Japs, you never know what'll happen next."

"How did you get out? I guess I'm confused. I didn't know guys were coming home," Smith asked.

"I was on my way to a work camp in Japan and the boat got scuttled. It's a long story. I got rescued."

Ernie joined the group at the table. He was carrying an *Athol Daily News*. "I found this in the back room. Does this guy look familiar to you?" Ernie stuck the paper under Hoctor's nose. Franny shook his head no.

"His name is Walter—Walter E. LaCoste, and his parents are Mr. and Mrs. Walter A. LaCoste of Ninety-five C Street. It says here he joined the service on his eighteenth birthday, on October 23, 1942, and was part of the Fifth Army invasion of Italy, which became the first American division to set foot on European soil in World War II. This guy can't be Frenchy. But this is the guy they're burying today."

"I'll tell the family. Thanks a million," Smith said and shook his hand again. "His mother and grandmother've been heartbroken since the war. Soldier, this is great news! I'll run down and tell the family." Smith patted Hoctor on the back, dropped a few dollars on the bar, and left.

Hoctor put his head between his hands and breathed deeply. Ernie went to the back room and came back with the club sandwich. He looked up as the food arrived. "Wow, this is great. Thanks."

"Thank Smith," Ernie said, retrieving the beer mug from the counter and setting it beside him. "He paid for it."

Hoctor gobbled up the sandwich as if he were starved. Just then, his buddies arrived.

"Franny," they shouted and waved.

"All your drinks are on the house," Ernie announced to the soldiers. "We're celebrating. Porky's alive!"

Hoctor braced his arms against the table to stand and then walked back to the bar and grabbed his duffel bag from the floor by the barstool. "I have to go. I've had enough to drink."

"But the party's just getting started," his friends protested.

"You drink. I'm on my way back home," he said. "Great sandwich," he shouted out to Ernie. As he opened the door to leave, the frigid wind blew in and held it wide open. He seemed stone-cold sober as he stepped outside, closed the door securely behind, and vanished.

End of Part 2

FDR arrives in Hawaii, July 1944
Courtesy FDR Library and Museum

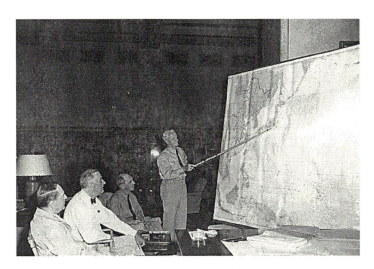

Pearl Harbor Conference, July 26, 1944.
Admiral Chester Nimitz briefs President Franklin D. Roosevelt, General Douglas MacArthur and Chairman of the Joint Chiefs of staff William Leahy on military actions in the Pacific. It was here that General MacArthur convinced President Roosevelt that the United States must liberate the Philippines for strategic as well as moral reasons. Courtesy FDR Library and Museum

General MacArthur and Admiral Chester W. Nimitz on deck of the USS Baltimore with President Roosevelt, July 1944. Courtesy FDR Library and Museum

October 20, 1944. Allied forces land at Leyte Island, fulfilling MacArthur's vow to return to the Philippines. The Battle of Luzon lasted from December 15, 1944 to July 1945. Courtesy Department of Defense

Part 3

Bilibid Prison, Manila
Courtesy National Oceanic &
Atmospheric Administration
(NOAA)

Chapter 29

Luzon
Fall 1944

Wind whipped torrents of rain through the jungle, snapped up branches, and pitched them across the muddy path of the ten-truck convoy journeying from Cabanatuan south to Manila and Bilibid Prison. Each of the ten-wheelers had wooden panels in the rear, covered with canvas and lashed down by rope. Porky was seated in the back end of the truck, a perfect observation place, and suffered an occasional slap as warm mud splashed up from the road. But the mud was soon washed away as wind flung the rain back in his direction. The driver of the truck in back was struggling to see. His wipers were not working properly and the windshield had fogged up. He stuck his head out and shouted at the guard seated next to him to do likewise, to guide him so he could pull his head back inside the cab. Guards were also stationed in the rear with the prisoners. But no one seriously expected a rebellion from the half-starved malaria- and dysentery-ridden prisoners as the convoy rumbled along the increasingly rutted road.

Japanese flag-decked cars (confiscated from the US Army) led the convoy with gun-toting guards on the alert, ready to spring into action if American and Filipino resistance fighters staged an attack. Farther back was another car and half-dozen prisoner-laden trucks. Several more heavily armed trucks took up the rear. And though by the first weeks in September the tide of war had begun to turn against the Imperial forces, an attack from resistance fighters seemed remote at this juncture in the war. The Japanese were still firmly entrenched in Luzon.

The Japanese concern was that the Philippine Islands were now an official war front for the first time since the fall of Corregidor on May 5, 1942. Merged forces of the United States Fifth and Thirteenth Air Forces, with Australian, Netherlands, and New Zealand air groups had begun fast, ferocious assaults on a variety of Japanese-held ports and airbases, and General MacArthur had pressed the Third Fleet into the emerging campaign. Meanwhile, back home in Japan, all able-bodied men had been enlisted in the war effort; the prisoners of war could be used to fill the void in a variety of industries.

Despite the weather, Porky was enjoying the ride and a chance to look at the countryside as they headed south, past San Fernando, the "Gateway to Manila," and on toward the fertile plains and marshland of the river region. The rain kept the pollen down, which had been causing no end of misery to him. After a while, he turned his attention back to the trucks. All the tires looked new, he noticed. The treads were deeply grooved, not threadbare as they had been after they were first captured. Of course, they were using old Philippine equipment back then, not their own. *I bet they've gotten plenty of supplies from Japan: trucks, tanks, food, medicine, ammunition—everything they need, when they need it*, he conjectured. If only the United States military had done the same for them. But the thought made him burn with anger, so he turned his attention back to the road. The villages they passed had Japanese trucks parked about as if they belonged—as if they had come to stay. He recalled the pretty Filipino girl who sold him the Cokes a lifetime ago and shuddered, realizing what might have happened to her and her family. The last time he had traveled this road, he was with an American convoy and Dynamite Dunn, who was now buried somewhere in a back field at Cabanatuan.

The thought of Dynamite made him depressed, so he turned his attention back to the Japanese trucks that had been shipped over along with other cargo. The snouts of the trucks weren't curved like the trucks back home, with little slits like whiskers, but were built like tapered wedges. Based on what little geometry he could remember, he observed the front ends were rectangles, with wider rectangles near the windshield. The sides and top narrowed toward the front. If he could turn the shape up vertically, it would turn into a wedge-shaped funnel. Maybe the style had changed in America too and cars and trucks featured geometric forms. Or maybe they weren't making stylish new cars anymore, and people were learning to make do with what they had. If they had any sense, the steel mills would be turning out steel for ships and jeeps and tanks and planes and guns—the war effort. Of course they were, or at least he hoped they were. At heart he still counted on Uncle Sam to come to the rescue. But he wasn't going to hold his breath waiting.

By late afternoon, the wind and rain tapered off, and the air turned humid as the convoy reached the outskirts of Manila. Porky's muscles ached and his clothes were still slightly damp. If only he could slide down and rest; but the prisoners were packed in too tightly. Exhaustion set in, a weariness so profound it settled in his bones as they passed through Manila, even now the Pearl of the Orient. By February 1945, Manila would become a broken shell of its former self as the Japanese ransacked and burned, looted and raped and murdered an estimated 111,000 men, women, and children in advance of the American liberation, which completed the city's destruction with widespread bombing.

Before long the convoy was headed down España Street and turned the corner at Rizal Avenue to Bilibid Prison, which stood about two hundred yards north of the Pasig River. Porky's allergies were acting up worse than ever. He could barely breathe as he got his first glimpse of Bilibid. It looked forlorn as the late afternoon shadows lengthened across the medieval façade, elevated turrets, and strong iron bars of the gate Japanese prison guards were pulling open as the convoy approached. He recalled how when he first arrived at Nichols Field, he had served as guard to Bilibid prisoners on a work detail. Now, thousands of Americans were held captive here, and Porky would become part of those statistics.

As the convoy passed under the vaulted archway into the prison courtyard, the trucks pulled up alongside the razor-wire-topped inner wall and parked. Drivers and guards hopped out and unhitched the wooden slabs at the rear of the truck. By now, Porky's eyelids were red and swollen and his nose was dripping. Everything was a blur as he hopped off the truck along with the other prisoners. Guards pushed rifle butts into the backs of the POWs to prod them along to the central area where the other prisoners had amassed. Altogether they totaled five hundred new inmates for the notorious Bilibid Prison complex.

The cars that had accompanied the convoy drove in front of the gathering prisoners and came to a halt. Armed guards jumped out and reassembled in a tight line perpendicular to the men, who were ordered to line up for "tenko"—roll call. A Japanese soldier stepped forward and shouted out the names of each of the POWs that had been trucked in. Each man in turn stepped forward and hollered, "Present," as his name was called. Once all the POWs were accounted for, the Japanese military personnel climbed back into the vehicles and drove off. To the POWs' surprise, American Navy personnel shut the gates, and a naval officer approached the crowd. "Follow me, men, we're in charge here," he said.

As the stunned "inmates" followed the officer into the main building, Porky whispered to a man next to him, "This is a pretty good deal." The man nodded in agreement, too startled to speak.

Inside the walls of Bilibid Prison.
Courtesy of the National Archives and the Bensing family
(Bataan Project)

The POWs entered an enormous hall and formed a semicircle around the officer, whose back was to a large extended passageway. "Look to your left," he instructed. "That's where you're going to bed down. Look to your right. See those tables over there," he said, pointing. "That's where you'll eat. You'll be notified when it's your turn. Now follow me."

The officer turned and walked toward the back corridor, then turned to face the men again as he put up his hand to halt. "We've got some clothes we're going to issue you for your next excursion. Now, I know you're all army, but don't be offended if we hand you navy uniforms, army uniforms, or even some Japanese uniforms. Just take what you get. We've broken it down to small, medium, and large."

The passageway was lined with tables and uniforms, reminiscent of Porky's first encounter with the military at Fort Slocum, four years earlier. GIs were stationed behind the tables as before, but instead of strong muscular enlisted men, these men were emaciated and looked far older than their years.

Each POW was handed a navy uniform, a set of wool army pants and shirt, suntans, coveralls, and a Japanese work outfit that looked something like a set of suntans. Toward the far end of the corridor, the table was stacked with shoes. Cartons more were stashed underneath the table. Each man was handed a new set of army shoes and several pairs of heavy wool socks. The end table was stacked with long heavy wool army overcoats—small, medium, and large. Porky was handed the smallest one in stock and followed the others to the area where they were to bed down. There, each man dropped his clothes in a heap, then sorted through and tried on the clothes.

Porky was curious about how he might look in a navy outfit. Before the war, they were the ones who got all the girls, or so he thought. As he buttoned up his pants, he swung his leg to check out the flap of the bell-bottoms and then pulled the jumper over his head. "It fits like it's tailor-made. I'm ready to go out on the town," Porky commented to a particularly scrawny man trying on clothes next to him.

"Yeah, good deal," the man said, glancing up. "I'm not as fortunate." His uniform hung as if he were a scarecrow. "I may be tall, but I'm no longer well built. Hope they give us some grub here that'll put some meat back on our bones." He picked through the pile and pulled up the wool pants and shirt from the bottom. "Say, what's all of these heavy clothes about?"

"Beats me," Porky admitted. "Suntans and overcoats, it's kind of screwy. What kind of place is this Japan anyway?"

The soldier to his left joined in. "Yeah, I've heard in parts of Japan it rains all the time, so why the winter overcoats?"

"Maybe they don't have blankets or bunks, so we're supposed to sleep on this."

Across the hall, there was a table crowded with POWs who were finishing their meal. "Looks like that bunch over there are about done," the man to the right commented as he fumbled with the buttons of his bellbottoms.

Porky sneezed. "Goddamn allergies!"

A Navy officer approached to alert them that they were up next. The soldiers, newly outfitted as sailors, grabbed their mess kits and made their way to the dining area. Before long, a Navy kitchen aide approached with a steaming bowl of white rice plus a large bowl of soup with vegetables.

"Pinch me, is this Christmas?" Porky asked as he dug in. "This is good quan."

"Good quan?" the POW next to him said with his mouth full, "Try great quan! All we need is a bottle of plum wine."

Porky sneezed again. "These GD allergies!" The kitchen aide put a hand on his shoulder and leaned in to speak.

"You ought to look into that."

"Look into what?"

"Your allergies."

"My allergies? Now who's going to do that?"

"The doctor. Why don't you check into the sick bay after supper? I'm sure he can do something for you."

"That'll be a change."

"Look, you're going to be shipping out before long. They want you as fit as can be."

"Any idea where we're headed? We know it's Japan, but why all the different clothes?"

"You want a travel guide? Let me tell you something. From what I hear, Japan has it all—sunny tropics, great beaches, snowcapped mountains, cities, the country, and lots and lots and lots of Japanese. But trust me. You'll miss the cozy atmosphere of Bilibid Prison."

"So how long are you here for?"

"Indefinitely. Our job is to take care of people as they come and go. Not a bad assignment," he said and walked back to the kitchen.

Porky finished eating and wandered back to his pile of clothes. He pulled a terry-cloth bathrobe out of his knapsack, put it on over his spiffy sailor's outfit, and loosely tied the belt in front. The bathrobe was one of the many lucky finds he discovered in a pile of belongings from the dead back at Cabanatuan. Plopping down atop his belongings, he slipped new socks on and slid them into new shoes, then got up to take a walk around the prison to check out the place before heading to the sick bay. One particularly eerie passageway he entered was dimly lit from barricaded windows within a small row of prison cells. Each cell contained an American serviceman cloaked in semidarkness. *What the hell are these guys in for?* Porky wondered.

Halfway through the passage, one of the men called out with a thick Bronx accent, "Hey, you, you with the bathrobe!"

Porky stopped in his tracks. "You mean me?"

"Yeah, who else would I be talking to?"

Porky wasn't sure whether he should talk to the guy or run. For all he knew, the man could be a psychopath, a murderer. Still, he was curious. "So what do you want?" he responded, trying to sound tough.

"Your bathrobe!"

"My bathrobe! Say, what are you in for anyway?"

"What's it to you?"

"Just curious. Most of the guys I know got in trouble over stealing food. Is that what happened to you?"

"No. Plenty of food here."

"So what happened? Did you beat up some guy, or hit an officer?"

"No, nothing like that."

"So—"

"Hell, we're all nuts!" The prisoner coughed up phlegm and spit in a corner.

"Nuts! You don't seem nuts."

"Don't let me fool you. I am as looney as a looney tune," he said, coughing again.

"Oh yeah, so does that mean you get to stay here? I suppose they don't want any nuts in Japan."

The prisoner laughed hysterically until he coughed violently, spit up more phlegm, and spit it into the same corner as before. He smiled a toothless smile and wiped his mouth with his hand, then rubbed his hand clean on the bottom of his sailor jumper. "Hey, I want your bathrobe," he insisted.

"Look, I like it myself."

"Oh yeah, look at what I've got here," the prisoner said as he maneuvered to the back of the cell and pulled an old tobacco can out from his piles of clothes. "Looky here," he said, beaming a toothless grin. The man slid his tongue along his lips and waited.

"What, so you have tobacco? I'm not interested. I can get plenty of tobacco."

The prisoner burst out in gales of laughter, then just as suddenly stopped and stared, his bloodshot eyeballs fixed on Porky. "Just taste it," he urged as he opened the can. "Wet your finger and dip it in," he demanded as he pressed the can against one of the cell bars, careful to hold it tight to prevent his would-be trading partner bolting, can and all.

Porky licked his finger and dipped it into the can. "I think I know what this is," he said as he withdrew his finger and placed it on his tongue. "Ah yes, it's pepper! That would make for some tasty meals," he admitted, nodding in approval.

"OK," the prisoner said. He pulled the can away from the bar and slid the top back on securely. "So do you want to barter?"

"It's a bargain." Porky slipped off the bathrobe and handed it through the bars to the prisoner, who passed the can through to him. "Thanks a lot," Porky said as he watched the prisoner try on the robe.

"Oh, this feels good. Takes the chill off. Thanks, soldier."

"Fair enough! See you later."

Porky continued through the passageway until he reached the sick bay. Inside, a doctor was seated at a table, writing into a large notebook. He looked up as Porky approached.

"So what is your problem, soldier?"

"Allergies. I came to get my nose scraped or whatever you think might work."

"Aren't you with that group that's due to leave shortly?"

"Yes, I believe so."

"Do you know where we're going?"

"No."

"The rumor is you'll be headed to northern Japan, the mountains of Japan. There's no need to treat your allergies because they'll disappear once you're in the mountains."

"Are you sure?"

"Soldier, you're in the tropics. Plants are blooming year-round. You're filled up with pollen."

"Oh," Porky sniffed.

The doctor stood and went to a medicine cabinet. He opened the glass case and pulled out a dingy tan handkerchief that had been made from threadbare suntans. "Here, use this," he said, handing the cloth to Porky. "There's snow up in the mountains. If you find yourself sniffling, trust me, it won't be from the pollen."

Privates O'Meara, Scherban and Mazerole (right) Pre-War 1941, Manila
Courtesy LaCoste/Thurber family

Chapter 30

About a week later, the Japanese returned and issued orders to the naval officer in charge. All the men recently brought to Bilibid from Cabanatuan were to gather their belongings and report to the front courtyard for roll call. After tenko, the Americans were lined up four abreast. Japanese guards opened the massive gate, then marched the POWs down Rizal Avenue over to Quezon Boulevard. As they were paraded down to the Manila docks, the prisoners passed bombed-out buildings, a former American warehouse filled with new tires, and one of the many apartment buildings rumored to be a *juro,* or brothel, where Caucasian and mestiza women were kept—forced from their families to serve the carnal tastes of Japanese officers. The U.S. Navy headquarters was now an enemy center of operations, housing the Japanese Imperial Forces; and streets that had once housed thriving businesses were now vacant, their windows shattered and interiors looted, their battered shop signs serving as silent testimony to the past.

The POWs struggled with balancing their bundles and keeping pace. Once they arrived at dockside, a Japanese officer shouted for them to break rank. Though some were puzzled by the order, enough men understood the command that several broke rank and gathered in front of him. The others quickly followed suit. As the Japanese officer continued, his back to Pier 7—one of the largest docks at the Manila port—an unmarked freighter turned transport vessel docked next to another freighter marked with a large red cross. However, the men coming down the gangplank appeared to be carrying box loads of ammunition, not medical supplies, while a crane maneuvered a Japanese military truck into place on the dock.

To the left of the men was a three-story warehouse from which dozens of Japanese soldiers carried bulky cardboard boxes filled with Red Cross care packages from home. After they piled the boxes in front of the assembled prisoners, the officer in charge motioned for one of the Japanese soldiers to come forward and handed him the stack of papers used earlier during the tenko. This man spoke English. "Jeffrey Adams, Thomas Atwater, Charles . . . ."

Eventually, Porky's name was called. He stepped forward to receive his package, but when he retreated back into the crowd a man called after him, "Frenchy, Frenchy! It's Leo, don't you remember me?" Porky dropped the package on top of his pile of clothes and gear and turned around and saw someone pushing his way through the crowd.

"Remember, we were in the same outfit at Nichols Field," Leo said as he pushed aside two men and extended his hand.

"Leo, how the hell are you?" Porky said, reaching out to shake his hand before dropping to his knees to open the package.

Leo looked down at Porky, who turned the package over to study the writing before opening it. "Looks like Christmas came early for you."

"I see you're surviving," Porky said, glancing up. Leo looked anxious as ever. "Things OK with you?"

"Not bad. Have you run into anyone else from the outfit?"

"Not lately. I hope they've managed. Of course, you knew about Billy Freeman and Bobby Dolan, my friends from back home."

"They're OK, aren't they?"

"I am afraid not. They both died of malaria; Bobby at Camp O'Donnell and Billy at Cabanatuan. I got to spend some time with Bobby in Bataan, but Billy died before I could reach him."

"Sorry to hear that," Leo gulped in some air before he spoke. "You know, the damnedest thing happened to me."

"What's that?" Porky asked as he pulled apart the flaps on the package.

"As I've told you before, Frenchy, I've had the damnedest life, what with my folks just about starving to death, so they gave me up during the Depression."

"Oh, that's right. Didn't you tell me about some foster mother who'd take you to bed as soon as her old man left for work?" The ears of a few standing nearby perked up, but they stood, arms folded, waiting for their names to be called, acting oblivious to the conversation.

"Yeah, and I haven't had a girlfriend since," Leo joked. With that, the men glanced over to get a good look at who was talking. One man's name was called, but he appeared torn between picking up his package and continuing to eavesdrop.

"Wow! The folks back home have been good to me." Porky whistled through his teeth and laughed out loud.

Leo tried to disguise his envy and appear pleased. "Why? Whatcha got?"

"Two tins of fifty cigarettes, one bag of Bull Durham tobacco, three packages of rolling papers, and two bars of chewing tobacco." Porky was delighted, but Leo was shocked.

"No food, no medicine?"

Porky checked through the package again and then closed the box. "Nope, there's only tobacco," he said as he stood back up and surveyed the scene. "The package is from Uncle Rosario. He knows me real well, and seeing that he was in France for the First World War, he knows how valuable this is."

"I doubt that I'll get anything. As far as I know, my parents are dead. I have no one. Besides, how do they know if we're dead or alive?"

"Beats me. Of course, there's always hope, and that's what they count on."

"You're the lucky one, Frenchy. You've got family, you've got friends, and the way you look, you've got your health too."

"Oh, I've had my moments. I've passed out a few times on work details, and they've put me on—"

"Well, I've passed out, and you would never guess from what." Leo glared at Porky in silence.

"I don't know, Leo. Tell me. You look fit enough to me."

"Epilepsy."

"Epilepsy? Jesus Christ, how did you pick that up? I didn't know it was catching."

"It's not something you catch. It is something you develop."

"I thought you had to be born with it."

"That's what I thought too, but I've got it. By Jesus, I've got it."

"Christ, I hope you haven't swallowed your tongue," Porky blurted out. Everyone within earshot turned and stared. One man was so uncomfortable with the topic he picked up his belongings and moved toward the back of the crowd. But Porky and Leo were oblivious to the reaction.

"So far, I've been lucky. Someone's always been close by with a spoon to hold my tongue down. One guy used a stick. So far, I've woke up from these seizures, but I've been lucky. Jesus, you never know when your luck'll run out."

As names continued to be called, a continual flow was created, with some leaving the group while others returned. Eventually, as more and more men opened their packages, the need to spread out forced the crowd to disperse along the dockside while gifts from home were stacked on the pavement and inventoried. Porky and Leo grabbed their belongings and moved to the side to make way but were faced with the prospect of standing closer to the Japanese guards, who maintained a watchful eye.

"Well, stick close by, and if you get in trouble, I'll take care of you," Porky said, dropping his gear, clothes, and package back onto the pavement. "Maybe we can fix it so we can go out on work details together."

"They won't let me work. The Japs won't let me. They're afraid of me. I don't know if they're superstitious or think they can catch it."

"Jesus, Leo, I hope you get a package. Everyone else seems to be getting a package."

"Not me. It's not my luck. I must have been standing behind the door when they passed out good luck. In fact, it's the damnedest thing, how I got this epilepsy," Leo began and was soon so carried away with his story that he grew louder and louder as he spoke and began to capture more and more attention.

"I was onboard a small boat back at Cabanatuan on a work detail. We were sent out to fish, and you must remember that typhoon during rainy season?"

"I remember it rained like hell," Porky said, scratching his head. "But I don't remember any strong winds, unless it was during one of those times I was at Ward Zero, passed out. And I was never assigned lake duty."

"I'm not sure when it happened, but I do remember we were pretty far out, and a typhoon came along. Jesus, we were tossed around like Ping-Pong balls."

Several men looking through packages stopped what they were doing to listen. Leo continued as if hypnotized, "It's a wonder we didn't capsize. We kept taking on water and bailing it out, but the worse part of all was how dark it got. Then pressure with the wind and the howling started building so bad I thought my ears would pop. But the pressure got worse and worse. It was all around. It kept on getting tighter and tighter. I thought my head was crushing in and my eyes were about to pop out. It was like a boa constrictor had wrapped itself around my body and was swallowing me whole."

Leo's eyes bugged out as he continued. "I must have stopped breathing because I passed out. I woke up after the storm was over, and maybe I got more luck than I give myself credit for. A young lieutenant, a doctor, was onboard with us. I woke to find him leaning over me. He said I was one lucky guy he was there. See, he had been carrying some kind of syringe on him since we were taken prisoners, so he shot me up and that brought me to."

"That's good. Thank God for that doctor."

"You know, I thought I was fine, until one day, I was out in a field on a work detail when all of a sudden this attack came over me."

As Leo continued, another unmarked transport docked at the pier. As Japanese soldiers walked to the vessel to assist in unloading cargo, a gangplank was extended for the human cargo that would soon be loaded into the hold.

"Wouldn't you know—I started losing control. My hands started flailing around," Leo said. As he thrashed his arms around to demonstrate, POWs stepped back to create space. "And it seems like the trees and ground was moving backward with the sky," he continued, as if onstage. "But it must have been my eyes rolling backward in my head." When Leo rolled his eyes backward to illustrate, a Japanese guard became so uncomfortable he moved away. "Then some guy stuck a spoon in my mouth," he said, straightening up. "I must have been swallowing my tongue. I fell down on the ground and passed out." Leo paused and there was total silence.

The men were spellbound as Leo continued. "At any rate, that's how it started. I can't tell you how many people I've scared half to death, but there is a bright side. The Japs don't want anything to do with me. They won't let me work. I haven't been on one detail since. If I don't watch it, I'm going to get fat and lazy."

"The way they starve us, there's no danger of that," one man shot back while in the background the Japanese officer continued calling off names.

Porky and Leo sat on their stack of clothes to listen. "Patrick Mackie, James McDonald, Leo Mazerole—"

"Mazerole. Leo, that's you."

"Are you sure? I thought he said my name, but maybe that was someone else."

One of the men eavesdropping tapped Leo on the shoulder. "Soldier, if your name's Mazerole, that's your package."

Porky yanked Leo to his feet. "Hurry up and claim it. They're about ready for us to start boarding the ship."

Leo pushed his way to the front to retrieve his package. Soon after, the guards ordered the men to gather their items and line up for a final count before boarding. As the last crates of rice and palm oil were hauled off the freighter, the POWs were force-marched across the gangplank onto the deck of the ship and made to hurry down the ladder into the cargo hold.

Arms and legs competed with someone else's hands and feet as the guards pushed them down with rifle butts. "Speedo, speedo," they screamed, shoving the men on top of one another. Many fell, unable to maintain their footing while others below pulled them out. Before long, there was hardly room to breathe, let alone stand, as bodies crushed against one another. Once they were inside, the hatch was dropped into place and fastened by thick cables. There was no escape. They were trapped inside a dark, dank space of extremely limited size. POWs screamed and swore obscenities against their captors. One thing was clear: they were caught, trapped in a living nightmare.

As the vessel churned into open waters, Porky blocked out the sound, smells, and sweltering heat with memories of when he was a green recruit traveling with his buddies to the Philippines. But when the freighter lurched and zigzagged to outfox Allied vessels bent on their destruction, he snapped back to reality. More often than not, the pitching and rolling combined with the stench of men's excrement and vomit, and the pungent odor of piss was impossible to escape. Yet despite their ordeal, during the first few days, the hundreds of POWs forced to share this experience were in better shape than others who had crossed. Most had canned ham and cheese, sardines and orange juice, candy and crackers, and anything else friends and relatives had thought might help them survive—hoping against hope that they were still alive—and if not, hoping some other wretched soul would benefit.

Porky's uncle Rosario was one of a kind. The care package he sent was chosen wisely. Porky held a near monopoly on the tobacco trade within the ship's hold. Chewing tobacco commanded the highest prices—virtually anything Porky wanted to barter for, he got, and Leo was also willing to share. As a boy growing up in Maine, Leo occasionally attended church with his grandparents, who had long since died. The aging pastor made it a habit to clip out notices of local men pressed into service by the war. Leo had long forgotten them, but the pastor and elders of the parish remembered the scrawny child, whose life seemed to go from bad to worse. So when the Ladies Fellowship prepared Christmas packages for the local boys overseas, they were more than happy to include him, packing the standard items the Red Cross recommended minus the cigarettes, substituting instead extra boxes of raisins and orange juice.

But there was nothing like a plug of tobacco to stave off hunger and refocus the mind. The prisoners had little to concentrate on during the day except personal misery and the tiny shaft of light that slipped through the hatch. It was how they tracked the rising and setting of the sun. For many, thoughts turned inward to loved ones or baseball or sex or dreams of sitting in an open field or fishing—leaning against a boulder, rod in hand, as a cool breeze ruffled the stillness of pooled water from a clear mountain stream. Others succumbed to the torture of grueling heat and thirst as they mentally as well as physically descended into hell. But with a plug of tobacco in your mouth, you could remember you were a man, to buck up and take it as best you could and to find comfort in knowing that this too shall pass.

Three buckets served as chamber pots for the men able to maneuver over to the make-do toilets. On the first and second days, the only thing they had been given for sustenance was hot water and a spoonful of sugar. Most still had food remaining from care packages but hesitated to polish it off, just in case. By late afternoon of the third day, their Japanese caretakers had not yet opened the hatch. A violent storm howled overhead as a steady drumbeat of rain pelted the ship and rocked it violently, pitching the men into one another, slamming them to one side, then to the other. Then the ship made a 180-degree pivot turn.

"Jesus Christ Almighty! That sea is rough," Leo blurted out as fellow passengers maneuvered to the pails to vomit.

"What the Christ are they doing?" someone shouted. "Are they turning around?"

"I don't care where they're bringing us," Porky yelled into Leo's ear. "It's been three days and still no food."

The ship's thrust kept the ship starboard but suddenly the stern turned portside and seemed to hold at a forty-five-degree angle. "Holy shit, what the fuck," men shouted as they fell into one another. Eventually, the ship began to right, which allowed the men to relax momentarily.

"At least most of us still have some food left," a POW commented, continuing a conversation he was having prior to the vessel nearly capsizing.

"If it weren't for those care packages, God knows what would have happened," the man next to him said.

"I've lost my appetite," Porky admitted to Leo.

Once the winds diminished, general conversation once again dominated. "I've heard tales that would make your flesh crawl. Let's hope we get to port before anything happens."

"Ain't this supposed to be a three-day journey?"

"Three days if you're lucky, but that was in peacetime."

"Look, there's a GD storm raging, and to top it off, we're dodging torpedoes. We'll be lucky *if* we make it to Japan."

"I bet the Americans are close by."

"If that's the case, someone, quick, hand me a white handkerchief. I want to surrender," Leo piped up.

"Don't we wish we could," Porky shouted, joining in the banter. "Hey, remember what it was like on the way over before the war? I remember sunning myself on deck with my buddies. Remember the floating crap games below deck? Hell, there's not enough room here to sleep, never mind play a game of craps. And remember the flying fish? We threw it back like it was garbage. I'd eat it now."

"Yeah, raw," another man called out from across the compartment. "Let's get serious," another hollered above the din. "What's the danger of being hit by one of our own?"

"The odds must be pretty good," someone ventured. "The way they're steering this sardine can, you'd think half of the U.S. Navy was on our tail."

"Oh yeah, we're so small no one's going to detect us."

"If they keep spinning around, we'll get swamped by our own waves."

"Maybe we have a bunch of drunken Japs at the helm," Leo joked.

"I could use some sake about now," Porky joined in, trying to make light of their dilemma.

"Did ya hear about that ship that was out three weeks?" the man to his left whispered hoarsely. "Men were starving and dying of thirst, so they ganged up on one of the weaker guys, slit his throat, and drank his blood."

"Soldier, would you shut up?" a man called from the back.

"Nothing like that is going to happen on this ship."

"Guess again. I've seen so much atrocity since the war began it makes my stomach turn."

"Yeah, remember back at Cabanatuan, those two guys who tried to escape?"

"Will someone shut him up?"

"The Japs gouged their eyes out, cut their balls off, and they were strung up on poles to serve as a warning for the rest of us."

Porky leaned over to Leo. "I remember hearing about that, but I didn't go out of my way to see it. I guess for a lot of guys it was a big attraction."

"I missed that one too. I'm with you, Frenchy. The less I see, the better I'll sleep."

"Remember how the Japs told us that if one man escapes, the next ten would be shot? The thing is, where would anyone go if they did escape? The Japs are everywhere. The Philippine villagers know they're dead if they harbor a prisoner, and if you steal a boat, where are you going to go? The Japanese control all of the islands."

Following Porky's comments there was silence, except for men moaning, the boat creaking, the wind howling, and the thud of waves collapsing on deck and pounding the hull.

"You know, I never did hear what happened to guys who escaped or ten men getting shot," Porky continued, breaking the silence.

"Maybe they didn't shoot them," the man with the hoarse voice shouted out. "Maybe they slit their throats instead."

"Where I was, in Ward Zero, we didn't need to be shot," Porky continued. "We were dying like flies. And who had the energy to escape? Though maybe I did escape. I escaped all of the action everyone talks about by being passed out half the time."

Leo turned to face his friend, whose head was dimly illuminated by a shaft of light. "Frenchy, maybe we're the lucky ones. Maybe someone upstairs is watching over us."

"I hope so." Porky placed a hand on Leo's arm. "Say, I am sick of smelling those shit pails," he announced. "I'm going to see if I can do something about it."

"Go ahead, just knock on the hatch," Leo suggested. "Who knows, you might get an answer. No one else has had the courage to try." Porky pushed past the men and grabbed the closest pail.

"Peeyoo! Whew!" the POWs hollered as they made way for Porky to march past to the ladder.

"Hey, I'm surprised you don't salute," Porky quipped back.

"We will salute if you dump that goddamn shit pail."

Porky climbed the ladder, bucket in hand. Once he was close enough, he raised a fist and knocked on the hatch. A guard lifted the metal cover, checked out the pot, and drew back in disgust. He gestured for Porky to climb out onto the deck. Once outside, Porky breathed deeply and glanced up at the sun, which was breaking through the clouds and haze. A brisk gust slapped his hair and beard back and forth and passed over his half-naked body. The guard pointed to the spot where he wanted Porky to dump the festering mixture, then remembered that he was never to leave a prisoner to fend for himself, no matter what the circumstances. He raised his rifle butt forward and pushed Porky along to the deck railing where he was to toss the contents of the pail.

The guard checked the wind direction, then placed a hand on Porky's arm and gestured for him to wait. Meanwhile, on the deck above, several soldiers trained their rifles on Porky—in case he did what, he wondered. Did they think he might jump overboard, trying to steal a pot full of shit and puke?

"Ma-te, Ma-te," the guard insisted.

"Don't worry. I'll wait," Porky tried to assure him. "Christ, I don't want this splashing back onto my face."

Porky held the pail as far away as possible. Both he and the guard averted their faces, which made them visible to the guards above, who broke out laughing at the sight. The more they wrinkled their lips and noses from the stench, the greater the howls from above. *I'm glad they find this amusing*, Porky quietly fumed but then noticed several Japanese sailors tucked into a corner about twenty feet away, standing by a cauldron of rice. The steaming pot was set on the square grill of an iron *shichirin*, an ancient portable cooking device. One man was working a small bellows, attempting to fan the flames of the smoldering firewood beneath. But the problem they encountered was soon obvious. Seawater began pouring out of the scuppers, followed by a gigantic wave that crashed over the deck and washed out the flame.

Porky braced himself against the railing, grabbed hold with one hand while he kept the pail at arm's length. Finally, the guard yelled, "Jootoo, jootoo." Porky tossed the contents of the pail into the ocean below and jumped back. Simultaneously, the guard jumped back too, which again evoked peals of laughter from the soldiers above. "Jootoo, Jootoo, de nai? Jootoo de nai?" the guard insisted as he shot a stern look up, then back to Porky, pointing at the hatch with his rifle. Just then, a wave swamped the area. Porky grabbed the railing and somehow managed to avoid smashing into the deck. He was drenched to the bone, which was what he had hoped for—a quick shower. He looked up at the sun, wiped his hands on his pants, breathed deeply, then walked back toward the hatch, the pail swinging loosely by his side. The guard stuck the rifle in his face as he opened the hatch. Porky turned to descend, tapping for the first rung with the tip of his shoe as he stepped back into the hole. When he reached the bottom, the hatch came crashing down and the cable scraped across, secured back into place. Porky turned to find a dozen or so men who had gathered. They stood at attention and saluted. He grinned and handed the pail to the last man in line.

"Here, soldier. Put it back where it came from," he said, then returned to his spot by Leo.

"Well, I found out one thing when I was on deck."

"What's that? They're dirty, rotten bastards?"

"The reason we've got no food is they can't cook it. Every time they get a fire going, a wave comes along and douses it. Men, pray for calm seas," he recommended to everyone within earshot.

Japanese 18th Century Ukiyo-e print
Courtesy Library of Congress

Chapter 31

According to legend, the Japanese islands were created as part of a mating ritual between the goddess Izanami-no-kami and god Izanagi-no-mikoto, who stood on the rainbow bridge of heaven, contemplating the sea beneath. The god took hold of a magnificent jeweled spear from the heavens and stirred the sea. When he lifted the spear, a salty drop dripped below and a great island rose like a pillar. The gods stepped from the Rainbow Bridge onto the island, danced, and mated; and the goddess gave birth to a chain of islands, which became a great nation—Nippon. A sacred tiger guards Nippon from the west. A sacred dragon holds sentry from the east. But despite their protection, the gods must have felt a growing sense of apprehension as 1944 drew to a close. The Allied powers grew stronger and the Japanese weaker with each attack. And in a place called Los Alamos, a monstrous apparatus was under construction, so deadly it would force hostilities to come to a close.

Two weeks after the Japanese freighter left Pier 7 with its human cargo, it passed the Ryukyu Islands—Amami, Okinawa, and Sakishima—that extend seven hundred miles southwest from Kyushu, the first of Japan's four major islands. The ship bobbed and weaved through the South China Sea into the East China Sea. The men entombed in the bowels of the vessel were terrified, imagining what was in store for them—that is, if they survived the journey. Porky had last seen his friend, Pint Lawson, at Cabanatuan. Little did he know that Pint was now working in a machine shop and foundry outside of Shenyang (Mukden), Manchuria, not far from the Korean Peninsula, while his friend from New Hampshire, Roland Stickney, was detained at Keijo, outside of Seoul. Roland busied himself in the military warehouse in the winter, untying knots to preserve straw ropes. During the summer, he stacked milled rice.

At Camp Hoten, where Pint spent his time, the prisoners were housed in Chinese barracks about three-quarters underground because of the subzero temperatures that at times reached fifty to sixty below. A potbelly stove in each of the fifty-man barracks served as a form of central heating and mattresses were made of wood. Adding to the misery, the latrines were outside. But though 350 men died that first winter, others were able to endure the extreme conditions dressed in wool-lined canvas outfits and heavy coats, heavy boots, and fur-lined caps. Their diet consisted mostly of soybeans that took about six or seven hours to cook, but it was a change from the rice diet of the Philippines and was more nutritious.

On the sixteenth day of the voyage to Japan, Porky's personal Hell Ship approached the island of Kyushu, which history tells us was involved in commercial trade for centuries. On the western coast of the island, Nagasaki was not only one of the oldest international ports but served as the only gateway open to foreign trade between 1639 and 1859. But Porky and company were not there as sightseers. There were no tour guides in the blackness of the ship's hold except the personal demons within each man as he clung to life and sanity. Their conditions rivaled the squalor and hardship endured thirteen centuries earlier by thousands of *nuhi* (奴婢) who served as slaves in the Ibaraki region, their final destination too.

Frank Batchelor, one of the Athol men Porky had run into shortly before the war, was serving time about a hundred miles north-northeast of Nagasaki, outside of the city of Fukuoka at Camp Number 1. The POW camp was set across from the railroad tracks, not far from the Sea of Japan. Here the men slept in unheated wooden barracks with tar-paper roofs and dirt floors. They worked ten-hour days at hard labor outside of camp, constructing airfield bomb shelters or working in the coal mines. Though there were active volcanoes on the island, the prisoners' worries were focused on daily survival. And they were blissfully unaware of a new form of fly ash—radioactive human and material debris—that would soon coat parts of the island.

An arm of the Pacific Ocean, *Seto Naikai* courses between the islands of Kyushu, Honshu, and Shikoku. The smallest of Japan's four major islands, Shikoku has a tip that extends not far from Hiroshima. As Porky's Hell Ship steamed past, approximately 223 Americans, 166 British, and 401 Dutch prisoners of war were stationed in and around Hiroshima. Ten downed American airmen were among the 130,000, mostly Japanese, who died during or soon after the Little Boy was dropped by the B-29 Superfortress bomber, the *Enola Gay*, on August 6, 1945. The seven-foot-eight-inch long Fat Man arrived in Nagasaki three days later, on August 9. Moments after the B-29 *Bockscar*'s bottom opened, the Fat Man's mushroom cloud was visible to all the nearly five hundred mostly Dutch and British prisoners based on the outskirts of the city. But that was in the future—a future in whose frightening shadow we live to this day.

Honshu, the largest of the islands, would soon be home to Porky and his cargo-hold mates in the late fall of 1944. They had long since finished the tasty morsels shipped by the Red Cross from family and friends and now subsisted on a handful of rice and a cup of filthy water a day, if they were lucky. During the darkness of the early morning hours of their seventeenth day at sea, the freighter churned into the Pacific Ocean. The distant snowcapped Fuji Mountain was visible by moonlight to all on deck. Hours later, the cities of Yokohama and then Tokyo were portside as they pushed northward to the Hitachi seaport. Herman Hausmann was imprisoned in the mountainous region due west of Tokyo, in the Nagano prefecture at Camp Hiraoka a.k.a. Mitsushima, in the village of Tenryu. There, 307 POWs—215 British and 93 Americans—aided in the construction of the Hiraoka Electricity Generation plant and dam.

Porky and Leo would soon be engrossed in their own adventure. The immediate destination was the southern end of the Abukuma Mountains in the Ibaraki Prefecture. Here they would spend Christmas 1944 and greet the New Year of 1945—a year that would witness some of the fiercest fighting as well as the climax and end of the war. But most of the men stowed away in the ship's hold had no idea what time it was, let alone what day it was. What they did know was that the shadow world they inhabited had turned cooler, and soon it would be time to bundle up.

Shortly before dawn, the ship docked at a village not far from the city of Hitachi, in northeast Japan. The guards pulled the cables off the hatch and lifted it, letting in the morning air. A Japanese soldier appeared above. He seemed otherworldly, shrouded in fog and the first glimmers of light. He spoke perfect English with an American accent and was to accompany the men to their next destination.

"Gather all of your goodies together from your family packages," he shouted down at them. "Grab your clothes, packs, everything. Come up on deck as soon as you grab everything. You will see the gangplank. Get in line and follow the leader."

The men scrambled to retrieve their things, grabbing their army and sailor outfits and coats and mess kits and the small personal items they clung to like lucky charms. Miraculously, all had survived though they were significantly weaker than when they first started out on the journey. One by one, they climbed the ladder—up and out of the hatch onto the deck. They stretched and rubbed their muscles and blinked as light grew brighter. The cool air felt like a refreshing bath against their skin. They gasped mouthfuls of fresh air, forcing out the stench of foulness that had permeated their lungs and infiltrated their bodies. After these few minutes of relaxation, the guards forced them to get in line. One by one they walked the gangplank to shore and what for a moment seemed like freedom. The prisoners looked around at the beach and in the distance the village poking through the mist.

Japanese soldiers waved the men onto the open-paneled trucks. As each truck filled with POWs, it would drive off and another truck would back in for more men. Porky and Leo stuck together and boarded the third truck, tossing in their clothes and parcels first. They sat near the back along the driver's side and watched the scenery—first shrubs, then birch and evergreens as they moved up a hill along a dirt road several miles to the base of a mountain. The ride ended at the Hitachi copper mining camp in the village of Motoyama. Suddenly, several long wooden buildings came into view, along with an open framed structure that looked like two attached fire ranger outposts. The men were ordered to disembark and count off in groups of ten.

At the far end of the barracks, which were constructed of unstained newly timbered wood, were straddle trench latrines. The interior of the barracks was also unstained wood and contained about fifty rooms, each a perfect sixteen-by-sixteen-foot square. Each room was divided into a three-foot-wide walking area and a three-foot-high elevated sleeping area, approximately sixteen feet long and thirteen feet wide. The sleeping area contained blankets and straw mats radiating like spokes of a wheel around a center section with a large clay pot three-fourths full of sand.

Before long the men settled into their new life, and the memory of their passage over dimmed. As dusk descended that first night, a Japanese veteran, Matsuda, entered with a pail full of cooked mush and a bucket of water for them to fill their canteens. One of Matsuda's legs was stiff and dragged as he limped, and there was a deep gash across his left cheek that sank into the corner of his mouth and distorted into a sneer.

The men froze as he served them, trying not to stare. "Shit. What the hell is this crap?" Sam blurted after Matsuda left.

"Looks like maize and half-cooked nuggets to me. Kaffir corn, someone said it was," Chet drawled with an Alabama twang. "One's going to bloat you so you're likely to burst, and the other's like eating BBs."

"Come night, you'll be awake hungry as hell and listen to them roll around in your stomach," another joked.

"Aw, don't worry. We'll get used to it like we got used to the rice," a balding POW managed to spit out between mouthfuls. "It's not too bad. And it's hot!" What they were eating was a sorghum grain used as cattle feed and in distilled liquor. Properly ground, it would have been an excellent flour for unleavened bread as it has been in parts of Africa and India since ancient times.

"So what's next?" Leo asked, looking around at his bunkmates. "What are we doing here?"

"Looked like mining equipment to me," Porky said. "Did you notice that structure by the base of the mountain—looked something like the upper section of an elevator? That's a mining shaft is my guess. We'll find out soon enough."

Leo looked confused. "A mine? What'd we be mining for so close to the ocean?"

"Maybe our luck has turned and it's a gold mine," Porky wisecracked.

"Yes, sir. Fool's gold," the Southerner piped up.

After the men finished eating and prepared for bed, Matsuda reentered with charcoal briquettes, placed them in the clay pot, and lit the fire.

"So this must be hospitality, Jap style," Porky commented.

"Look, there are no windows. I bet the room is close to airtight—should keep us warm for the night," another man explained. "I used to be a carpenter outside of Madison, Wisconsin, before I was drafted. The building's not that bad. I'd guess it was constructed—ah, maybe a couple of years ago."

Matsuda motioned for each man, one by one, to step onto a mat and lie down feetfirst toward the pot. As the men moved to their assigned place, he handed out a small round cloth pillow, stuffed with sawdust.

Chet lay down and covered himself with a blanket. "Great! If I get hungry during the night, I'll rip open the pillow and eat the stuffing." The men laughed, more in relief than at Chet's wit, as they bunked down for the first time in weeks.

The next morning, Matsuda woke the men at dawn. His shoulders were stooped, and he walked with a limp more discernable in the morning light than it had been the evening before. Once again, he carried in a pail of maize and kaffir corn and pail of water. As they ate, he returned with a third pail and gestured for the men to get their mess kits. "Hiruhan, hiruhan," he said.

"This must be lunch," Porky said, grabbing his mess kit. "At least we get to eat." The men stood in line as he filled their mess kits with the food.

"Emon," he said, pointing to their extra clothes and instructing them to get dressed. After squabbling about how it should be done, the men settled on putting their navy outfits on first, followed by their army outfits and coveralls or suntans. Once outfitted, they were instructed to line up. They followed the guard through the hall to the outside, down the hill to the building below where the interpreter was waiting, Mr. Kakei.

"Prisoners, you have come here to work for the Japanese government," Kakei said with a clipped, upper-crust American accent. "You will get an allotment of two cigarettes a day, and you will be assigned to a supervisor who will instruct you each day on where you will go and what you will do."

About thirty feet behind Mr. Kakei was a stone-arched entrance to the mine. There, Korean forced-labor supervisors were lined up, waiting to go in. Rail tracks were extended into the tunnel beneath arched beams, visible every twenty feet or so overhead. Japanese guards handed out lunch packets to the Koreans, and then the American POWs were ordered to move forward as Koreans grabbed them by the arm and lead them into the mine. The Korean captives and American POWs walked beside the train tracks toward an elevator shaft a hundred yards farther. The elevator consisted of a pulley with steel cables and a gate, which opened into a metal elevator that was large enough for eighteen to twenty men. Once the Korean and American workers stepped onto the platform and crowded close together, the operator closed the gate and started the elevator on the slow journey down. They passed two levels and then stopped on the third level. The gate opened and Korean teenagers, not more than fifteen or sixteen years of age, led each of the POWs to their assigned working area.

Porky and his Korean boss followed the railroad tracks through a dark tunnel. The boy guided them by the dim light of a glassed-in carbon lantern. Before long, they came to an area covered with loose ore and were soon joined by another POW accompanied by his Korean boy boss. Porky's boss disappeared around a corner in the tunnel. Shortly afterward, the dim light from the lantern could be seen bouncing off the cave-like walls, followed by another Korean teen, who appeared with an empty car that he pushed along the tracks. Porky's boss pointed to four metal pans and picked one up by its side handles.

"Buketsu," he said to Porky as he handed him a pan. "Buketsu," he said to the other American, handing him the other pan by the handle. He then bent down and picked one up for himself.

Porky's boss demonstrated the work to be done. He picked up a small hand rake, set the pan on the ground near the ore, and raked the ore into the pan. He then picked up the pan and dumped it into the empty ore car. The men followed suit and worked until the car was full.

"My breaking back," Porky said, straightening up as he pushed a fist into the curve of his back.

"This is slave labor," the other POW complained.

"No. We're government workers. We've been promised two cigarettes a day," Porky quipped.

"So what are we supposed to do now?"

"Your guess is as good as mine."

Porky's boss motioned for him to help push the cart. The other Korean boss gestured for his POW to rake up the remaining ore into a pile for the next load. At the end of the day, the POWs and their young Korean bosses walked down to the elevator shaft and waited their turn to ride up. As they exited from the mine, a Japanese soldier stood guard waiting to accompany them back to barracks.

Two weeks passed without incident. Despite the unappealing nature of their quan, it was food; and though the work was hard, the men slept well at night, breathing the clean mountain air. One particularly gray morning, Porky and his fellow POWs descended into the shaft with their Korean bosses, returned to the same work area, and carried on with their chores. At noon, the Koreans checked their watches and ordered the men to stop working and break for lunch. Porky sprinkled a small pinch of the pepper he had exchanged while at Bilibid prison onto his maize and kaffir corn and dug in, as did the other POWs, content that they were not starving. But as the young Koreans opened their lunch packets, they became agitated and soon grew angry. Porky's boss approached Porky and handed him his packet. He pointed to Porky and then to the food and gestured for him to eat it.

"Dame, dame, no good, no good."

"No good? You want me to eat it?"

Porky looked down at the rice, which had been steamed with potatoes. "Look at this, will you. They don't have enough rice to feed their own people, so they've started to fill lunch packets with potatoes," he said to an American seated on a stump nearby.

"So what's wrong with that? Why can't he eat it?"

"Who knows? Maybe it is against his religion," Porky said, rising to accept the packet from his boss. "Thank you, thank you," he said with a bow. "Their loss is our gain."

Soon the other Korean bosses followed suit, handing their lunch packets over to the POWs they were supervising. The men looked at one another in astonishment and then feasted on their bosses' food as the Korean teens returned to work.

Aerial view of Ashio POW camps
Courtesy National Archives

Chapter 32

The Japanese archipelago islands, referred to as Nippon by the people, spread elongated like a jagged sea creature, with a thick, truncated tail flipped south and a thin close-jawed fox head tipped back due north. Nippon's bony back arches at Honshu into the Pacific and is warmed by the first rays of the sun as its belly caves inward, washed by tides from the Sea of Japan. At Nippon's core is the toothed spine of the country—high, steep mountains lashed by monsoons in the summer and governed by seasonal winds. Winter brings a Siberian chill and heavy snow to the plains and mountain valleys of Honshu Island. Then the back roads of the interior are barely passable.

As fall slipped into winter, the Americans slipped into the rhythm of their new lives—ate, drank, worked hard, and slept soundly. At daybreak one morning, as the first light grew from the blue ridge of the Pacific, the short piercing shriek from the mine's whistle shook the men awake. One by one, they sat up and scooted forward toward the clay center stove. Soon, Matsuda entered, leaving rice and water by the door.

"Han-guri? Meshi. Hun-guri? Foodo!"

The men entered the hallway to retrieve their breakfast and noticed a convoy of trucks with wooden side panels, battened over with canvas tops. Matsuda pointed to the trucks and instructed them in both Japanese and halting English.

"Pikku issai. Pek up," he said, leaning over and scooping up to demonstrate. "Deru honjitsu. Move, move too-day. Speedo. Haar-ri, speedo, haar-ri." Again, he pointed to the trucks. "Move."

"Men, he's trying to tell us to pick up everything and pronto," Sam shouted with an edge to his voice. "Clean your mess kits. We are heading out. Only God knows where."

The men hurriedly ate, dressed, and cleaned themselves as best they could, packed their clothes and gear, then rushed outside and counted off. Japanese soldiers pointed rifles at the men then to the five trucks and menaced the prisoners until they were all onboard as the officers stood by to watch them board. One by one, back panels were slammed shut while the top halves remained open, like canvas-covered wagon trains of American pioneers embarking on an adventure into the wilds. Soon after, the convoy began a slow move away from the mining camp onto a narrow snow-packed road along the southern edge of the Abukuma Mountains. Here, the forest was a profusion of Konara oak and Sawtooth Beech, intermixed with an assortment of evergreens. As they rode out of the coastal Ibaraki Prefecture into the interior Tochigi-ken, the woods thickened into something ancient, primeval. The convoy was dwarfed by giant Shirakashi evergreen oak protruding out of the mists, with heights towering upward to ninety feet from an eight-foot-diameter base.

The trucks skirted past Utsunomiya, the capital of the district, and dipped south until they came to the time-honored prefecture road that swung in a northwest curve past the small rural towns of Niregi, Awano, and Nakakasuo to the valley of Kamikasuo, rich with rice paddies and flowers in season. The winding road passed through the foothills into the chilly depths of an even denser evergreen cover. Sweeping curves narrowed into barely passable mountain roads. The men soon realized that if the tires skidded too far to the left, they would have plunged to their deaths.

About an hour into the journey, they entered Kusagyu, where a cog railroad divided the tiny village in half. The trucks stopped and the Americans grabbed their belongings. The guards took up positions to cordon the prisoners away from the village and direct them onto the tramcars. Once on Board, the cog rail began a long, slow ascent up the side of a ruggedly forested mountain. Their destination was Ashio, home of the Copper Mountain, the Plum God, and Ashihara-shikoo, the god enshrined at the bald mountain, whose fiery wrath sent down burnt ashes that became gnats.

Due north along the main road through Ashio is the Hosoo Pass, which leads to hot springs and a stunning waterfall and Nikko, the home to Shinto and Buddhist mountain worship and thirteen temples and shrines. The most famous, Toshogu, is set in a cedar forest and has stood resplendent, clad in 2.4 million sheets of gold leaf, since 1617. Toshogu is the final resting place of Shogun Tokugawa Ieyasu, the founder of Edo, present-day Tokyo.

Nearby is the stable for sacred horses with its world-renowned carving of the three monkeys who hear no evil, speak no evil, and see no evil. They have maintained their silent vigil as the Japanese samurai was transformed into a soldier in the Japanese Imperial Army, and the monkeys' maxim was eclipsed by Emperor Hirohito's Yamato Damashi, "Never be captured, never break down, and never surrender."

Praying before a row of images of the God of Light, Nikko, Japan
Courtesy Library of Congress

For centuries, during the spring and autumn, the Procession of a Thousand Warriors passed from Nikko to Edo-Tokyo through Ashio, where the Copper Mountain had disgorged golden yellow to reddish black copper since 1610. Now the mountain was to become the encampment of captured Allied soldiers, who would work the mines as thousands had before them. They were needed for Japan's continued war effort. But the emperor and his modern warriors had little respect for the POWs, who strived to survive despite all hardships. For the Japanese who remained loyal to Hirohito, fear of disgrace was what drove them. For the POWs, endurance was their badge of courage. The thought of their loved ones waiting kept them going and would somehow, someday, bring them home.

The tramcars stopped at the Dozan Kanko station at Sunahata, a small village beneath a desolate, deeply gullied mountain. There were no villagers in sight. It appeared to be as devoid of people as the mountain was of vegetation. Porky and Sam had sat together for the ride. Leo was one seat behind. Porky looked out the window and up and down the street at the tin-roofed shacks intermingled with curved clay-tile-roofed houses and shops.

"Have you noticed how there's no people in the village?" Porky said after a long silence.

"They're just trying to keep us out of sight."

"But why?"

"They're probably so brainwashed they're terrified."

"Yeah. To them, we must look like a race of giants," Leo said as he readjusted his belongings into a satchel he could sling over his back.

"Giants? Not quite," Porky responded with a self-deprecating laugh.

Guards opened the tram doors and the POWs picked up their bundles and stepped onto the snow-packed street. From there, they were marched to a platform where the officers from the mining camp waited, and they were ordered to line up in rows four abreast. Approaching from the north were a dozen Japanese guards and one officer. The heavily armed contingent churned up clouds of snow as they marched lockstep toward the POWs and came to a halt. The officers entered into a brief conversation. Moments later, the officers and guards who had brought the POWs from Hitachi Motoyama boarded the tram and began their slow descent down the mountain to the village below.

The new guards took up positions around the POWs. The officer instructed them to count off, from 1 to 260, up and down the rows. The Americans were then marched through the main street and over a wooden pedestrian bridge. An ice-encrusted river flowed beneath. Their new camp lay a half mile down a steep road at Nojimata, Kamitsuga-gun. Bureaucratically designated as Tokyo 9B—Ashio-detached, the compound was surrounded by a high wooden fence with sharp pointed tops and four guard stations posted at each corner. As the men marched toward their new quarters, the snow-covered rooftop of one of the barracks was visible over the fence.

The camp guards must have been waiting and heard them approach because when they were about five hundred feet away, the large wooden gate opened. To the right were guardhouses and, in the distance, two large barracks that appeared to be newly constructed. One was for the Americans, and the other in the rear was for the British, West Indians, and any other POWs. Three smaller buildings set to the side were used for the commander, the interpreter, and the guard units.

The men entered the Ashio POW compound that gloomy winter afternoon and lined up for orientation. A middle-aged Japanese doctor, dressed as a civilian in a Western-style suit and tie, stepped forward to interpret as a slightly older Commander Sato, the base commandant, spoke.

"You are expected to do good work. You will be assigned two supervisors, and you are expected to follow their instructions," the doctor said, echoing the Japanese commandant with a crisp English accent.

Sato stopped speaking with a gulp as if he had swallowed too much air. His eyeballs bulged with repressed anger. He turned to his left with ironclad precision and headed down the packed-earth and snow-encrusted road for headquarters.

The interpreter pointed to the largest barracks. "That is to be your home, where you will have your meals. There are latrines at the other end," he explained with a slight smile. He could afford to smile. As the base doctor, his lodgings also served as the infirmary, which was the only heated building on the compound.

"You will have morning and evening meals there," he said, continuing the orientation. "If you have questions, do not feel afraid to ask me. I will be around at all times." Several prisoners coughed while others shifted from foot to foot as the doctor paused for questions. There were none. A sudden wind picked up and blew the cold and wisps of snow between the layers of their clothing. It was obvious the men were chilled, exhausted, and hungry from the journey.

"Relax for a while. We will let you know when your meal is ready." His smile dissolved as he continued, "Tomorrow, you will go to the mines. However, this evening, as with all evenings, you will hear a loud whistle and the commander and guards will enter the barracks for tenko, an inspection. All are to kneel at attention along the border of the bays and call off numbers in order." The interpreter-doctor took a hard look at the men. *A sorry lot*, he thought as he turned and walked away.

The guards ordered an about-face and the POWs were escorted to their quarters. There were doors at both ends. One served as an entrance, the other for egress. The prisoners were brought to the entrance and marched along the six-foot-wide crushed-rock floor that ran through the center. Three tables and a cast-iron potbellied stove were set in the middle of the walkway. They looked around at the open bays, which were to serve as living quarters and beds for the men. The lower bays to the left and right of the walkway were approximately two feet off the ground and five feet high. The foundations of the bays were constructed of wide planks that stretched from one end to the other, much like the wide plank boards of early colonial American homes, which were constructed out of timber from virgin forests. The upper bays were ten feet high and extended to the peaked roof. A slatted board served as a ladder to the top.

"Not quite as homey as the last place," Porky whispered to Leo, who looked around bug-eyed and fearful. But on this, their first day at the base of the Copper Mountain, most of the POWs felt a degree of confidence. They unpacked and were soon led down to the kitchen for their second and final meal for the day. This was a routine they could easily adjust to, they thought. After the whistle, they lined up and knelt for inspection. As the men quieted down and waited for the commander, rats scurried out as if on cue from all directions onto the walkway, which turned from gray to black—alive with hundreds and hundreds of fat black rats.

At dawn the next day, light filtered into the bays from an open triangle above the doors at the peak of the roof. The men had spent the night bundled up in all of their clothes and had spread canvas shelter halves over them in lieu of blankets. Each shelter-half covered two men. Rats had scurried over the canvas covers throughout the night and into the early morning. But when the loud morning whistle blew, the rats disappeared. The men rose and cussed and complained about the rats until an American Naval lieutenant stood and called them to attention.

"Men, I have been led to believe that you will be broken down into groups of a dozen or more and assigned various jobs in the mine. For your information, you will be working in Japan's famous Ashio copper mines," the lieutenant began. "The cooks have been busy preparing your meal and you can start lining up and exit to the kitchen. Return to your bays and eat your food as fast as you can. Then grab your mess kits and return to the kitchen for your lunch. Before long, Japanese guards will come to march you off to your work detail." The POWs began to line up to exit for the kitchen as the lieutenant added, "Men, it is my understanding you will be doing work similar to the work you did before at Hitachi."

After the men grabbed their food, they reentered the barracks, as instructed, sat and ate, and then exited once again to the kitchen to fill their mess kits for their noon rations. Soon, three Japanese guards appeared and called the men off four abreast to march the half mile to the mine. It was a static routine, but in sameness there was comfort, especially when your goal was to survive.

The POWs marched to the back of the compound to a narrow road through thickets that led to a clearing. In the distance, they could see several sheds, some larger buildings, and a gaping opening in the mountain, the entrance to the mine. At first glance, the view beyond the mine was stunning.

Several snowcapped mountain peaks towered in the distance. Cable cars rode up and over one of the closer mountains and looked to the men like a ski resort. However, the closer they got, the more desolate the scene became. The smelting, dressing plants, and mine operations had taken their toll through the years. Belching pollutants had eaten at leaves and roots until the vegetation disappeared. Even the snow had disappeared in spots, revealing the dirt beneath. The prisoners felt as forlorn as the scenery when they got closer and had a good look at the mine. Before long, the guards called out to halt.

As early as 1942, American soldiers captured on Guam and Wake Island were transported to the only POW camp established in Japan proper, the Zentsuji POW Camp at Zentsuji City, Kagawa Prefecture. But before the war ended, more than 36,000 prisoners of war had been held in 130 main camps, branch camps, dispatched camps, and detached camps. Within those, 3,500 POWs died mostly from malnutrition and its effects.

Some claim the Ashio Copper Mines were using Chinese forced labor prior to the war in 1940. What is known is that by 1942, the Furukawa Mining Company had discovered the skills of the Korean forced labor at Ashio and elsewhere. By November 1943, the Ashio Branch Camp was open for business for American, British, and Dutch prisoners "employed" by the honorable Furukawa Mining Company. The second camp at Ashio was established in June 1945. So while Japanese Army soldiers maintained discipline in the camps outside the mine, as in Hatachi, it was the Koreans who maintained discipline inside the mine.

The POWs stood and waited as dozens of Korean men and boys emerged from the opening of the mine and approached them. Meanwhile, the interpreter-doctor from the evening before mounted a wooden box. "Prisoners, each Korean supervisor will come over and select three men. He will be your boss for as long as you are here. Follow his signals and do what he demonstrates for you to do."

This said, the interpreter no longer seemed like a doctor to the Americans but part of central command for the camp. He dismounted and stood by the box while the Koreans came forward to select their crew. A Korean boy about five feet tall and fifteen years of age approached Porky and pointed to two other men, Sam and Pete, to follow him. The men tagged alongside their Korean boss into the mine. Once inside, the boy bowed before a small shrine, and the POWs followed suit. He then handed the men unlit carbide lamps, then lit each one while the men observed. They walked in about a hundred yards and came to an open metal cage which served as the elevator. The door hung above. The cage swung slightly as Porky, Sam, and Pete followed their honcho inside and waited for more crews to enter. Finally, the door was yanked down with a clunk and a thud and the elevator began to descend. Electric lights extended in intervals along the elevator shaft as they glided four hundred feet down to the third level, where the elevator stopped with a jolt. Everyone got off and the elevator cluttered and clanked and rose back to the top.

The other bosses demonstrated to their crews how to light the carbide lanterns. Each of the men lit his lamp as instructed then stepped back. The glow emitted an ethereal radiance, which recast their racial features as lamplight flicked against the subterranean cavern wall. For a moment, each appeared suspended in an ancient and mysterious past when all of mankind was one. But soon they went their separate ways and entered the four different passageways that were part of the 1,200-kilometer tunnel system that had once made Ashio and its Copper Mountain famous.

Porky's group turned left, followed by one of the other crews, and entered an eight-foot-wide-by-thirty-foot-high tunnel alone. They walked along the cart rail for about five hundred yards until they came to a fourteen-foot-wide opening directly above. A ladder, constructed of two-by-four beams with crossbeams for support, protruded into the opening. Next to the ladder was a pile of straw. The honcho placed his lantern down and sat down on the ground next to the straw. He gestured for the men to put down their lanterns, sit, and slip off their mess kits. He then proceeded to weave the straw into rope, stopping to demonstrate the technique to his students. After a while, he handed straw to the men and assisted them as they too learned to weave straw into rope the Korean way. After a while, they sat Buddha-style and practiced their newly acquired skill.

"Jesus Christ, I will never get the hang of this," George, a sailor to his left, confided. George had survived the sinking of a U.S. naval submarine hit by depth charges between the Gilbert Islands and Truk and was captured shortly afterward by a Jap patrol.

Porky gestured with his head to the right side of the tunnel. "You think this is bad. Did you get a load of those drills over in the corner? Pick your poison, sailor."

"They don't expect us to do the jackhammering? You've got to be kidding me," Sam said, eyes wide with apprehension. He had dropped about seventy pounds and at times could barely muster the strength to walk.

"Na, we're on the rope detail," Porky assured him.

Once the ropes were made, the boss picked up a drill bit and secured a piece of rope around it. He then picked up another bit and tied it to the other end. He crossed over to Porky and gestured for him to stand. Now it was Porky's turn to feel apprehensive. The Korean teen, who was about four inches shorter than Porky, reached up and placed the rope and bits over Porky's slender shoulders and then, stepping to his back, tied the loose ends together. The drill bits hung off him like a pair of very weighty knapsacks.

"Jesus, this is hell on my bones. It wouldn't be so bad if I had some meat on me."

"Ah, I think I can handle it," Pete said as the boss secured the rope and bits on him.

"Sure, you're five-foot eleven inches. I'm so short I'll trip on the damn things."

The honcho moved on to Sam. "Phew, it is heavier than it looks," Sam said, straining under the weight.

"Hope he doesn't expect us to carry these too far," Porky groaned. "With the quon we've been eating, I barely have enough strength to carry my mess kit."

Once he had outfitted his crew, the honcho put a rope and bit around his slender shoulders, secured it in back, then pointed to the opening above. He gestured for the men to follow him up the ladder. After he had climbed about ten feet, he turned to see that no one was following.

"Foro appu," he insisted, gesturing for them to follow him up the ladder.

"Mr. Honcho wants us up. So up we go," George said, resigned to the work ahead. He grabbed a rung above his head and started to ascend.

"Jesus Christ, what's next?" Pete spit out as he began the climb directly under Sam.

Porky grabbed the ladder and called up, "Hey, you guys, I don't want you slipping. Remember, I'm the low man on the totem pole."

Sam was about twenty-five feet above. "Jesus, I bet there are a hundred steps."

Porky strained but attempted to make light of the matter. "And I'm afraid of heights!" Beads of sweat appeared on his forehead. He managed to get halfway up, then came to a stop and clung on for dear life. "Hey, you guys, I'm not going to make it. I can't go any further," he yelled, frozen in place while the others continued on up to the top.

Up above, the honcho brushed the men aside to kneel by the opening. Spit rained down on Porky as he screamed and swore in Korean.

Porky looked up at the boy's contorted red face, framed in black locks. It had taken on a demonic look in the glow of the carbide light. "I can't make it. I can't do it," Porky screamed back.

His boss continued to rant but after a while removed the drill bits from around his neck and dropped them onto the floor of the cavern. Then he carefully descended the ladder, swearing at each step. When he reached Porky, he grabbed the rope and transferred the weight onto his slender neck and climbed back up as Porky followed behind.

The cavern at the top was enormous. Porky, Sam, and Pete followed their honcho over to another hole and watched as he demonstrated how they should squat down to pick up ore with both hands and then drop it down the hole. The men flinched as the ore hit the cart below with a thud. Their honcho continued to demonstrate while the POWs used the time to catch their breath. Each time he dropped the ore, the boy waited for the thud and would smile and grunt with satisfaction as if it were great sport. Finally, he turned and pointed to Pete and Sam and gestured for them to try. But the technique used by the boss was lost on the students. When they dropped the ore, it bounced along the sides of the hole, making a decreasing sound until a muted thud was heard below.

The honcho folded his arms and shook his head back and forth disapprovingly. "No yoroshii," he said and demonstrated once again the technique needed to drop the ore with precision as if it were a bowling ball scoring a direct hit. Porky, ever the sportsman, was tempted to try but valued the moment he had to rest and suspected picking up ore over and over again must be extremely exhausting. Besides, watching their boss in action was fascinating. He was so small he looked like a child, yet he had the skills and power of a man. When Porky was his age, his life was filled with football, basketball, baseball, camaraderie, and times spent having fun. The only work he did was as a paperboy and helping his family with chores around the house.

After a while, the task was turned over to Sam and Pete. The boss picked up his lantern and pointed to Porky to follow him. Porky grabbed the wire handle of his light and trailed behind as his young boss strode over to the far end of the cavern, which had a recently blasted area—the beginning of a new tunnel. There, a compressed air jackhammer and short and long drills were housed in a jack stand made from three-inch-diameter piping. A crowbar leaned against the stand. The boss grabbed the crowbar and probed along the top and sides of the blasted area, checking for loosened stones. He then pulled out a rock-shaped piece of chalk from inside his coveralls' top pocket and marked *X*s into six areas that were to be the next drill sites. Choosing a long drill for a deep hole, he placed a cutting bit into the drill and jammed it into the jackhammer, then steadied the unit by wedging it between the short ceiling and floor, which tightened the apparatus in place. After turning the jackhammer on with a twist of the air-control knob, he stood aside and watched for a moment, then turned the wheel attached to the jack to the left, which moved the jack deeper into the hole.

Finally, he turned to Porky. "Yuu torai," he said, ordering him to take over the task. The boss watched as Porky steadied the jack by pushing it forward and turned the wheel hammer so it drilled deeper into the rock.

"Yoroshii. OK, OK," the honcho said, then he turned and walked back to supervise Pete and Sam.

For the next hour or so, their honcho walked back and forth between the three men, overseeing their work. After the holes were drilled, he wandered deeper into the cavern, over to a large wooden crate. Porky watched as he placed the lantern over the open box and bent over and grabbed a few items. Once he returned, Porky understood what the next task would be. His boss was holding several sticks of dynamite and caps close to his chest, which he dropped by the edge of where the new tunnel was to be constructed.

The boss disassembled the jack, drill, and platform and moved it twenty feet to the side, where the dynamite was, then instructed Porky to stand and watch as he prepared the dynamite. "*Chuui shinasai*," he announced with a show of pride. Porky paid careful attention as the boss placed a cap and fuse on each stick of dynamite. In the past, someone else always handled the dynamite, but he suspected that in a few moments it would be his turn. As the boy secured the fuse to the cap by biting it, using his teeth as a clamp, Porky flashed back to memories of Dynamite Dunn and his buddy at Bataan, who had fished with sticks of dynamite instead of fishing poles.

"Boy, you guys don't know what you are missing," Porky yelled to Sam and Pete. "Want to trade jobs?"

Pete looked up and swore.

"Frenchy, that's a hell of a cap pistol he has there," Sam hollered back.

"I hope he knows what he is doing." Porky shouted, attempting to sound brave.

The young boss waved Porky on to join the others, then inserted sticks of dynamite into each of the drilled holes and lit the fuses. As he rushed back to the men, he gestured for them to go back down the ladder. "Hayaku, hayaku," he screamed.

Sam, Pete, and Porky descended as quickly as they could, hands and feet fumbling for the wooden rungs. The honcho had barely entered the hole and begun to descend when the dynamite went off with a deafening sound. The men held on for dear life as the ladder vibrated wildly, then continued their descent to the bottom as smoke and dust spewed forth through the opening. The men coughed and attempted to outrun the smoke and dust. After it had cleared a bit, their boss gestured for them to follow him back to the pile of straw where they had left their belongings. He sat and opened his lunch box and pointed for the men to sit down and grab their mess kits.

"Hiruhan," he said, maneuvering his chopsticks into the rice and up to his mouth.

"Hiruhan, to you," Porky responded with a slight bow as he wiped his hands on his coveralls and joined his friends, who had already sat to chow down.

That evening, as instructed, POWs from the upper and lower bays knelt for inspection before retiring. As they waited, rats scurried from every crack and crevice, hunting for food. The men reached down and grabbed a handful of rocks to fling at the rats until the guards came. Such as it was, this was their new home, and they were to remain there until the end of the war. The following day, Porky, Sam, and Pete walked through the same tunnel with their Korean boss, stopped at the same hole, and ascended the same ladder to the cavern above, carrying lanterns and drill bits as before. Once inside, it was obvious that the night crew had been there.

"Looks like someone's cleaned up most of the mess," Porky observed as he crawled up and out of the hole. He hoped the boss would keep him as an assistant and not put him in charge of dynamiting, or better yet, maybe he could make straw ropes throughout the day. Already concessions had been made. Porky carried only one bit, and it was fastened onto a shorter rope.

"You can bet there's plenty left to do," Pete countered, rolling his eyes.

The Korean boss pointed to Sam and Pete and escorted them to an area scattered with ore that was hidden by shadows. They were to continue their job of yesterday, tossing ore down a nearby hole into a cart below. Then with lanterns held high to cut through the darkness, Porky and his honcho walked over to the area they had dynamited the day before. There were few signs that the second shift had gotten to it. Giant chunks of rubble created a crazy obstacle course to the jack, drills, and platform.

The Korean boss grabbed the crowbar and checked for loosened pieces of ledge and ore and began to knock down anything that had been loosened by the blast. He then checked out an adjacent area to work on and motioned for Porky to help him set up the jackhammer at the new location. Again, Porky was instructed to drill out areas that the Korean boss marked with chalk. Once the holes were made, his boss retrieved dynamite from the crate, but this time, he handed the sticks, fuses, and caps to Porky, who froze with fear.

"Shuujin taan—yuu torai."

"Your turn, you try," Porky suspected he was saying as he gestured for Porky to put the dynamite down between them. After pushing a few rocks aside, the boss sat and invited Porky to sit and watch. He picked up a cap and fuse and carefully demonstrated how to attach the cap to the fuse and finally to the dynamite. Then it was Porky's turn. After the dynamite was prepared properly, they stood, and his honcho demonstrated the correct way to place the prepared sticks into the freshly drilled holes. Porky's heart raced, but he felt that he could handle it until his boss started pushing aside the rubble, apparently hunting for something. He turned to Porky, demanding to know where whatever he was looking for was. Porky shrugged, utterly confused, which further infuriated the boy, who pushed him aside and hunted in a manic state in the debris.

"Rantan—hi," he shouted, pointing to the lamps. Porky grabbed the lanterns and scrambled back to the excavation area to help in the search. Finally the boss spotted what he was after. He plucked a broom handle from the rubble and returned to the drilled holes to jam the dynamite to the end with the handle.

"Outo—Outo," he screamed to Sam and Pete, gesturing for them to get out and pronto. The men dropped what they were doing and made a mad dash for the ladder and scrambled down.

Porky was handed three matches, and his boss kept three for himself. Both held their lanterns high as his boss gestured for Porky to strike a match against the rock and light the fuse. After the six sticks were lit, they ran like hell to the ladder, but Porky didn't make it. The room was filling with smoke, which completely masked the debris. In his rush he had jostled the lantern and his light went out, then he stumbled on rubble and fell. He picked himself up and headed toward a dim light. Within moments, his boss realized he was missing and yelled for him to hurry. His voice resonated in the cavern as Porky stumbled again, smashing his frail legs against the sharp edges of the shattered ledge and ore. Porky began coughing but continued on. At last, he felt his boss's hand grabbing his, leading him to the escape hole. Porky grabbed the ladder and began to descend as his boss followed holding the lantern. They managed to get about twelve feet down when a large explosion rocked the cavern. The ladder vibrated wildly and smoke billowed down as they continued their descent to the base of the tunnel below.

Coast Guard-manned LSTs' on Leyte Island, PI during unloading operations, 1944.
Courtesy National Archives

Chapter 33

Prior to leaving Cabanatuan Prisoner of War Camp in the fall of 1944, Porky woke one morning feeling particularly homesick. After brooding half the morning, he decided to do something about it—to write home on the off chance the Japanese command would take pity and send the postcard out. They did send it, along with hundreds of other cards and letters. The tide of war was turning. POW messages home were a propaganda tool used to convince the world that the Japanese Imperial Military Command was abiding by international codes of conduct. So on January 17, 1945, months after it had been written, an item appeared in the *Athol Daily News* with the heading: "Cpl. LaCoste Writes from Jap Prison."

> From a Philippines military prison camp. Mrs. Rose LaCoste. 132 Swansey street received a card from her grandson Cpl. Franklin J. LaCoste, member of the ground crew taken prisoner while stationed at Nichols Field in Manila in 1941.
>
> The card read: I am interned at Philippines Military Camp, No. 1. My health is good.
>
> Message: Dear Mother, I am feeling well and hope that this reaches you feeling the same. Give my regards to Rose, Bertha and Yvonne and all my friends.

###

About the time Porky's family received his message, a tall, lanky Scotsman, a naturalized citizen by the name of James Baird, from Boston, Massachusetts, was arriving at Lingayen Bay, Luzon Island, in the Philippines. He was a member of a reconnaissance platoon, the 169th Infantry, Forty-third Division, under the command of Lt. Gen. Walter Krueger, commander of the Sixth Army, who had received responsibility for operations in the Luzon campaign.

Jim was born in Glasgow and had arrived in Boston at the age of three in the company of his parents, whose leisure time as he was growing up was spent playing the violin and piano and singing nostalgic tunes about dear old Scotland. Jim was caught up in the draft and now was spending his time trying not to get blown up.

A week earlier, Jim had been in New Guinea about to embark for the Philippines as a member of a Landing Craft Infantry (LCI). He now felt like a latter-day Jonah as he emerged from the belly of a landing craft into the waters of Lingayen Bay. He was driving a jeep. The night before had been spent encasing the engine in clay, hoping to waterproof it. But the proof was in the doing, and Jim hoped that as the Jap planes buzzed around, bombing and strafing, the jeep would perform as advertised and get him through the water, up and onto the beach to safety.

Fortunately, he was not the only target, he reasoned. After all, he was surrounded by American ships, great and small. Just then, Jap shelling hit a small landing craft next to him. But Jim had nowhere to go but up and out. He literally was up to his helmeted chin strap in South China Sea water. He stared straight ahead, his hands gripped tightly to the steering wheel and his foot planted firmly on the gas. The jeep gripped the sandy incline and slowly pushed forward against the tide, but as the hood emerged out of the water, the engine stalled. Then the shelling really got serious and another landing craft was hit. Jim turned around to hunt for his ship. The best idea might be to go back and wait for the shelling to subside, but the captain of his landing craft must have had a similar idea. It was nowhere in sight. All landing crafts had beaten a hasty retreat out of the bay, back toward open waters and the other vessels.

Jim put the jeep in gear, jumped into the water, and bolted for the beach. He slid headfirst under a bulldozer positioned near a clump of palm trees, and in the process nearly knocked himself out. Jim's helmet slammed into the helmet of the bulldozer operator, who was also hiding there, attempting to wait things out. Eventually the Jap planes flew off and the men grabbed a chain, dragged it into the water, and attached it to the jeep. Jim jumped back into the driver's seat and after several attempts managed to start the vehicle back up as the bulldozer pulled him out of the water onto dry land. Jim waved good-bye, and moments later, the shelling started up again. He pushed the vehicle to go faster—from five miles per hour to ten miles per hour and managed to put-put up to twenty miles per hour! But where was he supposed to go? Except for the bulldozer operator, he was alone as far as he could tell.

The night before, Jim's infantry sergeant explained that the initial landing party had chased the Japanese out and established a command center not too far inland. Directional signs were posted at varying intervals along the way, the sergeant claimed. Jim looked and looked and was close to despair when he finally spotted a sign ahead, half-hidden by shrubbery—169th Infantry, it read. Under the lettering was an arrow pointing toward what he prayed was the company headquarters established earlier.

Jim followed the sign to railroad tracks as the shelling continued and intensified. What were they shooting at, he wondered, and from where? There wasn't a plane in sight. Then it dawned on him: they must be holed up somewhere miles away and were shooting blindly, as a deterrent. Jim put his foot to the floor and gunned the engine up to about twenty-two miles per hour. Then in true Scots style, he did what came naturally. Pfc. James Baird threw his head back and laughed uproariously at the absurdity of it all until he reached the relative safety of the new encampment, a coconut and banana plantation ten miles up the road.

On February 1, another item appeared in the *Athol Daily News* under the heading: "Sgt. Hausmann Writes 50-Wd. Letter Home from Jap Prison Camp."

> Sgt. Herman W. Hausmann, 25, who has been a prisoner of war since the Japs took Bataan, has written to his mother, Mrs. Anton Hausmann of 566 Hapgood street, informing her that he is well treated and that he is served good food.
>
> The letter, containing 50 words from which one line was cut out by a Japanese censor, said that he had been receiving mail from home."
>
> Hausmann, along with William G. Freeman, Franklin J. LaCoste, Robert L. Doolan, and Francis Robichaud, enlisted in the Army on Oct. 2, 1940. Four of the five men were together at Clark

Field when Luzon Island was invaded. Later, Freeman was reported missing and LaCoste was taken prisoner. Doolan was reported killed in action. Robichaud, now a technical sergeant, went to Australia on a hospital ship. After serving there, he returned to the United States and now is a recruiter for the Air-WAC.

###

One month into their internment at Ashio, as the first light dawned, the men no longer dwelled on rats crawling over the tops of the covers, only that they were snuggled securely under them. The whistle blew. The rats scattered and the men got up and stretched. After a bowl of rice and hot cup of tea, the POWs marched to the mine in small assigned groups. Porky's group waited at the mouth of the mine for their honcho to arrive from the Korean POW camp. They finally spotted him chatting with several other bosses, who scattered to join their respective crews. When he approached, he pulled Porky aside.

"*Atchi itte changi atarashii hancho,*" he said, pointing to a small group of POWs standing by a cliff. "Go, new boss," he said in Pidgin English. Porky bowed in appreciation to his young honcho for saving his life. He then turned to join the new group. Porky made the fifth man, and they were soon joined by four more.

Another young Korean, about the same age as his last honcho, walked over to the crew and waved them on to follow him. They marched in loose formation to the tunnel exit where the ore carts emerged fully loaded. Each cart was marked from one to six, depending on the quality of the ore. Porky's new job was to ensure that the ore cart was moved to the appropriate chute. Each cart traveled thirty feet down toward an ore shed but was stopped at the bottom by a heavy steel grille that screened out large chunks, which fell to the side. Crews of Korean women waited below. As soon as the cart slammed into the grille, women who were stationed on both sides of the chute would move forward to smash the large chunks with small sledgehammers before it was stored in the shed. Each hammer had a flexible handle that absorbed the shock; otherwise the women's delicate wrists would not have withstood the job for long.

At noontime, the whistle blew and dozens of women gathered their cloth bags and sat in a large group on the rocks by the ore shed, chattering away as they removed bento lunch boxes from their bags. Though it was late February, there was a hint of spring in the air. Snows were melting, and the sun shone brightly as they relaxed for lunch. Each box contained rice, pickles, and greens on top. A bucket of water had been placed nearby. The clicking of chopsticks mixed with the chatter of snow birds flitting along the edge of the rooftop of the shed. As each of the women finished eating, she'd put the bento box back in the carryall bag and take out knitting or patches to sew onto cotton kimonos.

Porky and the crew of American POWs gathered at a nearby outbuilding to sit and eat. To Porky and the rest of the American prisoners of war, the Korean women were a sight for sore eyes. Most appeared youthful and energetic. However, they were strictly hands-off, and even if available, these men were too sickly, exhausted, and famished to have responded with anything but a passing nod and brief smile.

"It's amazing," Porky remarked to a fellow prisoner. "These are the first women I've seen since the Philippines, and I'm more interested in their lunch boxes than I am in them."

After lunch, Porky got up and got back in line to work. But this job demanded more exertion than the last. Several men were needed to successfully push an ore cart to a chute. They literally shouldered the task. They shoved their shoulders into the cart and with their free hand grabbed a knob, not with their hands but with a steel hook. The hook was oddly shaped, something like a hacksaw without a blade. This provided added leverage as the men pushed the cart along. Once a cart started rolling, the men continued to push, but the job was easier because the momentum helped keep it moving. Occasionally, the cart would stop, and then another man would be needed to help get it rolling again. As POWs used their shoulders to push the wheels, Korean boys walked back and forth, monitoring the activity.

An hour or so before it was time to break for the day, Porky and his fellow crew members were having a hard time with an overloaded cart that suddenly stopped. The men strained to get it going again. Beads of sweat formed on Porky's brow as he pushed and pushed, but the task seemed impossible. A Korean teenager, built like a diminutive sumo wrestler, approached to assist. He grabbed Porky's steel hook and grunted as he thrust a fat arm and shoulder against the cart. Porky took up the rear. The crew struggled to move it forward, pushing as hard as they could, but it still wouldn't budge.

Out of the blue, Porky doubled over with the first kidney attack he had had since the Philippines. The teenager yelled at Porky to continue working—to push harder, but Porky was in agony. His pain was so great he was unable to stand up straight. The boy grew red in the face and started swearing in Korean. Suddenly, he let out a holler and lifted the steel hook from the cart into the air. Porky looked up in horror. The boy came closer, swinging and menacing Porky with the steel hook. Porky lifted his right arm to his face in anticipation of the blow and feared he might be killed. The Korean took another step closer, enraged at Porky's seeming defiance. Falling back on gut instinct, Porky struck out with a right hook and connected to his eye. The teen screamed in anguish and opened his hand as he reached for his eye. The hook smashed to the ground with a thud.

Immediately, a dozen red-faced Korean teenagers descended on Porky and threw him down. One pulled his hair and smashed his head against the ground. Another grabbed his testicles and pulled. Others pounded his body with their fists. But this time Porky didn't resist, nor did he scream out in pain. Instead, he took a deep breath and went limp, and though he was conscious, he kept his eyes closed. The boys jumped back, their cropped black hair tossed and damp from the exertion. They feared they had killed him.

Word was sent back to the camp, and a Japanese guard came out to examine Porky. A crowd of American POWs and their Korean bosses had gathered round. As the guard entered the mine, the gang that had beaten Porky hid behind the cart. The guard ordered several of the Korean bosses to grab a couple of boards that were stashed by the ore shed below and fasten them together with rope to make a makeshift stretcher. Meanwhile, he put a hand on Porky's chest to check if he was breathing.

When the Koreans returned with the makeshift stretcher, the members of the American POW cart crew carefully lifted Porky onto the boards and started back for camp. Four men carried the load. They had marched a mile or so down the dirt road when Porky's eyes momentarily flickered open. The Japanese guard who was walking beside him stared back, then let out a holler, grabbed the side of the stretcher, and dumped Porky onto the road. Porky looked up to see the guard standing over him, screaming for him to stand up. Porky stood, and the guard threw him back down and then ordered him to stand again. Porky picked himself back up as the POWs moved out of the way.

The guard hooked his right foot in back of Porky's left foot and slapped him hard on the face. Porky fell again, scraping his knees on a rock and the coarse sand on the road. The guard forced him up again and continued to work him over for several minutes until he grew tired from the gruesome sport. Porky sprawled out on the road, coughing out dirt and blood from his mouth, when he was given the order to get up and march toward camp.

Porky put one knee on the ground and his right foot forward and attempted to stand. He braced his hands on his upper right leg, pushed himself up, and staggered forward as his fellow POWs walked behind. When they reached the camp, the guard marched Porky and the detail to the front of the commander's cabin. Commander Sato emerged and was briefed by the guard in Japanese. The commander pursed his lips and looked hard and long at Porky. Finally he approached, slipped off a sandal, held it by the heel, and whacked him across the face with the leather sole. Porky grimaced from the pain but remained motionless and silent. The commander scowled, looked him up and down, then turned and exited back into headquarters. Moments later, the interpreter emerged from the headquarters with his hands behind his back and approached Porky, looking very, very angry.

"Prisoners, you are dismissed," the interpreter said to the other POWs without looking at them. All his attention was focused on Porky. "LaCoste, you remain here." Sweat streamed down the dirt on Porky's face. "LaCoste, we are preparing a jail for you. You will remain there until further notice. There will be absolutely no smoking and no socializing. Go to the barracks and get your clothes and blankets and report back here immediately."

Porky walked back to the barracks to get his clothes and blankets as the interpreter reentered the commander's headquarters to discuss the case. As he entered the barracks, Sam approached him carrying his mess kit. He opened it to show Porky. "Frenchy, I got your mess kit and filled it with food. A couple of the guys are going to lend you some bigger clothes to fit over your other clothes. How are you doing?"

"I'll make it," Porky said, more grateful than he let on for their show of kindness.

Several POWs handed over their coveralls as Porky fought back tears. "Good luck," they offered and patted him on the back.

As Porky walked back to the command headquarters, he tried to focus on the clean air and birds flitting between birch trees near the fence; then he saw the interpreter standing on the porch, waiting. "Follow me," the interpreter shouted out as he stepped off the porch and headed down a path to the right of the headquarters. Porky struggled with his bedding as he followed him to the guardhouse, a simple Japanese-style building with tiny windows and a curved roof edge which protruded about seven feet along the sidewall. Several poles were secured in the ground in a straight line from both edges of the protrusion and chicken wire was strung from pole to pole, creating a rectangular enclosure. This was his cell? Porky suppressed a laugh when he noticed a separate length of chicken wire strung from the first pole to the edge of the building. This served as the cell door—chicken-wire door!

The interpreter ordered the guard to unhinge the door to allow the prisoner to enter. Most of the snow had melted, which left muddy puddles in spots. The guard grabbed a loose board leaning against the side of the building and tossed it into the five-by-nine-foot enclosure. "Here, you can sit on that," the interpreter said, pointing to the board, and then turned and walked away as the guard rehitched the chicken wire back onto the wall of the guard shack.

Porky settled into his specially prepared jail. He separated the clothes from the blankets and put them in neat stacks on the board about two feet apart. He sat between the piles and soon adjusted to his surroundings, relaxed, opened his mess kit, and began to eat as dusk settled and darkness descended. The guard turned on the bare bulb in the guardhouse and the light above his guard station. The soft glow fought the gloom of Porky's predicament. After eating, Porky folded his blanket into a thin mattress, sat on it, and after a while slowly stretched out, using his extra clothing as a pillow. The guard noticed Porky resting and hollered for him to sit up and not to sleep.

"Nai ikoi . . . Nai suimin. No rest. No sleep."

Porky bolted upright. He had considered his punishment a joke—solitary confinement under the stars, but now it dawned on him what his real punishment was—sleep deprivation. His only hope was if the guard nodded off, he could nod off too.

Porky stretched his legs out in front of him. The night settled in, but so too did the cold. He sorted through the extra clothes and began to put them on, one by one, until his shivers stopped. He sat back down, feeling warmer, but also more heated over a punishment he felt he didn't deserve. Several hours later there was a change of guards. The new guard was smoking. Porky relaxed, inhaling the aroma when, to his amazement, the guard tossed the butt in for him to grab and smoke.

"Arigatoo," Porky said standing to grab it, hoping he was pronouncing the words correctly. "Thank you, very much."

Porky stared up at the stars, hoping that someone, somewhere, knew the POWs were still alive and would come to rescue them. Without realizing it, he was staring up at Japan's Azure Dragon—the emerging eastern spring sky—then he swung his head around to find comfort in the North Star and Big Dipper. He knew where he was, but not how to get home. He settled back down again and stared straight ahead.

The next morning, the interpreter approached the makeshift jail and found Porky sitting bolt upright, staring straight ahead, his breath visible in the morning air. The interpreter spoke to the guard and instructed him to take Porky's mess kit down and get his rations. He then turned to Porky.

"After you eat, the commander wants to see you. I'll be back shortly to pick you up," he said, then walked back to headquarters.

Not long after Porky ate his breakfast rations of rice and tea, the interpreter returned and escorted him to the commander's office, a small room about eight feet by twelve feet. The office contained a small wooden table, four chairs, and two floor lamps. To the left was a door that led to additional quarters. The interpreter entered first, followed by Porky.

"LaCoste, show respect—take your shoes off," he instructed.

The interpreter took his sandals off as Porky unlaced his heavy GI boots and placed them by the entrance. The interpreter then motioned for Porky to sit beside him in a chair in front of the table. The two sat in silence. Porky's heart was racing as his thoughts ran wild, considering the possible punishment he might face. Finally, the commander entered from an adjoining room. The interpreter stood at attention and Porky followed suit.

"Chokuritsufudou, attention!" the interpreter ordered.

Sato sat with a stone face and deliberate formality on the other side of the table and nodded for the interpreter to continue.

"Sit," he said and sat as Porky followed suit.

Sato spoke in Japanese, "Isshiki kyosai." (I want full details.) "Ichimon'ittou." (I will interrogate.) "Yuu-intapurito." (You interpret.)

The interpreter nodded in agreement.

"Naze yuu-dageki Nicchuukan touken hukku?" the commander asked.

"Why did you strike the Korean guard with the steel hook?" the interpreter asked Porky.

"I didn't. I hit him with my fist. It was the knuckle that made the skin abrasion," Porky explained, showing him his knuckle.

"But why did you hit him?" the interpreter pressed.

"I was doubled over with pain with an attack," Porky began and pointed to the area of the pain. "The guard came over with a hook to strike me. I defended myself."

The interpreter offered Porky's explanation to the commander, who asked still more questions in Japanese.

"We do not believe you. Why did you attack?"

"I was sick and I was defending myself."

The men discussed Porky's explanation at length, but Sato did not accept the explanation, and the interpreter acquiesced.

"We do not believe you. You must tell the truth."

"I saw him coming at me with a steel hook and I must have snapped."

Once again the interpreter and commander conferred until the commander pointed at Porky and rattled off something in Japanese that sent a chill down Porky's spine.

"You will not leave here until we get to the bottom of this. You must confess," the interpreter shouted.

"I confess that I hit him, but I thought he was attacking me."

The discussion continued as Porky's fears mounted. He felt completely hopeless. *Perhaps it's official policy never to believe an American*, he thought. Finally, the discussion ended and he was told they could leave. Porky put his boots back on and the interpreter his sandals as the commander abruptly left the room.

The interpreter walked Porky back to the chicken-wire enclosure in silence. He motioned for the guard to open the enclosure. Porky entered listlessly, sat back down on his blanket, and stared straight ahead as the interpreter quietly left.

The next morning, Porky was beyond exhaustion, having been forced to remain awake for forty-eight hours. The interpreter approached and ordered the guard to let him out.

"Today, you will tell the truth. You will confess. We are sick of your excuses," the interpreter insisted as they marched toward headquarters.

On the third day, Porky was so completely fatigued he could barely sit up and would occasionally tumble over as his eyelids fluttered and closed. The guard stood, gripping the top of the chicken wire, screaming at Porky to stay awake as a delegation of seven military men approached, led by a Japanese major. The interpreter and camp commander soon joined the group, who spread out around the chicken-wire enclosure. They stared at Porky and conferred in Japanese. The interpreter walked around to the end of the fence, directly in front of Porky.

"Pile up your clothes neatly for the day. You are to come with us for additional interrogation," he said through the chicken wire. The delegation trekked back to headquarters as the interpreter stayed behind with Porky.

"I've brought you a clean set of clothes. Clean yourself up as best as you can," he said, tossing a clean uniform and GI suntans over the fence. The interpreter then headed back to headquarters to join the others.

Porky let himself out of the chicken-wire enclosure and walked back to the barracks as the guard looked on. He grabbed a towel and headed outside for the water spigot, washed his face off, then doused the towel with water and headed back into the barracks. He took off his overcoat, peeled off the layers beneath, starting with his outer coveralls, and shivered with cold as each layer was discarded. His teeth chattered as he grabbed the towel to wipe himself down. Afterward, he put on the clean uniform and overcoat, then sat on the wooden bay and wept. *What's next*, he asked himself, *the firing squad?* He stood up, walked back to the entrance, and braced himself against the door before opening it. *When was the last time I slept?* he wondered but was so groggy he was unable to remember.

While Porky was changing his clothes, the delegation had gone ahead to the mines. Porky pulled himself together enough to walk back to headquarters, where commander Sato, the interpreter, and one guard waited for him.

"Fall in behind. We're going to the mine," the interpreter ordered as he and the commander stepped ahead and Porky and the guard followed behind.

Porky staggered and struggled to keep up as the four men marched the mile up the hill to the opening of the mine where the ore carts were stored before unloading. But this was a day unlike others. All work activity had ceased as they waited for Porky's arrival. The Japanese major, who was about thirty-five years old and movie-star handsome, conversed with the top Korean honcho who served as the foreman for all of the Korean bosses. The POWs stood on one side and the Koreans on the opposite side, but all eyes were on Porky as he approached.

The interpreter walked over to the major and spoke to him in Japanese, then turned to Porky. "The major wants you to describe in full detail exactly what happened."

Porky breathed deeply and a basic survival instinct kicked in. His head cleared, and he was filled with a determination to get himself off the hook.

"I was attempting to push the cart, and I came down with an attack. I felt sharp pain in my stomach. I doubled over with pain," he said, pointing to his stomach and doubling over as if in pain.

"Just then, my Korean boss comes over. He must have thought I was loafing, and he starts yelling at me in Korean or maybe it was in Japanese—at any rate, I had no idea what he was saying. And as he was screaming at me, he was waving his arms about," Porky said, waving his arms frantically in the air.

"But he had this hook in his hand," Porky said as he grabbed the nearby hook to demonstrate. "He started toward me. I put my arms up over my face to shield my face," he said, shielding his face with his arm. "And the Korean's arm came down as if to strike me." Porky raised the hook high in the air. "So I defended myself," he said, bringing the hook back down. "You see, I thought he was going to attack me with the hook."

The interpreter explained what Porky had narrated to the major, who continued to question the interpreter in Japanese.

"The major wants to know why the skin is broken in two places on the Korean boy's face. You hit him with the hook, didn't you? Confess," the interpreter insisted.

"No, no, I didn't." Porky approached the major and extended his right fist toward him, showing off his bare knuckles. "See, see," he said, pointing to his knuckles. "Look at these two knuckles. That's what caught him under the eye."

The interpreter repeated Porky's defense in Japanese. The major turned to Commander Sato and other members of the delegation. They debated the incident among themselves, then abruptly turned and walked down the hill as Porky followed behind with the guard. The major dropped back to join Porky briefly. "Hey, where can I take a leak?" he asked Porky with an American accent.

"Behind any one of these buildings," Porky answered with a straight face though he was tempted to laugh out loud.

The major rejoined the delegation and spoke to the commander in Japanese as he pointed to a nearby building. The major allowed the delegation to continue as he waited for Porky and the guard to catch up. "Let's go," he said, grabbing Porky by the arm. The two men turned to the left and followed a path toward a shed that housed rice and other commodities. As they walked, the major reached into his jacket and pulled out a pack of Japanese cigarettes and matches. "Here, have a smoke while I take a leak." The men ducked behind the building as the major relieved himself and Porky lit up.

Porky had inhaled only three puffs before the major returned to his side. "OK, let's go. Just butt your cigarette and save it for later."

"Gee, thanks. That was nice of you," he responded as he snubbed out the cigarette and handed the matches and box of cigarettes back.

The major stuck the box back into his pants pocket and walked Porky back to the guard before rejoining the delegation in the march back to headquarters. Porky hoped the group would take some pity on him but realized his goose might be cooked. Despite his explanation, they still demanded that he confess. A shiver shot down his spine as they stopped in front of headquarters. He waited with the guard as the Japanese clustered in discussion. Finally, the interpreter approached.

"You will stay in your barracks tonight," the interpreter began. "Tomorrow morning, clean up as best as you can. Wear the suntan uniform again. After your morning meal, clean off your mess kit and march over to the kitchen.

The cook will prepare lunch for you, and then I will come to get you. You are to be court-martialed."

Porky entered the barracks and announced flatly, "I'm going to be court-martialed."

His barracks-mates looked stunned, then swarmed around and peppered him with questions. "Do you think you'll come back alive?"

"What kind of crazy Jap punishment are they going to dream up?"

"Did you hear about Joe? He was stealing potato vines and smoking 'em, and it looks like he's up for a court-martial too!"

"You heard about Leo didn't you?"

Porky was in a daze, but the word *Leo* shook him out of his stupor. "So what happened to Leo?" he asked, afraid of the answer.

The men created an opening for Porky to see. Leo was at the far end of the building, stretched out on the floor. His feet were tied to a two-by-four beam which supported one of the bays. His hands were tied together and laced onto another two by four, which was about five feet farther toward the back of the bay. Porky's jaw dropped as he approached.

"What the hell is this? Did you beat up someone too?"

"No, they think I am a weirdo."

Porky began to laugh, and the more he looked, the more he laughed, until he doubled over, gasping for air and wiped tears from his eyes.

"Hey, don't make me laugh, it hurts."

"Sorry, buddy, I don't mean to laugh. Jesus, what the hell . . . ?"

"It's my seizures. Maybe they think I am a sorcerer. I might conjure up devils and do weird things to them."

"Well, I'm off tomorrow. Only God and the GD Japs know where I'm going."

"I'll be thinking of you."

Porky knelt by his friend's side and said quietly, "And I'll say a prayer for you."

Tokyo Station restored during US Occupation
Courtesy G. Thomson Fraser
1951 postcard (public domain)

Chapter 34

The following morning, Porky put on his suntans and overcoat, ate breakfast and picked up his mess kit, and was soon escorted to the downtown Ashio station by two guards, Commander Sato, and the interpreter. It was the first of March, not that it mattered much to Porky. The Ashio Railway he now boarded was upscale in comparison with the cog rail that had brought him to the Copper Mountain. On the train, two seats faced one another all along the aisle, like in a diner but without the table between. Several elderly couples were scattered throughout the car. They looked up as Porky entered but quickly turned away. Porky was seated between the two guards, not far from the window, facing front. The interpreter sat across from Porky, and Commander Sato sat by his side, next to the aisle. They conversed softly in Japanese while Porky stared out the window. Ashio to Tokyo was less than an hour away and the track followed close to the Watarase River along the ravine, past Omama, Aioi, into the valley, past Kiryo, and onto the broad Kanto plain.

Their final stop, the Tokyo Station, was an impressive structure built of 8.9 million red bricks, built to replace an earlier station that had become too overcrowded. Three stories high, it housed ninety hotel rooms and featured an Imperial entrance with ornate cupolas and green awning for the emperor and guests who were frequent visitors. The building, which was opened in 1914, was designed by Kingo Tatsuno to be reminiscent of Amsterdam's central station, with Tuscan porticos and a domed façade. In 1921, the Tokyo train station gained notoriety when Japan's prime minister was stabbed to death there by a right-wing military officer. The building faced west toward the

Imperial Palace, the seat of the emperor, just as the Imperial Japanese soldiers in the Philippines had faced north toward the Imperial Palace as they bowed to Hirohito during those early mornings at Camp Cabanatuan.

Earlier Tokyo Train Station, 1905
Courtesy Library of Congress

The train bearing Porky and his military escort came to rest inside the massive structure, and the passengers disembarked. Inside were marble supports that held a fifty-foot-high ceiling. Arched marble walkways extended out from around the central ticket arena like spokes on a wheel. Thousands of people—from children to elders dressed in kimonos and Western-style clothing, soldiers and civilians—walked in all directions throughout the building or lined up in front of a dozen ticket stalls.

In the center of the building was a small octagonal wooden room about fifteen feet across with narrow vertical windows. The windows, which extended from its top to five feet from the floor, opened the room to public view. Commander Sato opened the door and entered, followed by the interpreter, Porky, and the two guards. Benches were placed inside along the remaining seven sides of the room. Immediately, a crowd began to gather and jockeyed for position to see in. The commander ignored the crowd, as did the interpreter, but Porky and the guards made the mistake of staring back at the onlookers, who behaved as if they regarded the men as caged animals in a zoo. The crowd laughed and pointed and chattered at the wonder of it all. The commander, interpreter, and guards opened their lunch boxes, which contained rice. Porky's was the same as always, the detested kaffir corn. He finished eating then turned to the interpreter.

"Hey, is there a toilet around here?"

The interpreter looked up from his meal. "The guards will take you there."

One guard opened the door; the other positioned himself behind Porky. The spectators cleared a path as the men exited and the guards repositioned themselves between the scrawny, bearded Caucasian prisoner in the American uniform. They then marched with great formality to the ornate marble lavatory used by both sexes. A short older man in a business suit looked up from the urinal. He adjusted his gold-framed pince-nez and stared as the scruffy American entered with the armed guards. Startled, he quickly zipped up and left.

By the time the commander and his entourage exited the Tokyo train station, they were treated like celebrities. The crowd crushed forward and impeded their progress as they struggled to get a peek at the American prisoner. The commander shouted orders, the crowd parted, and they continued to march lockstep toward a mid-1930s Buick. A chauffeur stood at attention by the front passenger door. The crowd pushed in once again at the sight of the car, completely enveloping the small procession. This time the guards yelled and pushed the people away then hurried toward the waiting car.

The commander jumped into the front passenger seat but almost got his foot clipped as the chauffeur quickly shut the door and moved to the driver's side. The guards and interpreter hurried into the back with Porky in the middle, slammed and locked the doors. People continued to spill out of the train station and poured onto the sidewalk as far as the eye could see. Porky had become an instant cause célèbre. The fifteen-year-old Buick was turning into a one-car parade. In the midst of the hullabaloo, Porky had one regret—if only he had his aviator sunglasses, then he'd really look like a movie star. If only his friends could see him now! But then he recalled why he was there—the trouble he was in. His cheeks turned hot, sweat broke out on his forehead, and he turned his attention elsewhere.

In the midst of the commotion, a small pickup truck approached with a potbelly stove in the rear. The vehicle was similar to a mid-1920s American truck. The chauffeur turned the key to start the Buick, pulled past the crowd, and headed onto the street. As the crowd faded from view, Porky pointed to the truck as it drew near.

"How do they operate that thing?"

"It's a charcoal burner," the interpreter explained. "The stove feeds a steam system and fires the engine."

"Wonders never cease."

"That's a civilian driving the truck. All of the gas and oil reserves are tied up with the military, but our people are very clever. They always manage."

"That is clever," Porky admitted.

The Buick made a turn and headed down the broad boulevard at right angles to the train station. The interpreter narrated as they passed what to him were familiar landmarks. To their left were the massive Marunouchi and Yusen office buildings, which between them housed nearly one thousand separate offices. On the right was the Kaijo building and straight ahead a moat and bridge to the Imperial Palace and Gardens.

Moat around the Imperial Palace Grounds
Courtesy Library of Congress

Porky turned to look out the back window but lost sight of the crowd as they turned left onto Babasaki Street and passed the townhouse-style Londontown section. What the interpreter did not know was that the Allied Occupation Army had earmarked the district for its future headquarters.

During the fire bombings that would soon engulf much of the city, the Marunouchi business district remained largely unscathed.

As Porky took in the sights, he observed the giant moat was now to the right. Straight ahead were the exquisite grounds of a park that the Japanese Imperial Army now used for drills, based on the number of military personnel he saw marching in formation past the front gate. The Hibiya Park grounds were originally earmarked for Meiji government ministry offices during the later part of the nineteenth century, but the terrain was too spongy, having once been a part of the Tokyo Bay inlet that was filled in centuries before. Imperial planners then turned to the west of the park, to the Kasumigaseki District, whose name meant Gate of the Mist. There, along the rim of the Imperial Moat and Gardens, they constructed gigantic Western-style ministry buildings with traces of Asian embellishments. The bureaucrats who filled these ministries served the dictates of a parliamentary monarchy and government, fashioned from the English and German systems to replace the 250-year feudal, clan-oriented rule of the Tokugawa family.

The chauffeur turned right at Hibiya Park onto Kasumigaseki's main avenue, which faced Sakuradamon, the ceremonial entrance of the Imperial Palace. As the car sped along, it passed the High Court, the Ministry of Justice, and the Navy Ministry, which had trained its modern navy along the lines of the Royal Navy. Porky had begun to enjoy the ride when the car slowed down. They were approaching the headquarters of the Imperial Japanese Army and several other institutions that overlooked the palace moats.

The driver pulled up alongside a large fenced-in area and high wall where armed guards walked back and forth in front of the main gate. One of the Imperial Army guards approached the Buick. Once he spotted the commander, he signaled for the other guard to unlock the gate and allow them to drive in. Inside the courtyard, a half-dozen old American Cadillacs, Buicks, and Fords were parked to the right alongside the wall. Without being told, Porky realized this must be the top military post. He spotted dozens of small and large Western-style buildings within the spacious grounds. Some were clearly administrative buildings and others, barracks.

The chauffeur drove through the narrow streets of the complex and stopped in front of a large stone-block building several stories high. As the men stepped out of the Buick, the interpreter took the lead and directed them to the side of the building, which extended fifty yards or so along a cement path. In the rear of the administrative building was a smaller building. They entered the smaller building and walked down a hallway. To the right were three jail cells. Seated at the desk to the left was the major who interrogated

Porky at the mine. He was shuffling through papers, waiting for the group to arrive. They approached the desk, stood before him, and bowed just as he looked up. The major stood and looked Porky up and down. He then turned his attention to the commander and interpreter, whom he spoke to in Japanese while Porky hung back with the camp guards.

"Senjin," he yelled, calling for the prison guards.

Shortly afterward two Japanese soldiers emerged from a hallway and relieved the camp guards of their duty. One was middle aged, with wisps of white hair peeking out from beneath his cap. The other was younger and wore wire-rimmed glasses. They grabbed Porky by the arms and marched him to the third cell, past the other cells, which housed one Japanese prisoner each. The older guard on Porky's right opened the cell door and all three entered.

"Sutorippu," he commanded.

Porky had no idea what he meant. He raised his hands, palms up, and shrugged his shoulders. "What? I don't understand," he explained.

The guard made motions as if he were taking off his clothes. "Kigae," he ordered, indicating that Porky was to change clothes.

The second guard produced a kimono he carried in a sack and handed it over. The kimono was a patchwork of shapes and patterns, ragged but thick. Porky took off his overcoat, suntans, boots, and socks. He shivered as he slipped it on and belted it tight, but he was still cold because it barely came to his knees. Pain spiked up his legs as he stood with bare soles on the cold cement floor. The older guard knelt on one knee and pulled back a wooden sliding door in the floor. Inside was a metal pot which served as a commode.

"Benjo," he said, looking up with a slight smile.

"Benjo," Porky repeated with a bow as the guard slid the door back shut.

Both guards gathered Porky's suntans, shoes, socks, and overcoat, tucked them under their arms, and exited, leaving Porky alone with his thoughts. Five minutes later they were back. They took Porky by the arms as before but this time led him to the back of the cell and forced him to kneel, facing the wall. Porky was kneeling in the same position three hours later, swaying with hunger and pain, when the older guard returned with supper and placed it by the cell door.

"*Tatte. Tabenasai,*" he said, indicating that Porky should rise and eat.

Porky looked up and attempted to stand but was too stiff. He fell back against the wall, hit his head, and slid back down onto the floor. The guard rushed over, helped him up, and walked him over to the food—a bowl of rice and cup of hot broth with greens.

"Thanks, thanks a lot," he said as the guard turned and left. "This is the best meal I've had in years," he muttered to himself.

After the first sip of broth, he relaxed. The rice was well cooked and tasty and the greens delicious and nourishing. Despite his predicament, he felt content and thoroughly enjoyed his supper. Once he finished, the guard returned to take the bowl and cup away and reemerged moments later with his companion. They each carried three quilted blankets. Porky stood, bowed, and accepted the bedding from the guard who had been kind to him. He piled the quilts on top of one another in the corner of the cell, then stepped back to admire his handiwork. *Perfect*, he thought, *they make a nice soft bed*. He turned and smiled at the second guard, bowed, and accepted the remaining quilts. The guards watched in amazement as he carefully placed the other three on top, allowing about a foot at the top for his head, and tucking the ends into the bottom.

As Porky knelt at the end of the "bed," patting and smoothing it down, the guards burst out laughing. They doubled over, slapping one another on the back, and yelled for the other guards to come see.

"Konna baka na koto minasai," they shouted.

Four guards came rushing through the hallway and skidded to a halt by Porky's cell. After one look, they laughed out loud and slapped Porky's guards on the back. The men fell against one another, doubled over with laughter. Porky was more than annoyed, he was angry and decided to ignore them as they tried this bizarre new form of torture on him. *They will not break me*, he thought as he crawled in between the covers, pulled them up under his chin, and closed his eyes. With that, the first guard fell to his knees, pounding the cement floor with his fist. His companion sat next to him. Tears ran down his face as he held his belly in pain from too much laughter. But instead of subsiding, the hilarity grew. Porky opened his eyes and turned to see them pointing at him. He turned away, stared up at the ceiling, and grew stiff with suppressed rage, then folded his arms with as much dignity as he could muster on top of the blankets.

After a while, the man who had brought him supper took pity. He stood and motioned for Porky to stand. Fearing a beating, Porky stood and bowed. His companion's laughter had died down to a chuckle as they walked to the makeshift bed and began kicking off the quilts one by one.

"Shiroo," they said, realizing it was their duty to teach him.

Porky watched as the men folded and then wove the quilts together into an airtight sleeping bag. *So that's the trick to avoid freezing to death*, he thought. They gestured for him to get inside.

Porky bowed and smiled. "Thank you, thank you."

The guards who had rushed over and were neglecting their own charges disappeared down the hallway, back to their responsibilities. Porky crawled into the sleeping bag as the older guard bent over to tuck in a stray end against the cold. After a while, Porky fell asleep and the guards quietly exited and closed the cell door behind them.

The next morning, Porky awoke deafened by the sound of a loud bell that rang and clanged for about a minute. Guards rushed down the hallway. One stopped at Porky's cell door, opened it, and beckoned for him to exit and stand against the wall opposite his cell. Two Japanese prisoners were standing against the wall further down. All three were in their bare feet and kimonos. Two guards conducted a body search on each of the men and, once they were determined not to be carrying weapons, dropped a pair of rubber shoes in front of each, which they quickly stepped into.

"Benjo," the guards said, motioning for each of the prisoners to reenter their jail cell and bring out the commode.

The men reentered their cells, knelt, drew back the sliding door in the floor, and grabbed their chamber pots. The guards marched them outside to a hand pump with a large trough filled with water. At the bottom of the trough, there was a larger container with frozen sewage, which the Japanese prisoners, being familiar with the drill, tapped with their commodes until the ice broke and then dumped the contents into the container. Porky observed the drill and followed suit and was led with the others back into the building and back into their cells.

About a half hour later, a guard returned with a bowl of rice and a cup of soup. Porky finished the meal and was instructed to face the wall and kneel, as before. That evening, the guards gathered to watch Porky make the blankets into a sleeping bag. They laughed and pointed as he inexpertly tried to duplicate what was done for him the night before. But just as Porky was starting to get hot under the collar, a siren sounded. Soon planes were heard overhead and the sound of antiaircraft fire. Porky's guard rushed to open the cell door and handed him his rubbers, which he quickly slipped on, only to be handcuffed seconds later. As he exited the cell, he saw the Japanese prisoners being pulled out of their cells and handcuffed by the guards. Then they all hurried down the corridor. "At least they're not playing favorites," he mumbled under his breath.

The prisoners were led outdoors into the dark and gingerly made their way to a large courtyard where foxholes had been dug. "Tobi-oriru," the guards screamed. The Japanese prisoners jumped into the foxhole as instructed.

Sweaty with anxiety, Porky held back. Jumping into a foxhole with your hands free was one thing, but with your hands cuffed behind your back was another. "Tobi-oriru," the guard screamed and gave him a push. Porky jumped and by a miracle landed on his feet and was shortly followed in by the guards.

All ducked as antiaircraft guns opened fire nearby in a furious assault, but eventually the men settled into the ditch. Porky counted fifty-one planes overhead, planes he was unfamiliar with—B-29s. They flew low, setting off searchlights and antiaircraft fire, but on that night, no bombs were dropped. That was to come less than a week later, on March 9, when incendiary bombs would light up the night sky, targeting the industrial district of the city. Tokyo sprawled along Tokyo Bay and was densely packed with factories, docks, and wooden homes—the hub of Japan's war industry. Within the space of two days, incendiary bombs would create a perfect firestorm that raged and howled and spread thousands-degree temperatures—a Dante's Inferno devouring over a hundred thousand residents and creating cinders of all else in its path.

"That's fifty-one. Fifty-one planes," Porky said out loud that early March evening, but he was ignored. *Jesus Christ what if I die here, killed by the Americans*, he thought gloomily. "Just hold on, it can't be much longer," he whispered to himself.

After the air raid, the men were led in total darkness back to their cells. The next morning, the prisoners underwent a routine similar to that of the day before. But on this day, the Japanese prisoners were taken out of their cells by the early afternoon to be court-martialed. By midafternoon it was Porky's turn.

Porky sat waiting on the floor, his back against the wall. He was wearing the jacket, suntans, overcoat, shoes, and socks he had arrived in. The kimono he had been wearing was neatly folded and stacked against the sidewall on top of the quilted blankets. Porky listened as a guard entered the hallway with one of the prisoners to lead him back to the cell. The door creaked open and slammed shut again. He heard footsteps, then the guard appeared at Porky's cell, key in hand. Porky got up and was escorted out of the building. They walked a short distance to a cinder-block-gray courthouse and entered the courtroom through a side door.

Commander Sato, the interpreter, and the camp guards were seated on a bench near the middle aisle. The prison guard walked Porky to the end of the bench and sat him next to the interpreter. The room was vast, with dozens of empty benches, but what riveted Porky's attention was the long judicial bench on a raised platform about thirty feet away. There, fifteen or so Japanese military officers were seated from various branches of service, judging from their uniforms. These were the judges. Each wore a dozen or more medals on his jacket. Several wore the customary steel-rimmed round glasses and busied themselves examining the papers spread out before them—his case, he soon realized. Porky looked around the room, but as he had feared, they were alone with the tribunal, not that an audience would have helped matters. Finally, one of the officers in the middle stood up and shouted. "Ippozenshin," he commanded, ordering the group to step forward closer to the bench.

Sato stood and approached the bench. The others followed close behind. All bowed. The commander addressed the group of officers, explaining the purpose of the trial. Immediately afterward, a conversation ensued between the commander and the presiding judge. The interpreter turned to Porky to explain. "You have been found guilty and have been fined ten thousand yen and 120 days hard labor."

The interpreter then turned to the presiding judge and in Japanese explained the incident in even greater detail, from the type of work Porky was engaged in to the nature of the assault and the incident on the stretcher where the accused faked a state of unconsciousness. The interpreter turned back to Porky. "I have explained the incident in full detail but informed the committee that you are a good worker. As a consequence, they have reduced your sentence. You will be fined sixty yen and made to serve twenty days of hard labor."

The interpreter and camp commander bowed, and Porky and the guard followed suit, turned, exited the courtroom, and walked back to the front of the building and into the waiting Buick. They drove back onto the street and headed back to the train station. Porky looked out the window to forget his troubles and soak in the magnificence of the Imperial Gardens that spread out past the moat. As they approached Hibiya Park, Porky turned to the interpreter.

"Did you hear the planes?"

"No."

"You must have heard them."

"Even if I did, it is nothing for you to worry about. If the Americans get to the point where they come ashore to fight, every man, woman, and child will be armed with sticks and stones and picks, axes, and anything they can get their hands on. The Americans will never take this island. They will never win. As far as all you prisoners are concerned, if that happens, you will go to the mines and we will blow them up with you inside."

Porky was stunned. The rest of the ride was spent in silence. Soon the Buick arrived in front of the train station, and the men left without further fanfare to catch the train. Porky rode back deep in thought, oblivious to the passing scenery, and was startled when he realized they were back at Ashio station. The men disembarked and marched back to the camp headquarters, but instead of heading back to the barracks, the interpreter had Porky join him in his private headquarters, which served as the infirmary.

The interpreter took off his sandals and Porky his military boots as they entered. Seven or eight prisoners lay across the floor, covered with blankets. Extra clothing propped up their heads. A potbelly stove set in the corner provided little heat against the chill. The interpreter opened the iron door, grabbed a poker, and stirred the embers before throwing in a few coals from a bin nearby. When he turned back to Porky, he softened for a moment and acted like the doctor he had been trained to be.

"LaCoste, take your shirt off. I want to examine you."

Porky did as he was told, and the interpreter-physician poked around his stomach.

"I think I know what your problem is. There's an ancient Chinese treatment that may help you."

"You're not talking about acupuncture, are you? I don't want any needles stuck in me."

"No. This is a burn treatment, but it is the same principle. It works on the nerves. Don't worry. Over fifty thousand physicians throughout Japan practice this technique. Lay down on the cot over there, on your stomach."

The cot was near the stove, the center of the heat that diminished significantly the farther you were back in the room. Whether or not Porky liked the treatment, at least he'd feel warm. He sprawled out on the cot, hands over his head, and tried to relax as the physician prepared the cotton, rolling it into tiny balls. He then placed the tightly packed balls on Porky's back, above his kidneys, and then lit a piece of punk wood.

"This will burn only for a moment."

The doctor touched the lighted punk to each of the balls. Porky flinched.

"LaCoste, turn over for a moment. I need to work on your ankles."

He placed a ball on each ankle and lit it. Porky flinched once again with pain but tried to relax, to believe in the treatment.

"OK, put your shirt back on and lie down and get some rest."

Porky not only put his shirt back on but his coat as well. He then curled up in the corner, not far from the stove, and fell asleep as the physician slipped out of the room and joined Commander Sato for their evening meal.

The next morning, kitchen help entered with their ration of food. Porky sat up and spoke to the POW next to him as he ate.

"Say, can you tell me something about this burn technique? Is this the first time you've been burnt?"

"Naw, second time."

"Did you get an infection from it, or were you given any medication?"

"No. I've talked to some of the other fellows. No one has had any problems with infections, and it's a good thing because there is no medicine to treat us."

The interpreter entered and surveyed the scene. "The commander will be here in a few moments. Everyone lie down."

Each of the POWs immediately bedded down again. Porky placed his overcoat over him just as the commander entered with a walking stick. He poked at each man as he walked and barked out commands in Japanese, which the interpreter translated.

"Back to work," he shouted, repeating what the commander had ordered in Japanese.

"You there, back to work," he yelled as his boss poked at another POW.

"Back to work," he barked as he stood over a third man, who was in pain from the severity of the poke from the commander's stick.

Sato approached Porky and poked hard into the overcoat with the stick.

"LaCoste, you son of a bitch," the commander screamed in perfect English. "You owe me sixty yen. I paid your fine. Now you go to work. Pay me back."

Porky looked up in surprise and caught sight of the commander's back as he marched out. He stood up as did the other POWs, put on his boots, and returned to the barracks.

Dropping bombs over Japan, 1945
Courtesy National Archives

Chapter 35

The rats scurrying across the canvas top ate away at Porky's nerves as he attempted to sleep in preparation for the morning's work. Despite the cold and torture of remaining awake, not one rat had crossed his path during the nights he spent outside in the chicken-wire prison, nor had he spotted any during his stay in the Tokyo army jail. He burrowed deep inside the covers and waited for dawn and the retaliation that was sure to come from the Korean bosses once he reentered the mines.

That morning, the steel gray sky overhead seemed especially bleak as snow melted off Ashio Mountain, revealing the dirt and sterility beneath. Porky was filled with dread as he trudged up the path leading to the worksite but did what he knew he must do and rejoined a work detail from his old job, pushing ore carts. As Porky grabbed a hook and joined the others as they maneuvered a cart along the rails, he noticed Korean men and teens picking up rocks, bits of steel, pieces of wood, and anything they could get their hands on. He squatted against the cart, hands shielding his head as they screamed and hurled objects at him. Hearing the commotion, a Japanese guard rushed in and pulled him out of the line of fire and into a nearby shack. They waited until the Koreans settled down and then walked back to the barracks.

The second-shift prisoners looked up as Porky entered, shaken and exhausted. Porky's misadventure was a word to the wise for all of them. They passed by in silence and hurried out to the mines. Some things were best left unsaid. Later that evening, the men were sitting on the edge of the bay as the interpreter entered and approached Porky, who was stuffing the last scraps of kaffir corn into his mouth.

"LaCoste, tomorrow morning you will be given a different assignment," he announced curtly, then sauntered over to several men he had treated recently to inquire about their health.

After the interpreter left, Leo approached. "I never thought I'd see you again," he said with emotion.

"You're looking good. When did they release you?"

"The day after you left, and I haven't had a seizure since. I think they must have been right. It must have been demons, and they excised them clean out of me. Either that, or I'm so scared shitless after what they pulled, my body won't let me have another attack."

"Amazing!"

"Sure in heck is," Leo acknowledged, looking as if he might smile.

But Porky was the bleak one now. "So where do I go next? After what the bosses tried to do to me today—Leo, they tried to kill me!"

"I heard."

"So what's next? That's what I'd like to know. If I can keep my nose clean, maybe I'll get out of this alive."

"So you think there's a chance we could go home?"

Porky nodded his head yes and then called out to the men. "Hey, guys, did dozens of planes fly overhead while I was gone?"

Several men looked up, and a few approached to hear the latest. "Jap planes?"

"No. I mean American planes."

"Have you been hitting the sake?" Leo asked with a snort.

"No. I was in Tokyo a couple of nights ago. Not in a fancy hotel, mind you, but a real Jap jail, and lo and behold, you'd never guess what happened."

He had them hooked. "You didn't see American planes? You are kidding, right?"

"I didn't see any. I heard them. It was dark. I was in a cell when of all things, the siren starts screeching away like it's an air raid."

Nearly all the men dropped what they were doing and crowded in to hear. Bony elbows pushed into bare ribs of fellow prisoners as they crushed Porky, trying to listen to the details. Leo pushed back.

"Stop squeezing. Give him some room," he yelled until they backed off.

"Well, next thing I know, a Jap guard shows up with handcuffs," Porky continued. "He lets me out of the cell, and we go running outside and into a foxhole."

"Jesus Christ, you could have been bombed."

"Strangest thing, I heard antiaircraft fire from the Japs, but all the planes did was fly overhead."

"How do you know they were ours?" Leo asked.

"The motors. You know the difference between how a Jap plane sounds and an American. American planes are smoother, quieter. I counted them. One by one, there were fifty-one planes."

"Fifty-one planes?"

"You counted that many?"

"That's over four dozen planes."

"Yes, fifty-one, and they were about ten seconds apart," Porky continued.

"I wonder if they were on surveillance," Leo ventured.

"I don't know. They seemed to be big planes. Nothing I'm familiar with."

"If they were small, they'd have to be stationed nearby. But bigger, who knows."

"Or maybe they took off from the deck of a carrier," Porky conjectured. "Remember how it is on a carrier. The planes take off one by one. Maybe I'm off base, but it seems to me they were maybe about ten seconds apart."

"They must be on bombing runs."

"Imagine if we survive all of this time and we end up dead because we were bombed by our own," Leo whispered to the crowd.

"It'll never happen. Who'd bomb a tiny village up in the mountains? Look, guys, we've got one task ahead of us, and that's to survive until we're rescued."

Sam entered the room and searched around for Porky, finally spotting him in the center of the gathering.

"Hey, LaCoste," he shouted as he pushed his way into the crowd. "You're coming with my gang tomorrow."

"So what kind of job is it this time?"

"Nothing too bad," Sam said with a laugh. "Not like the blasting you used to do. We work outdoors. We're the new mud men."

"The mud men?"

"Yeah, haven't you noticed the cable car traveling up to the other side of the mountain? Well, they're not filling the cars up with ore. They fill 'em with mud, and we're the ones who have to get the crap into the cars."

"What the hell do they do with the mud?"

"Get rid of it. It's the waste—the crap left over from the ore. The village people complain all of the fish have been dying and their crops won't grow. Our job is to get it to the other side of the mountain."

"Why? What's on the other side of the mountain?"

"A valley filled with mud," Sam said stoutly as the men burst out laughing.

"Jesus Christ, I'd better be good from now on."

"Why the hell start now?"

"It'd be the perfect murder weapon—quicksand. A valley filled with mud—and they'd never find my body."

"Well don't worry, LaCoste. There are no Koreans on the detail and we only work during the day," he said, realizing that Porky's concerns might be serious. "If you'd like, I'll keep a sharp eye out for you."

"Ah, don't bother. I can take care of myself," Porky replied with a touch of bravado once he realized his enemies would be nowhere near.

The Ashio copper mine was not only one of Japan's largest mining operations, it was one of the largest in the world. And though it was a source of national profit and pride, it was also infamous for labor unrest and pollution. In 1907, miners rioted for three days against the Furukawa Company owners, who were also plagued by complaints about poisonous byproducts that impacted the air, soil, and water of the region. Sulfurous gas emitted during refining combined with rain to form sulfuric acid that damaged forests and polluted rivers and streams, killed fish, and leached out metals from the soils. Today, you'd refer to the problem as acid rain. But for local inhabitants, the most visible problem was the slag. The mine lacked storage facilities for slag and untreated ore. Farmers argued that it was the slag from the mine that made the mountain villages downwind from the refinery nearly uninhabitable. What was worse, it leached into river water used to irrigate rice paddies.

The next morning, a Japanese guard led Porky, Sam, and eight other POWs onto a dirt road. After a mile or so they came to a fork in the road. The left led to the mines, the right to the mud detail. They marched to the right over a small wooden bridge where the spring melt had swollen the stream below, then walked round a boulder and up an embankment. Below was the work site. Large holding lagoons filled with a soapy mix of ore waste and water acted like moats, nearly surrounding several weather-beaten buildings that housed the equipment used in the operation. The guard stopped outside of an old building and the men entered.

Inside were four large machines. Each machine had two large rods, two inches in diameter, with fifty round steel plates that were three feet in diameter with two-inch holes in the center. The plates had a steel cradle that sat on top of the rods and functioned as vertical wheels. The wheels were covered with a canvas that had two-inch holes to match the holes in each plate. Slurry mixture from the lagoons was forced through the holes while the men used hooks to force the plates apart. Mud was formed by forcing water out between the plates.

Porky's job was to take a large paddle, scrape the mud off the canvas, and drop it into a waiting cable car below. Massive cables pulled the carts out from under the building and up over the mountain, where a device at the top caught and dipped the car so that the mud contents were dropped into the valley below. After each cart left, the men forced the plates back together again by pulling hard on the hooks while Sam turned a giant wheel. Soon more sludge from the lagoon was forced into the device as the men relaxed and waited for the machine to fill.

U.S. and Filipino Forces recapture Manila
Courtesy National Archives

Chapter 36

On March 2, U.S. Airborne troops recaptured Corregidor. The following day, U.S. and Filipino troops were in control of Manila. Two weeks later, an item of interest appeared in the *Athol Daily News*. It was a photo of Porky's old buddy, Franny, in a hospital bed. The caption under the photo read, "Shirley Temple visits Athol soldier—Patterson Field, Dayton, O., March 17.—T. Sgt. Francis W. Robichaud, Army Air Force, son of Mr. and Mrs. Charles W. Robichaud, of 110 Sanders street, Athol, Mass., is visited at the field hospital by Shirley Temple, Hollywood star, flanked by nurses' aides. Sergeant Robichaud was with the Air Force in the Philippines when the Japs struck, and was evacuated, ill and wounded on a hospital ship the day before Manila fell."

The following month, the focus was on Porky. "In Jap Camp," ran the heading along with a photo of a jaunty, smiling Porky in his formal army corporal's outfit, complete with cap, a belted uniform, shirt, and tie.

> ATHOL, April 18.—Corp. Franklin J. LaCoste of 132 Swanzey street, reported a year ago as a prisoner of the Japanese, is still in Jap hands but well and in good spirits, according to word received by his mother, Mrs. Rose Libby, and his grandmother, Mrs. Rose LaCoste, both of the same address.
>
> Word of an interception of an enemy broadcast in which Corp. LaCoste was mentioned came Saturday to Mrs. LaCoste from the Federal Communications Commission.

###

Whatever cherry trees were left unscorched in Tokyo from incendiary bombs were in full bloom by mid-April about the time President Franklin Delano Roosevelt died of a cerebral hemorrhage. So too were the petals of the Japanese Cherry trees in Washington, D.C., blossoming soft pink and white, quite beguiling despite the antipathy most Americans felt at the time towards the country they represented. But the American and other Allied Power prisoners of war in Japan were oblivious to the happenings great and small outside their confines.

By the end of the month, fraternizing with the village foremen had become routine for Porky in his new detail outside of the Ashio mines. The days were warmer, but the mountain nights were still cold. And though the season's growth was muted by the mines' pollutants, the detail Porky was now assigned allowed POWs to spend time out in the open and to wander a bit into the budding field. One afternoon, he sat on a rock sunning as he ate with two Japanese guards, along with Sam and Don, who had also made corporal before the war, as well as a few of the other prisoners. One of the guards was relatively tall, slightly cross-eyed, and slender. The other man was smaller than Porky and had a sensitive round face. Both were from a nearby village and spoke broken English and were usually pleasant and cooperative, but on this day, the shorter guard seemed withdrawn, pensive, and very sad. He caught Porky observing him. Porky smiled, and the guard opened up.

"My Ichiro, my *isshi* (only child) very *omoibyooki*, as you say, vewwy sickku. He fooah," he said, holding up four fingers. "My *aisai* and I *torai* (try) wad-ash ha (radish leaf) *wappu* him up. Needu *tokubetsu kusur* (special medicine) from tokubetsu *puranto*—(special plant). No find," he said with a shrug. "Needu Shakuyaku. It vewwy tall. *Wappu* on body get much *atsui*— wam. Need to *fixxu isshi* son."

Sam turned to Porky. "It sounds like pneumonia to me."

"You say your son's only four years old?" Porky asked the honcho.

"*Isshi,* little Ichiro," he said, choking with emotion. "He fooah."

"Does he have a cough?"

"That pwob-em. Vewwy deepu seki (cough). Sick deepu seki in Ichiro," he said, pounding his chest and coughing to demonstrate. "Ichiro vewwy baddu. No play. He no smile. My *aisai* and I know Ichiro die. We *torai* (try)—*besuto* with hoomu fixxu (home-made) medeshin (medicine) but not goodu. We needu *hontoo* (real) medeshin for my boy, my *isshi*."

Porky couldn't take his eyes off this man, who no more looked like an enemy than any of his friends back home. The guard turned away, his eyes brimming with tears.

"Say, I have a couple of pills that might help—sulfa pills."

"Sul-fa?"

Sam leaned over and whispered, "You're willing to give him your medicine? These nights are cold, real cold. You could get sick yourself."

"Yeah, I know, but this kid is real sick," Porky whispered back. "He's dying. Look, I'm tough. I'll survive."

"You're nuts."

Porky drew closer to the guard, who sat on a discarded toolbox. He knelt on one knee and looked up into his face.

"Look, I carry this medicine with me wherever I go. I have three sulfa pills left." Porky took the three tinfoil-wrapped pills out from his shirt pocket. His medic friend, Stickney, had slipped the pills to him along with some quinine back at Cabanatuan as a trade for his aviator glasses. "Now, I'm going to break these up into little pieces."

Porky unwrapped the pills and grabbed a nearby stick. He left each pill in its unfolded tinfoil and placed them on the rock he had been sitting on moments before. Grabbing the foil to steady the pill, he tapped each with the sharp end of the stick to break them up.

"Have your boy take one piece every half hour with water," he said, rewrapping the pieces in the foil. "If he refuses to take it that way, crush it into a powder and put it in a sweet drink."

Porky handed the medicine to the guard. "Be careful. Don't lose one precious piece of this. It will save your son's life," he said and bowed. Both honchos bowed to Porky, and Sam, Don, and the other prisoners bowed to the guards. Later, as they returned from the work detail to the barracks, Sam turned to Porky.

"I'm telling you. You're nuts!"

Two days later, birds chirped gaily and flitted about as dew on the tender grass shoots melted in the morning sun. The bleakness of winter had faded. It was the first day of May 1945. The day before, Adolph Hitler, together with his bride of only one day, Eva Braun, committed suicide in his Berlin bunker. On the first of May, Joseph Goebbels, the propaganda minister and newly named chancellor of Germany, followed suit. By May 2, the Battle of Berlin was over and on May 4, British field marshal Montgomery accepted the military surrender of all German forces. Three days later, on the seventh, the chief of staff of the German Armed Forces High Command signed the documents of unconditional surrender. The Axis was broken, but Japan's 124th emperor, Hirohito, and his cabinet ministers were unmoved. They were determined to fight to the last man.

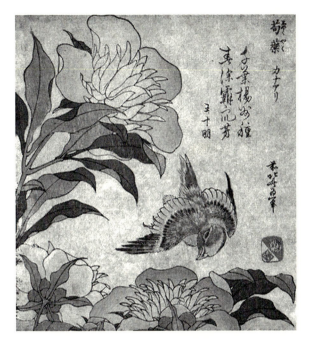

"Small Flowers" by Katsushika Hokusai (1760-1849)
Courtesy Library of Congress

Despite continued hardship, the POWs felt reinvigorated on this spring morning as the camp guard escorted them back to the mud relocation unit. They entered the mud room and the guard headed back down to camp. Outside, the foremen from a nearby village sat on stools, sunning themselves and smoking cigarettes. Porky joined the men working the mud machines. After the sluice was opened and the liquid tracings entered, the men went outside to sit and chat or wander around the grounds.

Porky approached the village guard with the sick son. "*Sochi, sochi,*" he said, rocking his arms as if holding the child. "*Isshi* son, Ichiro?"

The man smiled so broadly his gold teeth shone in the sun. "*Isshi yoshi*—well," he responded with a bow, then grabbed Porky's hand and held it for a moment. "*Doumo,*" he said, thanking Porky, "Thank to you."

The men looked deeply into one another's eyes in an exchange of warmth and mutual understanding as the Japanese villagers and POWs stood nearby to witness. Finally, Porky withdrew his hand and bowed.

The grateful father responded with a bow. "*Donmai ichirei*," he said and waved his hand as if to say, "No need to bow." Porky smiled broadly and then returned to his fellow prisoners.

"Thank God it worked, Frenchy," Sam said after the men returned to work. "Why, if the boy died, they would think you poisoned him."

"Well the medicine worked, and I'm grateful."

"Looks like you made a friend for life," Sam admitted.

"Look. Do you see what I see?" Porky asked, changing the subject.

"No," he said, looking around.

"I've got an idea."

"So tell me. I'm not a mind reader."

"Let's scout out this building," Porky said, leading the way into a ramshackle shack. "Hey, this bucket's in pretty good shape." Porky examined a vintage cast-iron cooking pot that had been used decades earlier when some work crews cooked their rice out in the field.

"So what?"

"Stick with me, pal. I've got something in mind," he said, holding the bucket by its handle. "But let's get back. We don't want them scouting for us."

When the men returned to the work site, the village honchos and bosses waved for them to return to the mud room. Porky dropped the bucket by the door and got back to work. He grabbed a hook to pull the metal plates apart and scraped the mud off into the carts below. A Japanese foreman flipped a switch and the carts began the slow journey along the tracks up the side of the mountain where the sludge was to be dumped; meanwhile, the POWs prepared the plates and then opened the sluice for the liquid tracings to slosh through.

When they took their work break, the Japanese foremen were curious. One picked up the vintage pot and followed Porky outside as he joined the POWs and honchos, who sat together as a group. The bosses sat on stools. Some of the American prisoners sat on the ground or on rock outcroppings warmed by the sun. Others rolled logs over to use as benches. The substandard timber had been thrust aside from an earlier forestry clearing. As the men chatted amiably among themselves, the village boss who had grabbed the bucket held it up for all to see.

"*Doushite?* What for?" he asked.

"Thought maybe we could cook with it," Porky responded. "Isn't that what it used to be used for?" The Japanese villagers laughed. Many still used cauldrons not unlike the one Porky had found. In remote mountainous regions, modern conveniences were hard to come by even before the war; oil and coal were in short supply and used primarily for industrial and military uses. Since the war, in the forestry and mountain villages people carried on as before, largely fending for themselves.

"Where food?" one of the honchos asked.

Suddenly the POWs sprang to life with plans, just as they had back on Bataan before the surrender when they were GIs fighting to survive and remain free. "Seeing we have an hour or so to waste, why don't we scout out for snakes or wild flowers or greens?" Don proposed.

"Let's cook anything we find," another said.

"We've got drinking water in the other pail. Maybe part of it could be used to cook stuff in. Afterward we could drink it—like a broth."

The Japanese foreman who had grabbed the pot pointed to the trees. *"Pikku gureenu fuudo.* arigato Chou," he said, pointing to the budding leaves of a tree that resembled the American scrub oak. He walked to the tree and plucked off a few leaves, popped them in his mouth, and began to chew. "OK, OK," he said after he swallowed.

"Not my first choice in a vegetable," Sam whispered under his breath.

"Beggars can't be choosers," Porky whispered back, then looked up and smiled at the Japanese boss.

The village honcho whose son Porky had saved got up from his stool and gestured for Porky to follow. As they reentered the mud room, he pointed to a chain balled up on the floor, and then pulled it out to check on the length. "Daibu, nice?" he asked with a smile. He looked up, searching along the ceiling for a hook, then pointed down to the cement floor.

"Chuukei. Hook," he said, pointing up. "Okibi. Jikayaki. Fire cook," he said, pointing down at the floor.

"Hang the pail from the chain and build a fire. Great idea!" Porky said with a bow.

His new friend gestured for Porky to follow him outside. They wandered through the field until they came to an old dilapidated building. The honcho pulled off two boards and broke them into smaller pieces. They tucked the boards under their arms and moved on to an adjacent building where he pointed out a pile of coal in a dark corner of the room.

"Daibu. Good."

"Very good, very useful," Porky agreed as they meandered back. He picked up his mess kit and the honcho's bentou-bako lunch box and rejoined the men, who were seated enjoying their lunch in the bright spring sunshine.

The next day, the men were anxious to finish their duties in the mud room and head outdoors. "OK, men, spread out and pick all of the wildflowers you see, but keep your eyes open for anything else that moves," the POW from Alabama instructed.

"Bingo," another shouted as he caught a brown mountain hare nibbling on a bit of rice dropped behind a shed for bait. Others were gathering leaves and flowers. Each leaf was checked for bitterness. Some were discarded, others saved for the pot. The POW from Alabama returned with a six-inch garden snake, minus its oval head, which had been sliced off with the sharp edge of a rock against a boulder.

"This will flavor things nicely," he said to a village boss, who looked on with approval. Snake soup gave energy to weakened bodies, according to local beliefs.

Porky stacked the scraps of half-rotten wood under the pail of water. The village boss lit the fire, and one by one, the men dropped their items into the pail until it was full.

"I suppose it's about time we got back to work," Porky admitted with a sigh.

"I, for one, can't wait 'til lunch. I'm drooling already," Sam said, staring into the flames leaping under the pail.

The Southerner turned to the village boss who had been assisting. "Mind if I borrow your knife?"

The boss handed him his knife without hesitation and Porky handed him a board. Before long, the decapitated snake was diced properly and scraped off the board into the steaming pail. The Japanese villager shook his head back and forth, as if in wonderment at the scene, and then shook with uncontrollable laughter.

"What's he laughing at?" Sam asked.

"He's laughing at us," Porky admitted, then joined his Japanese friend in laughing so hard he thought he would split a gut.

June and July are typically typhoon season in Japan. July 31 was particularly overcast. A typhoon was approaching the island nation. Cloud cover made visual bombing impossible, so the Allied Forces postponed a special mission and waited for the storm to pass.

Back in the POW barracks at Ashio Mountain, the moon peeped through the clouds and in through the triangular opening above as rats scampered about over the sleeping men. In the hallway, bare lightbulbs at each end of the barracks served sentry along with the faint glow of lit coals. A POW crew leader rose and put on his overcoat against the early morning chill and then woke the men on his work detail.

Porky was tossing and turning as the crew leader approached. "LaCoste, we're moving out in a few minutes. Better dress extra warm. It's a bit raw out tonight."

"Oh, I hate this graveyard shift," he complained as he yawned and stretched.

The men gathered at the door where the guard was waiting to lead them to the mud room detail. They fell in line and walked along the mountain road, guided by a dim flashlight and the occasional glow of moonlight that filtered through openings in the clouds. Porky kicked something and bent to pick it up. The wind picked up and a cloud floated past the moon, revealing a potato. Porky wondered how it had gotten there—abandoned in the middle of the road—until he spotted a shed nearby where the Korean food supplies were kept. He quickly pocketed it and continued the trek. *They'll never miss it, they hate these*, he rationalized.

A village boss was waiting at the work site and led them into the mud room, which was dimly lit by two bare bulbs hanging at the front and the back of the room. It was now around four in the morning; time for the men to begin preparations for their early morning meal. The pail and chain had been set down by the entrance of the mud room for use during the day. Porky hooked them up and headed to the building where the coal was stored. He pocketed a lump, grabbed some wood, and headed back to build the fire. He then checked to see that no one was looking and buried the potato in the embers and placed several pieces of wood on top.

"Guys, grab your mess kits," he announced. "I've got a good fire going now."

The men placed their mess kits around the fire and then walked outside to the spigot to fill their cups.

"Bakku job," the village boss yelled to the men who remained milling around the spigot, chatting.

About a half hour later, the Japanese barracks guard returned to the work site and entered the mud room unannounced. He stood by the fire to warm himself as the prisoners worked. After a moment, he caught a distinct aroma, sniffed about, then called the village boss over. They conferred in Japanese and looked around. The guard noticed a sharply pointed branch left against the wall, grabbed it, and began poking at the fire. At last, he found what he was looking for. He speared the potato and lifted it to his face for further inspection. Just then, Joe, an older POW the Japanese used as a snitch, walked in. Ratting out his fellow POWs earned him rice and other treats normally reserved for the Japanese. The guard pointed at Joe and called him over.

"Hanzaisha. Who potato?" he asked, wanting to know who the culprit was.

Joe shook his head as if to say he didn't know. To squeal with everyone watching was not a wise thing to do. The guard raised his rifle as if to strike.

"Who, who?" he screamed.

Joe ducked and held his hand up against a blow, then pointed to Porky—not that he knew for sure it was him, but he thought Porky was a wise guy and had it coming. The guard smiled sadistically and sauntered over to the work area. The men scattered as the guard raised his leg, then pushed Porky against it, tripping him. He kicked him as he sprawled on the cold cement floor, then forced Porky up and slapped him across the face several times and tripped him again and kicked him when he was down. Finally, he walked away swearing and stopped at the entrance to confer once again with the village boss. Before leaving, the guard picked up the skewered potato, turned, and smiled at Porky, then sauntered down the road eating the roasted potato.

Dawn cast a rosy glow above the mountains as the men finished work and sat down to eat. Later, when the men marched back to the barracks, two guards accompanied the crew. One of the guards marched in front of Porky, and the other marched behind. As they marched in lockstep, Porky slowly pulled out the lump of coal he had pocketed earlier, opened his mess kit, and shoved the stolen item into the container. He knew that once he got back to the barracks, the guards would conduct a body search. What he had not anticipated, however, was what occurred as they approached the compound. The gate guard was stopping each man to check his mess kit. Porky was attempting to reopen the mess kit and repocket the coal but fumbled with the latch, just as the guard grabbed the kit. Worse still, the barracks guard who had beaten him earlier over the stolen potato suddenly appeared from behind the guardhouse and conversed briefly with the gate guard. The game was over. The gate guard opened the kit and spotted the coal as the barracks guard looked smugly on, barely able to stop himself from laughing out loud. The gate guard called Porky to attention.

"Chokuritsufudouate," he called sharply as Porky froze in attention. The gate guard grabbed the mess kit and instructed the guards to return to barracks with the rest of the men. As the others marched away, he closed and locked the kit with the coal inside, then handed it back to Porky, who was forced to extend his arms out straight and hold the mess kit until further instructions.

As Porky took his punishment, the gate guard sat while the sadistic barracks guard remained standing and offered him a cigarette. The guards smoked and watched as Porky strained to remain standing at attention, facing the guardhouse, with his arms outstretched. After an hour or so, the barracks guard had had his fill of amusement for the day and returned to the compound. Porky remained at attention for another four hours. Periodically, work details marched by and laughed. By noon, he was allowed to relax and return to quarters for lunch. Porky entered the barracks, opened his mess kit, and dumped the stolen coal into the stove, then sat on the edge of the bay and stared straight ahead. He felt utterly dejected and was completely exhausted as he crawled into his bunk area to sleep.

That evening, Porky got up for supper and joined the men walking toward the kitchen. As they entered, they noticed the smell of ammonia permeated the room. Two cauldrons were boiling over at the far end of the building. One contained kaffir corn and the other shark heads.

"Peeyoo."

"Jesus. That stuff stings your eyes."

"They don't expect us to eat whatever it is?"

"Where the hell did it come from?"

"I could have sworn I heard bombing."

"Maybe Uncle Sam is bombing boats in the harbor and they end up killing sharks," Sam whispered to Porky.

"And they expect us to eat it? It's so strong, I feel like I am going to pass out."

Porky's depression had passed. He was starting to feel like part of the group again. The men sat at the table and the kitchen staff dropped kaffir corn and a spoonful of a slimy substance into each of their mess kits. Soon Leo joined them.

"Ugh. This is the worse crap. It is gruesome."

"You said it. What a day!"

Courtesy Department of Defense

Chapter 37

By the next week, Porky was back on the day shift. The men were in the mud room, emptying the mud into the carts when the taller village Japanese boss entered.

"Hitoyasumi. Stop job," he said, shutting the machines off.

The men went outside and sat down at their favorite rest area, where they had rolled over logs to use as benches months before.

"While we're on a break, I might as well scout for some food," Porky offered.

"There's nothing left to pick," Sam replied.

"Oh sure there is. I spotted a few flowers in back of the outbuilding."

"Hey, hey, hold up," Sam warned. "The Jap guard's coming."

"Holy shit," Porky said with a grimace.

"Jesus Christ, Frenchy, what the hell have you gotten yourself into now?"

"I'm innocent. I swear to God I'm innocent."

"Sure you are."

The army guard approached the civilian Japanese boss and they conferred briefly in Japanese, keeping their voices low.

"Ke-oski, Ke-oski," the Japanese guard ordered.

The POWs jumped in line and began to count off. After they were finished, the guard put up his hand.

"Yoi, ka, good," he said as he waved them on to march back to the camp while he took up the rear.

When the men arrived back at the compound, they discovered that all of the POWs had been brought back. The men wandered around or talked in clusters; others went back to the barracks to grab a bit more rest. The next morning, the rats exited as the day broke and the men rose, relieved themselves outside at the straddle trench, cleaned up for the day, grabbed their mess kits, and marched to the kitchen for their morning rations. As they waited to enter, the gossip was at fever pitch. They all had their theories but feared something bad was about to happen as they hoped for something good.

"No tenko last night," Porky commented to Sam. "*No* lineup. *No* guard last night, nothing this morning."

"Did I miss the morning whistle?" Sam asked.

"No, it never happened," Leo said and informed them he was so anxious he had stayed awake half the night, listening to the rats pounce.

"Judging from the sky, it has to be at least seven," Porky remarked.

A POW standing nearby butted in. "My watch says seven thirty."

"So what are we supposed to do?" Leo asked nervously.

"Nothing, take life easy," Porky said with a smile. "But what I'd like to know is . . . where the hell is the interpreter? I haven't seen him in two days."

"I've seen the commander," Sam offered.

"The guards are walking around," Leo added.

Finally Sam dared to say what was on everyone's mind. "Maybe the war's over!"

"Maybe you're right," Porky admitted with a short laugh.

But Leo was more frightened than before. "Do you think we're in danger?"

Porky pulled his friends close and whispered, "After I was court-martialed, I was told if the Americans invaded, every man, woman, and child would fight, and we'd be taken into the mines and blown up."

"So is that what you think is about to happen?" Leo's eyes were as big as saucers.

"Maybe if the war is over, they will have to kill us . . . so we don't squeal, tell the world how we were treated," Porky responded glumly.

"But if we're all dead, wouldn't that prove we were treated badly?"

Sam had had enough. "Jesus Christ, enough of this. I'd like to know what the frigging hell is really going on."

With that, the men scattered and wandered off to join another cluster of men, who were debating just as hotly what was up. But as the morning wore on, they were getting hungry. Men filtered into the mess hall, and some wandered into the kitchen. As they had begun to suspect, if they wanted to eat, they'd have to prepare the grub themselves. Having worked at the kitchen at Cabanatuan, Porky was about to volunteer when a tall blond Swede came rushing in. For a second, Porky was reminded of his long-lost buddy, Pint

Lawson, who might be dead for all he knew. "Hey guys, guess what? They want us to make a giant POW sign on the roof," the young man blurted out. "Any volunteers?"

Porky abandoned the kitchen to others more focused on eating and rushed outside to scout out where the Japs might have stored paint cans. He wanted to be the one who painted the sign, but there was a crush of volunteers with the same thought in mind. One man began to climb a ladder and was followed up by a balding lieutenant, who made an announcement.

"Men, we've found the paint cans," he shouted. "Thanks for volunteering, but I don't want any of you to break your necks. We've got matters in hand. Hey, Johnson, Smith, Riley, Springer," he shouted to a few friends below. "Quit chewing the rag. I need your sweat up here on the roof. We'll hand you the paint from below."

On August 14, following the atomic bombing raids on Nagasaki and Hiroshima the previous week, Japan capitulated and President Truman declared a two-day holiday to celebrate America's victory over Japan. The following day, the Japanese listened in shock as they heard their emperor's voice for the first time. Hirohito announced, in a radio broadcast, the end of hostilities and ordered cooperation with occupying forces. Several days later, a special military and diplomatic envoy was flown to Gen. Douglas MacArthur's Manila headquarters in the Philippines to receive Allied instructions concerning surrender arrangements.

From August 28 through September 2, the Allied forces staged amphibious landings in Tokyo Bay. Demolition experts checked potential landing areas to ensure that Japanese fortifications had been neutralized. Marine and sailor landing parties came ashore and destroyed small arms held by the enemy forces, such as rifles, light field guns, and other weapons. The occupation of Japan had begun. Strategic positions were quickly established and the U.S. Army airborne forces began aerial reconnaissance to scout out POW camps for eventual liberation.

By August 28, conditions at the POW compound had not changed significantly. Around noontime, the men wandered around outside or in the barracks, chatting or resting, grateful there was enough rice left to feed them and wondering if they would ever be rescued. Then out of the blue the sound of approaching airplanes brought everyone to their feet and outside to scan the sky as the sound grew louder and louder. Four navy pursuit planes appeared over the mountains and made a dive toward the camp. The men

Aerial view of Niigata, Japan prisoner of war camps
Courtesy National Archives

ducked, then just as suddenly the planes climbed high and put on a fancy air show. There were loop de loops and dives. They leveled off in formation, then broke formation to fly in a giant circle. The men broke out in loud cheers and tossed their hats in the air.

The planes broke out of the circle and flew closer. Doors were opened, but instead of parachutists, navy bags popped out and sprouted parachutes that gently drifted downward toward the compound. Each bag was filled with magazines, hard candy, candy bars, and cigarettes. As the planes took off, the men rushed toward the packages. The lieutenant once again stepped forward.

"I'll take charge of the bags," he shouted, stepping next to a supply shed. "Just bring them over here. No crowding, men. There's enough here for everyone."

Porky tried to push his way in but was crushed up against too many other POWs, so he tried to push his way back out. "Hey, this is just a sample. Now that they've found us, I'm sure there'll be lots more," he said to a man beating a similar retreat.

The lieutenant opened a sack filled with magazines and pulled them out one by one.

"Here's a *Life* magazine, and here's a *Time*," the lieutenant shouted, handing the magazines out to outstretched hands. "Pictures from home," he continued. "See what's been happening back home."

Before long the bags were emptied, the candy and cigarettes distributed, and whoever had grabbed himself a magazine was now surrounded by a dozen or more men straining to see. Pages were quickly flipped, searching for photos of food, but whoever was holding the magazine paused at the photos of smiling stylishly dressed women so that his fellow readers might gawk and dream for a moment. Sam grabbed a *Saturday Evening Post* while Porky went searching for his old-time favorite—a *National Geographic*.

"What would you want this thing for?" one unfortunate man asked, who was more than happy to pass it over to Porky.

"The pictures," Porky said, wolfing down a Hershey bar as he fumbled through the pages. "Hey, I've been gypped. Where are the native girls?" he spouted off to Leo.

"I'm afraid they're all prisoners of war," Leo replied soberly, sucking on a Tootsie Roll.

Sam grabbed the magazine and flipped through quickly. "Wow. Look at this."

"What?" Porky asked, peering over his shoulder. "Was an American city bombed?"

"I have no idea, but look at that cake," he said, flipping the page around so that Porky and Leo could see.

"Aw, forget the cake. Is there a picture of rhubarb pie?" Porky asked.

Sam flipped through the magazine, looking for photos of food as the others looked on.

"This is worse than torture," Leo agonized. "I want real food, not pictures of food."

Noontime the next day, men were seated on the bay reading magazines; others were outside, smoking or just lounging about. Once again, the sound of American planes brought everyone to their feet and outdoors, scanning the sky. Four navy planes appeared from the east and began an air show. Suddenly, they climbed to a very high altitude as the deafening sound of an enormous plane was heard approaching. It was the men's first glimpse of the B-29, the Superfortress that had been used to drop incendiary bombs over Tokyo and other Japanese cities. The plane appeared up over the trees about five hundred feet above the ground. It looked like a flying battleship to the men.

15079 Over Japan: PW Camp Ashio #1 36-38'N 139-25'E 45/09/05

Aerial view of Ashio prisoner of war camp #1, September 6, 1945
Courtesy National Archives

"Jesus Christ Almighty," Leo exclaimed.

"God, what the hell is that?" Porky echoed as his heart beat wildly, frightened at the specter.

Some of the men drew back as a giant shadow crawled on the ground. The bomber followed the course of the river, passed the POW camp, and disappeared.

"I wonder why . . . ? Leo began.

"What the hell is happening?" Porky said, suddenly frightened.

"That was strange," Sam said, screwing up his face as he scanned the sky. "Look. Look up above," he said, pointing straight up. "Look. The navy planes are still up there. They must have known the ship was coming. Why else would they move to such a high altitude?"

"Well, they're not descending," Porky observed. "So maybe that flying battleship is coming back."

A scrawny POW standing nearby joined the discussion. "Maybe it's going to pick us up."

"But how?" Porky asked. "Where's it going to land? We're on the side of a mountain."

The sound of the flying battleship grew louder. "It's headed back," Porky yelled. He shielded his eyes from the glare of the sun as it shone off the tail of the plane. "Jesus Christ, is that a big sucker."

Leo was growing more anxious by the minute. "Yeah, it's almost scary. Are you sure it's American?"

Porky was insistent. "I saw a flag."

Leo disagreed. "I only saw camouflage."

As the jumbo plane approached, Porky pointed upward. "See. It's an American flag."

Just then the bomb bays opened, dropping its payload.

"Jesus Christ, will you look at those parachutes. There's got to be hundreds."

"So what are we waiting for?" Sam slapped them on the back to get going as he made a dash toward the cargo drop.

POW Camp Fukuoka. Supplies were dropped at every prisoner of war camp across Japan. Courtesy National Archives

The supply crates landed about a hundred feet outside the compound. All hell broke loose as the entire company of POWs rushed forward, sprinted out past the opened gate, and encircled the crates entangled with nylon parachutes and lines tied securely to each crate. Without thought, they pried them open with their bare hands, and their efforts were rewarded. Each crate was filled with gallon cans of meat, veggies, fruit, beans, plus bags of candy, cigarettes, and gum. Dozens of men too weak to participate stood back and watched. Several had tears streaming down the sunken features of their cadaverous faces.

"Why, there's so much food and cigarettes here we could live like kings for a month!" Porky shouted, laughed, and grabbed his friends around the shoulders in a gesture more reminiscent of his high school football days than the past forty-two months they'd spent in captivity. "What more could a guy ask for?"

The men headed toward the kitchen, carrying as much as they could handle. Many of the cans were damaged and leaking from the airdrop. As they sorted through the cans, all broken cans were opened immediately. There were several 250-gallon pots in the kitchen. Meat and beans and veggies went into one pot, and the fruit went into the other pot. All of the rest was stacked in the kitchen, except for the food and cigarettes some men stashed away in their pockets. Coffee, tea, and sugar were set in one pile, Spam and beef in another, and various cheeses in a separate area. The cigarettes were displayed on an open shelf easily accessible to all. Soon, the fires were lit and the stew began to simmer as the men lined up to gorge themselves. Before long, their mess kits were filled to overflowing and they wandered back to the barracks to eat. After stuffing themselves, they returned and refilled their mess kits with more food. This continued for several hours. As the sun set over Ashio Mountain, men were still wandering back into the kitchen to sample more food. Others wanted nothing more than to relax and settle back with candy bars and cigarettes.

At midmorning on August 31, Porky approached one of his former guards and asked if he would scout out some paper and a pencil so he could write home. The guard returned a short while later with cheap yellow gum-seal paper and a short stub of a pencil the interpreter felt he could spare from a drawer in the infirmary. Porky accepted the items with a bow, telling the guard to be sure to thank the interpreter for him. He then made his way back to the barracks to stash the writing supplies with his belongings.

When he stepped back outside, the jarring noise from a flying Superfortress signaled its arrival, and it soon appeared over the trees. A second load of crates was soon parachuted to a spot outside the compound. As before, the men rushed forward to pry open the crates and gather the canned goods and packages. Some they grabbed for themselves, some to share as they had days earlier, while other goods were set aside for the kitchen. After the commotion died down, Porky scouted around the camp looking for the interpreter. He found him talking to a group of POWs outside the kitchen, impeccably dressed in a white linen suit and black tie.

"Say, could I have a word with you?"

The interpreter excused himself and walked over to talk with Porky in private.

"I want you to find my honcho," Porky began. "You know the one, the villager who had the sick kid."

"Ah, the one with the boy you cured with American medicine you saved for yourself," the interpreter said as he looked into Porky's eyes.

Porky blushed. "I have something I want to give him."

"I will do what I can," the interpreter said, then turned and walked out of the compound and headed toward the village.

Porky headed to the supply depot, grabbed two empty navy bags that had been tossed from the American planes, and then walked back to the barracks. He was stuffing his overcoat, coveralls, and suntans into one of the bags as Sam approached.

"LaCoste, what the hell are you doing? Packing to go home?"

"Don't I wish!"

"So what are you doing?"

"I felt like that honcho with the kid treated me as good as we could be treated, so I want to give him some food and clothes and some candy and cigarettes. I bet he could use some Spam and cheese too. What do you think?"

"He was a great guy. He always did what we wanted."

Several men who overheard the conversation joined in, grabbing whatever they felt they could spare and dumping the items into oversize knapsacks. Before long, both bags were filled to the top with clothing and food. They carried the bags outside, sat on the grass to have a smoke and wait. Finally, the interpreter returned, accompanied by their honcho, who was carrying a "yo-yo" stick—a pole used to carry items at each end. Porky and Sam stood in greeting. The villager smiled and bowed to Porky.

"Pokey, Pokey, *arigato,* thank you."

The men hoisted the overloaded bags onto the ends of the stick. The villager bowed again and then attempted to lift the yo-yo stick, now weighted down by the bags. Porky and Sam stood at either end and helped lift the stick up onto the villager's shoulders. It was a heavy load, but once balanced, it was bearable.

"Arigato, thank you," he said, then turned to walk back to the gate accompanied by the interpreter, who waved him through. Porky felt positively upbeat as he set out for the kitchen. But after supper, a depression set in as bitter memories of beatings, hunger, and despair flooded over him. When he returned to the barracks, he remembered his earlier plan to write home. He grabbed the yellow paper and pencil, lit a cigarette to relax, and began to write, using a *Time* magazine as a writing board.

"I don't know how to start this letter or just what to say," he wrote to his mother.

> It's been so long, since I've been able or been in a position to do this the way I wanted to, that I'm in a fog.
>
> Since we've known the war was over, I have mailed two cards to you and this is the first letter. The reason I haven't written sooner is because I haven't been able to obtain any paper from these rotten, slant eyed XXXs. I was very lucky even to get this piece of paper and envelope this afternoon. Paper is as scarce as 1946 automobiles are at home right now.
>
> I have just eaten supper and that makes three American meals we have eaten today. A few days ago, Army and Navy planes dropped us food, tobacco, magazines and candy. Everyone was so happy the roof of the barracks almost came off when the first shouts were let out. I have never seen a sight like that before. When a few of the packages were opened, the men started walking about the compound telling friends about what there was in the boxes, and I wish that you could have seen it. Many of them I believe still doubt it.
>
> It has been 16 days that we have been lying around now, and I have gained eleven pounds. I lost about 35 pounds the first ten days as a prisoner, and this is the first time I have shown any signs of getting back to normal. However, when I return, and the first time you see me, I think I will still be and look like the same boy that left home in 1940—except maybe a little fatter around the middle.
>
> Some of the magazines we received had stories about prison life in them so I won't waste any space in trying to tell you about some of it. I also hope that you have saved many papers and magazines, as I intend to do lots of reading when I get back, so as to know what took place in the last four years. I feel as though ten years have passed instead of four.

Porky put down his letter to join a buddy who had rushed into the barracks to shout that a radio had been set up in the kitchen to keep the men updated on the latest developments. When Porky returned to his task, he continued, "Just now received news from Tokyo that September 1 all prisoners of war enter in the regular status of the United States service and so this is the last time I will write POW on my mail, and I hope that—" Just then, he was interrupted again by friends who were hotly debating merits of the latest rumors about when they would be released. The evening's sunset was glorious—all pink and salmon, with a vibrancy he had never noticed before. Porky went back to his writing, finished with endearments, and signed, sealed, and addressed the letter just as the interpreter entered the barracks and approached.

"Your honcho has returned. He's at the gate and wants to see you." Porky handed the letter to the interpreter to post and accompanied him to the gate where his Japanese friend stood holding a plate with a small melon and two small potatoes.

"Your honcho wants to reciprocate. He has come with gifts."

Porky was profoundly moved by the gesture. He bowed deeply and accepted the plate. Fresh produce was more precious than money and would be a delicious addition to his diet of canned items. But this time he would insist that he was the one who got to eat the potato.

"You didn't need to do this, but thanks, thanks." Tears welled up in Porky's eyes. He wanted to give the guy a big hug but smiled instead. The interpreter, who remained quite formal, relayed his message back to the honcho. Porky stood by the interpreter's side and watched his gentle friend walk up the mountain road. As the sun set and the moon appeared on the horizon, his small figure gradually disappeared as he crossed to the path that led to the village, his dear wife, and little son. No, this man was not the enemy. The enemy was the power that compels men to do evil and those who willingly comply.

POWs evacuated from Ashio POW Camp
Courtesy National Archives

14046 Home made flag exhibited by POWs who have been evacuated from Ashio Camp, 90 miles west of Yokohama.

Chapter 38

At twilight the next morning, before the full company of former POWs awoke, a small but significant ceremony was performed. A U.S. Navy lieutenant gathered a dozen or so men to accompany him to the gate. There the Japanese guards, two officers, and the commander had assembled. Commander Sato gave an order, and one by one, the Japanese guards handed their weapons over to the Americans.

As the weapons were collected, the lieutenant's thoughts strayed to one particular moment at twilight two years earlier. He was onboard a battle-worn submarine as it surfaced off the Malay coast to attack a Japanese merchant ship. Instead, it was strafed by a Japanese plane. The men began burning confidential documents as the sub sank and then abandoned ship. The enemy was convinced that the Americans held military secrets that were of vital importance to the Imperial Navy. The lieutenant recalled how the Japanese rescuers meted out particularly harsh treatment to the officers who survived the blast. They were eventually separated, then passed from POW camp to POW camp.

Now the tables were reversed, but it was not his place to mete out revenge but to return to an order based on international law and laws established under the U.S. Constitution. Once the rifles were collected, the ex-POWs turned back to the lieutenant, who stood at attention on behalf of the United States and its allies. Imperial Japanese Army Commander Sato and his officers bowed in surrender, and the gathering of American soldiers, sailors, and marines handed over the enemy's weapons to the American lieutenant.

Later that morning, the lieutenant entered the barracks. Men were lounging around, eating, and chatting. Many had regained weight as well as strength; some were even boisterous. *Before long*, he thought, *they'll look like your average red-blooded American GIs.* But still, there were men lying prostrate in sick bay who needed to be rescued—and pronto! They needed immediate medical attention. He cleared his throat for an important announcement.

"Men, gather your things. We're moving out in the afternoon. A special train will be arriving from Tokyo, and we'll all be moving out."

The announcement was met by a cheer so loud it was a wonder the roof didn't cave in, he thought. Jack, a fellow Navy man, approached.

"So this is it. We're going home. We're finally going home."

The lieutenant squeezed his arm. "That's right. We're finally going home. Pack your bags, sailor. And that's an order!" The lieutenant turned on his heels and quickly left the barracks, afraid he would dissolve in emotion.

14044 POWs being evacuated from Ashio camp, 90 miles west of Yokohama. These men have been working in copper mines.

Rescue train leaving Ashio.
Courtesy National Archives

The men scrambled to pack, gathering all they could carry. Porky borrowed a chapter from his experiences back at Cabanatuan. He made bags out of his suntan pant legs and filled them to the top with canned goods, candy, cigarettes, cheese, and other items. The men then lined up and marched out of the compound, over the five-foot-wide bridge, and back onto the main road leading into Ashio. But this time, they weren't headed to the cog tramcars but waited at the main station, with its wide platform and wooden overhang, for a special train that had been sent up from Tokyo. After a while, the train arrived and the men lined up to get onboard. But the long faces and fear in their eyes had long since passed and were replaced with smiles as they climbed onboard—except for Leo.

"What is wrong with you? Did you eat too much?"

"No. It's just that you're all going home to someone. I have no one." "What do you mean? You got a package, don't you remember? You got it while we were at Bilibid—just before we boarded the ship to go to Japan."

Leo looked even more downcast. "Yeah, I got a package, but who was it from?"

"It had your name on it. Someone knows you're here. Besides, how do I know my family's still alive? It's been almost five years since I left. My Grandma Rose is quite old. She could be dead by now. None of us knows what we're walking into. Some of these guys are married. Their wives could have run off."

Leo brightened. "You know, Porky, you sure know how to cheer a guy up."

"You're a rugged guy," Porky said, patting him on the back and gesturing for him to get onboard before him. "I have a feeling you're going to be rich and famous."

"Yeah, rich and famous," Leo repeated as he maneuvered onto a seat. He dropped his gear onto the floor of the car and Porky slid in beside him, perching his suntan suitcase on his lap.

"Let's see—as a private, you'll get thirty-one dollars a month times forty-two. Hm, that's over $1,300."

"And as a corporal, you get sixty-four dollars a month. You're the one who is going to be rich."

Porky chuckled at the thought of the wealth that waited once he got home. "Look, Leo, you're going to be rich enough. As a matter of fact, I bet you'll be so rich that the girls will be crawling all over you."

"I doubt it," he replied, looking out the window as the rest of the men moved on to the next car to board.

"Leo, you are a war hero, wake up. You are a big shot. It's time you learned to act like one."

Once the former prisoners of war were onboard, the Japanese contingent was placed in the last car. Americans now guarded both the front and back doors of the train. As the train pulled out, not one Japanese villager or Korean was in sight. The men relaxed as the locomotive descended into the valley below, through farm country along the Watarase River ravine. Every now and then they passed isolated groups of Japanese villagers, who stood not far from the tracks to watch the train go by. Their clothes were shabby and they looked gaunt and hungry. These were victims of their emperor's hubris, not perpetrators of war crimes.

Children clutched their mothers' legs as the whistle of the steam engine sounded the train's approach. The villagers waved as they passed. But Porky was shaken by their appearance.

"God, do they look hungry," Porky said, then turned to Leo. "Let's trade seats. I want to sit by the window."

"What the—," Leo began. But it was too late. Porky was already crawling over him to open the window.

"Look. I want to help these folks out. Hey, I don't need this stuff. We're going to a place where there'll be plenty."

Porky untied one pant leg and then the other of his suntan trousers and began tossing items out every time he spotted a small gathering of bedraggled Japanese. Soon the zeal of his mission caught on. A whole carload of reinvigorated GIs joined in. One by one, the former prisoners lowered the windows and began tossing out food and candy bars and cigarettes for the natives, who scrambled to retrieve them. But when the train approached Tokyo, there were no more Japanese in sight, and the train came to a sudden stop. After a few seconds, it went in reverse. The men grew silent and fearful.

"Oh my God! Don't tell me we are going back," Leo blurted out, daring to say what the others feared.

"What is this, a cruel joke?" Porky barked out.

The train stopped with a jolt. Lieutenant Hardy rose from his seat to address the men.

"Calm down, men. The war really is over and you are going home," the lieutenant began. "All that's happening is the crew is changing the old steam engine for a more modern engine. We're going to the Tokyo railroad station nearest the harbor. From there, God knows what's going to happen. All I know is we're all going home."

That said, the train started up again and lurched forward. Soon after, they arrived at the railroad station, which was completely boarded up. As they disembarked, they were led through a hastily constructed tunnel. Sam hurried to catch up to Porky and Leo.

"I wonder why it's all boarded up," Sam commented as he peeked through the cracks. What he saw peering back were eyeballs. "People are staring at us," he said, jumping back.

Unable to resist, Porky peeked too. "You're right," he said, hurrying to catch up with the crowd. "I guess they want to see us, but whoever's in charge doesn't want them to see us."

"Or attack us," Leo blurted out. "Jesus, this is creepy."

An attractive army nurse greeted the men at the end of the tunnel. She stood in front of a redbrick building handing out cigarettes and candy. As they entered the building, they were met by army officers who led them to a room with a large sign overhead, "Delousing Unit." The men were instructed to strip and shower with special chemicals, scrub down, and shave. That task completed, the naked men were led to another room and instructed to form a line and wait outside.

"What's this about?" Leo asked.

"Do we want to know?" Porky responded but was relieved when they were handed clean uniforms and led into an adjoining room to dress. Once properly outfitted, they exited to the outside and gathered to wait for further instructions.

"After you leave here," the lieutenant began, "you're going to that big boat over there." He pointed to a large vessel. "It's an English ship where you'll get supper. Once onboard, go to the kitchen dining area. Before you leave the ship, you'll receive further instructions."

After boarding the English ship, the anticipation of sitting down to the first decent meal since the war began quickly faded. The recently rescued were treated to porridge and bread minus the butter. Now, a true Scot prefers his rolled-oat porridge with a sprinkle of salt where the English prefer it with a bit of sugar or honey and a spot of milk. But dairy products were not offered, and these red-blooded Americans would have none of it.

"Hey, where's the butter?" Leo shouted.

"Rations, mate, all's we 'ave left is rations," the cook explained in a thick Cockney accent.

"We ate better back at the prison camp," Porky hyperbolized.

An English sailor with a mouthful of porridge pushed away from the table, swallowed, and sauntered over to a nearby porthole and pointed with the crook of his thumb. "See that boat out there, docked at the harbor?" The men looked out the porthole. "They're feeding the Americans over there."

"You mean they're feeding them real food?" Porky asked, oblivious to the insult he had just hurled.

"If that's what you call it," the man retorted.

"What are we waiting for guys," Porky said to his associates. "Let's go."

The Americans were soon outside, hiking over to the gangplank of a ship flying Old Glory, and scrambled onboard. Before long, they spotted a long line of men and took up the rear.

"Do you smell what I smell?" Porky said, inhaling deeply. "I must have died and gone to heaven."

"Bacon—mouthwatering bacon!" Leo exclaimed in exaggerated ecstasy.

"Oh, and home fries," another said, closing his eyes and breathing deeply. "This is worth waiting for."

After stuffing themselves with eggs, bacon, home fries drowned in ketchup, and cup after cup of freshly brewed coffee, the men sauntered back to the first building by the tunnel. The sky was an intense blue, and a mild breeze was blowing off the water. They were well fed and full of hope as an army private directed them to the interrogation room where they would be debriefed. It was time to give their name, rank, and serial number to military personnel who were assigned to fill in the gaps between when the war started to the date they were rescued.

The interrogation room was filled with army and navy personnel seated at desks. Next to each desk was a chair on which sat an American GI, leaning in as he answered a dozen or more questions that were shot at him. Before long, an Army WAC pointed to Porky, "GI, you're next."

Porky quickly moved to the assigned desk, where a short-haired brunette, trim and pert in her WAC uniform, sat writing on a manila file folder. As he sat, she looked up without a smile and asked, "What's your name?"

She's much too stern for me, Porky thought, *though she's pretty enough*. "Franklin J. LaCoste," he said with a smile, hoping she'd warm up to him if he warmed up to her.

"Outfit," she asked coolly.

"Twenty-seventh material," he said as a sharp pain struck in the area of his kidneys.

"The next question has to do with—"

But before the Army WAC completed her sentence, Porky passed out and collapsed onto the floor. When he woke, he was on a cot in the back of

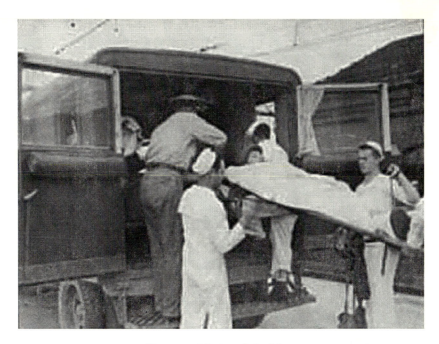

Courtesy National Archives

a panel truck with ten other GIs. A captain and a snub-nosed, red-headed nurse were in attendance. Before long they arrived at the airfield and scouted out a plane with a pilot and crew dozing beneath. Porky sat up, shook himself until his vision cleared, and climbed out of the truck along with the others. The nurse pulled Porky to one side to check his pulse.

"Don't worry. I'm OK now—especially with a good-looking nurse like you to hold my hand."

The nurse dropped his wrist and rolled her eyes. "My guess is, you're doing better," she said, trying not to smile. She shook down the thermometer and stuck it in his mouth, just as he started to say, "Can't blame a guy for trying." She put her finger on his pulse and concentrated on her watch as Porky studied the freckles on her cheeks. Finally, she looked up and pulled the thermometer out to check. "You're better, but we still need to get you to a hospital. We're flying you and the others out to be treated."

The captain tucked his head under the belly of the plane. "Lieutenant, lieutenant," he shouted to wake the pilot. The pilot opened his bloodshot eyes and stared blankly at the captain as the crew snored on, oblivious. "I need you to fly these men out," he said, handing him an envelope. "Your instructions are in the letter."

"I'm not flying this thing," the pilot responded, as adamant as the captain was insistent. "This plane hasn't been checked for God knows how long. It's not fit to fly."

The captain reached for his pistol. "I'm not asking you. I'm ordering you. These men here are emergency cases."

"You can order all you want. Not me. I'm not flying this damned plane. It hasn't been checked for five hundred hours."

The captain drew his pistol and pointed it at the pilot and crew, who were now fully awake and beginning to grasp the situation.

"These are special orders from General MacArthur. Take them to Okinawa tonight."

"No, Captain, I don't care if you threaten me."

At that, the captain scooted under the plane and pushed the cold steel barrel of the Commando revolver against the man's sweaty forehead. "I want these men boarded now. You are flying to Okinawa."

The lieutenant finally understood the captain's order and scrambled with his crew to prepare for flight. Porky and the rest of the ailing GIs boarded with the nurse as the crew unloaded boxes of food and medicine from the truck and hauled them onboard the plane. Shortly into the flight, Porky began to feel sick again. Sitting up was too painful and standing was impossible. The nurse gently assisted him into the middle of the aisle and hooked up a portable oxygen tank. There he rested, stretched out and breathing comfortably, grateful he was headed back to civilization, as the potential gravity of his situation finally sunk in. The plane made its final circle before landing just as Porky managed to sit up. The nurse unhooked the apparatus and allowed him to breathe on his own.

Kadena Air Base in Okinawa was to serve as their layover and refueling depot before they headed on to Manila. The airfield had been captured by the Americans on April Fools' Day but was in dire need of upgrading. But first, the seventy-mile-long island needed to be secured. The battle to take Okinawa had been particularly fierce. Since the start of the war, American forces had experienced kamikazes, and antishipping swimmers had been utilized in the waters near Iwo Jima. At Okinawa, the Allied forces encountered suicide attacks on a whole different level. Here were *Kikusui* (Floating Chrysanthemums)—massed suicide air strikes—against the British Pacific Fleet. Here, 450,000 Army and Marine Corps personnel landed to engage 130,000 Japanese Army troops entrenched in concealed positions and caves. What ensued proved to be the largest amphibious campaign in the Pacific, the largest battle of the campaign, and the bloodiest. Hostilities lasted from late March to June

1945. And though Japanese organized resistance had officially ended in July, Kadena had been the focus of attention only days earlier when documents were signed there that brought the Battle of Okinawa to an official close.

But for the former POWs fresh out of Tokyo, the Okinawa airfield was a sight to behold. Massive reconstruction had transformed the base into a major airfield. Thousands of aircraft of various sizes and shapes sported colorful insignias, cartoons, and signs. It was a whole new world, full of vibrancy and activity. But the best was yet to come. They were treated like heroes in the mess hall—served real meat, red, juicy meat and all they could eat—and they were served before the GIs so they would be sure to have their pick. The next day when they boarded the plane to fly to Manila, the nurse handed Porky the oxygen mask, but this time he was able to make it on his own, belted down and seated.

At Manila, the men were brought into a large mess hall where the Japanese prisoners served as cooks and waiters. But rather than enjoying the fact that the tables were now turned, Porky was disturbed by the sight and began to flash back to the worst moments of his internment.

"Let's get away from these sons of bitches," he said, turning to one of the men who had accompanied him on the flight. "We've been their prisoners for years. I don't want anything more to do with them."

Porky exited the mess hall and went straight to the officer on duty, who arranged to have a meal brought to him. He had been on an emotional high since the end of the war, and now he was starting to crash. As he sat in the hallway, picking at his food, a lieutenant approached.

"Corporal, I've got some good news and some bad news. Which do you want to hear first?"

Porky was in a funk. "Give me the bad news."

"OK. There's not a plane around we can trust to fly to the States." Porky was shocked. All he wanted was to go home. "The good news is there's a boat—a brand-spanking-new ship, and the captain and crew are determined to try and set a record nonstop to 'Frisco. Not only that, onboard there's someone on duty twenty-four hours a day to prepare food. Anything you want, it's yours—steaks, sandwiches, macaroni and cheese, anything."

"Stop it, I'm drooling," Porky said with a laugh.

"You can eat ten times a day, if that's what you want."

September 2, 1945—The Japanese surrender documents are signed by General MacArthur onboard the USS Missouri in Tokyo Bay as 1,000 carrier-based planes fly overhead; President Truman declares VJ Day.
Courtesy Department of Defense

Chapter 39

Today the guns are silent. A great tragedy has ended.
A great victory has been won . . .
General Douglas MacArthur,
Supreme Allied Commander

Porky made it to San Francisco. There he learned that what few records the military had on him were lost once again. He was reinterrogated, but this time with better results. He remained conscious throughout the interview. Afterward, the men lined up and boarded a shuttle bus to the hospital. After the man ahead of him entered and turned to the left to be seated, Porky looked up to see a woman dressed in a dark blue uniform and cap seated in the driver's seat.

"I'm not riding with a woman driver," he said to the man in back.

The driver glared down at Porky. "Soldier, you get in here and pronto. What do you think we gals have been doing while you guys were off to war? Sitting on our hands? No, siree, we've been working."

With that, Porky boarded the bus and kept his mouth shut for the ride. "Not bad, for a woman," he quipped as he stepped off onto the sidewalk.

General MacArthur had written special orders to ship the POWs who were sick or injured to the hospital nearest their families. After a thorough examination, it was determined that Porky needed an operation to remove kidney stones and would have to wait a few days before he could be flown home. The next day word came that the men would be brought by bus to Seals Stadium to see the San Francisco Giants play against the St. Louis Browns.

Pete Gray, the one-armed outfielder, was in the lineup. Porky boarded the bus wearing his hospital greens. When he got to the stadium and stood in line, waiting to go in, the crowd of strangers talking and laughing and going about their lives made him feel out of place. Of course, the guys who had flown back with him were there too, but he wasn't friends with any of them. They weren't part of the old crowd.

"Hey, Frenchy, let's cut out of here and see the town," Tom said. He had been held prisoner closer to Tokyo and had witnessed the firebombing.

"Great idea, but let's wait 'til we're inside. We don't want one of our wardens to catch on that we're missing," he said, referring to the hospital staff assigned to accompany the men back and forth to the game. The two let the others push into the interior of the bleacher and they sat on the outside.

"Strike three!" the empire hollered, and the crowd stood and booed. It was a perfect moment to escape. Porky and Tom stood with the crowd, then walked up the steps of the bleacher and out the side door. The crowd was still screaming by the time they made it down to the street level and out of the stadium. They slipped into the first bar they came across.

"Hey, you guys medics?" the bartender asked.

"No, patients. We're just back from Jap prison camps."

"Drinks are on the house."

A man seated at the bar handed them his pack of Lucky Strikes. "Here, take these," he said, getting up to buy another pack at the cigarette machine.

Porky and Tom smoked and downed a few beers. "Thanks, guys. This is our first night on the town since before the war, and the night is young," Porky explained as they prepared to leave. Tom shouted, "Adios, amigos!" Moments later they were back out on the street, scouting out the next barroom.

After a few more pit stops, they came to an entertainment area awash in bright festival colors, with sparkling lights that blinked on and off and loud carnival music. Inside, soldiers and sailors shouted, cursed, and laughed. Some played pinball while others gambled, dropping coin after coin into the slot machines, then slamming their fists into the sides to force some winnings. Tom and Porky fumbled drunkenly in their pockets, looking for change. Suddenly, two hulking men in trench coats stood in their path. They tried to move around them to get to the machines but were stopped.

"Hey, guys, having a good time?"

"Sure," Porky said, hoping that they weren't about to be rolled, but sure he'd feel no pain if they were.

"Aren't you two supposed to be in the hospital?" the other asked.

"There's nothing wrong with me," Tom said. "What about you, Frenchy?"

"Right as rain," Porky said, nodding his head drunkenly.

"How come you're dressed in hospital greens? Shouldn't you be back on base?"

"Where do you get off?" Porky wanted to know.

The muscle men flipped open the top flap on their trench coats and discretely displayed three items. Each had a holstered gun, a badge, and handcuffs.

"Time to go back to the hospital, fellas. They've got to patch you up and get you back home."

A late-model sedan was parked outside the door to the establishment. Their escorts opened the passenger door and pulled the seat back. Porky and Tom slipped into the back, and the officers handed them a couple of blankets to ward off the early evening chill. As the car rolled into traffic, Tom and Porky fell sound asleep. They were out cold from exhaustion, booze, and the lingering effects of years of starvation and ill treatment. When they arrived back at the hospital, the officers got a couple of aides to help move them onto stretchers and back into their hospital rooms where they were put into bed for the night.

The next evening, Porky was on post, enjoying a movie in the theater compound when his name was called out on the loudspeaker.

"Corp. Franklin LaCoste, please report to the lobby."

Porky bolted out the door, not knowing what to expect, and made his way to the theater lobby. There, to his amazement, was his first cousin, Walter Porter, from Athol, standing with his cousin from California, Irene Fox.

"Porky," Irene called and ran to him. She burst into tears as they embraced.

"Irene, Walter," he said, shaking Walter's hand. "I can't believe my eyes."

"Hey, there's a couch. You two sit and play catch-up, I'll get some Cokes," Walter said, then headed off toward the concession stand.

Before long, the cousins were so immersed in conversation they barely noticed when the crowd left the theater and the concession stand was shut down for the evening. Finally, a janitor approached, sorry he had to kick them out. Irene and Walter linked arms with Porky and walked him back to the hospital lobby where they kissed him and said goodbye for now. His mother and grandmother and uncle were all fine and could barely wait to see him again. Yes, he hadn't changed a bit. He still had his boyish good looks and charm, Irene assured him as she hugged him one more time. Porky barely spoke of Bataan and his stay in prison camps. For the most part, he decided, he would keep his thoughts to himself. Why dwell on what he couldn't change? Besides, the world that he had so recently escaped from was so far outside of their reality, they would never understand, he realized as he walked the corridor back to his hospital room plagued by memories of departed friends.

The next day, he was on a plane bound for home, with two more stops. One of them was in Cincinnati, Ohio, where armed guards watched over the latest super-bomber that had tires taller than Porky. From Cincinnati, he flew to Bedford Army Air Base in Massachusetts and then was driven with other New England servicemen to Fort Devens, about thirty miles from his home. There, at a base hospital, he was operated on and remained for a month until he recovered. The surgeon took out one very large kidney stone but left in two smaller ones he felt weren't worth digging after and risking an infection. After surgery came the shocker—a surprise even to the surgeon. Porky had only one kidney and was ineligible for the service. He was 4F! He enjoyed telling that to his grandmother when she arrived for a visit with his aunt Yvonne. When his grandmother entered his hospital room, they took one look at one another and their eyes filled with tears.

"Grandma . . ." He could barely get out the word.

"How's my good little soldier?" she managed to ask before they embraced.

"Doing just fine," he choked out.

"I baked a little something for you."

The old woman plunked down her black handbag on the bedside table and sat on the wooden folding chair next to his bed. His aunt sat by his foot.

"Aw, Grandma . . . ," he said as Rosanna opened a Christmas candy tin now filled with cookies.

His grandmother and aunt alternately smiled, cried, and chatted happily as they watched Porky eat cookie after cookie. By a miracle, her precious grandson had returned and would never again stray far from her watchful gaze—that is, if she had anything to do with it!

After he arrived home and settled back in, Porky picked up a job at the post office. A few weeks later, Pint arrived back home. One afternoon after Thanksgiving, they ran into one another on Main Street and dropped into the Rexall drugstore for a soda.

"She's interested. I know she's interested. Look, there's no harm in dropping by. We're having a get-together tomorrow after church. The family, a few relatives, some friends," Pint coaxed.

"Hey, don't make a big deal out of it. Oh brother—I wish I hadn't brought the subject up."

Porky was embarrassed. It wasn't that Pint had actually promised his sister to him. Of course, the stipulation was that he would keep his nose clean—no loose women. *The war sure fixed that*, he thought. The next day, Porky considered dropping by the church the Lawson family attended in Orange, but decided against it. He didn't want to be a hypocrite. He wasn't a goody-

goody, just an average guy. He stood in front of the mirror and adjusted his tie. After his bath, he had dusted himself with the talc Bobby had bought him as a present so long ago. Bobby—the thought of him brought tears to Porky's eyes. *Help me out, buddy. You were always so good at getting the girl.*

On his way to Orange, Porky thought of picking up some roses at the shop across from the Café Royale on Exchange Street, but picked up candy instead. *A gift for the family, that's the way to do it. Nothing too obvious*, he decided. He didn't want to look too eager. Just a regular guy, a nice guy, not the wise guy his uncle used to accuse him of being way back when. *So I'm kind of short, but hell, I'm a war hero,* he thought, boosting his ego as he rang the doorbell.

Pint's sister, Helen Lawson
Courtesy LaCoste/Thurber family

Helen answered. Sunlight glistened on her blond curls as her shapely figure filled the doorway. She wore a pink top and gray skirt. *A sharp dresser*, he thought. He had never really looked at her close up, just waved at a distance when they passed on the street—so long ago—when he was a high school football jock and she was a kid. Her face was pale except for red lipstick and lightly rouged cheeks. *Hi, gorgeous*, he wanted to say. But instead he said, "Pint invited me over. Mind if I come in?"

Helen blushed, "Of course not."

"Hope you like candy," he said, handing her the box. "I thought the family might like it," he corrected himself.

For Christ's sake, this isn't a date, you ass, he thought as she brought him to the couch and asked what he'd like to drink.

"Water's fine."

"No coffee?"

"Coffee's fine too," he said with a smile.

Pint was relieved he hadn't asked for a beer. He came over, shook his hand, and sat next to him. "Athol's playing Gardner next week."

"That right?" Porky said, accepting the coffee but afraid to look at her again.

"Cream, sugar?"

"Sugar. Thanks. I like things sweet," he said, looking into her clear blue eyes. She blushed and dropped a lump into his cup, then sat demurely in an overstuffed chair adjacent to where her aunt sat discussing a recipe with a neighbor. Pint tried not to laugh.

Porky's eyes followed her every move. She was so beautiful he was transfixed. *Helen*, he thought and watched as her gray flannel skirt slipped up slightly when she twisted in the chair. Her soft pink sweater clung lightly against her breasts but hid as much as it revealed. Sweet and sexy and petite—she was everything he had ever hoped for, had ever dreamed of, and he didn't need to travel halfway round the world. She was right here in his backyard. Pint kept up his end of the small talk, and several hours later, when Porky stumbled out the door on his way home, he knew he was in love.

A week later, he dropped by to visit Bobby Doolan's mother, Eudora. She was a widow now. She had sold the Athol House Hotel and moved from her Victorian home to the Furbush Building, a four-story brick apartment building on Exchange Street near the Miller's River bridge. Her two eldest sons had families and careers, and her husband had died not long after learning of Bobby's death. Her daughter lived in Ohio and was married to the president of a bank, so she was alone with her memories and the charity work that kept her busy.

"Have a seat, Franklin. What can I get you? Coffee, soda?"

"Water is fine, Mrs. Doolan."

Porky sat on the couch as Eudora brought a pitcher of water in from the kitchen and placed it on the coffee table. "You're all settled in, I hear. And you've found yourself a job with the post office?" she asked, pouring a glass of water and popping in some ice.

"Yes. Things are working out well," he admitted, trying not to sound too happy, considering that for Bobby the fates were not as kind. "I see you've sold the business."

"Yes, not much point in keeping it."

"Well, you've got a swell place here," Porky said, looking around. So much was familiar: the photographs of Bobby as a boy and his graduation photo and a framed picture from his brief career as a soldier.

"Bobby had planned to attend the University of Manila. Had he told you?"

"Tell me? He wanted me to take classes too, but I was a high school dropout. Didn't matter, he said. 'You're a GI. You can take special classes.'"

"He wrote to ask for my permission to attend. Graduate work can be quite expensive. I wrote back and told him he had my permission if he didn't mind my calling the president of the college every week to make sure he was keeping his grades up."

Porky laughed and sipped his water. "He sure was a great guy, my very best buddy."

"You were with him when he died?"

"Yes, but he didn't suffer. It just got hard for him to eat."

"So he slipped away peacefully?"

"Very peacefully, he didn't suffer."

"And they buried him—"

"In a very beautiful spot. Palm trees and tall grass, flowers nearby. One of the most beautiful and peaceful places, now that the war's over. The mountains are nearby, and the ocean."

Eudora studied her hands for a moment, looked up, and changed the subject.

Graves of American servicemen in the Philippines
Courtesy Department of Defense

William Freeman 1940
Photo credit: Hames Photo Shop.
Courtesy Richard Chaisson

Chapter 40

One month later, Porky climbed the steps to the Athol City Hall, determined to make up to Billy for his failure to reach him before he died. He took a right and headed down the hall to the veterans' agent who was waiting for him. The day before, when he visited Billy Freeman's mother, she shared the Western Union telegram that had arrived on March 29—three years after his death.

> MRS. SARAH FREEMAN = 252 UNION ST. = I AM DEEPLY DISTRESSED TO INFORM YOU CORRECTED REPORT JUST RECEIVED STATES YOUR SON PRIVATE FIRST CLASS WILLIAM H FREEMAN WHO WAS PREVIOUSLY REPORTED MISSING IN ACTION DIED TEN JULY NINETEEN FORTYTWO IN PHILIPPINE ISLANDS AS THE RESULT OF CEREBRAL MALARIA WHILE A PRISONER OF WAR OF THE JAPANESE GOVERNMENT PERIOD THE SECRETARY OF WAR ASKS THAT I EXPRESS HIS DEEP SYMPATHY IN YOUR LOSS AND HIS REGRET THAT UNAVOIDABLE CIRCUMSTANCES MADE NECESSARY THE UNUSUAL LAPSE OF TIME IN REPORTING YOUR SON'S DEATH TO YOU CONFIRMING LETTER FOLLOWS = DUNLAP BRIGADIER GENERAL ACTING THE ADJUTANT GENERAL OF THE ARMY.

Billy's poor mother was being shafted as far as he could see, and Porky was hopping mad. She was entitled to be reimbursed for her lost son's possessions, and Porky was determined to see that she got it. The veterans' agent looked up as Porky entered, grabbed a piece of typing paper, popped up the metal bar over the rubber roll bar, and slipped the paper in. After scrolling up to the proper height, he began typing as Porky spoke:

TO WHOM IT MAY CONCERN:

This is to certify that I, Franklin J. LaCoste, 132 Swanzey St., Athol, Mass. entered service Oct. 2, 1940, and served with William H. Freeman at Fort Slocum, N.Y. until Jan. 4, 1941, went overseas with him, and was stationed at Nichols Field, Manila, P.I. from Feb. 20, 1941 to Dec. 8, 1941 and that I have personal knowledge that William Freeman had in his possession the following personally owned articles:

   Wrist watch (Elgin)
   Class ring
   Black suit (one yr. old)
   Athletic sweater
   $80 civilian clothes purchased in Philippines
   Bicycle
   Camera
   Tennis racket
   Music
   Pen and pencil set.

Porky married Helen Lawson at the Bethany Lutheran Church in Orange on April 28, 1948. Mrs. Eudora Doolan was present, along with many other family and friends. Her gift to the happy couple was a wedding card with a $50 bill enclosed. One year later Porky and Helen had their first child, a daughter they named Caryl, and later a son, Larry, was born. Porky became the superintendent of mail at the Athol post office. In 2006, after waiting 60 years, he was awarded the Purple Heart. His brother-in-law, Winston "Pint" Lawson, married and went to work for the L. S. Starrett Company and had two daughters and a son.

Herman Hausmann was released as a prisoner of war on September 25, 1945. He testified at the war crimes trials in Tokyo and became an executive board member of the defenders of Bataan and Corregidor. Herman married, had three children, and worked as a tool and die maker and piano teacher.

Porky and his firstborn, Caryl, with his grandmother Rosanna and mother, Rose.
Courtesy LaCoste/Thurber family

Herman Hausmann 1946
Photo credit: Hames Photo Shop. Courtesy Richard Chaisson

Francis Robichaud moved to California and became a lawyer. He married and had nine children.

Philip "Pinky" Dower May 1944
(Photo taken while on leave home)
Photo credit: Hames Photo Shop.
Courtesy Richard Chaisson

Pinky Dower survived the bombing of Pearl Harbor and became a pilot. By the time he was discharged at the end of the war, he was a major and had earned the Distinguished Flying Cross, an Oak Leaf Cluster, the European-African-Middle Eastern Service Medal, and the World War II Victory Medal. He also married and had children.

Billy Freeman's body was returned for burial on October 20, 1949. The train carrying his flag-draped casket made a brief stop in Greenfield before traveling on to Athol. His sweetheart had requested that she be allowed a few moments alone with the casket. Days later, the town of Athol showed up in full force for the celebration of High Mass and Billy's burial service.

On that day in late October—in the heart of football season—the men who had survived the war now stood together to bury one of their dead. As the body of Billy Freeman was lowered into the cold ground of Gethsemane Cemetery, the women cried but the men sobbed. The sound poured out loud, deep, and sustained as the emotional wounds of war tore open once again and then were closed over and laid to rest. Billy's sweetheart never imposed on his family, and their relationship remained a secret except to a chosen few. But her love endured through the decades as witnessed by the flowers that were placed year after year on his grave.

William Freeman gravesite, Gethsemane Cemetery
Courtesy G. Thomson Fraser

Bobby Doolan's remains are buried in the Philippines, not far from where he died. But if you find your way to the Silver Lake Cemetery in Athol—where people who lived in the eighteenth, nineteenth, and twentieth centuries are buried not far from their ancestors—look for a hillock across from the ancient burial chamber. There, beneath a Civil War monument, is a long gray headstone marking the burial site of members of the Pratt, Lee, Fay, and Doolan families. Near the inscription that marks the passing of his parents, Frank and Eudora Doolan, is a simple statement carved in stone:

> 1917 Sgt. Robert L., son 1942
> 3rd Pursuit Sqdn AAF
> Died at Prison Camp O'Donnell
> Philippine Islands

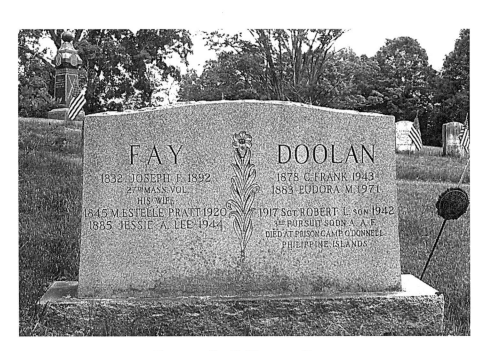

Photo credit: G. Thomson Fraser

4th of July Celebrations in Athol 1946

Marking the end of World War II

July 4, 1946 Athol Victory Parade and Fairground Celebration
Photo credits: Hames Photo Shop. Courtesy Richard Chaisson

Courtesy FDR Library and Museum

Appendix

Three Fireside Chats—Franklin D. Roosevelt

Courtesy of the Franklin D. Roosevelt
Library Digital Archives

* *FDR's On the Declaration of War with Japan—December 9, 1941*

* *FDR's Report on the Home Front—October 12, 1942*

* *FDR's State of the Union Message to Congress—January 11, 1944*

Courtesy FDR Library and Museum

On the Declaration of War with Japan

December 9, 1941

Address of the President, Broadcast from the Oval Room of the White House, Nationally and Over a World-Wide Hookup

MY FELLOW AMERICANS:

The sudden criminal attacks perpetrated by the Japanese in the Pacific provide the climax of a decade of international immorality.

Powerful and resourceful gangsters have banded together to make war upon the whole human race. Their challenge has now been flung at the United States of America. The Japanese have treacherously violated the longstanding peace between us. Many American soldiers and sailors have been killed by enemy action. American ships have been sunk; American airplanes have been destroyed.

The Congress and the people of the United States have accepted that challenge.

Together with other free peoples, we are now fighting to maintain our right to live among our world neighbors in freedom, in common decency, without fear of assault.

I have prepared the full record of our past relations with Japan, and it will be submitted to the Congress. It begins with the visit of Commodore Perry to Japan eighty-eight years ago. It ends with the visit of two Japanese emissaries to the Secretary of State last Sunday, an hour after Japanese forces had loosed their bombs and machine guns against our flag, our forces and our citizens.

I can say with utmost confidence that no Americans today or a thousand years hence, need feel anything but pride in our patience and in our efforts through all the years toward achieving a peace in the Pacific which would be fair and honorable to every nation, large or small. And no honest person, today or a thousand years hence, will be able to suppress a sense of indignation and horror at the treachery committed by the military dictators of Japan, under the very shadow of the flag of peace borne by their special envoys in our midst.

The course that Japan has followed for the past ten years in Asia has paralleled the course of Hitler and Mussolini in Europe and in Africa. Today, it has become far more than a parallel. It is actual collaboration so well calculated that all the continents of the world, and all the oceans, are now considered by the Axis strategists as one gigantic battlefield.

In 1931, ten years ago, Japan invaded Manchukuo—without warning.

In 1935, Italy invaded Ethiopia—without warning. In 1938, Hitler occupied Austria—without warning.

In 1939, Hitler invaded Czechoslovakia—without warning. Later in '39, Hitler invaded Poland—without warning. In 1940, Hitler invaded Norway, Denmark, the Netherlands, Belgium and Luxembourg—without warning.

In 1940, Italy attacked France and later Greece—without warning.

And this year, in 1941, the Axis Powers attacked Yugoslavia and Greece and they dominated the Balkans—without warning. In 1941, also, Hitler invaded Russia—without warning. And now Japan has attacked Malaya and Thailand—and the United States—without warning.

It is all of one pattern.

We are now in this war. We are all in it—all the way. Every single man, woman and child is a partner in the most tremendous undertaking of our American history. We must share together the bad news and the good news, the defeats and the victories—the changing fortunes of war.

So far, the news has been all bad. We have suffered a serious setback in Hawaii. Our forces in the Philippines, which include the brave people of that Commonwealth, are taking punishment, but are defending themselves vigorously. The reports from Guam and Wake and Midway Islands are still confused, but we must be prepared for the announcement that all these three outposts have been seized.

The casualty lists of these first few days will undoubtedly be large. I deeply feel the anxiety of all of the families of the men in our armed forces and the relatives of people in cities which have been bombed. I can only give them my solemn promise that they will get news just as quickly as possible.

This Government will put its trust in the stamina of the American people, and will give the facts to the public just as soon as two conditions have been fulfilled: first, that the information has been definitely and officially confirmed; and, second, that the release of the information at the time it is received will not prove valuable to the enemy directly or indirectly.

Most earnestly I urge my countrymen to reject all rumors. These ugly little hints of complete disaster fly thick and fast in wartime. They have to be examined and appraised.

As an example, I can tell you frankly that until further surveys are made, I have not sufficient information to state the exact damage which has been done to our naval vessels at Pearl Harbor. Admittedly the damage is serious. But no one can say how serious, until we know how much of this damage can be repaired and how quickly the necessary repairs can be made.

I cite as another example a statement made on Sunday night that a Japanese carrier had been located and sunk off the Canal Zone. And when you hear statements that are attributed to what they call "an authoritative source," you can be reasonably sure from now on that under these war circumstances the "authoritative source" is not any person in authority.

Many rumors and reports which we now hear originate, of course, with enemy sources. For instance, today the Japanese are claiming that as a result of their one action against Hawaii they have gained naval supremacy in the Pacific. This is an old trick of propaganda which has been used innumerable times by the Nazis. The purposes of such fantastic claims are, of course, to spread fear and confusion among us, and to goad us into revealing military information which our enemies are desperately anxious to obtain.

Our Government will not be caught in this obvious trap—and neither will the people of the United States.

It must be remembered by each and every one of us that our free and rapid communication these days must be greatly restricted in wartime. It is not possible to receive full and speedy and accurate reports front distant areas of combat. This is particularly true where naval operations are concerned. For in these days of the marvels of the radio it is often impossible for the Commanders of various units to report their activities by radio at all, for the very simple reason that this information would become available to the enemy and would disclose their position and their plan of defense or attack.

Of necessity there will be delays in officially confirming or denying reports of operations, but we will not hide facts from the country if we know the facts and if the enemy will not be aided by their disclosure.

To all newspapers and radio stations—all those who reach the eyes and ears of the American people—I say this: You have a most grave responsibility to the nation now and for the duration of this war.

If you feel that your Government is not disclosing enough of the truth, you have every right to say so. But in the absence of all the facts, as revealed by official sources, you have no right in the ethics of patriotism to deal out unconfirmed reports in such a way as to make people believe that they are gospel truth.

Every citizen, in every walk of life, shares this same responsibility. The lives of our soldiers and sailors—the whole future of this nation—depend upon the manner in which each and every one of us fulfills his obligation to our country.

Now a word about the recent past and the future. A year and a half has elapsed since the fall of France, when the whole world first realized the mechanized might which the Axis nations had been building up for so many years. America has used that year and a half to great advantage. Knowing that the attack might reach us in all too short a time, we immediately began greatly to increase our industrial strength and our capacity to meet the demands of modern warfare.

Precious months were gained by sending vast quantities of our war material to the nations of the world still able to resist Axis aggression. Our policy rested on the fundamental truth that the defense of any country resisting Hitler or Japan was in the long run the defense of our own country. That policy has been justified. It has given us time, invaluable time, to build our American assembly lines of production.

Assembly lines are now in operation. Others are being rushed to completion. A steady stream of tanks and planes, of guns and ships and shells and equipment—that is what these eighteen months have given us.

But it is all only a beginning of what still has to be done. We must be set to face a long war against crafty and powerful bandits. The attack at Pearl Harbor can be repeated at any one of many points, points in both oceans and along both our coast lines and against all the rest of the Hemisphere.

It will not only be a long war, it will be a hard war. That is the basis on which we now lay all our plans. That is the yardstick by which we measure what we shall need and demand; money, materials, doubled and quadrupled production—ever-increasing. The production must be not only for our own Army and Navy and air forces. It must reinforce the other armies and navies and air forces fighting the Nazis and the war lords of Japan throughout the Americas and throughout the world.

I have been working today on the subject of production. Your Government has decided on two broad policies.

The first is to speed up all existing production by working on a seven day week basis in every war industry, including the production of essential raw materials.

The second policy, now being put into form, is to rush additions to the capacity of production by building more new plants, by adding to old plants, and by using the many smaller plants for war needs.

Over the hard road of the past months, we have at times met obstacles and difficulties, divisions and disputes, indifference and callousness. That is now all past—and, I am sure, forgotten.

The fact is that the country now has an organization in Washington built around men and women who are recognized experts in their own fields. I think the country knows that the people who are actually responsible in each and every one of these many fields are pulling together with a teamwork that has never before been excelled.

On the road ahead there lies hard work—grueling work—day and night, every hour and every minute.

I was about to add that ahead there lies sacrifice for all of us.

But it is not correct to use that word. The United States does not consider it a sacrifice to do all one can, to give one's best to our nation, when the nation is fighting for its existence and its future life.

It is not a sacrifice for any man, old or young, to be in the Army or the Navy of the United States. Rather it is a privilege.

It is not a sacrifice for the industrialist or the wage earner, the farmer or the shopkeeper, the trainmen or the doctor, to pay more taxes, to buy more bonds, to forego extra profits, to work longer or harder at the task for which he is best fitted. Rather it is a privilege.

It is not a sacrifice to do without many things to which we are accustomed if the national defense calls for doing without it.

A review this morning leads me to the conclusion that at present we shall not have to curtail the normal use of articles of food. There is enough food today for all of us and enough left over to send to those who are fighting on the same side with us.

But there will be a clear and definite shortage of metals for many kinds of civilian use, for the very good reason that in our increased program we shall need for war purposes more than half of that portion of the principal metals which during the past year have gone into articles for civilian use. Yes, we shall have to give up many things entirely.

And I am sure that the people in every part of the nation are prepared in their individual living to win this war. I am sure that they will cheerfully help to pay a large part of its financial cost while it goes on. I am sure they will cheerfully give up those material things that they are asked to give up.

And I am sure that they will retain all those great spiritual things without which we cannot win through.

I repeat that the United States can accept no result save victory, final and complete. Not only must the shame of Japanese treachery be wiped out, but the sources of international brutality, wherever they exist, must be absolutely and finally broken.

In my Message to the Congress yesterday I said that we "will make very certain that this form of treachery shall never endanger us again." In order to achieve that certainty, we must begin the great task that is before us by abandoning once and for all the illusion that we can ever again isolate ourselves from the rest of humanity.

In these past few years—and, most violently, in the past three days—we have learned a terrible lesson.

It is our obligation to our dead—it is our sacred obligation to their children and to our children—that we must never forget what we have learned.

And what we have learned is this:

There is no such thing as security for any nation—or any individual—in a world ruled by the principles of gangsterism.

There is no such thing as impregnable defense against powerful aggressors who sneak up in the dark and strike without warning.

We have learned that our ocean-girt hemisphere is not immune from severe attack—that we cannot measure our safety in terms of miles on any map any more.

We may acknowledge that our enemies have performed a brilliant feat of deception, perfectly timed and executed with great skill. It was a thoroughly dishonorable deed, but we must face the fact that modern warfare as conducted in the Nazi manner is a dirty business. We don't like it—we didn't want to get in it—but we are in it and we're going to fight it with everything we've got.

I do not think any American has any doubt of our ability to administer proper punishment to the perpetrators of these crimes.

Your Government knows that for weeks Germany has been telling Japan that if Japan did not attack the United States, Japan would not share in dividing the spoils with Germany when peace came. She was promised by Germany that if she came in she would receive the complete and perpetual control of the whole of the Pacific area—and that means not only the Far East, but also all of the Islands in the Pacific, and also a stranglehold on the west coast of North, Central and South America.

We know also that Germany and Japan are conducting their military and naval operations in accordance with a joint plan. That plan considers all peoples and nations which are not helping the Axis powers as common enemies of each and every one of the Axis powers.

That is their simple and obvious grand strategy. And that is why the American people must realize that it can be matched only with similar grand strategy. We must realize for example that Japanese successes against the United States in the Pacific are helpful to German operations in Libya; that any German success against the Caucasus is inevitably an assistance to Japan in her operations against the Dutch East Indies; that a German attack against Algiers or Morocco opens the way to a German attack against South America and the Canal.

On the other side of the picture, we must learn also to know that guerilla warfare against the Germans in, let us say Serbia or Norway, helps us; that a successful Russian offensive against the Germans helps us; and that British successes on land or sea in any part of the world strengthen our hands.

Remember always that Germany and Italy, regardless of any formal declaration of war, consider themselves at war with the United States at this moment just as much as they consider themselves at war with Britain or Russia. And Germany puts all the other Republics of the Americas into the same category of enemies. The people of our sister Republics of this Hemisphere can be honored by that fact.

The true goal we seek is far above and beyond the ugly field of battle. When we resort to force, as now we must, we are determined that this force shall be directed toward ultimate good as well as against immediate evil. We Americans are not destroyers—we are builders.

We are now in the midst of a war, not for conquest, not for vengeance, but for a world in which this nation, and all that this nation represents, will be safe for our children. We expect to eliminate the danger from Japan, but it would serve us ill if we accomplished that and found that the rest of the world was dominated by Hitler and Mussolini.

So we are going to win the war and we are going to win the peace that follows.

And in the difficult hours of this day—through dark days that may be yet to come—we will know that the vast majority of the members of the human race are on our side. Many of them are fighting with us. All of them are praying for us. But, in representing our cause, we represent theirs as well—our hope and their hope for liberty under God.

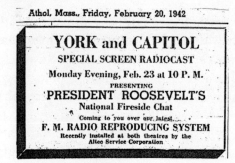

Athol Advertisement
Courtesy Richard Chaisson

Report on the Home Front

October 12, 1942

Radio Address of the President

MY FELLOW AMERICANS:

As you know, I have recently come back from a trip of inspection of camps and training stations and war factories.

The main thing that I observed on this trip is not exactly news. It is the plain fact that the American people are united as never before in their determination to do a job and to do it well.

This whole nation of one hundred and thirty million free men, women and children is becoming one great fighting force. Some of us are soldiers or sailors, some of us are civilians. Some of us are fighting the war in airplanes five miles above the continent of Europe or the islands of the Pacific—and some of us are fighting it in mines deep down in the earth of Pennsylvania or Montana. A few of us are decorated with medals for heroic achievement, but all of us can have that deep and permanent inner satisfaction that comes from doing the best we know how—each of us playing an honorable part in the great struggle to save our democratic civilization.

Whatever our individual circumstances or opportunities—we are all in it, and our spirit is good, and we Americans and our allies are going to win—and do not let anyone tell you anything different.

That is the main thing that I saw on my trip around the country—unbeatable spirit. If the leaders of Germany and Japan could have come along with me, and had seen what I saw, they would agree with my conclusions. Unfortunately, they were unable to make the trip with me. And that is one reason why we are carrying our war effort overseas—to them.

With every passing week the war increases in scope and intensity. That is true in Europe, in Africa, in Asia, and on all the seas.

The strength of the United Nations is on the upgrade in this war. The Axis leaders, on the other hand, know by now that they have already reached their full strength, and that their steadily mounting losses in men and material cannot be fully replaced. Germany and Japan are already realizing what the inevitable result will be when the total strength of the United Nations hits them—at additional places on the earth's surface.

One of the principal weapons of our enemies in the past has been their use of what is called "The War of Nerves." They have spread falsehood and terror; they have started Fifth Columns everywhere; they have duped the innocent; they have fomented suspicion and hate between neighbors; they have aided and abetted those people in other nations—(even) including our own—whose words and deeds are advertised from Berlin and from Tokyo as proof of our disunity.

The greatest defense against all such propaganda, of course, is the common sense of the common people—and that defense is prevailing.

The "War of Nerves" against the United Nations is now turning into a boomerang. For the first time, the Nazi propaganda machine is on the defensive. They begin to apologize to their own people for the repulse of their vast forces at Stalingrad, and for the enormous casualties they are suffering. They are compelled to beg their overworked people to rally their weakened production. They even publicly admit, for the first time, that Germany can be fed only at the cost of stealing food from the rest of Europe.

They are proclaiming that a second front is impossible; but, at the same time, they are desperately rushing troops in all directions, and stringing barbed wire all the way from the coasts of Finland and Norway to the islands of the Eastern Mediterranean. Meanwhile, they are driven to increase the fury of their atrocities.

The United Nations have decided to establish the identity of those Nazi leaders who are responsible for the innumerable acts of savagery. As each of these criminal deeds is committed, it is being carefully investigated; and the evidence is being relentlessly piled up for the future purposes of justice.

We have made it entirely clear that the United Nations* seek no mass reprisals against the populations of Germany or Italy or Japan. But the ring leaders and their brutal henchmen must be named, and apprehended, and tried in accordance with the judicial processes of criminal law.

There are now millions of Americans in army camps, in naval stations, in factories and in shipyards.

Who are these millions upon whom the life of our country depends? What are they thinking? What are their doubts? (and) What are their hopes? And how is the work progressing?

The Commander-in-Chief cannot learn all of the answers to these questions in Washington. And that is why I made the trip I did.

It is very easy to say, as some have said, that when the President travels through the country he should go with a blare of trumpets, with crowds on the sidewalks, with batteries of reporters and photographers—talking and posing with all of the politicians of the land.

But having had some experience in this war and in the last war, I can tell you very simply that the kind of trip I took permitted me to concentrate on the work I had to do without expending time, meeting all the demands of publicity. And—I might add—it was a particular pleasure to make a tour of the country without having to give a single thought to politics.

I expect to make other trips for similar purposes, and I shall make them in the same way.

In the last war, I had seen great factories; but until I saw some of the new present-day plants, I had not thoroughly visualized our American war effort. Of course, I saw only a small portion of all our plants, but that portion was a good cross-section, and it was deeply impressive.

The United States has been at war for only ten months, and is engaged in the enormous task of multiplying its armed forces many times. We are by no means at full production level yet. But I could not help asking myself on the trip, where would we be today if the Government of the United States had not begun to build many of its factories for this huge increase more than two years ago, more than a year before war was forced upon us at Pearl Harbor?

We have also had to face the problem of shipping. Ships in every part of the world continue to be sunk by enemy action. But the total tonnage of ships coming out of American, Canadian and British shipyards, day by day, has increased so fast that we are getting ahead of our enemies in the bitter battle of transportation.

In expanding our shipping, we have had to enlist many thousands of men for our Merchant Marine. These men are serving magnificently. They are risking their lives every hour so that guns and tanks and planes and ammunition and food may be carried to the heroic defenders of Stalingrad and to all the United Nations' forces all over the world.

A few days ago I awarded the first Maritime Distinguished Service Medal to a young man—Edward F. Cheney of Yeadon, Pennsylvania—who had shown great gallantry in rescuing his comrades from the oily waters of the sea after their ship had been torpedoed. There will be many more such acts of bravery.

In one sense my recent trip was a hurried one, out through the Middle West, to the Northwest, down the length of the Pacific Coast and back through the Southwest and the South. In another sense, however, it was a leisurely trip, because I had the opportunity to talk to the people who are actually doing the work—management and labor alike—on their own home grounds. And it gave me a fine chance to do some thinking about the major problems of our war effort on the basis of first things first.

As I told the three press association representatives who accompanied me, I was impressed by the large proportion of women employed—doing skilled manual (work) labor running machines. As time goes on, and many more of our men enter the armed forces, this proportion of women will increase. Within less than a year from now, I think, there will probably be as many women as men working in our war production plants.

I had some enlightening experiences relating to the old saying of us men that curiosity—inquisitiveness—is stronger among women. I noticed (that), frequently, that when we drove unannounced down the middle aisle of a great plant full of workers and machines, the first people to look up from their work were the men—and not the women. It was chiefly the men who were arguing as to whether that fellow in the straw hat was really the President or not.

So having seen the quality of the work and of the workers on our production lines—and coupling these firsthand observations with the reports of actual performance of our weapons on the fighting fronts—I can say to you that we are getting ahead of our enemies in the battle of production.

And of great importance to our future production was the effective and rapid manner in which the Congress met the serious problem of the rising cost of living. It was a splendid example of the operation of democratic processes in wartime.

The machinery to carry out this act of the Congress was put into effect within twelve hours after the bill was signed. The legislation will help the cost-of-living problems of every worker in every factory and on every farm in the land.

In order to keep stepping up our production, we have had to add millions of workers to the total labor force of the Nation. And as new factories come into operation, we must find additional millions of workers.

This presents a formidable problem in the mobilization of manpower.

It is not that we do not have enough people in this country to do the job. The problem is to have the right numbers of the right people in the right places at the right time.

We are learning to ration materials, and we must now learn to ration manpower.

The major objectives of a sound manpower policy are:

First, to select and train men of the highest fighting efficiency needed for our armed forces in the achievement of victory over our enemies in combat.

Second, to man our war industries and farms with the workers needed to produce the arms and munitions and food required by ourselves and by our fighting allies to win this war.

In order to do this, we shall be compelled to stop workers from moving from one war job to another as a matter of personal preference; to stop employers from stealing labor from each other; to use older men, and handicapped people, and more women, and even grown boys and girls, wherever possible and reasonable, to replace men of military age and fitness; to train new personnel for essential war work; and to stop the wastage of labor in all non-essential activities.

There are many other things that we can do, and do immediately, to help meet (the) this manpower problem.

The school authorities in all the states should work out plans to enable our high school students to take some time from their school year, (and) to use their summer vacations, to help farmers raise and harvest their crops, or to work somewhere in the war industries. This does not mean closing schools and stopping education. It does mean giving older students a better opportunity to contribute their bit to the war effort. Such work will do no harm to the students.

People should do their work as near their homes as possible. We cannot afford to transport a single worker into an area where there is already a worker available to do the job.

In some communities, employers dislike to employ women. In others they are reluctant to hire Negroes. In still others, older men are not wanted. We can no longer afford to indulge such prejudices or practices.

Every citizen wants to know what essential war work he can do the best. He can get the answer by applying to the nearest United States Employment Service office. There are four thousand five hundred of these offices throughout the Nation. They (are) form the corner grocery stores of our manpower system. This network of employment offices is prepared to advise every citizen where his skills and labors are needed most, and to refer him to an employer who can utilize them to best advantage in the war effort.

Perhaps the most difficult phase of the manpower problem is the scarcity of farm labor in many places. I have seen evidences of the fact, however, that the people are trying to meet it as well as possible.

In one community that I visited a perishable crop was harvested by turning out the whole of the high school for three or four days.

And in another community of fruit growers the usual Japanese labor was not available; but when the fruit ripened, the banker, the butcher, the lawyer, the garage man, the druggist, the local editor, and in fact every able-bodied man and woman in the town, left their occupations, (and) went out gathering(ed) the fruit, and sent it to market.

Every farmer in the land must realize fully that his production is part of war production, and that he is regarded by the Nation as essential to victory. The American people expect him to keep his production up, and even to increase it. We will use every effort to help him to get labor; but, at the same time, he and the people of his community must use ingenuity and cooperative effort to produce crops, and livestock and dairy products.

It may be that all of our volunteer effort—however well intentioned and well administered—will not suffice wholly to solve (the) this problem. In that case, we shall have to adopt new legislation. And if this is necessary, I do not believe that the American people will shrink from it.

In a sense, every American, because of the privilege of his citizenship, is a part of the Selective Service.

The Nation owes a debt of gratitude to the Selective Service Boards. The successful operation of the Selective Service System and the way it has been accepted by the great mass of our citizens give us confidence that if necessary, the same principle could be used to solve any manpower problem.

And I want to say also a word of praise and thanks (for) to the more than ten million people, all over the country, who have volunteered for the work of civilian defense—and who are working hard at it. They are displaying unselfish devotion in the patient performance of their often tiresome and always anonymous tasks. In doing this important neighborly work they are helping to fortify our national unity and our real understanding of the fact that we are all involved in this war.

Naturally, on my trip I was most interested in watching the training of our fighting forces.

All of our combat units that go overseas must consist of young, strong men who have had thorough training. (A) An Army division that has an average age of twenty-three or twenty-four is a better fighting unit than one which has an average age of thirty-three or thirty-four. The more of such troops we have in the field, the sooner the war will be won, and the smaller will be the cost in casualties.

Therefore, I believe that it will be necessary to lower the present minimum age limit for Selective Service from twenty years down to eighteen. We have learned how inevitable that is—and how important to the speeding up of victory.

I can very thoroughly understand the feelings of all parents whose sons have entered our armed forces. I have an appreciation of that feeling and so has my wife.

I want every father and every mother who has a son in the service to know—again, from what I have seen with my own eyes—that the men in the Army, Navy and Marine Corps are receiving today the best possible training, equipment and medical care. And we will never fail to provide for the spiritual needs of our officers and men under the Chaplains of our armed services.

Good training will save many, many lives in battle. The highest rate of casualties is always suffered by units comprised of inadequately trained men.

We can be sure that the combat units of our Army and Navy are well manned, (and) well equipped, (and) well trained. Their effectiveness in action will depend upon the quality of their leadership, and upon the wisdom of the strategic plans on which all military operations are based.

I can say one thing about (our) these plans of ours: They are not being decided by the typewriter strategists who expound their views in the press or on the radio.

One of the greatest of American soldiers, Robert E. Lee, once remarked on the tragic fact that in the war of his day all of the best generals were apparently working on newspapers instead of in the Army. And that seems to be true in all wars.

The trouble with the typewriter strategists is that while they may be full of bright ideas, they are not in possession of much information about the facts or problems of military operations.

We, therefore, will continue to leave the plans for this war to the military leaders.

The military and naval plans of the United States are made by the Joint Staff of the Army and Navy which is constantly in session in Washington. The Chiefs of this Staff are Admiral Leahy, General Marshall, Admiral King and General Arnold. They meet and confer regularly with representatives of the British Joint Staff, and with representatives of Russia, China, the Netherlands, Poland, Norway, the British Dominions and other nations working in the common cause.

Since this unity of operations was put into effect last January, there has been a very substantial agreement between these planners, all of whom are trained in the profession of arms—air, sea and land—from their early years. As Commander-in-Chief I have at all times also been in substantial agreement.

As I have said before, many major decisions of strategy have been made. One of them—on which we have all agreed—relates to the necessity of diverting enemy forces from Russia and China to other theaters of war by new offensives against Germany and Japan. An announcement of how these offensives are to be launched, and when, and where, cannot be broadcast over the radio at this time.

We are celebrat(e)ing today the exploit of a bold and adventurous Italian—Christopher Columbus—who with the aid of Spain opened up a new world where freedom and tolerance and respect for human rights and dignity provided an asylum for the oppressed of the old world.

Today, the sons of the New World are fighting in lands far distant from their own America. They are fighting to save for all mankind, including ourselves, the principles which have flourished in this new world of freedom.

We are mindful of the countless millions of people whose future liberty and whose very lives depend upon permanent victory for the United Nations.

There are a few people in this country who, when the collapse of the Axis begins, will tell our people that we are safe once more; that we can tell the rest of the world to "stew in its own juice"; that never again will we help to pull "the other fellow's chestnuts from the fire"; that the future of civilization can jolly well take care of itself insofar as we are concerned.

But it is useless to win battles if the cause for which we fight these battles is lost. It is useless to win a war unless it stays won.

We, therefore, fight for the restoration and perpetuation of faith and hope and peace throughout the world.

The objective of today is clear and realistic. It is to destroy completely the military power of Germany, Italy and Japan to such good purpose that their threat against us and all the other United Nations cannot be revived a generation hence.

We are united in seeking the kind of victory that will guarantee that our grandchildren can grow and, under God may live their lives, free from the constant threat of invasion, destruction, slavery and violent death.

*Note:

- President Roosevelt suggested the name, United Nations, to Winston Churchill in August 1941, during the Atlantic Charter meeting.
- "The governments of the United States, the Soviet Union, the United Kingdom, and China formalized the Atlantic Charter proposals in January 1942, shortly after the United States entered the war. In the Declaration of the United Nations, these major Allied nations, along with 22 other states, agreed to work together against the Axis powers (Germany, Japan, and Italy), and committed in principle to the establishment of the United Nations after the war."
- "The United Nations officially came into existence on October 24, 1945, after the United States, the Soviet Union, the United Kingdom, China, and France, as well as a majority of the other signatories, had ratified the United Nations Charter." U.S. Department of State

President Roosevelt 1944

State of the Union Message to Congress

January 11, 1944

Address of the President Broadcast Nationally

Ladies and Gentlemen:

Today I sent my Annual Message to the Congress, as required by the Constitution. It has been my custom to deliver these Annual Messages in person, and they have been broadcast to the Nation. I intended to follow this same custom this year.

But, like a great many other people (of my fellow countrymen), I have had the "flu" and, although I am practically recovered, my Doctor simply would not permit me to leave the White House to (and) go up to the Capitol.

Only a few of the newspapers of the United States can print the Message in full, and I am (very) anxious that the American people be given an opportunity to hear what I have recommended to the Congress for this very fateful year in our history—and the reasons for those recommendations. Here is what I said:

This Nation in the past two years has become an active partner in the world's greatest war against human slavery.

We have joined with like-minded people in order to defend ourselves in a world that has been gravely threatened with gangster rule.

But I do not think that any of us Americans can be content with mere survival. Sacrifices that we and our Allies are making impose upon us all a sacred obligation to see to it that out of this war we and our children will gain something better than mere survival.

We are united in determination that this war shall not be followed by another interim which leads to new disaster—that we shall not repeat the tragic errors of ostrich isolationism.

When Mr. Hull went to Moscow in October, (and) when I went to Cairo and Teheran in November, we knew that we were in agreement with our Allies in our common determination to fight and win this war. (But) There were many vital questions concerning the future peace, and they were discussed in an atmosphere of complete candor and harmony.

In the last war such discussions, such meetings, did not even begin until the shooting had stopped and the delegates began to assemble at the peace table. There had been no previous opportunities for man-to-man discussions which lead to meetings of minds. And the result was a peace which was not a peace.

And right here I want to address a word or two to some suspicious souls who are fearful that Mr. Hull or I have made "commitments" for the future which might pledge this Nation to secret treaties, or to enacting the role of a world Santa Claus.

Of course, we made some commitments. We most certainly committed ourselves to very large and very specific military plans which require the use of all allied forces to bring about the defeat of our enemies at the earliest possible time.

But there were no secret treaties or political or financial commitments.

The one supreme objective for the future, which we discussed for each nation individually, and for all the United Nations, can be summed up in one word: Security.

And that means not only physical security which provides safety from attacks by aggressors. It means also economic security, social security, moral security—in a family of nations.

In the plain down-to-earth talks that I had with the Generalissimo and Marshal Stalin and Prime Minister Churchill, it was abundantly clear that they are all most deeply interested in the resumption of peaceful progress by their own peoples—progress toward a better life.

All our Allies have learned by experience—bitter experience that real development will not be possible if they are to be diverted from their purpose by repeated wars—or even threats of war.

The best interests of each nation, large and small, demand that all freedom-loving nations shall join together in a just and durable system of peace. In the present world situation, evidenced by the actions of Germany, and Italy and Japan, unquestioned military control over the disturbers of the peace is as necessary among nations as it is among citizens in any (a) community. And an equally basic essential to peace—permanent peace—is a decent standard of living for all individual men and women and children in all nations. Freedom from fear is eternally linked with freedom from want.

There are people who burrow—burrow through the (our) nation like unseeing moles, and attempt to spread the suspicion that if other nations are encouraged to raise their standards of living, our own American standard of living must of necessity be depressed.

The fact is the very contrary. It has been shown time and again that if the standard of living of any country goes up, so does its purchasing power—and that such a rise encourages a better standard of living in neighboring countries with whom it trades. That is just plain common sense—and (it) is the kind of plain common sense that provided the basis for our discussions at Moscow, and Cairo and Teheran.

Returning from my journeying, I must confess to a sense of being "let down" when I found many evidences of faulty perspectives here in Washington. The faulty perspective consists in over-emphasizing lesser problems and thereby under-emphasizing the first and greatest problem.

The overwhelming majority of our people have met the demands of this war with magnificent courage and a great deal of understanding. They have accepted inconveniences; they have accepted hardships; they have accepted tragic sacrifices.

However, while the majority goes on about its great work without complaint, we all know that a noisy minority maintains an uproar, an uproar of demands for special favors for special groups. There are pests who swarm through the lobbies of the Congress and the cocktail bars of Washington, representing these special groups as opposed to the basic interests of the Nation as a whole. They have come to look upon the war primarily as a chance to make profits for themselves at the expense of their neighbors—profits in money or profits in terms of political or social preferment.

Such selfish agitation can be and is highly dangerous in wartime. It creates confusion. It damages morale. It hampers our national effort. It prolongs the war.

In this war, we have been compelled to learn how interdependent upon each other are all groups and sections of the whole population of America.

Increased food costs, for example, will bring new demands for wage increases from all war workers, which will in turn raise all prices of all things including those things which the farmers themselves have to buy. Increased wages or prices will each in turn produce the same results. They all have a particularly disastrous result on all fixed income groups.

And I hope you will remember that all of us in this Government, including myself, represent the fixed income group just as much as we represent business owners, or workers or (and) farmers. This group of fixed-income people include: teachers, and clergy, and policemen, and firemen, and widows and minors who are on fixed incomes, wives and dependents of our soldiers and sailors, and old age pensioners. They and their families add up to more than a (one) quarter of our one hundred and thirty million people. They have few or no high pressure representatives at the Capitol. And in a period of gross inflation they would be the worst sufferers. Let us give them an occasional thought.

If ever there was a time to subordinate individual or group selfishness for (to) the national good, that time is now. Disunity at home, and (—) bickering, self-seeking partisanship, stoppages of work, inflation, business as usual, politics as usual, luxury as usual—and sometimes a failure to tell the whole truth—these are the influences which can undermine the morale of the brave men ready to die at the front for us here.

Those who are doing most of the complaining, I do not think that they are deliberately striving to sabotage the national war effort. They are laboring under the delusion that the time is past when we must make prodigious sacrifices—that the war is already won and we can begin to slacken off. But the dangerous folly of that point of view can be measured by the distance that separates our troops from their ultimate objectives in Berlin and Tokyo—and by the sum of all the perils that lie along the way.

Over confidence and complacency are among our deadliest of all enemies.

And that attitude on the part of anyone—Government or management or labor—can lengthen this war. It can kill American boys.

Let us remember the lessons of 1918. In the summer of that year the tide turned in favor of the Allies. But this Government did not relax, nor did the American people. In fact, our nation's effort was stepped up. In August, 1918, the draft age limits were broadened from 21 to (-) 31 all the way to 18 to (-) 45. The President called for "force to the utmost," and his call was heeded. And in November, only three months later, Germany surrendered.

That is the way to fight and win a war—all out and not with half-an-eye on the battlefronts abroad and the other eye-and-a-half on personal selfish, or political interests here at home.

Therefore, in order to concentrate all of our energies, all of our (and) resources on winning this (the) war, and to maintain a fair and stable economy at home, I recommend that the Congress adopt:

First, (1) A realistic and simplified tax law—which will tax all unreasonable profits, both individual and corporate, and reduce the ultimate cost of the war to our sons and our daughters. The tax bill now under consideration by the Congress does not begin to meet this test.

Secondly, (2) A continuation of the law for the renegotiations of war contracts—which will prevent exorbitant profits and assure fair prices to the Government. For two long years I have pleaded with the Congress to take undue profits out of war.

Third, (3) A cost of food law—which will enable the Government ((a)) to place a reasonable floor under the prices the farmer may expect for his production; and ((b)) to place a ceiling on the prices the (a) consumer will have to pay for the necessary food he buys. This should apply, as I have intimated, to necessities only; and this will require public funds to carry it out. It will cost in appropriations about one percent of the present annual cost of the war.

Fourth, (4) An early re-enactment of the stabilization statute of October, 1942. This expires this year, June 30th, 1944, and if it is not extended well in advance, the country might just as well expect price chaos by summertime.

We cannot have stabilization by wishful thinking. We must take positive action to maintain the integrity of the American dollar.

And fifth, (5) A national service law—which, for the duration of the war, will prevent strikes, and, with certain appropriate exceptions, will make available for war production or for any other essential services every able-bodied adult in this whole Nation.

These five measures together form a just and equitable whole. I would not recommend a national service law unless the other laws were passed to keep down the cost of living, to share equitably the burdens of taxation, to hold the stabilization line, and to prevent undue profits.

The Federal Government already has the basic power to draft capital and property of all kinds for war purposes on a basis of just compensation.

And, as you know, I have for three years hesitated to recommend a national service act. Today, however, with all the experience we have behind us and with us, I am convinced of its necessity. Although I believe that we and our Allies can win the war without such a measure, I am certain that nothing less than total mobilization of all our resources of manpower and capital will guarantee an earlier victory, and reduce the toll of suffering and sorrow and blood.

As some of my advisers wrote me the other day:

"When the very life of the nation is in peril the responsibility for service is common to all men and women. In such a time there can be no discrimination between the men and women who are assigned by the Government to its defense at the battlefront and the men and women assigned to producing the vital materials that are essential to successful military operations. A prompt enactment of a National Service Law would be merely an expression of the universality of this American responsibility."

I believe the country will agree that those statements are the solemn truth.

National service is the most democratic way to wage a war. Like selective service for the armed forces, it rests on the obligation of each citizen to serve his nation to his utmost where he is best qualified.

It does not mean reduction in wages. It does not mean loss of retirement and seniority rights and benefits. It does not mean that any substantial numbers of war workers will be disturbed in their present jobs. Let this (these) fact(s) be wholly clear.

There are millions of American men and women who are not in this war at all. That (It) is not because they do not want to be in it. But they want to know where they can best do their share. National service provides that direction.

I know that all civilian war workers will be glad to be able to say many years hence to their grandchildren: "Yes, I, too, was in service in the great war. I was on duty in an airplane factory, and I helped to make hundreds of fighting planes. The Government told me that in doing that I was performing my most useful work in the service of my country."

It is argued that we have passed the stage in the war where national service is necessary. But our soldiers and sailors know that this is not true. We are going forward on a long, rough road—and, in all journeys, the last miles are the hardest. And it is for that final effort—for the total defeat of our enemies—that we must mobilize our total resources. The national war program calls for the employment of more people in 1944 than in 1943.

And it is my conviction that the American people will welcome this win-the-war measure which is based on the eternally just principle of "fair for one, fair for all."

It will give our people at home the assurance that they are standing four-square behind our soldiers and sailors. And it will give our enemies demoralizing assurance that we mean business—that we, one hundred and thirty million Americans, are on the march to Rome, and Berlin and Tokyo.

I hope that the Congress will recognize that, although this is a political year, national service is an issue which transcends politics. Great power must be used for great purposes.

As to the machinery for this measure, the Congress itself should determine its nature—as long as (but) it is (should be) wholly non-partisan in its make-up.

Several alleged reasons have prevented the enactment of legislation which would preserve for our soldiers and sailors and marines the fundamental prerogative of citizenship—in other words, the right to vote. No amount of legalistic argument can becloud this issue in the eyes of these ten million American citizens. Surely the signers of the Constitution did not intend a document which, even in wartime, would be construed to take away the franchise of any of those who are fighting to preserve the Constitution itself.

Our soldiers and sailors and marines know that the overwhelming majority of them will be deprived of the opportunity to vote, if the voting machinery is left exclusively to the States under existing State laws—and that there is no likelihood of these laws being changed in time to enable them to vote at the next election. The Army and Navy have reported that it will be impossible effectively to administer forty-eight different soldier-voting laws. It is the duty of the Congress to remove this unjustifiable discrimination against the men and women in our armed forces—and to do it just as quickly as possible.

It is our duty now to begin to lay the plans and determine the strategy. More than the winning of the war, it is time to begin plans and determine the strategy for (the) winning (of) a lasting peace and the establishment of an American standard of living higher than ever (before) known before.

This Republic had its beginning, and grew to its present strength, under the protection of certain inalienable political rights—among them the right of free speech, free press, free worship, trial by jury, freedom from unreasonable searches and seizures. They were our rights to life and liberty.

We have come to a clear realization of the fact, however, that true individual freedom cannot exist without economic security and independence. "Necessitous men are not free men." People who are hungry, people who are (and) out of a job are the stuff of which dictatorships are made.

In our day these economic truths have become accepted as self-evident. We have accepted, so to speak, a second Bill of Rights under which a new basis of security and prosperity can be established for all—regardless of station, or race or creed.

Among these are:

The right to a useful and remunerative job in the industries, or shops or farms or mines of the nation;

The right to earn enough to provide adequate food and clothing and recreation;

The right of (every) farmers to raise and sell their (his) products at a return which will give them (him) and their (his) families (family) a decent living;

The right of every business man, large and small, to trade in an atmosphere of freedom from unfair competition and domination by monopolies at home or abroad;

The right of every family to a decent home;

The right to adequate medical care and the opportunity to achieve and enjoy good health;

The right to adequate protection from the economic fears of old age, and sickness, and accident and unemployment;

And finally, the right to a good education.

All of these rights spell security. And after this war is won we must be prepared to move forward, in the implementation of these rights, to new goals of human happiness and well-being.

America's own rightful place in the world depends in large part upon how fully these and similar rights have been carried into practice for all our citizens. For unless there is security here at home there cannot be lasting peace in the world.

One of the great American industrialists of our day—a man who has rendered yeoman service to his country in this crisis—recently emphasized the grave dangers of "rightist reaction" in this Nation. Any clear-thinking business men share that (his) concern. Indeed, if such reaction should develop—if history were to repeat itself and we were to return to the so-called "normalcy" of the 1920's—then it is certain that even though we shall have conquered our enemies on the battlefields abroad, we shall have yielded to the spirit of fascism here at home.

I ask the Congress to explore the means for implementing this economic bill of rights—for it is definitely the responsibility of the Congress so to do, and the country knows it. Many of these problems are already before committees of the Congress in the form of proposed legislation. I shall from time to time communicate with the Congress with respect to these and further proposals. In the event that no adequate program of progress is evolved, I am certain that the Nation will be conscious of the fact.

Our fighting men abroad—and their families at home—expect such a program and have the right to insist on (upon) it. It is to their demands that this Government should pay heed, rather than to the whining demands of selfish pressure groups who seek to feather their nests while young Americans are dying.

I have often said that there are no two fronts for America in this war. There is only one front. There is one line of unity that (which) extends from the hearts of (the) people at home to the men of our attacking forces in our farthest outposts. When we speak of our total effort, we speak of the factory and the field and the mine as well as (of) the battlefield (ground)—we speak of the soldier and the civilian, the citizen and his Government.

Each and every one of them (us) has a solemn obligation under God to serve this Nation in its most critical hour—to keep this Nation great—to make this Nation greater in a better world.

President Franklin D. Roosevelt laid to rest at his Hyde Park estate, April 15, 1945.
Courtesy FDR Library and Museum